The Politics of
American Federalism

*STUDIES IN HISTORY AND POLITICS*
Under the editorial direction of Gerald E. Stearn

RUSSIA AND THE WEST FROM PETER TO KHRUSHCHEV
Edited by L. Jay Oliva, New York University

CHURCH AND STATE IN AMERICAN HISTORY
John F. Wilson, Princeton University

THE AMERICAN IMAGE,
PAST AND PRESENT
Edited by G. D. Lillibridge, Chico State College

SOLDIERS AND STATES
CIVIL-MILITARY RELATIONS IN MODERN EUROPE
Edited by David B. Ralston, Massachusetts Institute of Technology

THE DEVELOPMENT OF THE COMMUNIST BLOC
Edited by Roger Pethybridge, University College, Swansea

BRITISH POLITICS
PEOPLE, PARTIES AND PARLIAMENTS
Edited by Anthony King, University of Essex

FRENCH POLITICS
Edited by Martin Harrison, University of Keele

THE POLITICS OF AMERICAN FEDERALISM
Edited by Daniel J. Elazar, Temple University
Other Volumes in Preparation

# The Politics of American Federalism

Edited with an introduction by

*Daniel J. Elazar*

Temple University

D. C. HEATH AND COMPANY

*A DIVISION OF RAYTHEON EDUCATION COMPANY*

*Lexington, Massachusetts*

Library of Congress Catalog Number 68–31285

PRINTED IN THE UNITED STATES OF AMERICA

# Table of Contents

# Introduction

## The Meaning of American Federalism

A perceptive British student of American government recently observed, "The United States is a federal country in spirit, in its way of life, and in its constitution."[1] This insight into the American political system would not have surprised the founding fathers of our nation in the least. Today its accuracy is again becoming widely acknowledged.

### The Origins of American Federalism

For all intents and purposes, federalism as modern men know it is an American invention. As the literature of the Constitutional ratification campaign (both federalist and anti-federalist) indicates, federalism was created and designed by the founding fathers to be more than a structural compromise devised to make possible the unification of the several states under a single national government. It was also to be more than a geographic division of power for expediency's sake.

Federalism, to its American creators, represented a new political alternative for solving the problems of governing civil societies, an alternative that from the first embraced the whole panoply of political theories, institutions, and patterns of behavior that must be brought together in order to form a political system. The federalism of the founders was designed to provide substantially new means for the development of a viable system of government, a successful system of politics, a reasonable approach to the problems of popular government, and a decent means for securing civil justice and morality. Moreover, its inventors conceived of federalism as a uniquely valuable means for solving the perennial problems of any civil society seeking to transform itself into a good commonwealth, particularly one which is built on the rock of popular government — the problems of balancing human liberty, political authority, and governmental energy so as to create a political system at once strong, lasting, democratic, and just. They believed that their invention was capable of solving those problems because it was based on valid fundamental principles and was constructed to employ proper, if new, political techniques necessary to at least approximately effectuate those principles. They were convinced of this — and were soon joined in this conviction by the American people as a whole — not because their invention directly solved important substantive questions but because it provided correct procedures for dealing with the substantive questions which they anticipated would confront the United States. The essence of their solution was the application of the federal principle not only to relations between governments but to the over-all political relationships of groups ("factions" in Madison's terminology) and individuals to government.

[1]M.J.C. Vile, The Structure of American Federalism, Oxford University Press, 1961.

Their own sources try to justify their stand by telling us why the founders felt as they did. Unfortunately, current myths prevent many from considering those sources on their own terms. For one thing, there are too many who believe American federalism is the product of circumstances alone, that Nature itself (or at least prior experience) dictated that the American Republic be built on the rock of diffused governmental powers so that any discussion of a "federal principle" is an *ex post facto* attempt to discover a unique or original political invention when common political considerations actually sufficed. Pointing to the vast expanse of land under the American flag even in 1787, the great diversity of peoples gathered together under its protection, the general commitment to popular government prevalent in the land, and the pre-existence of the thirteen colonies, many people conclude that a formal distribution of power among "central" and "local" governments was inevitable if there were to be any union at all and that the founders of the Republic simply worked out the mechanisms needed to make the *status quo* politically viable.

This view has become widespread in the twentieth century because it is particularly useful to those who accept two companion views of American federalism current today. One is the notion that the framers of the Constitution were hostile to popular government and used federalism to limit "democracy" by distributing powers undemocratically. This school views subsequent American history as the struggle to establish popular government against the will of the founders' Constitution. Accordingly, they believe that the Constitution's system for the distribution of power becomes increasingly obsolete as the nation becomes more "democratic." The other accepts the premise that the founders were anti-democratic but "excuses" them on the grounds that problems of of communication over such a vast and diverse area then required the federal distribution of powers. Their claim is that as problems of fast communications are lessened, this distribution of powers becomes increasingly obsolete.

At first glance, history appears to support the current myths. The implantation of settlements on the American shore under different regimes and charters had led to the emergence of at least thirteen firmly rooted colonies-cum-states by 1776. The new nation did inherit the basis for some type of federal plan and, it might even be said, had no choice in the matter. Recent research has heightened the plausibility of this view by indicating the extent to which the American colonies enjoyed a *de facto* federal relationship with the English King and Parliament prior to independence.

The existence of states, however, was no guarantee that they could be united under one government. Moreover, there was no guarantee that unification could take any form other than loose confederation so long as the states remained intact as sovereign civil societies, or any form other than consolidation if they did not. In this respect, the factors of size and diversity were in no way determinative. Distribution, as opposed to concentration of power, is not a function of size and diversity *per se* but a function of republican political inclinations.

Students of comparative government — from the days of Aristotle to our own and including the generation of the founders of the Republic — have been fully aware of the possibilities for centralized government in even the largest and most diverse empires. In Aristotle's day the Persian Empire extended for over three thousand miles "from India to Ethiopia" and included over a hundred different nationality and ethnic groups, each located in its own land, yet throughout its two hundred years of existence, it was governed by a despotism which, while maintaining a benevolent attitude toward the maintenance of local customs and civil laws, carefully concentrated as much political power as possible in the hands of the emperor.

Locke, Montesquieu, and the founding fathers were acquainted with the similarly organized Ottoman Empire. They, like our own generation, also encountered one of the greatest centralized despotisms of all time in the form of the Russian empire. When Cortez was viceroy in Mexico, the Russian Empire under Ivan the Terrible already covered an area larger than the original United States (888,811 square miles in 1789). The Russians began their march eastward in the sixteenth century and at the time the Puritans were settling New England, they reached the Pacific. By the year of the Glorious Revolution and the establishment of parliamentary supremacy in England, the Russians had consolidated their centralized rule over some seven million square miles and dozens of nations, peoples, and tribes. An eighteenth-century Russian, if asked about the political consequences of a large domain, would have been likely to say that an expanse of territory is useful in protecting absolutism since the difficulties of internal communication that it creates help prevent popular uprisings on a nationwide scale.

A Frenchman of the same century, if asked the best method of creating a nation out of a number of smaller "sovereignties," would undoubtedly have recalled the history of France and advocated the complete political and administrative subordination of the entities to be absorbed under a central government and the elimination of all vestiges of their local autonomy so as to minimize the possibilities of civil war. Even an eighteenth-century Englishman, aware of the centuries-old problem of absorbing Scotland within Great Britain, would have been likely to approach the problem of national unification in a somewhat similar manner, except that he might have added a touch of decentralization as a palliative to libertarian sentiments. Thinking Americans were aware of all these examples in 1787. It is no accident that *The Federalist* had to concentrate heavily on refuting the argument that a stronger national government would inevitably open the door to centralized despotism.

Closer examination of the situation between 1775 and 1801 provides convincing evidence to the effect that, regardless of the factors present to encourage some form of division of power between national government and the state governments, the development of a federal system stronger than that embodied in the Articles of Confederation was by no means foreordained. What such an examination does reveal is the extent to which the founders of the United States were committed to the idea of popular government and were really involved in a search for the best form of organization—the best constitution—for the republic, one that would secure the liberties of the people while avoiding the weaknesses of past experiments in popular government.

Even here the founders had little precedent to guide them. Not only were there no extant examples of the successful government of a large territory except through a strong centralized government, but there were few small territories governed in a "republican" manner and none offered the example of federalism as Americans later came to know it. The two nations then existing that had come closest to resolving the problems of national unity without governmental centralization were the United Provinces of the Netherlands and the Swiss Confederation. Not only were both very small republics indeed (each covered about 15,000 square miles at that time), but the failure of the former to solve its constitutional problems and its consequent lapse into government by an incompetent executive and an anti-republican oligarchy was well-known while the latter was hardly more than a protective association of independent states with little national consciousness. Neither could be an attractive example to the American nation builders who were committed to both republicanism and the common nationality of all Americans.

In one sense, then, the founding fathers had only two contemporary models to choose from, both of which showed great weakness and promised little for the perpetuation of popular government. They could have attempted to bring the several states together into a single unified but decentralized state on the order of the government of Great Britain, or they could have been satisfied with a loose confederation of sovereign states, united only for purposes of defense and foreign relations which, while barely able to govern adequately even in the areas of its responsibility, would offer minimal opportunities for national despotism.

There were those who advocated the former course, particularly among the younger officers of the Continental Army. At various times, they urged Washington to establish a constitutional dictatorship (which possibly could have led to a political system akin to the kind of totalitarian democracy established by Napoleon in France during the 1790's) or assume the crown as a constitutional monarch (which presumably would have led to a political system akin to the kind of aristocratic oligarchy that existed in eighteenth century England). While Washington effectively subdued most of them on several occasions during the war itself (the most famous of which was his farewell at Fraunces Tavern), one of their number, former lieutenant colonel Alexander Hamilton, continued to advocate the latter position as much as he dared right through the Constitutional Convention.

The second course was the one followed during the war as a natural outgrowth of the Continental Congresses assembled from 1765 through 1775. If the founders had been content with a "foreordained" system, one "dictated" by the actual status of the United States in 1776, they would have accepted this alternative and retained the Articles of Confederation which were adopted to ratify just that kind of confederacy. That system has been most frequently compared to the various Hellenic leagues which united several city-states only insofar as they shared a common purpose—invariably that of defense. Such leagues embraced small despotisms as well as small democracies. They had no role to play in determining the internal regimes of member states and were in no sense protectors of human liberties or popular government.

Among those who advocated this course of action were some of the most notable patriots of the early Revolutionary struggle. Above all, they feared despotism in large governments and distrusted any notion that a national government with energy could be kept republican. Whatever their views as to the potential tyranny of the majority, they were more willing to trust smaller governments with supervision of the people's liberties on the grounds that they were more accessible to the people. Patrick Henry was the most outspoken of this group. He held his ground to the bitter end, uncompromising in his belief.

## Popular Government and the Federal Solution

As we all know, the founders chose neither alternative but, rather, invented a third alternative of their own. Their alternative was animated by a desire to perfect the union of what they believed to be an already existing nation, to give it the power to act as a government while keeping it republican and democratic. In developing their solution, they transcended the limits of earlier political thought in order to devise a way to protect the people's liberties from every threat.

Their alternative reflected a great step forward in thinking about popular government because they refused to accept the simplistic notion that the possibilities for despotism increased in direct proportion to the size of the country to be governed. They were fully convinced by history and personal experience that small governments, in their case the states, could be as despotic as large ones.

Moreover, the founders were convinced by history and experience that democratic governments could be as tyrannical as autocratic ones if they were based on simple and untrammeled majoritarianism. Pure democracies, in particular, were subject to the sway of passion and hence to the promotion of injustice, and even republics were susceptible if faction was allowed to reign unchecked. As friends of human liberty and popular government, they felt it necessary to create a political system that would protect the people from despotic governments whether they be large or small, democratic or not.

Their solution, federalism, was designed to deal with all these contingencies by balancing them off against one another so as to create a number of permanent points of tension that would limit the spread of either popular passion or governmental excess; break up or weaken the power of factions; and require broad based majorities to take significant political actions. Locating all sovereignty in the people as a whole while dividing the exercise of sovereign powers among several governments — one general, the others regional — was, to the founders, a means of checking the despotic tendencies, majoritarian or other, in both the larger and smaller governments, while preserving the principle of popular government. The interdependence of the national and state governments was to ensure their ability to check one another while still enabling them to cooperate and govern energetically. In the words of *Publius*, they advocated a republican remedy for republican diseases.

In organizational terms, the perennial tug-of-war between centralization and decentralization was to be avoided by the introduction of the principle of noncentralization. The difference is a crucial one. Decentralization, even as it implies local control, assumes the existence of a central authority which has the power to concentrate, devolve, or reconcentrate power more or less at will. Non-centralization assumes that there is no central authority as such but that power is granted to several authorities, national and regional, directly by the people and, even though the national authority may enjoy an ultimate preeminence that is very real indeed, that those authorities cannot legitimately take basic power away from each other.

True federal systems must be non-centralized systems. Even when, in practical situations, there seems to be is only the thin line of the spirit between non-centralization and decentralization, it is that thin line which determines the extent and character of the diffusion of power in a particular regime.

The American people and their leaders were to extend this aspect of federalism, which is partially described in common parlance as the "checks and balances" system, into most other areas of their political life. Both the state governments and the national government have powers which cannot be taken from one another, even when both planes share in their exercise. The principle was further applied to relations of the various branches of government — executive, legislative, and judicial — within each plane even before the invention of federalism. It was subsequently applied to the structure and organization of the party system which consists of two national coalitions of substantially independent state and local party organizations further checked by the independence of action reserved to the "congressional parties" within each of the two coalitions. It was applied to the other processes of politics and even to the nation's economic system in ways too numerous to mention here.

The federal principle sets the tone for American civil society, making it a society of balanced interests with equalitarian overtones, just as the monarchist principle makes British civil society class- and elite-oriented despite democratic pressures, and the collectivist principle sets the tone for Russian civil society, making it anti-individualistic even when equalitarian. In political terms, this is because the federal principle establishes the basic power relationships and sets the basic terms for the processes of distributing power within American civil society. The founders understood the role of such central principles in setting the framework for the development of a political system. They knew that, while the roots of the central principle of every civil society are embedded in its culture, constitution-makers do have a significant opportunity to sharpen the principle's application and the direction of its future growth.

In sum, federalism as the founders conceived it was an effort to protect the rights of men by consciously creating institutions and procedures that would give government adequate powers while, at the same time, forcing the governors to achieve a high level of consent from all segments of the public they served before acting in other than routine ways. Requiring extraordinary majorities for great actions, the Constitution was based on the idea that there is a qualitative difference between a simple majority formed for a specific issue and the larger consensus that allows governments to continue to function from generation to generation.

## The Covenant Idea and the Federal Principle

The creation of the American federal system was, at one and the same time, a new political invention and a reasonable extension of an old political principle; a considerable change in the American *status quo* and a step fully consonant with the particular political genius of the American people. Partly because of their experiences with the model before them and partly because of the theoretical principles they had derived from the philosophic traditions surrounding them, the American people rejected the notions of the general will and the organic state common among their European contemporaries. Instead, they built their constitutions and institutions on the *covenant* principle, a very different conception of the political order and the one most conducive to the theory and practice of federalism.

This notion of covenant, of a lasting yet limited agreement between free men or between free families of men, entered into freely by the parties concerned to achieve common ends or to protect common rights, has its roots in the Hebrew Bible. There the covenant principle stands at the very center of the relationship between man and God and also forms the basis for the establishment of the holy commonwealth. The covenant idea passed into early Christianity only after losing its political implications. Its political sense was restored during the Protestant reformation, particularly by the Protestant groups influenced by Calvin and the Hebrew Bible, the same groups that dominated the political revolutionary movements in Britain and America in the seventeenth and eighteenth centuries. Much of the American reliance upon the covenant principle stems from the attempts of religiously-inspired settlers on these shores to reproduce that kind of covenant in the New World and to build their commonwealths upon it. The Yankees of New England, the Scotch-Irish of the mountains and piedmont from Pennsylvania to Georgia, the Dutch of New York, the Presbyterians, and to a lesser extent, the Quakers and German Sectarians of Pennsylvania and the Middle States were all nurtured in churches constructed on the covenant principle and subscribing to the federal theology as the means for properly delineating the relationship between man and God (and, by extension, between man and man) as revealed by the Bible itself.

By the middle of the eighteenth century, however, the covenant idea had been plucked from its religious roots and secularized by men like Hobbes, Locke, and Rousseau. The transformed it into the concept of the *social compact*, the freely-assumed bond between man and man that lifted men out of an unbearable state of nature and into civilization. In the Lockean view widely admired by Americans, it was this social compact that made popular government possible. The availability of the covenant idea in two forms meant that those Americans who did not acknowledge the political character of the covenant between man and God inevitably recognized the political character of the social compact between man and man and built their constitutions upon that.

The evidence is overwhelming that the covenant principle translated into the larger political realm as part of the development of modern popular government produced the idea of federalism. The history and meaning of the term itself reveals this. The word *federal* is derived from the Latin *feodus* which means covenant. It was first used in 1645, in the midst of the English Civil War to describe covenantal relationships of both a political and a theological nature. Apparently, as its theological usage would indicate the term implied a closer or a more permanent relationship than its slightly older companion, *confederal*, a Middle English derivative of the same Latin root. At first the two words were so closely related that they were used synonymously until the American Civil War added an additional dimension to the theory of federalism by sharpening the distinction between them. *Federal* was not used in its present sense until 1777 during the American Revolution. Its modern usage, then, is an American invention. The creation of the term *federalism* to indicate the existence of a "federal principle or system of political organization" (quoting the Oxford Universal Dictionary), did not come until 1793 after the principle was already embodied in a great work of political theory and the constitution of a potentially great nation.

Covenant (or federal) theory was widely appreciated and deeply rooted in the American tradition in 1787 because it was not the property of philosophers, theologians, or intellectuals alone. In its various adaptations, it was used for a variety of very public enterprises from the establishment of colonial self-government to the creation of the great trading corporations of the seventeenth century. Americans made covenants or compacts to establish new civil societies regularly. Witness the Mayflower Compact (1620):

*IN The name of God, Amen. We whose names are under written, . . . Having undertaken for the Glory of God, and Advancement of the Christian Faith, and the Honour of our King and Country, a Voyage to plant the first colony in the northern Parts of Virginia; Do by these Presents, solemnly and mutually in the Presence of God and one another, covenant and combine ourselves together into a civil Body Politick, for our better Ordering and Preservation, and Furtherance of the Ends aforesaid . . .*

the Virginia Bill of Rights (1776):

*[A]ll men are by nature equally free and independent, and have certain inherent rights, of which, when they enter into a state of society, they cannot by any compact deprive or divest their posterity, namely, the enjoyment of life and liberty, with the means of property, and pursuing and obtaining happiness and safety.*

the Vermont Declaration of Independence (1777):

*We, . . . the inhabitants, [of the New Hampshire grants] are at present without law or government, and may be truly said to be in a state of nature; consequently a right remains to the people of said Grants to form a government best suited to secure their property, well being and happiness.*

the Constitution of Massachusetts (written by none other than John Adams in 1779):

*The body politic is formed by a voluntary association of individuals. It is a social compact by which the whole people covenants with each citizen and each citizen with the whole people, that all shall be governed by certain laws for the common good. It is the duty of the people, therefore, in framing a Constitution of Government, to provide for an equitable mode of making laws, as well as for an impartial interpretation and a faithful execution of them, that every man may, at all times, find his security in them.*

Covenant-making remained a part of the settlement process throughout the days of the land frontier. Men gathered together in every one of the thirty seven states admitted to the Union after the original thirteen to freely frame constitutions for their government in the manner of the first compacts establishing local self-government in the New World. Cities and towns were created by compact whenever bodies of men and their families joined together to establish communities devoted to common ends.

With the rise of organizations, the covenant principle was given new purpose. Scientific and reform societies, labor unions, and professional associations, as well as business corporations covenanted with one another to form larger organizations while preserving their own integrities. They initiated a new kind of federalization which continues to this day.

As a consequence of these manifold uses of the covenant idea, the American "instinct" for federalism was extended into most areas of human relationship shaping American notions of individualism, human rights and obligations, Divine expectations, business organization, civic association and church structure as well as their notions of politics. While there were differences in interpretation of the covenant principle among theologians, political leaders directly motivated by religious principles and those within a secular political outlook; among New Englanders, residents of the Middle States, and Southerners; and from generation to generation, there was also a broad area of general agreement which unified all who subscribed to the principle and which set them and their doctrine apart within the larger realm of political theory. All agreed on the importance of popular or republican government, the necessity to diffuse power, and the importance of individual rights and dignity as the foundation of any genuinely good political system. At the same time, all agreed that the existence of inalienable rights was not an excuse for anarchy just as the existence of ineradicable human passions was not an excuse for tyranny. For them, the covenant provided a means for free men to form political communities without sacrificing their essential freedom and without making energetic government impossible.

The implications of the federal principle are brought home forcefully when it is contrasted with the other conception of popular government developed in the modern era. Other revolutionaries in the "Age of Revolutions" that has existed since the late eighteenth century—most prominent among them the Jacobins—also sought solutions to some of the same problems of despotism that perturbed the Americans. But, in their efforts to hurry the achievement of the millennium, they rejected what they believed to be the highly pessimistic assumptions of the American constitution-makers that unlimited political power could even corrupt "the people" and considered only the problem of autocratic despotism. They looked upon federalism and its principles of checks and balances as subversive of the "general will," their way of expressing a commitment to the organic unity of society, which, like their pre-modern predecessors, they saw as superior to the mere interests of individuals. They argued that, since their "new society" was to be based on "the general will" as a more democratic principle, any element subversive of its organic unity would be, *ipso facto*, anti-democratic.

By retaining notions of the organic society, the Jacobins and their revolutionary heirs were forced to rely upon transient majorities to establish consensus or to concentrate power in the hands of an elite that claimed to do the same thing. The first course invariably led to anarchy and the second to the kind of totalitarian democracy which has become the essence of modern dictatorship. While the "general will" was undoubtedly a more democratic concept than the "will of the monarch," in the last analysis it has proved to be no less despotic and usually even more subversive of liberty.

The history of the extension of democratic government since the eighteenth century has been a history of the rivalry between these two conceptions of democracy. Because of the challenge of Jacobinism, the meaning of the American idea of federal democracy takes on increased importance.

### The American Federal Consensus

The framers of the Constitution capitalized on the American instinct for federalism which had already revealed itself in the nationwide organization for the revolutionary struggle and in the first constitution of the United States. In one sense, they simply tried to improve the American political system within the framework of the covenant idea by creating—as they put it—a "more perfect union."

The results of their work were not accepted uncritically at the time nor did the results remain unmodified after the ratification of the Constitution. Their emphasis on the "national" as distinct from "federal" aspects of the new Union (the terms are those of *The Federalist*) did not sit well with the majority of the American people who felt keenly that emphasis on the federal aspects was necessary to keep government limited, taxes low, and liberties secure.

The anti-federalists lost their fight to prevent ratification of the Constitution but, by immediately accepting the verdict and entering into the spirit of the new consensus, they soon won over a majority of the American people. After the Jeffersonian victory in 1800, the dominant theoretical emphasis around the nation was to be on the primacy of the states as custodians of the nation's political power, an emphasis that was to be dented from time to time—substantially between 1861 and 1876—but not altered until the twentieth century. This emphasis provided a very hospitable environment for the development of the "states rights" heresy that colored the actions of Southerners during the Civil War generation.

In reality, the debate over the meaning of the American covenant and its federal principles began anew under the Constitution, has continued ever since, and will no doubt continue so long as the American people remain concerned with constitutional government as an essential element of the American mystique.

Its very existence adds to the health of the body politic. Yet, from first to last, it has remained a debate over interpretation of the meaning of the federal principle and not over the validity of the principle as such.

Though the debate has involved vital questions of the first magnitude, it has been carried on within the context of a political consensus that is all the more remarkable for having changed so little in some two hundred years. Rarely, if ever, given verbal expression as a whole, the existence of this consensus is attested to by scores of commentators on the American scene from Crevecouer to Max Lerner and from de Toqueville to D. W. Brogan. More impressive testimony is found in the behavior of the American people when that consensus has been threatened. Abandoning their more transient allegiances, they have invariably responded to the call, changing their "normal" patterns of behavior—often to the amazement of observers lacking historical perspective—for others more appropriate to the situation. It is this instinctive understanding of the basics of the American political system that sustains popular government despite the mistakes of transient majorities. The consensus itself is imbued with the spirit of federalism through and through, though it extends much beyond a concern with the strict institutional aspects of the federal system to embrace the ideas of partnership and blance which, put together, give birth to the federal principle.

### The Purpose of This Book

This volume, then, is designed to explore the American system of government as a federal system, one with governments operating on three planes—federal, state, and local—yet functioning as one integrated and interdependent governmental system imbued with the federal principles of cooperation and negotiation in all its parts. The central theme of this book is that the governments on all three planes have a share in virtually all governmental activities in the United States. Consequently, we will be concerned with viewing their interrelationship, investigating its causes and support, understanding how the system operates in practice, and briefly examining the relationship between federal theory and federal practices in American political life.

Considering the pervasiveness of federal principles and their accompanying processes in the American political system, a book on federalism, strictly speaking, would have to encompass a discussion of every aspect of American government and politics. Such an undertaking would require more space and demand more detail than desirable in an introduction to the subject. In this brief volume I have sought to highlight certain aspects of the American political scene which reflect the politics of federalism most directly and explicitly and to provide some examples of the impact of federal principles and the federal spirit in fields not generally associated with federalism as it is formally perceived.

The following articles deal with such problems as the relationship between law, politics, and administration in a federal system; the functions of political parties in the maintenance of non-centralized government; "states rights," centralization, and federal power; and the reciprocal impacts of the federal government on state and local governments and vice versa. The emphasis is on the politics of federalism; hence, discussions of legal and constitutional material, administrative operations, judicial proceedings, and the like, are subsumed under a larger concern with the making of policy, the representation of interests, and the filling of political offices.

The book is divided into three parts. Part One is designed to present an historical and theoretical framework within which to view the American federal system as it is presently constituted and functions. Part Two examines the federal system in action. Through a series of case studies, consideration is given to the party system, the politics of congressional-executive relations, the role of federal aid in the political matrix of American federalism, the view from the states and localities and the operational patterns of the system. Part Three is concerned with the meaning of federalism in the United States and the ways in which the federal system is maintained as a political system responsive to changing times and conditions.

The reader will notice that this book, unlike other efforts to discuss the American political system which present the opposing views of differing observers, does not attempt to present an argument and a counter argument, either as to the nature of the system or as to its desirability or utility. While the editor appreciates the point of view of those who argue that the federal system was created in such a way as to assign each level of government its own sphere of activity with a minimal amount of overlapping and understands the position of those who advocate "restoration" of that separation by diminishing the federal role, the historical and empirical evidence against their position is so overwhelming that there cannot be two sides to the question of fact, even though it is perfectly reasonable to argue that the facts are disappointing or even deserving of change. Nor do those who advocate greater centralization of power in the hands of Washington on the grounds that the states have failed to get much of a hearing, since their argument is based on premises equally as erroneous as their orthodox "states rights" counterparts. Since this volume seeks to describe the system as it is rather than discuss what it ought to be, arguments of centralizers or decentralizers must be ruled out of place, no matter how legitimate they might appear to the editor or his readers.

By the same token, discussions of the utility or desirability of the federal system are avoided, though it is impossible not to detect a general pattern of support or even endorsement of American federalism as it is presently constituted on the part of the authors of the selections that are included. Perhaps it is inevitable that those men who have pioneered in the study of American federalism should tend to be sympathetic towards the system they seek to understand. The editor acknowledges his own bias in that direction. At the same time, he has concluded, in as unbiased a manner as possible, that those who have tried to examine the system from a more negative standpoint, have, with a few exceptions, failed to achieve the first requisite of honest criticism—that of understanding.

One final note: While the American system is generally—and justifiably —considered the prototype for all federal systems, the patterns evolved in this country are not the only possible ones. Both Canada and Switzerland, though influenced by the American model, have developed prototypes of their own which have, in turn, influenced other federal systems where such patterns are more applicable than ours. Moreover, every country with a federal system has its own unique combinations and variations of patterns generally common to all. The American conception of federalism is tied intimately to a frontier society that is constantly directed toward change and "progress." Political institutions in this dynamic society play a dual role; they act as conservative forces in a society dedicated to "the tradition of the new" and, at the same time, they are expected to adjust themselves rapidly to accommodate major technological and social changes. Almost every major question that has been raised over the efficacy or propriety of the American federal system has been related directly to the emergence of new "frontier" problems or the aggravation of old ones by changing frontier conditions. Most other federal systems, particularly those of the old world, are predicated on the maintenance of the *status quo* or something quite akin to it. At the very least, they are geared for social orders in which change is not considered the fundamental reality. Thus they tend to rely more heavily on legal theories and constitutional devices to maintain the diffusion of power rather than on the political process. Whether, as their societies become more dynamic they, too, will show tendencies previously manifested in the American federal system is as yet uncertain.

# I. *The American System: an Historical and Theoretical Framework*

The relationship between constitutionalism, the political process and the larger environment in the United States is a matter of perennial interest. In the very first years of the Republic and again in the last decade, numerous students of federalism have tried to come to grips with the web of relationships that tie the three together. The following selections represent four variations of the dominant view of the relationship over the years. The first, that of *The Federalist*, projects the vision of the relationship conceived by the best spokesmen for the framers of the Constitution itself. The other selections, by students who have examined the system as it actually operates, are agreed that intergovernmental cooperation is not only pervasive but fully compatible with the maintenance of the federal system. Nevertheless, the reader will note differences in their respective approaches, based, in part, on the questions which they raise.

In many respects the thesis presented by Morton Grodzins is the underlying thesis of this volume. The pervasiveness of sharing, to use Grodzins' terminology, is the keynote of American federalism and the understanding of how things are shared is the key to understanding American federalism.

William Anderson, one of the pioneers in the study of American federalism, explores the contemporary constitutional basis for the sharing system by analyzing the overall direction of constitutional interpretation today. This selection is taken from the book he published as a "minority report" on the work of the Commission on Intergovernmental Relations headed by Meyer Kestnbaum, which was appointed by President Eisenhower in 1953 to investigate the federal system with a view to restoring the place of the states and localities within that system. The work of the Kestnbaum Commission represented a landmark step in the revival of scholarly and public concern for the problems of federalism, yet its conventional conclusions have had considerably less impact than the forward-looking minority report which Professor Anderson wisely chose to publish separately.

"The Shaping of Intergovernmental Relations in the Twentieth Century," written at the beginning of the recent expansion of federal activities, emphasizes the devices which have been developed to expand and routinize the cooperative relationships. It contrasts the shifting patterns of intergovernmental rela-

1

tions with the continuing emphasis on sharing that has been characteristic of the system in any age.

Herbert Wechsler discusses the role of the electoral system as a powerful force working for non-centralization by introducing federal principles into the national government. While some of his figures have changed in the decade since the original publication of his essay and the United States Supreme Court has seen fit to step into the redistricting issue, the thrust of his argument remains as powerful today as ever. The selection included here is one of several in this book taken from the Columbia University bicentennial symposium on American federalism which, coming in the same year as the publication of the reports of the Commission on Intergovernmental Relations, had a major impact on subsequent consideration of the problems of American federalism. The Columbia symposium essentially confirms the perspective offered by Professors Anderson (a participant) and Grodzins.

*John Jay*

## THE FEDERALIST NO. 2

October 31, 1787

*To the People of the State of New York.*

WHEN the people of America reflect that they are now called upon to decide a question, which, in its consequences, must prove one of the most important, that ever engaged their attention, the propriety of their taking a very comprehensive, as well as a very serious view of it, will be evident.

Nothing is more certain than the indispensable necessity of Government, and it is equally undeniable, that whenever and however it is instituted, the people must cede to it some of their natural rights, in order to vest it with requisite powers. It is well worthy of consideration therefore, whether it would conduce more to the interest of the people of America, that they should, to all general purposes, be one nation, under one federal Government, than that they should divide themselves ·into separate confederacies, and give to the head of each, the same kind of powers which they are advised to place in one national Government.

It has until lately been a received and uncontradicted opinion, that the prosperity of the people of America depended on their continuing firmly united, and the wishes, prayers, and efforts of our best and wisest Citizens have been constantly directed to that object. But Politicians now appear, who insist that this opinion is erroneous, and that instead of looking for safety and happiness in union, we ought to seek it in a division of the States into distinct confederacies or sovereignties. However extraordinary this new doctrine may appear, it nevertheless has its advocates; and certain characters who were much opposed to it formerly, are at present of the number. Whatever may be the arguments or inducements, which have wrought this change in the sentiments and declarations of these Gentlemen, it certainly would not be wise in the people at large to adopt

From *The Federalist*, ed. Jacob E. Cooke (Wesleyan University Press: 1961), pp. 8–10.

these new political tenets without being fully convinced that they are founded in truth and sound Policy.

It has often given me pleasure to observe, that Independent America was not composed of detached and distant territories, but that one connected, fertile, wide spreading country was the portion of our western sons of liberty. Providence has in a particular manner blessed it with a variety of soils and productions, and watered it with innumerable streams, for the delight and accommodation of its inhabitants. A succession of navigable waters forms a kind of chain round its borders, as if to bind it together; while the most noble rivers in the world, running at convenient distances, present them with highways for the easy communication of friendly aids, and the mutual transportation and exchange of their various commodities.

With equal pleasure I have as often taken notice, that Providence has been pleased to give this one connected country, to one united people, a people descended from the same ancestors, speaking the same language, professing the same religion, attached to the same principles of government, very similar in their manners and customs, and who, by their joint counsels, arms and efforts, fighting side by side throughout a long and bloody war, have nobly established their general Liberty and Independence.

This country and this people seem to have been made for each other, and it appears as if it was the design of Providence, that an inheritance so proper and convenient for a band of brethren, united to each other by the strongest ties, should never be split into a number of unsocial, jealous and alien sovereignties.

Similar sentiments have hitherto prevailed among all orders and denominations of men among us. To all general purposes we have uniformly been one people — each individual citizen every where enjoying the same national rights, privileges, and protection. As a nation we have made peace and war — as a nation we have vanquished our common enemies — as a nation we have formed alliances and made treaties, and entered into various compacts and conventions with foreign States.

A strong sense of the value and blessings of Union induced the people, at a very early period, to institute a Fœderal Government to preserve and perpetuate it. They formed it almost as soon as they had a political existence; nay at a time, when their habitations were in flames, when many of their Citizens were bleeding, and when the progress of hostility and desolation left little room for those calm and mature enquiries and reflections, which must ever precede the formation of a wise and well balanced government for a free people. It is not to be wondered at that a Government instituted in times so inauspicious, should on experiment be found greatly deficient and inadequate to the purpose it was intended to answer. . . .

*Alexander Hamilton*

# THE FEDERALIST NO. 9

November 21, 1787

The utility of a confederacy, as well to suppress faction and to guard the internal tranquillity of States, as to increase their external force and security, is in reality not a new idea. It has been practiced upon in different countries and ages, and has received the sanction of the most applauded writers, on the subjects of politics. The op-

From *The Federalist*, ed. Jacob E. Cooke (Wesleyan University Press: 1961), pp. 52-56.

ponents of the PLAN proposed have with great assiduity cited and circulated the observations of Montesquieu on the necessity of a contracted territory for a republican government. But they seem not to have been apprised of the sentiments of that great man expressed in another part of his work, nor to have adverted to the consequences of the principle to which they subscribe, with such ready acquiescence.

When Montesquieu recommends a small extent for republics, the standards he had in view were of dimensions, far short of the limits of almost every one of these States. Neither Virginia, Massachusetts, Pennsylvania, New-York, North-Carolina, nor Georgia, can by any means be compared with the models, from which he reasoned and to which the terms of his description apply. If we therefore take his ideas on this point, as the criterion of truth, we shall be driven to the alternative, either of taking refuge at once in the arms of monarchy, or of splitting ourselves into an infinity of little jealous, clashing, tumultuous commonwealths, the wretched nurseries of unceasing discord and the miserable objects of universal pity or contempt. Some of the writers, who have come forward on the other side of the question, seem to have been aware of the dilemma; and have even been bold enough to hint at the division of the larger States, as a desirable thing. Such an infatuated policy, such a desperate expedient, might, by the multiplication of petty offices, answer the views of men, who possess not qualifications to extend their influence beyond the narrow circles of personal intrigue, but it could never promote the greatness or happiness of the people of America.

Referring the examination of the principle itself to another place, as has been already mentioned, it will be sufficient to remark here, that in the sense of the author who has been most emphatically quoted upon the occasion, it would only dictate a reduction of the SIZE of the more considerable MEMBERS of the Union; but would not militate against their being all compre-

hended in one Confederate Government. And this is the true question, in the discussion of which we are at present interested.

So far are the suggestions of Montesquieu from standing in opposition to a general Union of the States, that he explicitly treats of a CONFEDERATE REPUBLIC as the expedient for extending the sphere of popular government and reconciling the advantages of monarchy with those of republicanism.

"It is very probable (says he) that mankind would have been obliged, at length, to live constantly under the government of a SINGLE PERSON, had they not contrived a kind of constitution, that has all the internal advantages of a republican, together with the external force of a monarchial government. I mean a CONFEDERATE REPUBLIC.

"This form of Government is a Convention, by which several smaller *States* agree to become members of a larger *one*, which they intend to form. It is a kind of assemblage of societies, that constitute a new one, capable of increasing by means of new associations, till they arrive to such a degree of power as to be able to provide for the security of the united body.

"A republic of this kind, able to withstand an external force, may support itself without any internal corruption. The form of this society prevents all manner of inconveniencies.

"If a single member should attempt to usurp the supreme authority, he could not be supposed to have an equal authority and credit, in all the confederate states. Were he to have too great influence over one, this would alarm the rest. Were he to subdue a part, that which would still remain free might oppose him with forces, independent of those which he had usurped, and overpower him before he could be settled in his usurpation.

"Should a popular insurrection happen, in one of the confederate States, the others are able to quell it. Should abuses creep into one part, they are reformed by those that remain sound. The State may be destroyed on one side, and not on the other; the confederacy may be dissolved, and the confederates preserve their sovereignty.

"As this government is composed of small republics it enjoys the internal happiness of each, and with respect to its external situation it is possessed, by means of the association of all the advantages of large monarchies."

I have thought it proper to quote at length these interesting passages, because they contain a luminous abridgement of the principal arguments in favour of the Union, and must effectually remove the false impressions, which a misapplication of other parts of the work was calculated to produce. They have at the same time an intimate connection with the more immediate design of this Paper; which is to illustrate the tendency of the Union to repress domestic faction and insurrection.

A distinction, more subtle than accurate, has been raised between a *confederacy* and a *consolidation* of the States. The essential characteristic of the first is said to be, the restriction of its authority to the members in their collective capacities, without reaching to the individuals of whom they are composed. It is contended that the national council ought to have no concern with any object of internal administration. An exact equality of suffrage between the members has also been insisted upon as a leading feature of a Confederate Government. These positions are in the main arbitrary; they are supported neither by principle nor precedent. It has indeed happened that governments of this kind have generally operated in the manner, which the distinction, taken notice of, supposes to be inherent in their nature—but there have been in most of them extensive exceptions to the practice, which serve to prove as far as example will go, that there is no absolute rule on the subject. And it will be clearly shown, in the course of this investigation, that as far as the principle contended for has prevailed, it has been the

cause of incurable disorder and imbecility in the government.

The definition of a *Confederate Republic* seems simply to be, an "assemblage of societies" or an association of two or more States into one State. The extent, modifications and objects of the Fœderal authority are mere matters of discretion. So long as the separate organisation of the members be not abolished, so long as it exists by a constitutional necessity for local purposes, though it should be in perfect subordination to the general authority of the Union, it would still be, in fact and in theory, an association of States, or a confederacy. The proposed Constitution, so far from implying an abolition of the State Governments, makes them constituent parts of the national sovereignty by allowing them a direct representation in the Senate, and leaves in their possession certain exclusive and very important portions of sovereign power. This fully corresponds, in every rational import of the terms, with the idea of a Fœderal Government.

In the Lycian confederacy, which consisted of twenty three CITIES or republics, the largest were entitled to *three* votes in the COMMON COUNCIL, those of the middle class to *two* and the smallest to *one*. The COMMON COUNCIL had the appointment of all the judges and magistrates of the respective CITIES. This was certainly the most delicate species of interference in their internal administration; for if there be any thing, that seems exclusively appropriated to the local jurisdictions, it is the appointment of their own officers. Yet Montesquieu, speaking of this association, says "Were I to give a model of an excellent confederate republic, it would be that of Lycia." Thus we perceive that the distinctions insisted upon were not within the contemplation of this enlightened civilian, and we shall be led to conclude that they are the novel refinements of an erroneous theory.

PUBLIUS.

James Madison

# THE FEDERALIST NO. 37

January 11, 1788

Stability in Government, is essential to national character, and to the advantages annexed to it, as well as to that repose and confidence in the minds of the people, which are among the chief blessings of civil society. An irregular and mutable legislation, is not more an evil in itself, than it is odious to the people; and it may be pronounced with assurance, that the people of this country, enlightened as they are, with regard to the nature, and interested, as the great body of them are, in the effects of good Government, will never be satisfied, till some remedy be applied to the vicissitudes and uncertainties, which characterize the State administrations. On comparing, however, these valuable ingredients with the vital principles of liberty, we must perceive at once, the difficulty of mingling them together in their due proportions. The genius of Republican liberty, seems to demand on one side, not only that all power should be derived from the people; but, that those entrusted with it should be kept in dependence on the people, by a short duration of their appointments; and, that, even during this short period, the trust should be placed not in a few, but in a number of hands. Stability, on the contrary, requires, that the hands, in which power is lodged, should continue for a length of time, the same. A frequent change of men will result from a frequent return of electors, and a frequent change of measures, from a frequent change of men: whilst energy in Government requires not only a certain duration of power, but the execution of it by a single hand. How far the Convention may have succeeded in this part of their work, will better appear on a more accurate view of it. From the cursory view, here taken, it must clearly appear to have been an arduous part.

Not less arduous must have been the task of marking the proper line of partition, between the authority of the general, and that of the State Governments. Every man will be sensible of this difficulty, in proportion, as he has been accustomed to contemplate and discriminate objects, extensive and complicated in their nature. The faculties of the mind itself have never yet been distinguished and defined, with satisfactory precision, by all the efforts of the most acute and metaphysical Philosophers. Sense, perception, judgment, desire, volition, memory, imagination, are found to be separated by such delicate shades, and minute gradations, that their boundaries have eluded the most subtle investigations, and remain a pregnant source of ingenious disquisition and controversy. The boundaries between the great kingdoms of nature, and still more, between the various provinces, and lesser portions, into which they are subdivided, afford another illustration of the same important truth. The most sagacious and laborious naturalists have never yet succeeded, in tracing with certainty, the line which separates the district of vegetable life from the neighboring region of unorganized matter, or which marks the termination of the former and the commencement of the animal empire. A still greater obscurity lies in the distinctive characters, by which the objects in each of these great departments of nature, have been arranged and assorted. When we pass

From *The Federalist*, ed. Jacob E. Cooke (Wesleyan University Press: 1961), pp. 234–238.

from the works of nature, in which all the delineations are perfectly accurate, and appear to be otherwise only from the imperfection of the eye which surveys them, to the institutions of man, in which the obscurity arises as well from the object itself, as from the organ by which it is contemplated; we must perceive the necessity of moderating still farther our expectations and hopes from the efforts of human sagacity. Experience has instructed us that no skill in the science of Government has yet been able to discriminate and define, with sufficient certainty, its three great provinces, the Legislative, Executive and Judiciary; or even the privileges and powers of the different Legislative branches. Questions daily occur in the course of practice, which prove the obscurity which reigns in these subjects, and which puzzle the greatest adepts in political science. The experience of ages, with the continued and combined labors of the most enlightened Legislators and jurists, have been equally unsuccessful in delineating the several objects and limits of different codes of laws and different tribunals of justice. The precise extent of the common law, the statute law, the maritime law, the ecclesiastical law, the law of corporations and other local laws and customs, remain still to be clearly and finally established in Great-Britain, where accuracy in such subjects has been more industriously pursued than in any other part of the world. The jurisdiction of her several courts, general and local, of law, of equity, of admiralty, &c. is not less a source of frequent and intricate discussions, sufficiently denoting the indeterminate limits by which they are respectively circumscribed. All new laws, though penned with the greatest technical skill, and passed on the fullest and most mature deliberation, are considered as more or less obscure and equivocal, until their meaning be liquidated and ascertained by a series of particular discussions and adjudications. Besides the obscurity arising from the complexity of objects, and the imperfection of the human faculties, the medium through which the conceptions of men are conveyed to each other, adds a fresh embarrassment. The use of words is to express ideas. Perspicuity therefore requires not only that the ideas should be distinctly formed, but that they should be expressed by words distinctly and exclusively appropriated to them. But no language is so copious as to supply words and phrases for every complex idea, or so correct as not to include many equivocally denoting different ideas. Hence, it must happen, that however accurately objects may be disciminated in themselves, and however accurately the discrimination may be considered, the definition of them may be rendered inaccurate by the inaccuracy of the terms in which it is delivered. And this unavoidable inaccuracy must be greater or less, according to the complexity and novelty of the objects defined. When the Almighty himself condescends to address mankind in their own language, his meaning, luminous as it must be, is rendered dim and doubtful, by the cloudy medium through which it is communicated. Here then are three sources of vague and incorrect definitions; indistinctness of the object, imperfection of the organ of conception, inadequateness of the vehicle of ideas. Any one of these must produce a certain degree of obscurity. The Convention, in delineating the boundary between the Federal and State jurisdictions, must have experienced the full effect of them all.

To the difficulties already mentioned, may be added the interfering pretensions of the larger and smaller States. We cannot err in supposing that the former would contend for a participation in the Government, fully proportioned to their superior wealth and importance; and that the latter would not be less tenacious of the equality at present enjoyed by them. We may well suppose that neither side would entirely yield to the other, and consequently that the struggle could be terminated only by compromise. It is extremely probable also, that after the ratio of representation had been adjusted, this very compromise must have produced a fresh struggle between the same parties, to give such a turn to the organization of the Government, and to the distribution of its powers, as would encrease the importance of the branches, in forming which they had respectively obtained the greatest share of influence. There are features in the Constitution which warrant each of these suppositions; and as far as either of them is well founded, it shews that the Convention must have been compelled to sacrifice theoretical propriety to the force of extraneous considerations.

Nor could it have been the large and small States only which would marshal themselves in opposition to each other on various points. Other combinations, resulting from a difference of local position and policy, must have created additional difficulties. As every State may be divided into different districts, and its citizens into different classes, which give birth to contending interests and local jealousies; so the different parts of the United States are distinguished from each other, by a variety of circumstances, which produce a like effect on a larger scale. And although this variety of interests, for reasons sufficiently explained in a former paper, may have a salutary influence on the administration of the Government when formed; yet every one must be sensible of the contrary influence which must have been experienced in the task of forming it.

Would it be wonderful if under the pressure of all these difficulties, the Convention should have been forced into some deviations from that artificial structure and regular symmetry, which an abstract view of the subject might lead an ingenious theorist to bestow on a Constitution planned in his closet or in his imagination? The real wonder is, that so many difficulties should have been surmounted; and surmounted with a unanimity almost as unprecedented as it must have been unexpected. It is impossible for any man of candor to reflect on this circumstance, without partaking of the astonishment. It is impossible for the man of pious reflection not to perceive in it, a finger of that Almighty hand which has been so frequently and signally extended to our relief in the critical stages of the revolution.

*James Madison*

## THE FEDERALIST NO. 51

February 6, 1788

*To the People of the State of New York.*

To what expedient then shall we finally resort for maintaining in practice the necessary partition of power among the several departments, as laid down in the constitution? The only answer that can be given is, that as all these exterior provisions are found to be inadequate, the defect must be supplied, by so contriving the interior structure of the government, as that its several constituent parts may, by their mutual relations, be the means of keeping each other in their proper places. Without presuming to undertake a full developement of this important idea, I will hazard a few general observations, which may perhaps place it in a clearer light, and enable us to form a more correct judgment of the principles and structure of the government planned by the convention.

In order to lay a due foundation for that separate and distinct exercise of the different powers of government, which to a certain extent, is admitted on all hands to be essential to the preservation of liberty, it is

From *The Federalist*, ed. Jacob E. Cooke (Wesleyan University Press: 1961), pp. 347–353.

evident that each department should have a will of its own; and consequently should be so constituted, that the members of each should have as little agency as possible in the appointment of the members of the others. Were this principle rigorously adhered to, it would require that all the appointments for the supreme executive, legislative, and judiciary magistracies, should be drawn from the same fountain of authority, the people, through channels, having no communication whatever with one another. Perhaps such a plan of constructing the several departments would be less difficult in practice than it may in contemplation appear. Some difficulties however, and some additional expence, would attend the execution of it. Some deviations therefore from the principle must be admitted. In the constitution of the judiciary department in particular, it might be inexpedient to insist rigorously on the principle; first, because peculiar qualifications being essential in the members, the primary consideration ought to be to select that mode of choice, which best secures these qualifications; secondly, because the permanent tenure by which the appointments are held in that department, must soon destroy all sense of dependence on the authority conferring them.

It is equally evident that the members of each department should be as little dependent as possible on those of the others, for the emoluments annexed to their offices. Were the executive magistrate, or the judges, not independent of the legislature in this particular, their independence in every other would be merely nominal.

But the great security against a gradual concentration of the several powers in the same department, consists in giving to those who administer each department, the necessary constitutional means, and personal motives, to resist encroachments of the others. The provision for defence must in this, as in all other cases, be made commensurate to the danger of attack. Ambition must be made to counteract ambition. The interest of the man must be connected with the constitutional rights of the place. It may be a reflection on human nature, that such devices should be necessary to controul the abuses of government. But what is government itself but the greatest of all reflections on human nature? If men were angels, no government would be necessary. If angels were to govern men, neither external nor internal controuls on government would be necessary. In framing a government which is to be administered by men over men, the great difficulty lies in this: You must first enable the government to controul the governed; and in the next place, oblige it to controul itself. A dependence on the people is no doubt the primary controul on the government; but experience has taught mankind the necessity of auxiliary precautions.

This policy of supplying by opposite and rival interests, the defect of better motives, might be traced through the whole system of human affairs, private as well as public. We see it particularly displayed in all the subordinate distributions of power; where the constant aim is to divide and arrange the several offices in such a manner as that each may be a check on the other; that the private interest of every individual, may be a centinel over the public rights. These inventions of prudence cannot be less requisite in the distribution of the supreme powers of the state.

But it is not possible to give to each department an equal power of self defence. In republican government the legislative authority, necessarily, predominates. The remedy for this inconveniency is, to divide the legislature into different branches; and to render them by different modes of election, and different principles of action, as little connected with each other, as the nature of their common functions, and their common dependence on the society, will admit. It may even be necessary to guard against dangerous encroachments by still further precautions. As the weight of the legislative authority requires that it should be thus divided, the weakness of the executive may require, on the other hand, that it should be fortified. An absolute negative, on the legislature, appears at first view to be the natural defence with which the executive magistrate should be armed. But perhaps it would be neither altogether safe, nor alone sufficient. On ordinary occasions, it might not be exerted with the requisite firmness; and on extraordinary occasions, it might be perfidiously abused. May not this defect of an absolute negative be supplied, by some qualified connection between this weaker department, and the weaker branch of the stronger department, by which the latter may be led to support the constitutional rights of the former, without being too much detached from the rights of its own department?

If the principles on which these observations are founded be just, as I persuade myself they are, and they be applied as a criterion, to the several state constitutions, and to the federal constitution, it will be found, that if the latter does not perfectly correspond with them, the former are infinitely less able to bear such a test.

There are moreover two considerations particularly applicable to the federal system of America, which place that system in a very interesting point of view.

*First.* In a single republic, all the power surrendered by the people, is submitted to the administration of a single government; and usurpations are guarded against by a division of the government into distinct and separate departments. In the compound republic of America, the power surrendered by the people, is first divided between two distinct governments, and then the portion allotted to each, subdivided among distinct and separate departments. Hence a double security arises to the rights of the people. The different governments will controul each other; at the same time that each will be controuled by itself.

*Second.* It is of great importance in a republic, not only to guard the society against the oppression of its rulers; but to guard one part of the society against the injustice of the other part. Different interests necessarily exist in different classes of citizens. If a majority be united by a common interest, the rights of the minority will be insecure. There are but two methods of providing against this evil: The one by creating a will in the community independent of the majority, that is, of the society itself; the other by comprehending in the society so many separate descriptions of citizens, as will render an unjust combination of a majority of the whole, very improbable, if not impracticable. The first method prevails in all governments possessing an hereditary or self appointed authority. This at best is but a precarious security; because a power independent of the society may as well espouse the unjust views of the major, as the rightful interests, of the minor party, and may possibly be turned against both parties. The second method will be exemplified in the federal republic of the United States. Whilst all authority in it will be derived from and dependent on the society, the society itself will be broken into so many parts, interests and classes of citizens, that the rights of individuals or of the minority, will be in little danger from interested combinations of the majority. In a free government, the security for civil rights must be the same as for religious rights. It consists in the one case in the multiplicity of interests, and in the other, in the multiplicity of sects. The degree of security in both cases will depend on the number of interests and sects; and this may be presumed to depend on the extent of country and number of people comprehended under the same government. This view of the subject must particularly recommend a proper federal system to all the sincere and considerate friends of republican government: Since it shews that in exact proportion as the territory of the union may be formed into more circumscribed confederacies or states, oppressive combinations of a majority will be facilitated, the best security under the republican form, for the rights of every class of citizens, will be diminished; and consequently, the stability and independence of some member of the government, the only other security, must be proportionally increased. Justice is the end of government. It is the end of civil society. It ever has been, and ever will be pursued, until it be obtained, or until liberty be lost in the pursuit. In a society under the forms of which the stronger faction can readily unite and oppress the weaker, anarchy may as truly be said to reign, as in a state of nature where the weaker individual is not secured against the violence of the stronger: And as in the latter state even the stronger individuals are prompted by the uncertainty of their condition, to submit to a government which may protect the weak as well as themselves: So in the former state, will the more powerful factions or parties be gradually induced by a like motive, to wish for a government which will protect all parties, the weaker as well as the more powerful. It can be little doubted, that if the state of Rhode Island was separated from the confederacy, and left to itself, the insecurity of rights under the popular form of government within such narrow limits, would be displayed by such reiterated oppressions of factious majorities, that some power altogether independent of the people would

soon be called for by the voice of the very factions whose misrule had proved the necessity of it. In the extended republic of the United States, and among the great variety of interests, parties and sects which it embraces, a coalition of a majority of the whole society could seldom take place on any other principles than those of justice and the general good; and there being thus less danger to a minor from the will of the major party, there must be less pretext also, to provide for the security of the former, by introducing into the government a will not dependent on the latter; or in other words, a will independent of the society itself. It is no less certain than it is important, notwithstanding the contrary opinions which have been entertained, that the larger the society, provided it lie within a practicable sphere, the more duly capable it will be of self government. And happily for the *republican cause*, the practicable sphere may be carried to a very great extent, by a judicious modification and mixture of the *federal principle*.

PUBLIUS.

## Morton Grodzins

## THE SHARING OF FUNCTIONS

The American form of government is often, but erroneously, symbolized by a three-layer cake. A far more accurate image is the rainbow or marble cake, characterized by an inseparable mingling of differently colored ingredients, the colors appearing in vertical and diagonal strands and unexpected whirls. As colors are mixed in the marble cake, so functions are mixed in the American federal system. Consider the health officer, styled "sanitarian," of a rural county in a border state. He embodies

the whole idea of the marble cake of government.

The sanitarian is appointed by the state under merit standards established by the federal government. His base salary comes jointly from state and federal funds, the county provides him with an office and office amenities and pays a portion of his expenses, and the largest city in the county also contributes to his salary and office by virtue of his appointment as a city plumbing inspector. It is impossible from mo-

From Morton Grodzins, "The Federal System" in *Goals for Americans* by The American Assembly, Columbia University, New York, © 1960, pp. 265-267, 268-271. Reprinted by permission of Prentice-Hall, Inc., Englewood Cliffs, New Jersey.

11

ment to moment to tell under which governmental hat the sanitarian operates. His work of inspecting the purity of food is carried out under federal standards; but he is enforcing state laws when inspecting commodities that have not been in interstate commerce; and somewhat perversely he also acts under state authority when inspecting milk coming into the county from producing areas across the state border. He is a federal officer when impounding impure drugs shipped from a neighboring state; a federal-state officer when distributing typhoid immunization serum; a state officer when enforcing standards of industrial hygiene; a state-local officer when inspecting the city's water supply; and (to complete the circle) a local officer when insisting that the city butchers adopt more hygienic methods of handling their garbage. But he cannot and does not think of himself as acting in these separate capacities. All business in the county that concerns public health and sanitation he considers his business. Paid largely from federal funds, he does not find it strange to attend meetings of the city council to give expert advice on matters ranging from rotten apples to rabies control. He is even deputized as a member of both the city and county police forces.

The sanitarian is an extreme case, but he accurately represents an important aspect of the whole range of governmental activities in the United States. Functions are not neatly parceled out among the many governments. They are shared functions. It is difficult to find any governmental activity which does not involve all three of the so-called "levels" of the federal system. In the most local of local functions—law enforcement or education, for example—the federal and state governments play important roles. In what, *a priori*, may be considered the purest central government activities—the conduct of foreign affairs, for example—the state and local governments have considerable responsibilities, directly and indirectly.

The federal grant programs are only the most obvious example of shared functions. They also most clearly exhibit how sharing serves to disperse governmental powers. The grants utilize the greater wealth-gathering abilities of the central government and establish nation-wide standards, yet they are "in aid" of functions carried out under state law, with considerable state and local discretion. The national supervision of such programs is largely a process of mutual accommodation. Leading state and local officials, acting through their professional organizations, are in considerable part responsible for the very standards that national officers try to persuade all state and local officers to accept.

Even in the absence of joint financing, federal-state-local collaboration is the characteristic mode of action. Federal expertise is available to aid in the building of a local jail (which may later be used to house federal prisoners), to improve a local water purification system, to step up building inspections, to provide standards for state and local personnel in protecting housewives against dishonest butchers' scales, to prevent gas explosions, or to produce a land use plan. States and localities, on the other hand, take important formal responsibilities in the development of national programs for atomic energy, civil defense, the regulation of commerce, and the protection of purity in foods and drugs; local political weight is always a factor in the operation of even a post office or a military establishment. From abattoirs and accounting through zoning and zoo administration, any governmental activity is almost certain to involve the influence, if not the formal administration, of all three planes of the federal system.

A POINT OF HISTORY

The American federal system has never been a system of separated governmental activities. There has never been a time when it was possible to put neat labels on discrete "federal," "state," and "local" functions. Even before the Constitution, a statute of 1785, reinforced by the Northwest Ordinance of 1787, gave grants-in-land to the states for public schools. Thus the national government was a prime force in making possible what is now taken to be the most local function of all, primary and secondary education. More important, the nation, before it was fully organized, established by this action a first principle of American federalism: the national government would use its superior resources to initiate and support national programs, principally administered by the states and localities.

The essential unity of state and federal financial systems was again recognized in the earliest constitutional days with the assumption by the federal government of the Revolutionary War debts of the states. Other points of federal-state collaboration during the Federalist period concerned the militia, law enforcement, court practices, the administration of elections, public health measures, pilot laws, and many other matters.

The nineteenth century is widely believed to have been the preeminent period of duality in the American system. Lord Bryce at the end of the century described (in *The American Commonwealth*) the federal and state governments as "distinct and separate in their action." The system, he said, was "like a great factory wherein two sets of machinery are at work, their revolving wheels apparently intermixed, their bands crossing one another, yet each set doing its own work without touching or hampering the other." Great works may contain gross errors. Bryce was wrong. The nineteenth century, like the early days of the republic, was a period principally characterized by intergovernmental collaboration.

Decisions of the Supreme Court are often cited as evidence of nineteenth century duality. In the early part of the century the Court, heavily weighted with Federalists, was intent upon enlarging the sphere of national authority; in the later years (and to the 1930's) its actions were in the direction of paring down national powers and indeed all governmental authority. Decisions referred to "areas of exclusive competence" exercised by the federal government and the states; to their powers being "separate and distinct"; and to neither being able "to intrude within the jurisdiction of the other."

Judicial rhetoric is not always consistent with judicial action, and the Court did not always adhere to separatist doctrine. Indeed, its rhetoric sometimes indicated a positive view of cooperation. In any case, the Court was rarely, if ever, directly confronted with the issue of cooperation *vs.* separation as such. Rather it was concerned with defining permissible areas of action for the central government and the states; or with saying with respect to a point at issue whether any government could take action. The Marshall Court contributed to intergovernmental cooperation by the very act of permitting federal operations where they had not existed before. Furthermore, even Marshall was willing to allow interstate commerce to be affected by the states in their use of the police power. Later courts also upheld state laws that had an impact on interstate commerce, just as they approved the expansion of the national commerce power, as in statutes providing for the control of telegraphic communication or prohibiting the interstate transportation of lotteries, impure foods and drugs, and prostitutes. Similar room for cooperation was found outside the commerce field, notably in the Court's refusal to interfere with federal grants in land or cash to the states. Although research to clinch the point has not been completed, it is probably true that the Supreme Court from 1800 to 1936 allowed far more federal-state collaboration than it blocked.

Political behavior and administrative action of the nineteenth century provide positive evidence that, throughout the entire era of so-called dual federalism, the many governments in the American federal system continued the close administrative and fiscal collaboration of the earlier period. Governmental activities were not extensive. But relative to what governments did, intergovernmental cooperation during the last century was comparable with that existing today.

Occasional presidential vetoes (from Madison to Buchanan) of cash and land grants are evidence of constitutional and ideological apprehensions about the extensive expansion of federal activities which produced widespread intergovernmental collaboration. In perspective, however, the vetoes are a more important evidence of the continuous search, not least by state officials, for ways and means to involve the central government in a wide variety of joint programs. The search was successful.

Grants-in-land and grants-in-services from the national government were of first importance in virtually all the principal functions undertaken by the states and their local subsidiaries. Land grants were made to the states for, among other purposes, elementary schools, colleges, and special educational institutions; roads, canals, rivers, harbors, and railroads; reclamation of desert and swamp lands; and veterans' welfare. In fact whatever was at the focus of state attention became the recipient of national grants. (Then, as today, national grants established state emphasis as well as followed it.) If Connecticut wished to establish a program for the care and education of the deaf and dumb, federal money in the form of a land grant was found to aid that program. If higher education relating to agriculture became a pressing need, Congress could dip into the public domain and make appropriate grants to states. If the need for swamp drainage and flood control appeared, the federal government could supply both grants-in-land and, from the Army's Corps of Engineers, the services of the only trained engineers then available.

Aid also went in the other direction. The federal government, theoretically in exclusive control of the Indian population, relied continuously (and not always wisely) on the experience and resources of state and local governments. State militias were an all-important ingredient in the nation's armed forces. State governments became unofficial but real partners in federal programs for homesteading, reclamation, tree culture, law enforcement, inland waterways, the nation's internal communications system (including highway and railroad routes), and veterans' aid of various sorts. Administrative contacts were voluminous, and the whole process of interaction was lubricated, then as today, by constituent-conscious members of Congress.

The essential continuity of the collaborative system is best demonstrated by the history of the grants. The land grant tended to become a cash grant based on the calculated disposable value of the land, and the cash grant tended to become an annual grant based upon the national government's superior tax powers. In 1887, only three years before the frontier was officially closed, thus signalizing the end of the disposable public domain, Congress enacted the first continuing cash grants.

A long, extensive, and continuous experience is therefore the foundation of the present system of shared functions characteristic of the American federal system, what we have called the marble cake of government. It is a misjudgment of our history and our present situation to believe that a neat separation of governmental functions could take place without drastic alterations in our society and system of government.

William Anderson

# NATIONAL-STATE RELATIONS TODAY: THE CONSTITUTIONAL ESSENTIALS

"The Constitution, in all its provisions, looks to an indestructible Union, composed of indestructible States."

This statement in a Supreme Court decision of 1869 sets forth succinctly the basic fact about national-state relations under the Constitution of the United States—the importance and permanence of both the national and the state governments.

It is true of course [ . . . ] that the national government has been established as supreme. No state may constitutionally nullify or obstruct the acts of the national government. Every state stands under the compulsory jurisdiction and process of the nation's Supreme Court to decide on the state's rights and duties under the United States Constitution and laws. The constitutional acts of Congress are also binding on the states. National citizenship is the primary citizenship for all the people in the United States—above state citizenship—and the national government may reach with its laws any and every citizen (as well as all aliens and other persons) in any state. The national Constitution is the highest written law for all the people of the United States, for the nation as a whole and for each of its parts—for the national government and for the state and local governments as well. The Constitution is without qualification the "supreme law of the land."

It is true also that the activities of the national government have increased manyfold in the century and a half since the nation's beginning. These activities are not all specifically mentioned in the Constitution. But that document has proved to be a very flexible and adaptable instrument. It can, when necessary, be formally amended—and has been, twenty-two times. More important perhaps, it contains "implied powers" which can be interpreted by the Congress and the Supreme Court in the light of new needs. From the war powers, the commerce power, the postal powers, and the taxing power, all granted explicitly to the national government, Congress has, by implication, drawn the authority to do many things.

A power that has been especially adaptable to new needs is the power of Congress to tax (and, *ergo*, to spend) for the "general welfare of the United States." It merits special attention.

The Constitution does not mention a separate or distinct "spending power," although it does regulate congressional appropriation of funds out of the treasury. It is recognized, however, that from taxation and other sources the national government will have revenues, and that the taxing power is used primarily though not entirely to provide revenues. This being the case, the power delegated to Congress "To lay and collect taxes, duties, imposts, and excises; to pay the debts and provide for the common defense and general welfare of the United States" is widely interpreted in practice to imply a power to spend the money so raised "for the common defense and general welfare." There is no point in raising a revenue unless it is to be spent for such public purposes as the common defense and the general welfare.

This has not always been the favored view. But in 1936, in a case involving an

*The Nation and the States, Rivals or Partners?* by William Anderson, pp. 127–136. University of Minnesota Press, Minneapolis. Copyright 1955 by the University of Minnesota.

attack upon a taxing law, the Supreme Court accepted the broad view of Congress's power to spend for the general welfare. In the decision in United States v. Butler (297 U.S. 1), Justice Roberts (conservative, Republican, a former Philadelphia lawyer) wrote:

Since the formation of the nation, sharp differences of opinion have persisted as to the true interpretation of the phrase "general welfare" in the taxing power. Madison asserted it amounted to no more than a reference to the other powers enumerated in the subsequent clauses of the same section; that, as the United States is a government of limited and enumerated powers, the grant of power to tax and spend for the general welfare must be confined to the enumerated legislative fields committed to the Congress. In this view the phrase is mere tautology, for taxation and appropriation are or may be necessary incidents of the exercise of any of the enumerated legislative powers. Hamilton, on the other hand, maintained the clause confers a power separate and distinct from those later enumerated, is not restricted in meaning by the grant of them, and Congress consequently has a substantive power to tax and to appropriate, limited only by the requirement that it shall be exercised to provide for the general welfare of the United States. . . . Mr. Justice Story, in his Commentaries, espouses the Hamiltonian position. We shall not review the writings of public men and commentators or discuss the legislative practice. Study of all these leads us to conclude that the reading advocated by Mr. Justice Story is the correct one. While, therefore, the power to tax is not unlimited, its confines are set in the clause which confers it, and not in those of section 8 which bestow and define the legislative powers of Congress. It results that the power of Congress to authorize expenditure of public moneys for public purposes is not limited by the direct grants of legislative power found in the Constitution.

Even so, as Justice Roberts said for the Court, the power is not unlimited. The tax and the expenditure must be for the general welfare, for national as distinguished from local welfare.

The question remains, then, what is for the general or national welfare? This is for Congress, not the Court, to decide.

In recent decades Congress has, in the interests of general welfare, appropriated money for many functions and services not mentioned in the Constitution—public housing, for example, a wide range of other public works, emergency relief for the unemployed, old age and survivors' insurance, the support of agricultural prices, research in a wide range of subjects.

Congress has entered the field of education, too. Without adequate basic education a people cannot long preserve or wisely use their system of self-government. Furthermore, the defense of the nation depends upon having a citizenry with the essentials of education to understand and to use properly the weapons of modern warfare. The national safety and security may depend upon having enough men and women adequately trained in science, technology, economics, and public affairs. A surprising number of men have had to be rejected from the draft because of the lack of an adequate elementary education. The maintenance of the nation's productive capacity and its commerce also depends upon education, both literary and vocational.

In short, there are important national interests in having all citizens educated up to at least a minimum standard, and in having a large number trained and educated beyond the minimum level for scientific work, the professions, business, and public affairs. And Congress, under its general welfare power, has provided land grants, money grants, and direct services to education, a considerable stimulation to public schools, land-grant colleges, and instruction in particular vocational fields—notably in agriculture.

The Constitution says nothing about how to maintain reasonably full employment in the land or about how to ensure the economic health of the nation by protecting basic industries like agriculture or by making possible at least a minimum of income for the unemployed, the aged, dependent children, and other handicapped classes. These are functions that seem to invade the time-honored roles of families, voluntary groups, local governments, and the states, but nevertheless they are functions that have been accepted by the national government because they are national in their scope and their impact, they affect the nation's commerce and welfare, and they are far beyond the powers of forty-eight states individually to plan, finance, and administer. The maintenance of the economic health of the nation is now recognized as having a close relationship to the nation's security.

The commerce power is another that, alone and in combination with other powers, has enabled Congress to enter areas not specifically mentioned in the Constitution. For example, in order to protect and regulate commerce, Congress has found it necessary or expedient to regulate such matters as industrial disputes, wages and hours, and the production of coal, oil, and agricultural products.

Public health is linked to interstate commerce and to the postal system. Deleterious foods and impure or fraudulent drugs have been sent far and wide through interstate commerce and by mail. Railroads, steamship lines, airlines, and truck and bus systems, all interstate carriers under congressional regulation, may easily become carriers of contagion. And so Congress has enacted various measures to safeguard the nation's health.

For interstate commerce, for postal purposes, and for national defense, all of which are authorized national functions, a good modern highway system throughout the land is essential. And, as we have seen, the national government has become very important in planning and financing the construction of roads.

The original framers intended, I believe, that the powers they granted to the national government should be expanded "by implication" as national needs arose. And the later framers have by and large accepted the implied powers. Both major parties have had a hand in their development. Presidents of both political parties, and not a few state officials as well, have proposed various of the measures that Congress has passed. Congress has approved and passed the various laws, usually with bipartisan

support and in many instances by large majorities. The Supreme Court has accepted a broad interpretation of the commerce power, has upheld a broad federal spending power for the general welfare, and has declined to interfere with grant-in-aid measures. The state legislatures have accepted the federal grant-in-aid laws, all forty-eight state legislatures in many cases, by passing laws of their own to put the services into effect. State administrations have taken up the work of administering the grant-in-aid laws, and no governor has resigned in protest against the unconstitutionality of what was being done. The people also have generally accepted the laws.

But the original framers, no less than their successors, were well aware of the dangers in unrestrained governments, and they worked out a system of government that is unusually complicated and replete with various "checks and balances." Certain powers, for example, are reserved to each of the branches of the national government, and no one branch may act with impunity against the will of the others. The division of powers between the states and the national government is another "check." The framers also placed effective limits on the powers of all government in favor of individual liberties—and further restrictions were imposed by the Bill of Rights and later amendments.

All things considered, there is no country in the world that imposes as many and as varied written constitutional restrictions on government action as are to be found in the United States. The underlying principle is that the freedom, the responsibility, and the moral and intellectual development of individuals constitute the primary purpose for which governments exist.

Those who sometimes criticize the United States system of government for its great complexity should be reminded that the purpose of this complexity was largely to protect the liberties of the people. They should not overlook the fact that the American system provides more freedom and more varied opportunities for the citizen to bring his ideas and influence to bear upon government than any other known system of government in the world. This is a characteristic feature that is not often emphasized. To bring out this fact it is almost necessary to go outside the formal constitutional rules and documents, and to summarize the whole system.

Practically all adult men and women may vote. Popular elections are frequent at all levels and in all units of government, and through them the voters choose not only legislative and executive officers but in most states they elect the judges as well. Education is free and widespread though not universal. There is freedom to get information from a wide array of communications media. All persons have a right to criticize public officials and their acts; to assemble and to associate together freely for all lawful purposes; to organize political parties, committees, and other groups; to speak and publish their views without any prior restraint; to petition government for the redress of grievances; to run for and hold public office. Grievances can be directed against particular units and officers of government with considerable ease and accuracy. People on each side can appeal from the legislature or the executive to the courts, from the courts to the legislature, and even back to the courts. If state services are deemed unsatisfactory, the people can appeal to the national government; or appeal for state action if national services do not satisfy. Within each state there can be appeals from local governments to the state legislature, or to the state executive, or to the courts. If the party in power does not give satisfaction the voters can turn to its major rival, and through it get new persons into government. If anything unconstitutional is done or proposed it can be attacked at elections, in legislative bodies, and in the courts.

By these and other related devices and procedures an alert citizenry can play one part of the governmental system against another, or one political party against another, and so keep the various parts of the government "on their toes," alert, active, and responsible, while also keeping the entire government under fairly effective control.

This apparent looseness in the governmental system, with its many opportunities for appeal from one center of power to another, is perhaps the outstanding characteristic of government in the United States, and it has a significant effect on national-state relations.

For one thing, it prevents any single official or department or branch from speaking finally and conclusively for the government, either national or state. The "tidelands" issue mentioned earlier is an excellent example. The states appealed from national executive action to the Supreme Court, and then to Congress when an election brought a change in administration.

Something like this happened also in the Southeast Underwriters insurance case. After the federal Justice Department had won from the Supreme Court a decision that certain insurance companies, operating under state laws, were engaged in interstate commerce and were subject to the nation's antitrust laws, the states appealed to Congress to protect state control over the insurance business. This Congress and the President obligingly did, but on condition that the states themselves would take certain steps to prevent monopolies and private rate-fixing in insurance. Thus the states again appealed successfully from one branch of the national government to another.

One aspect of this complex system of government that many foreign observers and perhaps many Americans also do not understand is defined approximately by the terms "autonomy" and "free initiative." Congress and the President, the national policy-making authorities, may go ahead and act for the general welfare upon their own interpretation of the national powers without consulting or getting the consent of either the United States Supreme Court or the state governments. Each state government may do the same in acting for the welfare of its state without consulting the President, Congress, or the Supreme Court. If not sovereign the states are at least autonomous.

This apparent looseness of governmental structure strengthens the importance of each part of the system: each part, though subordinate to the whole, has certain "checks" on the other parts and on the whole. At the same time, paradoxical though this seems, it also ties the nation and its parts permanently together. For the threads between the President and the Congress, Congress and the Supreme Court, the Supreme Court and the state legislatures, the state legislatures and the Congress, Congress and the state governors, state governors and national executive agencies, national executive agencies and state divisions, state executive divisions and state legislatures, and so on, are so intricately interwoven that a break at any point would only temporarily snarl the threads; it cannot unravel the whole.

The relationship between the states and the nation that emerges from the complex governmental structure of the United States is sometimes called a partnership. I have used the term "partners" in the title of this volume, and in a way I believe it is a very apt term. But I want to make perfectly clear the sense in which I am using "partners" and "partnership."

It seems to me that there is between the nation and the states nothing like an ordinary business-partnership arrangement in which the partners have equal status and voting powers. Each state, being but a part of the entire people, is not an equal partner of the nation; at the same time, all the states combined *are* the nation and cannot be called its partners.

On the other hand the national government and the state governments are the agents of the nation to perform their respective functions and responsibilities for the nation and for its several parts, the states. They share the responsibility to promote the general welfare of all the people. In this sense they form a partnership, though not a partnership of equals, and not a partnership in any transient sense.

For what I have in mind it would be hard to find a more eloquent expression than that of Edmund Burke when he was criticizing the contract theory of the state. Said he:

Society is, indeed, a contract . . . [B]ut the state ought not to be considered as nothing better than a partnership agreement in a trade of pepper and coffee, calico or tobacco . . . to be dissolved by the fancy of the partners. It is to be looked upon with other reverence . . . It is a partnership in all science, a partnership in all art, a partnership in every virtue and in all perfection. As the ends of such a partnership cannot be obtained in many generations, it becomes a partnership not only between those who are living, but between those who are living, those who are dead, and those who are to be born.

As the distinct and separate agents of the people of the United States, a great nation among nations and one that we hope will endure to promote human welfare through many generations, the national government and the state governments have a joint responsibility to respect each other, to consult with each other, and to cooperate with and assist each other to promote the national security and the general welfare. It is in this broad meaning that I speak of a partnership in national-state relations.

An "indestructible Union" of indestructible States" is, then, the constitutional pattern of our government. It makes a certain amount of controversy inevitable—even desirable, so far as it protects individual liberties by bringing every major public action up for discussion before the court of public opinion. While the constitutionality of the activities of the Union, acting through the national government, cannot, as I think I have shown, be seriously challenged, there is a broad area in which the deciding factor is one of policy.

It is largely because the constitutional powers of the national government are now so great that the questions of policy are so important. To be sure the people want their public services well administered, and want to have them available and as nearly uniform as possible throughout the nation. In many cases direct administration by the national government is the best way to achieve these results.

But there are other values also, other things that people want. Among these are the maintenance in full vigor of suitable state and local governments under local popular control. They desire a considerable amount of local freedom to conduct their public services and the ability to vary them and adapt them to local ideas and conditions. When Congress considers any new measure, therefore, it needs to consider carefully whether it is necessary or even desirable to push national action to the limits of national power. In many situations it may be better, as a matter of public policy, to assist and induce the state and local governments to perform the service up to at least a minimum standard.

*Daniel J. Elazar*

# THE SHAPING OF INTERGOVERNMENTAL RELATIONS IN THE TWENTIETH CENTURY

One very practical manifestation of the political changes that have characterized the twentieth century has been the great increase in government activity, much of it in the form of new intergovernmental programs. Despite popular views to the contrary, intergovernmental collaboration is not a new phenomenon. Co-operative federalism—the patterned sharing of governmental activities by all levels of government—has been characteristic of the American federal system since its establishment. American governments have traditionally assumed responsibilities only in response to public demands but, where governments have acted, federal, state, and local governments usually have acted in concert. Whether this "co-operative federalism" was intended by the founders of the Union or not, it was quickly demonstrated to be necessary. Governments operating in the same territory, serving the same people, generally sharing the same goals, and faced with the same demands could not maintain a posture of "dual federalism" (the separation of functions by levels of government).[1]

[1]For a discussion of federal-state co-operation before 1913, see Daniel J. Elazar, *The American Partnership* (Chicago: University of Chicago Press, 1962).

## THE AMERICAN PARTNERSHIP

By the mid-twentieth century, certain basic principles and mechanisms for intergovernmental collaboration have become part of the American governmental tradition, most of which came into existence a century ago and persist to color the character of American federalism today. Among the principles are: national supremacy, broad national legislative and appropriation powers, noncentralized government, and maximum local control. Among the mechanisms are: a nondisciplined, noncentralized party system; routinized legislative "interference" in administration; regular intergovernmental consultation; and a system of grants-in-aid from higher to lower levels of government.

From the very first, Congress has acquired the authority to legislate very broadly under the Constitution. Although this authority was frequently diluted by the Supreme Court and by Congress itself until the 1930's, it was nonetheless apparent in the general expansion of federal activities in the intervening years. Also demonstrated from the first was the inherent superiority of the federal government as a

From Daniel J. Elazar, "Intergovernmental Relations in the Twentieth Century," *The Annals of the American Academy of Political and Social Science*, Vol. 359 (May, 1965), pp. 11–22. Reprinted by the American Academy of Political and Social Science.

raiser of revenue because of the tax sources available to it and the reluctance of the people to allow equally substantial state and local tax levies. For these reasons, federal funds provided the stimulus for new programs in a majority of the states throughout the nineteenth century.[2]

These two trends, coupled with the great political decisions of the nineteenth century, firmly established the principle of national supremacy. Along with it, however, the equally important principle of noncentralized government was also established. If the general government was early cast in the role of stimulator and partial supporter of such major governmental functions as education, internal improvements, and public welfare, the states — either directly or through their local subdivisions — were simultaneously cast in the role of managers and administrators of these functions. Policy-making for these programs became a joint state-federal activity.

This arrangement is often mislabeled decentralization. Decentralization implies the existence of a central authority having a legitimate monopoly of governmental power which can concentrate, devolve, or reconcentrate functions more or less as it pleases. Noncentralization — on the other hand, the keystone of every true federal system — implies the constitutional coexistence of a general government and governments with more particularized authority which share governmental power. In the American case, the basic authority of the states is delineated in the Constitution and cannot be withdrawn except with their consent, thus making dynamic federal action possible without concomitant reduction of local self-government by protecting the less formal institutions that deconcentrate power.

The American commitment to noncentralization has forced federal authorities to seek ways to develop nationwide programs with minimum national requirements within the framework of the co-operative system and has enabled the states to secure federal assistance without fearing any real loss of their integrity.

Thus it has always been the prerogative of the states to decide whether or not to accept any federal aid proffered under formal grant programs. And, despite the prevalent idea that no state can resist federal subsidies, few, if any, states have ever taken advantage of every grant offered them. The strong record of state participation, particularly in the major programs in any given period, is really a reflection of the nationwide consensus as to their value and necessity. Such programs represent only a few of the over a hundred available to the states and localities today. Moreover, many states do not take advantage of all the funds available to them under grants they have accepted. In both cases, state policy-decisions rule.[3]

Even more important, noncentralization means that the states, as of right, share in the initial development of most co-operative programs before they are written into law. They share in the shaping of policies from the first and throughout the existence of each program, and develop their own patterns of program implementation within the framework of agreed-upon guidelines.[4]

The sharing process has worked both ways. The states have become involved in the fields of foreign affairs, interstate commerce, defense, and monetary policy just as the federal government has become involved in the fields of education, health

[2]Adequate statistical data for most of the nineteenth century is lacking, but the author's sampling based on the available data confirms this. The figures usually cited show state-local expenditures as exceeding federal expenditures by an approximately two-to-one margin until 1933. However, when the value of federal land grants to states, localities, corporations, and individuals is included in the calculations of federal expenditures and the share of state and local expenditures derived from federal endowments is eliminated, the result is quite different.

[3]As of April 1964, 115 programs were available, as listed in the *Catalog of Federal Aids to State and Local Governments* prepared for the Subcommittee on Intergovernmental Relations of the Senate Committee on Government Operations (Washington, D.C., 1964). The most current and comprehensive published information on the extent of state participation in federal grant programs is available from the Advisory Commission on Intergovernmental Relations.

[4]For a brief, yet thorough discussion of this aspect of American federalism, see Morton Grodzins, "Centralization and Decentralization in the American Federal System," *A Nation of States*, ed. Robert A. Goldwin (Chicago: Rand, McNally, 1963).

and welfare, agriculture, and urban development.[5]

Moreover, local governments, public nongovernmental agencies, and private interests have acquired roles of their own as partners in the process because they have made an effort to become involved and have found ways to "pay the ante" required to sit in on the great game of government in the United States.[6]

THE FORMS OF THE PARTNERSHIP

Intergovernmental co-operation has taken on a variety of forms, all of which have histories as old as the sharing system itself.[7] Among the most common and recurring are those of *informal co-operation* through conferences, the provision of advisory and training services, the exchange of general services, the lending of equipment and personnel, and the performance of services by one government in place of another. Such collaboration is barely visible to the general public except when a conference is sponsored by the White House or when a public-health team moves into a community on the heels of an epidemic. The informal luncheon meeting, no matter how important, attracts no attention whatsoever.

Formal co-operative activities, on the other hand, are based on *contracts and compacts for co-operative action.* In the largest sense, contractual relationships are basic to a federal system which is founded upon a

fundamental compact to begin with. In essence, it is the contractual relationship that makes possible large-scale intergovernmental co-operation to achieve common ends. Every formal co-operative relationship involves some form of contractual tie. The flexibility of the contract as a device enhances its usefulness and allows it to be adapted for many purposes. There are contractual relationships for co-operative research, for the division of costs to support shared activities, for provision or exchange of services, to prevent conflict or misunderstanding, for exchange of personnel, for joint enforcement of laws, for sharing revenues, and for lending agreements.

Recurring informal contracts are often formalized to the point of receiving statutory recognition and contractual ratification through *contracts for simple sharing.* These are relationships that involve nothing more than a formal agreement to share resources without formal transfers of funds or personnel from one government to another. They are often used to prevent needless duplication of time, money, and effort or to enhance the possibilities for more comprehensive execution of particular programs. State-federal crop reports, Bureau of Labor Statistics calculations, state regulation of nuclear installations, formal agreements for the exchange of tax information or co-operative inspections of public utilities are examples of this type of relationship.

Another form of co-operation involves the interchange of *personnel.* This includes the provision of "services-in-aid," that is, arrangements by one government to lend its personnel to assist another; jointly paid agents; joint inspections by personnel of more than one government; and the deputization of personnel of one government by another for co-operative purposes. Under this type of co-operative activity, federal engineers are lent to states and localities to plan projects; county sanitarians are paid with federal, state, and local funds and have special obligations to all three governments; banks are jointly inspected by state and federal officers; and state hospital

[5]See, for example, Dennis J. Palumbo, "The States and American Foreign Relations" (Unpublished doctoral dissertation, Department of Political Science, University of Chicago, 1960); Morton Grodzins, "The Federal System," *Goals for Americans,* ed. President's Commission on National Goals (Englewood Cliffs, N.J.: Prentice-Hall, 1960); and Edward C. Banfield (ed.), *Urban Government* (New York: Free Press of Glencoe, 1961).

[6]For further elucidation of the role of local and private interests, see Daniel J. Elazar, "Local Government in Intergovernmental Perspective," *Illinois Local Government,* ed. Lois Pelakoudas (Urbana: University of Illinois, 1960) and Morton Grodzins, "Local Strength in the American Federal System: The Mobilization of Public-Private Influence," *Continuing Crisis in American Politics,* ed. Marian D. Irish (Englewood Cliffs, N.J.: Prentice-Hall, 1963).

[7]The following outline was suggested in part by Jane Perry Clark's important study, *The Rise of a New Federalism* (New York: Columbia University Press, 1938), which, as the first work to attempt to catalog the entire range of federal co-operative activities, established some essential guidelines that are still quite relevant.

guards are deputized by the local police.

The pervasiveness of the partnership has led to the development of *interdependent activities* in which one government depends upon another (or both depend upon each other) for the enforcement of laws or the administration of programs otherwise not apparently "shared." The administration of elections is one good example of this. The election of national officials is contingent upon state implementation of the constitutional requirements. In this case, there is federal dependence upon state action. States, on the other hand, may depend upon federal authorities to exclude the transportation of prohibited goods (liquor, oleo, firecrackers) across their boundaries.

First in importance among the forms of intergovernmental co-operation are the grants-in-aid: federal transfers of funds to the states and federal or state transfers to local governments for specified purposes usually subject to a measure of supervision and review by the granting government. They are particularly distinctive because they involve the transfer of funds from one government to another in order to attain certain agreed-upon ends. The first grants-in-aid were generally transfers of land to be sold to finance specific programs. Supervision of these grants was relatively loose by today's standards but still significant; conditions attached to them governed disposition of the lands and use of the proceeds earned.

Cash grants-in-aid, like land grants, date from the nineteenth century — six were established before 1900 — but did not flower until the twentieth. Since 1911 some sixty-five new federal grant-in-aid programs have been established, fourteen of which have since been discontinued. In general, they have been more rigorously administered by all governments concerned.

Grants-in-aid are of three kinds: (1) flat grants, which provide each recipient government with an equal sum regardless of local conditions or deviations from the national means, and without requiring formal matching of funds by the recipient governments — although recipients may have to shoulder administrative costs; (2) proportionate grants, as with road-building, made to recipient governments in proportion to their own contributions to the program or project in question, and often allocated on the basis of preset formulas which take the need and capabilities of the recipient into account; and (3) percentage grants, allocated like proportionate grants but with the granter's contribution fixed as a set percentage of the cost to the grantee for maintaining a particular program. Among the best known of these are the federal public welfare grants and some state grants to local school districts. Grants-in-aid may also include grants in kind, which generally resemble flat grants and are rarely subject to extensive supervision.

Other forms of intergovernmental sharing include tax offsets (used when nationwide compliance is necessary as in the unemployment compensation program), shared revenues (such as timber and mineral royalties and shared license fees), and grants or contracts awarded on similar terms to public and private applicants (such as federal research grants to universities). These all represent variations of the grant-in-aid principle, developed to meet conditions which would frustrate simpler grant mechanisms.

Supplementing the regular channels of co-operative control, the sharing system is strengthened through the maintenance of a nondisciplined, noncentralized party system which encourages elected representatives to follow the interest of their districts — from wards through states — rather than maintain party responsibility. This system encourages them to frame programs in such a way as to guarantee the maintenance of local control, thereby increasing their own power. One of the consequences of this has been the development of routinized mechanisms for continuous legislative "interference" (used in the neutral sense) in the administration of government programs, further enhancing local control over program execution as well as policy-making.[8]

The record of the partnership since approximately 1913 has been one of maintaining and appropriately modifying the patterns established earlier, in the face of a continually increasing "velocity of government"—the amount of total government activity in relation to the total activity of society—through the formal institutionalization of the co-operative system.[9]

This has meant (1) the development of more complex and sophisticated techniques for administering co-operative programs to secure better financial control by the granting government, (2) improved sharing of policy formation by all participants, including the panoply of interest groups that contribute so much to policy-making in the United States, (3) expansion of the range and variety of shared activities so that today one is hard-pressed to find any area of public concern that does not somehow involve government and in turn, federal-state-local collaboration, and (4) the adjustment of the theories and mechanisms of federalism to meet new times, situations, and demands. This, in turn, has led to growing public recognition of the co-operative system for what it is and an increased interest on the part of public officials and scholars in understanding how American federalism really functions.

The course of intergovernmental relations in this century can be traced through four periods and into a fifth. Understandably, the trends in intergovernmental rela-tions are closely tied to the larger political and economic movements on the American political scene.

By 1913 the era of virtually unregulated enterprise capitalism was coming to an end. During the next generation, government regulation was progressively extended over an even more complex corporate economy while an ideological battle over the legitimacy of government's new role was being fought.

The first period may be characterized as one of *progressive agrarianism*. It was actually inaugurated when the Republican party, whose national majority status had been consolidated in the critical elections of 1892 and 1896, briefly gave way to a progressive and activist Democratic administration in 1913.[10] It reflected the first concerted national response to the Populist-Progressive-Liberal agitation for positive government action to meet the problems of an industrialized society, and laid the foundations for co-operation in the subsequent periods. Growing government activism, begun in part under Theodore Roosevelt, brought with it revival of large scale co-operative activity. The magnitude of this revival is seen in the more than six-fold increase in federal grant expenditures and the near doubling of the number of formal grant programs between 1912 and 1920 (see tables)[11] and the development of "many other forms of formal and informal cooperative activities as government at all levels took on expanded roles in American life."

This period saw three important developments that were to influence the course of intergovernmental relations thereafter: (1) the beginning of clear public recogni-

[8]See Grodzins, in *Goals for Americans, op. cit.,* for a discussion of this and Kenneth E. Gray, "Congressional Interference in the Executive Branch" (Paper delivered at the annual meeting of the American Political Science Association, September 1962) for a detailed analysis of its operation at the federal level.

[9]While no single date for the real beginning of the "twentieth century" is precisely accurate, 1913 is chosen as the most appropriate, since it was the first year of Woodrow Wilson's "New Freedom," which represented the first great and co-ordinated nationwide response to the problems of the new century and the beginning of a five-year period of great changes in American life.

[10]A "critical election" has been defined as one in which substantial shifts occur in the voting behavior of major electoral blocs, shifts which become sufficiently "permanent" to set the voting patterns for a generation. The United States has experienced critical elections at the national level in pairs every twenty-four to thirty-two years. Every two generations, they have reflected a shift of the voting majority from one political party to the other.

[11]The figures cited here and subsequently—unless otherwise indicated—are from the report of the Advisory Commission on Intergovernmental Relations, "Periodic Congressional Assessment of Federal Grants-in-Aid to State and Local Government" (June 1961).

TABLE 1: TWENTIETH-CENTURY PATTERNS OF AMERICAN FEDERALISM

| Year | Period | Economic Era | Political Condition | State of Intergovernmental Relations |
|------|--------|--------------|---------------------|--------------------------------------|
| 1900<br><br><br><br>1910 | Transition (1895–1911)[a] | Concentrated Enterprise Capitalism (1877–1913)[a]<br>\|<br>↓ | GOP majority party<br>\|<br>\|<br>↓ | Passing of nineteenth-century co-operative programs. New experiments in collaboration under T. Roosevelt. Widespread state experimentation has important influence on public. |
| 1920 | Progressive Agrarianism (1911–1921)[a] | Transition Era (1913–1933)[a]<br>\|<br>\| | (Democratic Administration, 1913–1921)[a]<br>\| | Wilson's "New Freedom" lays foundation for twentieth-century co-operative federalism. |
| 1930 | Normalized Entrenchment (1921–1931)[a] | \|<br>\|<br>\|<br>\|<br>\| | \|<br>\|<br>↓<br>1928<br>Critical Elections<br>1932 | GOP restoration starts second period. Existing co-operative programs continued and improved but no significant new federal starts. State experimentation again significant. |
| 1940 | Crisis-oriented Centralism (1931–1945)[a] | \|<br>\|<br>\|<br>\|<br>\|<br>↓ | Democrats forge majority coalition, become majority party.<br>\|<br>\| | New Deal "explosion" in federal-state co-operation, heading off centralization through temporary concentration of power in Washington. Expansion of federal-local and unilateral federal programs along with co-operative ones. |
| 1950<br><br><br><br>1960 | Noncentralist Restoration (1946–1961)[a] | Regulated Capitalism (1946–   )[a]<br>\|<br>\|<br>\| | \|<br>(GOP Administration, 1953–1961)[a]<br>\|<br>1956<br>Critical Elections<br>1960 | Fourth period brings great expansion of small co-operative programs, great expansion of state government expenditures, and increased concern with states' role. |
| | Concentrated Co-operation (1961–   )[a] | ↓ | Democratic Majority coalition reforged | Fifth period brings new emphasis on federal stimulatory action and new threat of centralization from outside of the co-operative system. |

[a]Dating of periods is approximate.

tion of the possibilities inherent in an intergovernmental partnership to meet the nation's new governmental needs, (2) the inauguration of modernized forms of federal-state collaboration particularly through the grant-in-aid system, and (3) the first efforts to develop a more sophisticated understanding of the functioning of the American federal system. Woodrow Wilson set the tone for all three. Concerned simultaneously with expanding the federal role and with preserving the federal-state relationship, his public expressions and the programs enacted during his administration reflected the idea that the federal government was to assist the states in developing and maintaining programs already approved or requested by a substantial number of them.[12] The agricultural-extension, highway-construction, and vocational-education grant programs—the major ones inaugurated in Wilson's administration—all reflect this. In the case of the first two, and of the forest-protection program expanded under Wilson, formal co-operative relationships were actually established to replace or prevent unilateral federal action. These new grant programs betrayed the agrarian bent of Wilsonian Progressivism, being specifically designed to benefit the declining rural American majority.[13]

TABLE 2: Federal Grants to State and Local Governments, 1902–1964 (Selected Years)[a]

| Year | Total in $ '000s | Number of Grant Programs in Operation |
|------|-----------------|----------------------------------------|
| 1902 | 3,001 | 5[b] |
| 1912 | 5,255 | 7[b] |
| 1920 | 33,886 | 11 |
| 1925 | 113,746 | 12 |
| 1933 | 192,966 | 12 |
| 1937 | 2,663,828 | 26 |
| 1942 | 1,819,574 | 27 |
| 1946 | 894,625 | 28 |
| 1953 | 2,762,912 | 38 |
| 1957 | 3,816,404 | 45 |
| 1961 | 7,103,983 | 46 |
| 1964 | 9,864,000 | 51 |

[a]Sources: Advisory Commission on Intergovernmental Relations, Statistical Abstract of the United States, 1964.
[b]Exclusive of fifteen land grant programs.

As both federal and state governments became involved in the same general areas of activity, it became profitable for them to work out appropriate cooperative relations, even for apparently unilateral programs. This was particularly true in matters involving government regulation. Bank regulation had been a co-operative activity since 1865; regulation of railroads became increasingly co-operative as it became more meaningful. There was even some cooperation in the administration of antitrust legislation. Law enforcement had always led to a great deal of co-operative activity which was intensified after passage of the spate of federal criminal legislation to assist in handling interstate crimes, in this period. Perhaps the foremost "temporary" co-operative program of the period was selective service for World War I.[14] In some cases federal-state collaboration was explicitly authorized by law. In others, collaboration just grew informally because it was mutually advantageous.

The second period was one of *normalized entrenchment.* It began when the Republicans resumed power in Washington in 1921, and was characterized by a general reluctance to increase the role of government coupled with a negative attitude toward intergovernmental collaboration. Despite the hostile political climate, this period saw the expansion of existing programs and refinements in their co-operative administration. Actual expenditures for co-operative programs increased six-and-a-half times between 1920 and 1932. After an initial period of intensive federal supervisory activity to get the new programs under way, administrative arrangements began to take on a significantly noncentralized character.

At the same time, the number and scope of administrative decisions required to implement complex grant programs gave those who made the programs work substantial influence in shaping the character of intergovernmental co-operation. The professional associations of state and federal officials engaged in the same tasks, and national associations of state officials, such as the American Association of State High-

[12]See John Wells Davidson (ed.), *A Crossroads of Freedom* (New Haven: Yale University Press, 1956), the most complete edition of Wilson's campaign addresses available.
[13]For a comprehensive review of federal-state relations under the formal grant-in-aid programs in this period and a discussion of the sectional bases for their support, see Austin F. Macdonald, *Federal Aid* (New York: The Macmillan Company, 1928). Statutes restricting these programs to rural areas have been progressively modified, since 1921, reflecting the increased urbanization of American society. These first programs were primarily supported by the representatives of the generally rural and relatively poor Southern and Western states as a means for partial redistribution of the national wealth concentrated in the Northeast.

[14]The story of how the draft was made a co-operative activity is told by Hugh Johnson in his autobiography, *The Blue Eagle from Egg to Earth* (Garden City, N.Y.: Doubleday, 1935). It is a highly significant illustration of the utility of the sharing system in a time of crisis.

way Officials and the Association of Land Grant Colleges and Universities, whose memberships cut across all levels of government and all jurisdictions, began to assume important policy-making duties. These developments further limited the potential role of the federal bureaus to set policy unilaterally.[15]

The second period was one of considerable activity in the states, activity that would later win the period designation as the "seedtime of reform." Whereas federal expenditures rose by only $503 million between 1922 and 1932, state-local expenditures rose by $2,752 million. The expansion of state activity invariably meant an increase in state involvement in previously "local" problems. The expenditure figures are revealing. State transfers of payments to localities rose from $312 million in 1922 to $801 million in 1932, exceeding the growth of all federal transfers in the same period both proportionately and absolutely. Increases in established federal-aid programs in the 1920's and new state-initiated programs in the welfare field precipitated this growth.[16]

The third period, characterized by *crisis-oriented centralism*, coincided with Democratic achievement of majority party status. Their inauguration of the New Deal as a governmental response to the massive depression problems of a society by then over 56 per cent urban, and later a global war, brought great expansion of new federal programs, co-operative and otherwise. Some of these were in response to state and local pressures; others were developed by reformers eager to stimulate state and local action. The great acceleration of the velocity of government made cooperative federalism all-pervasive. The crisis broke down much of the resistance to federal aid. As a result, existing co-operative programs were made more national in scope, and new ones were broadly oriented from the first.

The co-operative system was subtly reoriented toward Washington, as that city became the nation's unrivaled center of political excitement, if not of governmental inventiveness. "Bright young men" of all ages were brought into the federal government to plan new schemes to meet the problems of the day, many of whom had no particular attachment to the principles of federalism, *per se*. The sheer fact of state and local dependence on federal aid meant that they were willing to tolerate pressures from Washington which they might have rejected forcefully in other times.

Yet the most significant fact that stands out in all this is the way in which the application of accepted techniques and principles of co-operative federalism prevented the tremendous growth in national government activity from becoming an excuse for an equivalent centralization of power. Regardless of the growth of federal influence, the unwillingness of some New Deal planners to develop co-operative programs rather than unilateral ones, and the notions of some political theorists popular in that day that federalism was obsolete, the entrenched forces of American politics directed most new federal programs into co-operative channels. Thus, all but one of the great public welfare programs originally designed by Roosevelt's "brain trust" to be directly administered by federal officials, were reshaped by other administration leaders and by Congress into shared programs in which state and local roles were central. So it was with virtually all the other programs inaugurated in this period that did not absolutely have to be centrally administered.

Indeed, while the New Deal brought formerly unilateral state programs into the sharing system, it also brought in several initially unilateral federal programs as well.[17] Often, experienced public servants

[15]See Macdonald, *op. cit.*; V. O. Key, *The Administration of Federal Grants to States* (Chicago: University of Chicago Press, 1937) for discussions of the development of these programs in the second period.
[16]See Clarke Chambers, *Seedtime of Reform* (Minneapolis: University of Minnesota Press, 1963); U.S. Census Bureau, *Historical Statistics of the United States* (Washington, D.C., 1960).

[17]Morton Grodzins discusses this in "American Political Parties and the American System," *Western Political Quarterly*, Vol. XII (December 1960), pp. 974–998.

(among them FDR himself) were plucked from successful agencies in progressive states and brought to Washington to manage new programs. Their understanding of state and local needs helped maintain the sharing system. Within the states themselves, new co-operative programs were generally subject to modification to meet special local needs.[18] In many cases of erstwhile "centralization," first appearances are deceiving. Consider the Hatch Act requiring states to establish merit systems for federal-aided programs. While this law was greeted by many as a serious limitation of state autonomy, its requirement that states adopt a single merit system of their own design in lieu of federally-imposed program-by-program controls (common in earlier grants-in-aid) helped maintain their integrity as political systems.[19]

The third period featured an expansion of direct federal-local relationships. Partly through urban assistance programs, partly through emergency relief activities, and partly through expanded agricultural programs, the federal government undertook formally to assist local communities in the same spirit of partnership that had animated other forms of intergovernmental relations.[20] This, of course, exacerbated the already complex problems of the states' co-ordination of their internal affairs, even while bringing local relief in a time of crisis.

The growing institutionalization of the intergovernmental partnership was reflected in the development of new institutions to enhance the ability of the states and localities to participate in the development of policy and the improvement of administrative procedures. The Council of State Governments and the complex of "conferences"

of state officials connected with it came into being. Headquartered in Chicago, they provided the states with an able instrument to use in negotiating with Washington and a means to further interstate co-operation, providing a measure of "federalism-without-Washington." Local officials, similarly organized, were also called upon to help shape the co-operative programs of the new era.[21]

By the end of the third period, the role of government in a mixed economy had been firmly established and generally accepted. With the beginning of the fourth period a new generation of regulated capitalism, in which government played a positive role in the economy, began. But the fourth and fifth periods reflect this new generation. A Republican interlude during most of the fourth period served to consolidate and assimilate the changes of the New Deal; then it gave way to a restoration of the Democratic majority coalition through the critical elections of 1956 and 1960. The Democrats' return to office in 1961 inaugurated the fifth period in a burst of renewed federal activism.

The fourth period was one of *noncentralist restoration*, marked by a resurgence of the states as spenders and policy-makers and great expansion of local government. Its public image was set by Dwight D. Eisenhower, who repeatedly called for increased reliance on state efforts in place of federal "intervention." However, its real tone was not one of federal "retrenchment" or unilateral state assumption of previously shared responsibilities, as the President and his advisors suggested, but of continued expansion of intergovernmental collaboration—some twenty-one new grant programs were established between 1946 and 1960—with the states and localities assuming a stronger position in the federal system.

This took four forms. There was a substantial shift in the balance of government expenditures for domestic purposes, with

---

[18]A study of one such case which has become classic is Paul Ylvisaker's *The Battle of Blue Earth County* (Washington, D.C., 1950).

[19]See George C. S. Benson, "Federal-State Personnel Relations," THE ANNALS, Vol. 207 (January 1940), pp. 38–43.

[20]Raymond S. Short, Municipalities and the Federal Government," THE ANNALS, Vol. 207 (January 1940), pp. 44–53; Robert H. Connery and Richard H. Leach, *The Federal Government and Metropolitan Areas* (Cambridge, Mass.: Harvard University Press, 1960).

[21]*See* Clark, *op. cit.* and Key, *op. cit.*, for discussion of these developments.

the states and localities coming to outspend the federal government by a two-to-one margin. There was also a marked relaxation in detailed federal supervision of state handling of established grant programs, a reflection of the increased professionalization of state and local program administrators and the growing willingness of their federal counterparts to trust their judgment. The states and localities, through their representatives in Congress, were responsible for the initiation of most of the new programs, which generally involved small grants to give them greater leverage in expanding their services. Finally, the states and localities again became centers of experimentation, developing "pilot projects" of all sorts, often aided with foundation grants or small doses of federal funds.

The states also began to concern themselves with acquiring some control over the unilateral federal programs carried on within their boundaries and, in some very important cases, a role in the federal-local programs. In some cases, this was a matter of informal intervention to co-ordinate programs or to render supplementary services. In others, it involved the acquisition of very real power over the implementation of programs within the state.

An added impetus to the resurgence of the states was the increased interest in studying the federal system and its functioning by government commissions for the first time in American history and by academic scholars who continued the tradition begun in the Progressive period.[22] The official studies sponsored by the President suffered somewhat from the disability of starting with the mistaken assumption that the ideal federal system demanded maximum separation of government functions by level.[23] Those sponsored by Congress, on the other hand, were directed toward understanding how the existing co-operative system worked without questioning its legitimacy.[24] The most important direct products of these studies were the relatively small but continuing efforts by the federal administration and Congress to smooth over the rough edges of intergovernmental relations, as evidenced by the establishment of the Advisory Commission on Intergovernmental Relations.[25] As the period ended, public discussion turned to consider the problems of co-ordinating diverse federal assistance programs within the state and metropolitan areas so as to allow both to better maintain their governmental and social integrity.

With the return of the Democrats to power in 1961, a fifth period of *concentrated co-operation* was inaugurated. Increased federal activity in a number of fields was coupled with an intensification of the debate over "states rights" on one hand and widespread acknowledgment of intergovernmental collaboration on the other. While this period is not yet sufficiently advanced to be fully characterized, it seems clear that it will be one of considerable governmental expansion, particularly at the federal level, to deal with the problems of a metropolitan society. Part of this represents

[22]A list of even the important publications on the subject of intergovernmental relations would be prohibitively long. There are, however, several good bibliographies that may be consulted, among them: *Intergovernmental Relations in the United States: A Selected Bibliography*, prepared for the Intergovernmental Relations Subcommittee of the Senate Committee on Government Operations (Washington, D.C., 1956); Glen L. Bachelder and Paul C. Shaw, *Federalism: A Selected Bibliography*, Michigan State University Institute for Community Development and Services, Bibliographic Series No. 1 (March, 1964).

[23]These studies included: The [Kestnbaum] Commission on Intergovernmental Relations, *A Report to the President*, with attachments (Washington, D.C., 1955), and Joint Federal-State Action Committee, *Progress Reports* (Washington, D.C., 1958, 1959). An excellent critique of the first study commission can be found in William Anderson, *The Nation and the States: Rivals or Partners?* (Minneapolis: University of Minnesota Press, 1955). The second is equally well treated in Grodzins, "Centralization and Decentralization in the American Federal System," *op. cit.* The first [Hoover] Commission on Reorganization of the Executive Branch of the Government also sponsored a study of federal-state relations by Mr. Hoover's own decision. The study report was prepared by Grodzins for the Council of State Governments and set forth the outlines of his later work on federalism, but the Commission's recommendations ignored his conclusions and called for a restoration of dual federalism. See *Federal-State Relations by the Council of State Governments* (Washington, D.C., 1949).

[24]These studies included those of the [Fountain] Intergovernmental Relations Subcommittee of the House Committee on Government Operations issued in 1956 and those of the [Muskie] Intergovernmental Relations Subcommittee of the Senate Committee on Government Operations, issued beginning in 1963.

[25]The contributions of this body are just now beginning to be felt. They have issued some eighteen reports to date, on a number of phases of intergovernmental relations, available from the Washington, D.C., offices.

federal "picking up the slack" after the fourth period and part, the extension of government in new ways.

Most of the new federal domestic programs have been resurrected from New Deal days, but recently some potentially new departures have been proposed. They are of two different kinds. There is a movement underway to raise federal minimum requirements in some programs unilaterally in a way that would seriously limit state discretion to adjust them to local needs. At the same time, serious proposals have been made to provide some federal aid through block grants and shared revenues to be used as needed at the states' discretion, thus widening their policy-making powers. However, most of the new programs enacted as of this writing, including the two most revolutionary ones (the Civil Rights Act of 1964 and the antipoverty program) are being implemented so as to continue the established traditions of intergovernmental collaboration. Both provide for substantial state and local participation and maximum possible local control. The antipoverty program, for example, is designed to provide federal money for locally sponsored projects and gives the states veto power over most projects proposed for within their limits.

### THE MAINTENANCE OF THE PARTNERSHIP

The foregoing description of the successful maintenance of the traditional system of noncentralized co-operation to date should not obscure the great centralizing pressures operating within the American political system today which may have a decisive impact before the century's end. Nor should it obscure the rough edges within the co-operative system itself that could contribute to a drastic change in the character of the American partnership. The need for managing a national economy, meeting foreign pressures, and securing the constitutional rights of all citizens, as well as the pressures toward elimination of diversity within the country—all these operate to centralize governmental power even when steps to prevent centralization are taken within specific programs. With the constitutional barriers to centralization lowered, the pressures of reformers to secure their reforms and of politicians to secure their rewards wherever it is easiest, without regard for the principles of federalism, further complicate the situation. Finally, the great growth of direct federal relations with private parties through defense and veterans' expenditures, agricultural subsidies, and loan guarantees, none of which are susceptible to organization along traditional co-operative lines, cut into the old patterns even when they are brought into the co-operative system by the back door.

Within the co-operative system, there are problems—for example, weak state and local governments unwilling or unable to uphold their share of the partnership and proliferating "red tape" required by federal administrators to meet federal requirements. There is another problem in that the public information system, as it is presently constituted, tends to focus public attention on Washington to the exclusion of the states and localities.

Logic tells us that noncentralized co-operative federalism is not an easy system to maintain, particularly in a nation that prides itself on being pragmatic—less concerned with form than with function and willing to try anything if it "works." Yet the system has been maintained despite the pressures and in the face of all logic because it has continued to satisfy most of the particular interests in this country more often than not. If not one of them gets everything he wants, each gets something, re-enforcing their attachments to a system they feel they can hope to influence.

*Herbert Wechsler*

# THE POLITICAL SAFEGUARDS OF FEDERALISM: THE ROLE OF THE STATES IN THE COMPOSITION AND SELECTION OF THE NATIONAL GOVERNMENT

Federalism was the means and price of the formation of the Union. It was inevitable, therefore, that its basic concepts should determine much of our history. The more important fact is that they shape government, law, and politics today. Nor is this merely illustration of the insight that the lives of nations, like the lives of individuals, are permanently influenced by the experience of infancy. In a far flung, free society, the federalist values are enduring. They call upon a people to achieve a unity sufficient to resist their common perils and advance their common welfare, without undue sacrifice of their diversities and the creative energies to which diversity gives rise. They call for government responsive to the will of the full national constituency, without loss of responsiveness to lesser voices, reflecting smaller bodies of opinion, in areas that constitute their own legitimate concern.

No form of government can serve these values with complete efficiency, no set of mechanisms can perfectly discriminate between the polar claims so patently involved. No single form or mechanism will give equal service under different circumstances or function with the same results at different times. But in a time when federalism must appear to many peoples as the sole alternative to tyranny, there is a special value in examining American experience, the more so since we face important issues of direction ourselves.

I

Our constitution makers established a central government authorized to act directly upon individuals through its own agencies—and thus they formed a nation capable of function and of growth. To serve the ends of federalism they employed three main devices:

They preserved the states as separate sources of authority and organs of administration—a point on which they hardly had a choice.
They gave the states a role of great importance in the composition and selection of the central government.
They undertook to formulate a distribution of authority between the nation and the states, in terms which gave some scope at least to legal processes for its enforcement.

Scholarship—not only legal scholarship—has given most attention to the last of these enumerated mechanisms, perhaps because it has been fascinated by the Supreme Court and its interpretations of the power distribution clauses of the Constitution. The continuous existence of the states as governmental entities and their strategic role in the selection of the Congress and the President are so immutable a feature of the system that their importance tends to be ignored. Of the Framers' mechanisms, however, they have had and have today the larger influence upon the working balance of our federalism. The actual extent of central intervention in the governance of our affairs is determined far less by the formal power distribution than by the sheer existence of the states and their political power to influence the action of the national authority.

The fact of the continuous existence of

From *Federalism: Mature and Emergent*, ed. Arthur W. MacMahon (Columbia University Press: 1955), pp. 95–109. Reprinted by permission of the Trustees of Columbia University in the City of New York.

31

the states, with general governmental competence unless excluded by the Constitution or valid act of Congress, set the mood of our federalism from the start. The first Congress did not face the problem of building a legal system from the ground up; it started with the premise that the standing *corpus juris* of the country was provided by the states. As with the law, so with the courts. One federal Supreme Court was essential and the Constitution gave a mandate that it be established. But even the establishment of lower courts was left an open question by the Framers, as was the jurisdiction to be vested in any such courts as Congress might establish — within the limits that the Constitution set. Congress was free to commit the administration of national law to national tribunals or to leave the task to the state courts, sworn to support the national supremacy within its proper sphere. Even the appellate jurisdiction of the Supreme Court was subject to congressional control.

National action has thus always been regarded as exceptional in our polity, an intrusion to be justified by some necessity, the special rather than the ordinary case. The point of view cuts even deeper than the concept of the central government as one of granted, limited authority, articulated in the Tenth Amendment. National power may be quite unquestioned in a given situation; those who would advocate its exercise must none the less answer the preliminary question why the matter should not be left to the states. Even when Congress acts, its tendency has been to frame enactments on an *ad hoc* basis to accomplish limited objectives, supplanting state-created norms only so far as may be necessary for the purpose. Indeed, with all the centralizing growth throughout the years, federal law is still a largely interstitial product, rarely occupying any field completely, building normally upon legal relationships established by the states. As Henry Hart and I have put it elsewhere: "Congress acts . . . against the background of the total *corpus juris* of the states

in much the way that a state legislature acts against the background of the common law, assumed to govern unless changed by legislation." As a state legislature views the common law as something to be left alone unless a need for change has been established, so Congress has traditionally viewed the governance of matters by the states.

The tradition plainly serves the values of our federalism in so far as it maintains a burden of persuasion on those favoring national intervention. New York, for example, faced the need for rent control after the need was deemed to have passed in most parts of the country. Should a national program have been continued when New York and every other state was competent to launch a program of its own, adapted to its special needs? Under such circumstances national action has consequences that are plainly undesirable. On the one hand, it is likely to impose control in areas where the politically dominant local judgment finds control unnecessary. On the other hand, it is likely to attenuate the rigor of control in areas where it is really needed. For if the need is not severe the country over, the terms of national legislation will be shaped by a Congress in which the hostile sentiment has a large influence, rather than by a legislature more generally sensitive to the need. This was, of course, the actual experience with federal control of rent throughout the later post-war years.

The political logic of federalism thus supports placing the burden of persuasion on those urging national action. Though the explanation is the same, it is more difficult to find support for the commonly fragmentary quality of many national enactments, with their resultant ambiguity as to how far they supersede state law entirely and how far they call for integration with it. This is a point that has a special visibility to lawyers, for the federal-state adjustments called for by such ambiguities present problems of enormous difficulty to the courts. The issue is perhaps most striking in the common case where federal law defines powers, rights, or duties without attention to resulting liabilities or remedies, raising the question whether these are matters to be governed by state legal systems or determined by the independent judgment of federal courts. To explore these matters is beyond my present purpose. I adduce them only to support my thesis that the existence of the states as governmental entities and as the sources of the standing law is in itself the prime determinant of our working federalism, coloring the nature and the scope of our national legislative processes from their inception.

## II

If I have drawn too much significance from the mere fact of the existence of the states, the error surely will be rectified by pointing also to their crucial role in the selection and the composition of the national authority. More is involved here than that aspect of the compromise between the larger and the smaller states that yielded their equality of status in the Senate. Representatives no less than Senators are allotted by the Constitution to the states, although their number varies with state population as determined by the census. Though the House was meant to be the "grand depository of the democratic principle of the government," as distinguished from the Senate's function as the forum of the states, people to be represented with due deference to their respective numbers were *the people of the states*. And with the President, as with Congress, the crucial instrument of the selection — whether through electors or, in the event of failure of majority, by the House voting as state units — is again the states. The consequence, of course, is that the states are the strategic yardsticks for the measurement of interest and opinion, the special centers of political activity, the separate geographical determinants of national as well as local politics.

Despite the rise of national parties, the shift to popular election of the Senate, and

the difficulty of appraising the precise impact of such provisions on the legislative process, Madison's analysis has never lost its thrust:

The State governments may be regarded as constituent and essential parts of the federal government; whilst the latter is nowise essential to the operation or organization of the former.
A local spirit will infallibly prevail much more in the members of Congress, than a national spirit will prevail in the legislatures of the particular States.
Even the House of Representatives, though drawn immediately from the people, will be chosen very much under the influence of that class of men, whose influence over the people obtains for themselves an election into the State legislatures.

To the extent that federalist values have real significance, they must give rise to local sensitivity to central intervention; to the extent that such a local sensitivity exists, it cannot fail to find reflection in the Congress. Indeed, the problem of the Congress is and always has been to attune itself to national opinion and produce majorities for action called for by the voice of the entire nation. It is remarkable that it should function thus as well as it does, given its intrinsic sensitivity to any insular opinion that is dominant in a substantial number of the states.

## III

The point is so clear in the Senate that, as Madison observed of the equality accorded to the states, it "does not call for much discussion." The forty-nine votes that will determine Senate action, even with full voting, could theoretically be drawn from twenty-five states, of which the combined population does not reach twenty-nine millions, a bare 19 per cent of all state residents. The one-third plus one that will defeat a treaty or a resolution of amendment could, equally theoretically, be drawn from seventeen states with a total population little over twelve millions, less than that of New York. I say theoretically since, short of

33

a combination to resist an effort to impair state equality within the Senate (which the Constitution purports to place beyond amendment) or to diminish the political power of the smaller states in other ways, a coalition in these terms is quite unthinkable. The fact remains that in more subtle ways the Senate cannot fail to function as the guardian of state interests as such, when they are real enough to have political support or even to be instrumental in attaining other ends. And if account is taken of the operation of seniority within the Senate, of the opportunity of Senators to marshal individual authority, not to speak of the possibility of filibuster, this power of negation, vested in the states without regard to population, multiplies in many ways. Given a controversy that has any sectional dimension, it is not long before the impact of this power is perceived.

Nor is it only power of negation. To be sure, on any direct show of strength in passing legislation, a Senate majority based on the states must be supported by a House majority based on population and must also avoid a veto by the President. But power to enact is rarely based on such a test—and when it seems to be, there sometimes is involved a merely token process. Legislation rests in practice on a balancing of interests, a give and take that calls for coalition and for compromise, a strategy that may involve a present sacrifice to hold or win future support. In this dynamic interchange, a latent power of negation has much positive significance in garnering the votes for an enactment that might otherwise have failed. This is the point at which state equality may well present the largest difficulties, but the issue is beyond the range I have undertaken to explore. It is enough for present purposes to show how far the composition of the Senate is intrinsically calculated to prevent intrusion from the center on subjects that dominant state interests wish preserved for state control.

IV

Even the House is slanted somewhat in the same direction, though the incidence is less severe. This is not due appreciably to the one seat reserved for every state regardless of its population, nor to the mechanics or the mathematics of congressional apportionment, though they present their problems. It is due rather to the states' control of voters' qualifications, on the one hand, and of districting, on the other.

The position with respect to voters' qualifications derives from the constitutional provision that fixes the electorate of Representatives (and of Senators as well since the Seventeenth Amendment) as those persons who "have the qualifications requisite for electors of the most numerous branch of the State Legislature." Subject, then, to the prohibition of the denial of franchise because of color, race, or sex, embodied in the Fifteenth and Nineteenth Amendments and the radiations of the equal protection clause of the Fourteenth, the states determine—indirectly it is true—the electorate that chooses Representatives. The consequences of contracting the electorate by such devices as a poll-tax are, of course, incalculable, but they tend to buttress what traditionally dominant state interests conceive to be their special state position; that is the point of the contraction. This sentiment, reflected in the Representatives that these constituencies send to Congress, is not ordinarily conducive to support for an adventurous expansion of the national authority, though there have been exceptions, to be sure.

The Fourteenth Amendment purports to put in the hands of Congress a remedy for such diminution of the electorate. It directs that the census figure determinative of the number of a state's representatives be reduced on the apportionment to the extent that the right to vote "is denied to any of the male inhabitants of such state, being twenty-one years of age and citizens of the United States, or in any way abridged, except for participation in rebellion, or other crime." The remedy has proved unworkable in practice by reason of the difficulty of the quantitative investigation needed, not to speak of the political problems that an effort to employ it would present. Federal abolition of the poll-tax is periodically urged in Congress, with extensive hearings on the measure, but there are grave doubts with respect to its constitutionality and no real prospect of its passage.

State control of congressional districting derives from the constitutional provision that the "times, places and manner of holding elections for Senators and Representatives, shall be prescribed in each State by the Legislature thereof." The same clause provides, however, that "Congress may at any time by law make or alter such regulations. . . ." Though the matter has been disputed, it seems plain that state control thus rests entirely on the tolerance of Congress. Until congressional action was taken in 1842, there was variation in state practice. Alabama, Georgia, Mississippi, Missouri, New Hampshire, New Jersey, and Pennsylvania elected Representatives on a state-wide basis by general ticket, while Maryland, Massachusetts, New York, Virginia, and South Carolina were committed early to the district basis. The act of 1842 made districts "composed of contiguous territory" mandatory, though leaving districting to the respective states. Even this mandate was initially defied in four of the general-ticket states, with the House seating their elected Representatives despite the state's recalcitrance as to the method of selection. Omitted in 1850, the mandate was repeated in later acts and was extended in 1872 to require that the districts contain "as nearly as practicable an equal number of inhabitants." The requirement of contiguity was further supplemented in 1901 to call for districts of "compact territory." These provisions were repeated in 1911 but the Congress failed to reapportion after the census of 1920. The legislation of 1929, as amended, establishing the present framework, provides for an automatic reapportionment upon the President's report (unless Congress directs otherwise). It directs the course that must be followed in the election of Representatives when a change from prior methods is required by an alteration of their number as a consequence of the apportionment and the state has failed to prescribe what the change shall be. Beyond this, however, it lays down no requirements at all. The district system thus rests wholly upon state initiative at the present time. More important, the delineation of the districts rests entirely with the states.

It is well known that there are great discrepancies in district size in many multi-district states, paralleling for Congress the discrepancies, to forego harsher terms, that prevail in districting for the state legislatures. . . .

It may be said, and perhaps rightly, that the situation with respect to districting, while detracting from the equality of popular representation in the House, has little bearing on the role of Congress in preserving federalist values. I am not so sure. It is significant, for one thing, that it is the states that draw the districts; one can hardly think the district lines would be the same had they been drawn from the beginning by Congress. Beyond this, however, the general motive and tendency of district deviations has quite clearly been to reduce urban power, not in the meaning of the census classification but in the sense of the substantial cities. The tendency is so appreciable that a recent article assures the readers of a small town magazine that while cities or towns of under 10,000 coupled with the farms account for only 51 per cent of the entire population, residents of such areas are numerically dominant in 265 of the 435 congressional districts, accounting for the choice of 61 per cent of the House (including 18 of the 21 committee chairmen) in addition to their numerical dominance in the choice of 75 per cent of the Senate. Traditionally, at least, a more active localism and resistance to new federal intrusion centers in this 51 per cent of Americans than in the other 49 per cent. I should suppose that this is likely to continue; and that the figures, therefore, have some relevancy to an understanding of why presidential programs calling for the extension of national activity, and seemingly supported by the country in a presidential election, may come a cropper notwithstanding in the House. Such hostility to Washington may rest far less on pure devotion to the principle of local government than on opposition to specific measures which Washington proposes to put forth. This explanation does not make the sentiment the less centrifugal in its effects. Federalism would have few adherents were it not, like other elements of govenment, a means and not an end.

v

If Congress, from its composition and the mode of its selection, tends to reflect the "local spirit" predicted by Madison, the prime organ of a compensating "national spirit" is, of course, the President—both as the Chief Executive and as the leader of his party. Without the unifying power of the highest office, derived from the fixed tenure gained by his election and the sense that the President speaks for and represents the full national constituency, it would be difficult to develop the centripetal momentum so essential to the total federal scheme. No modern President can doubt that one of his essential functions is to balance the localism and the separatism of the Congress by presenting programs that reflect the needs of the entire nation, building the best coalitions that he can for their enactment, using the prerogatives and prestige of his office to that end. That this has been accomplished, on the whole, despite the role allotted to the states in the selection of the President yields more support than Bagehot realized for his great dictum that

"the men of Massachusetts could . . . work *any* Constitution."

Familiar though they are, the constitutional provisions governing our presidential choices should be noted. The electors, in whom the initial choice is vested, are appointed by the states in the manner provided by each state's legislature. Their number reflects the compromise concerning representation in Congress, being determined by the number of Representatives allotted to the state on the apportionment plus the two Senators that each state is assured. A majority of all the votes is necessary for election by electors. If it is not obtained by any candidate, the choice among the three who lead in electoral votes devolves upon the House of Representatives voting not as individuals but by states, with each state granted equal voice and a majority of all required for election.

Had these provisions worked out as the Framers contemplated, with the electors as an independent agency of choice, it is hard to think that there would often have been an electoral majority; the electors would have functioned merely as a nominating body, with selection falling mainly to the House voting under the rule of state equality. It is not comfortable to conjecture how far this result might have reduced the President to a mere agent of the states, exacerbating the intrinsic localism of the Congress, losing the unifying thrust for which the Presidency stands. It is uncomfortable also to reflect that only the rise and success of the two-party system, buttressed by the general ticket method of selecting the electors (under which a state's votes are cast as a unit), prevents that result today.

The drift to the general ticket was inevitable, given the demand for popular participation in the choice and the fact that the choice of electors by districts, which Madison averred the Framers mainly contemplated, would normally divide the state's electoral votes. The states that used the district method early found themselves forsaking it, unwilling to accept such diminution in their influence on the election, unless the method that effected the division were decreed for all. The most important consequence for present purposes is that the casting of the electoral votes in state units yields electoral majorities despite third party candidates, as in 1860 and 1912, while any system that reflects internal differences of opinion in the states might send the election to the House. Minority opinion is washed out within the states; it works no fragmentation of their electoral votes. . . .

In net result, the present practice with respect to electoral votes seems likely to endure; and since the House vote by states on failure of an electoral majority is probably unchangeable alone, that feature of the system will probably remain as well, despite the weight and historicity of the objections to it.

Federalist considerations thus play an important part even in the selection of the President, although a lesser part than many of the Framers must have contemplated. A presidential candidacy must be pointed towards the states of largest population in so far as they are doubtful. It must balance this direction by attention to the other elements of the full coalition that is looked to for an electoral majority. Both major parties have a strong incentive to absorb protest movements of such sectional significance that their development in strength would throw elections to the House. Both must give some attention to the organized minorities that may approach balance of power status in important states, without, however, making promises that will outrun the tolerance of other necessary elements of their required strength. Both parties recognize that they must appeal to some total combination of allegiance, choice, or interest that will yield sufficient nationwide support to win elections and make possible effective government.

The most important element of party competition in this framework is the similarity of the appeal that each must make.

This is a constant affront to those who seek purity of ideology in politics; it is the clue, however, to the success of our politics in the elimination of extremists—and to the tolerance and basic unity that is essential if our system is to work.

The President must be, as I have said above, the main repository of "national spirit" in the central government. But both the mode of his selection and the future of his party require that he also be responsive to local values that have large support within the states. And since his programs must, in any case, achieve support in Congress—in so far as they involve new action—he must surmount the greater local sensitivity of Congress before anything is done.

VI

If this analysis is correct, the national political process in the United States—and especially the role of the states in the composition and selection of the central government—is intrinsically well adapted to retarding or restraining new intrusions by the center on the domain of the states. Far from a national authority that is expansionist by nature, the inherent tendency in our system is precisely the reverse, necessitating the widest support before intrusive measures of importance can receive significant consideration, reacting readily to opposition grounded in resistance within the states. Nor is this tendency effectively denied by pointing to the size or scope of the existing national establishment. However useful it may be to explore possible contractions in specific areas, such evidence points mainly to the magnitude of unavoidable responsibility under the circumstances of our time.

It is in light of this inherent tendency, reflected most importantly in Congress, that the governmental power distribution clauses of the Constitution gain their largest meaning as an instrument for the protection of the states. Those clauses, as is well known, have served far more to qualify or stop intrusive legislative measures in the Congress than to invalidate enacted legislation in the Supreme Court.

This does not differ from the expectation of the Framers quite as markedly as might be thought. For the containment of the national authority Madison did not emphasize the function of the Court; he pointed to the composition of the Congress and to the political processes. So in his letter to Everett, written in 1830, he summarized the views that he had often stated:

as a security of the rights and powers of the states in their individual capacities ag[ainst] an undue preponderance of the powers granted to the Government over them in their united capacity, the Constitution has relied on 1. The responsibility of the Senators and Representatives in the Legislature of the U.S. to the Legislatures & peoples of the States. 2. The responsibility of the President to the people of the U. States; & 3. The liability of the Ex. and Judiciary functionaries of the U.S. to impeachment by the Representatives of the people of the States, in one branch of the legislature of the U.S. and trial by the Representatives of the States, in the other branch; the State functionaries, Legislative, Executive & judiciary, being at the same time in their appointment & responsibility, altogether independent of the agency or authority of the U. States.

The prime function envisaged for judicial review — in relation to federalism — was the maintenance of national supremacy against nullification or usurpation by the individual states, the national government having no part in their composition or their councils. This is made clear by the fact that reliance on the courts was substituted, apparently on Jefferson's suggestion, for the earlier proposal to give Congress a veto of state enactments deemed to trespass on the national domain. And except for the brief interlude that ended with the crisis of the thirties, it is mainly in the realm of such policing of the states that the Supreme Court has in fact participated in determining the balances of federalism. This is not to say that the Court can decline to measure national enactments by the Constitution when it is called upon to face the question in the course of ordinary litigation; the supremacy clause governs there as well. It is rather to say that the Court is on weakest ground when it opposes its interpretation of the Constitution to that of Congress in the interest of the states, whose representatives control the legislative process and, by hypothesis, have broadly acquiesced in sanctioning the challenged act of Congress.

Federal intervention as against the states is thus primarily a matter for congressional determination in our system as it stands. So too, moreover, is the question whether state enactments shall be stricken down as an infringement on the national authority. For while the Court has an important function in this area, as I have noted, the crucial point is that its judgments here are subject to reversal by Congress, which can consent to action by the states that otherwise would be invalidated. The familiar illustrations in commerce and in state taxation of federal instrumentalities do not by any means exhaust the field. The Court makes the decisive judgment only when — and to the extent that — Congress has not laid down the resolving rule.

To perceive that it is Congress rather than the Court that on the whole is vested with the ultimate authority for managing our federalism is not, of course, to depreciate the role played by the Court, subordinate though it may be. It is no accident that Congress has been slow to exercise its managerial authority, remitting to the Court so much of what it could determine by a legislative rule. The difficulties of reaching agreement on such matters, not to speak of drafting problems of immense complexity, lend obvious attractiveness to the *ad hoc* judicial method of adjustment. Whether Congress could contribute more effectively to the solution of these problems is a challenging and open question. The legislative possibilities within this area of our polity have hardly been explored.

# II. *Federalism in Action: Some Cases in Point*

Part Two is divided into six sections. The first considers noncentralization and the party system; the second examines some of the processes of federalism from the vantage point of the states; while the last three look at the functioning of the system in three specific fields: civil rights, education, and water resources. The perspective of all five is simultaneously national and local. All the selections are in some way concerned with the role of federalism in determining the structure and functioning of the national government and, beyond that, of the nation as a civil society. Our concern here, then, is as much with the way federalism influences national actions serving the country as a whole as with the way in which it influences the maintenance of local self-government. Indeed, this aspect of federalism is just as important as the maintenance of traditional local control. The infusion of the national government with the spirit of federalism is a primary goal of the Constitution. The founders of the American federal system were particularly aware of this need. Their argument was that federalism, if it created a strong national government and infused the operations of that government with federal principles, could be the salvation of republicanism by limiting the possibility for demagogues and tyrants to seize power.

## NONCENTRALIZATION AND THE PARTY SYSTEM

David B. Truman's article on "Federalism and the Party System" describes one very important way in which the political process serves to infuse the spirit and principles of federalism into every part of the American system. Many observers view the role of political parties in this regard as absolutely crucial to the maintenance of federalism. The political meaning of noncentralization in the party system is illustrated in the selection from Bernard Hennessy's case study, *Dollars for Democrats*, an examination of the unsuccessful effort made by Paul Butler as chairman of the Democratic National Committee to strengthen the hand of his national party organization through increasing its financial independence. Butler, strongly influenced by the views of certain political scientists that the American party system would be made more responsible if the parties were more centralized, failed in his effort because of the very nature of his party as part of the system.

David B. Truman

# FEDERALISM AND THE PARTY SYSTEM

I

To speak loosely of "the party system," especially when dealing with federalism in the United States, is to run the risk of begging the central question in this inquiry, for the nature of the party enterprise rests on the extent to which the elements collectively designated by the term actually constitute a system. Differentiating factors of structure and function bisect the "system" from various directions and in bewildering fashion, creating patterns of autonomy and subordination, some stable and some fluid, which seriously embarrass generalization.

The structural elements of party can be classified in the conventional fashion—following the formal, frequently statutory provisions for the diversity of committees, conventions, and individual functionaries—by national, state, and local levels. Such classification, while formally appropriate, is likely to take insufficient account of the extent to which the persistent and effective relationships among men and groups of men active in party affairs are clustered around one or a number of individual offices located on one or two or all three levels of the formal hierarchy.

It is a commonplace to point out that the party on the national level in the United States is, and throughout the country's history has been, focused on the presidency. Such national or interstate machinery as exists is primarily, though not exclusively, concerned with the nomination and election, perhaps especially the renomination and reelection, of a President. So much is this the case that, despite the practice by both parties since 1928 of maintaining at least a nuclear national headquarters in continuous operation and despite the normal efforts of the defeated presidential candidate to give substance to his titular leadership, the party which has failed to win the White House presents a somewhat truncated, if not fractionated, appearance, which it is likely to retain until after the next nominating convention. Moreover, when the presidency is not at stake both parties show strong symptoms of "mid-term atomization."

The essential supportive structures for members of the Congress typically are not national or interstate. The chairmen and staffs of the national committees provide some services and assistance for duly nominated candidates for the Congress. The organizationally separate and often jealously independent campaign committees maintained by the "parliamentary" parties in the Senate and the House of Representatives seem to perform much the same sort of function, although their activities have never been closely studied.

The party in the Senate and the House of Representatives is not without significance as a means of allocating positions of power and influence in the legislative branch or even as a vehicle for the formulation of public policy, and the "record" of the congressional parties is not irrelevant to the fortunes of aspirants for election or reelection to the Congress. But the risks and sanctions to which most members of Congress are particularly sensitive have their focus within the states and localities. The relationships which the legislator has es

From *Federalism: Mature and Emergent*, ed. Arthur W. MacMahon (Columbia University Press: 1955), pp. 115–125, 129–134. Reprinted by permission of the Trustees of Columbia University in the City of New York.

tablished and maintained within the constituency are primary and crucial; others are secondary and incidental. This seems to be the case despite the evidence that, especially in the case of the House of Representatives, the bulk of the voters in general elections cast their ballots on the basis of party preference rather than attachment to the personal qualities of individual candidates for the national legislature; that is, party percentages in most districts tend to shift in the same direction. This is the case in presidential years, when the party is in a sense symbolized in the person of the chief candidate, but is equally apparent in the midterm elections. This paradox seems to point to the underlying significance of the nominating as against the electoral function of party structure, of which more will be said below.

At the state and local levels the structural patterns are varied and complicated, but not essentially different in kind. The significant organizations in the states may be centered upon the governorship, with control reaching down effectively into the counties and municipalities, or upon the United States Senators or upon both in some form of combination. Specialization in the localities may be built individually or in combination around the positions of mayors, sheriffs, or other prime sources of patronage and power such as the office of surrogate in the counties of New York State. Such specialized structures may include a variety of other elective offices, such as seats in the state legislature, in the United States House of Representatives, and even in the Senate. As often as not, however, congressional candidates will operate through more or less independent organizations of their own creation, even in the general election campaign. In the case of Representatives, this is often a reflection of the relative indifference of the more inclusive state and local organizations toward the congressional ticket, as compared with more lucrative sources of patronage. Senators may function independently for quite different reasons. Not only are they more conspicu-

ous in the political affairs of their constituencies and secure in their positions for a longer period of time, but also they are likely to command other means of political power in greater abundance, including federal patronage.

The structural scheme of parties in the American federalism thus displays a confusing complexity, both in its formal aspects and in its informal operation. The system, to the extent that it can be given the name, is composed of a tremendous variety of elements imperfectly and rather unpredictably articulated, capable of showing a remarkable degree of separatism and autonomy. Moreover, the degree of articulation which exists to make the system is of a peculiar sort. The relationships between the more obscure and the more prominent elements in the system show a defensive, unilateral quality. In areas where general elections mean anything, it is a rare local or state party unit which, personal and factional feuds aside, is indifferent to the vote-pulling power of those occupying the principal positions on the ticket. But the concern is in a sense parasitic, to derive support from the leading figure on the ticket rather than to supply it. Given the tendency of voters, even when the form of the ballot does not help, to simplify their tasks by voting a "straight ticket," state and local elements are understandably interested in a nominee at the top of the list who may carry the whole slate into office with him. But these segments of the system are able, in marked degree, to cut themselves off from the head of the ticket when the latter is regarded as a handicap and succeed with remarkable frequency in checking the effects upon them of a swing of voting sentiment adverse to the occupant of the top place. Similarly, there are significant relationships between the presidential party and the "constituency parties," illustrated by the common appeal by a member of the Congress for executive adoption of a particular policy or for a favorable presidential announcement in order to improve the prospects of hard-pressed candidates in special areas, but these carry no guarantee of reciprocal support either on the floor of the Congress or in subsequent election campaigns.

II

Although the system—made up of the presidential parties, the "parliamentary" parties, the constituency parties, and the various other state and local aggregations—is structurally unstable and disjointed, the distribution of power within it is not even or merely haphazard. Here again, however, the danger of hasty generalization is great. It is customary to refer to the distribution of power within the American party system as decentralized. This is the generally accepted view, yet its implications in the context of federalism and for possible future trends are not clear unless some account is taken of the relative significance of the various functions of the party and of the degree of decentralization of power in connection with the most important of them. Parties, in any representative system, perform a composite of functions, including nominating candidates for public office, mobilizing an electorate for their support, distributing patronage and other perquisites of public position, developing and protecting those formulas for social adjustment and accommodation which we collectively refer to as public policies, and a host of less obvious and self-conscious services. In different places and at different times one or another of these may be more conspicuous than the rest, which vastly complicates the tasks of historians and comparative analysts of the political process. Except perhaps in those political situations where a basic consensus is lacking or is being challenged, however, the nominating function seems to be the most fundamental or at least the most persistently focal. This has been strikingly the case in the United States since at least as far back as the caucuses and juntos of the later colonial years and, especially on the national level, conspicuously so since the

great changes in the period associated with the name of Andrew Jackson, when the presidential party assumed most of the characteristics it displays today. It is around the nominating function that the states in recent decades have constructed the most elaborate and complicated systems of statutory regulation, and the intensity of feeling associated with the spread of the direct primary in the first decade of the present century reflected in part a recognition of the fundamental importance of the nomination process. James Bryce made no more acute observation concerning the American scene than he did when he noted that the nomination of candidates for public office was not only the most important but the most distinctively American function of party organization.

It is in connection with the nominating of candidates that the decentralization of power in the American party system is most apparent. Looking at the presidency it is clear that the changes in practice which developed in the eighteen-twenties—changes largely of degree, perhaps, but of such measure that their significance can scarcely be exaggerated—involved an increase in the importance of localism in the selecting process. The congressional caucus had been the instrument of a limited and comparatively homogeneous national elite disposing of an office which had little of the quality of popular symbolism that it possesses today. Its members were not, of course, lacking in attachment to states and sections, but theirs was a national and central power reflecting the effects of close association in the institutional frame of the national legislature. The shift of initiative to the state legislatures and later to the national delegate conventions was a response to demands from more heterogeneous elements in the population and eventuated in a shifting of the power of decision, if not of initiative, from the national to the state or local level.

In Jackson's day, and for decades thereafter, the utility of the national convention lay not only in the announcement of a defensible nomination, but also in the sharpening of an effective electoral mechanism. In fact, the first national convention of the Democratic party was apparently more a rally to spur Jackson's state and local cohorts into vigorous activity than a device for selecting the candidate, as, in fact, conventions in which incumbent Presidents have sought renomination have usually been ever since. In later years the leaders of state and factional delegations had not only convention votes to market among the managers of aspiring candidates but also a canvassing and electoral organization as well. Both were needed, even though the former were of more immediate importance.

Perhaps the most significant, if largely undocumented, change in recent years, a change which may account for some of the recent criticism of the national convention, is that the electioneering functions of the presidential party have become increasingly centralized while the power over nominations remains decentralized. Although those voters who alter their choices late in the campaign may be strongly influenced, as the survey studies indicate, by personal solicitation, the presence of the presidential candidates in every living room, by way of radio and television, reduces the need for an army of canvassers in presidential campaigns as the development of the metropolitan press alone never did. In recent presidential elections both the behavior and the informal testimony of many urban functionaries support this interpretation; the circulars and posters are still distributed to the local clubs and headquarters, but the effort necessary to put them in the hands of individual voters is recognized as being of little or no value. State and local leaders are not powerless or completely unnecessary in the electioneering efforts of the presidential party, but both central direction and central execution of a presidential campaign have become in recent years not only a possibility but in large measure an actuality.

Yet the nomination function, excepting the renomination of an incumbent President, remains essentially decentralized. Despite such devices as the presidential primary and the centrally directed preconvention efforts of the leading aspirants, local and frequently extraneous considerations not only enter into but even dominate the selection of delegates and the horse-trading decisions behind the scenes at the convention. In fact, the evidence clearly suggests that in areas where one-party dominance, as in the South, operates to avoid disturbance to distinctive local practices, the only significant function of a state party may be to select reliable delegates to interstate party councils. The leaders of the presidential party may no longer need to rely heavily upon a decentralized machinery for conducting an election campaign, but they are still dependent on forging a cohesive coalition of state and local leaders for the opportunity to conduct one.

Decentralization of the nominating function is more striking and more significant as it affects Senators and Representatives. Regardless of the method of selection, by one or another form of the predominant direct primary or by convention, the influences which are chiefly responsible for the selection of candidates are local rather than national. The importance of this fact is merely underscored by the evidence that, under normal conditions, in about half the congressional constituencies, success in the primary is tantamount to election. This is typically due to the "one-party" complexion of many such areas, but it may result as well from the individual candidate's effectiveness in creating or associating himself with an organization within the constituency which can assure his selection or redesignation. The implications for the party system are much the same in either case.

Even a casual glance at the career lines of Senators and Representatives, as well as of state and local officials from whose ranks they are normally recruited, will indicate that most of them have had long and intimate association with the areas which they represent, more than is required by the symptomatically significant custom demanding residence in the district from which the legislator is chosen. No precise data on this point exist in the literature, but the impression is that a member of Congress is more likely than the average of the population to have been born, raised, educated, and trained in the area from which he is chosen. A constituency, perhaps especially an urban one, may take up a comparative newcomer who has achieved sudden prominence, but his survival is likely to depend ultimately upon his knowing his constituency, not in abstract, intellectual terms, but through supportive associations with individuals and groups. He must have satisfactory "connections," either with the leadership of a dominant party organization or with influential individuals primarily concerned with assuring his continuance in office or a combination of the two.

These connections may not be able to assure his election; the fortunes of the national party may be ebbing so rapidly that nothing can assure his individual survival or the nominee of the opposing party may more successfully exploit local dissatisfactions. But the aspirant will have no chance even to face these risks, except as he chooses to attempt a normally unsuccessful "independent" candidacy, unless he has the support necessary for nomination.

The structure responsible for nominating the legislative candidate need not be parochial or anti-national in its attitudes. This is not its principal significance but rather the fact that it is the locus of discretion in the nominating process. In its operations it need display no dependence upon, no functional association or identification with, the leadership of the presidential or the "parliamentary" party. Bryce made the point effectively in a brief comparison of local party organizations in Britain and the United States:

An organization which exists, like the political associations of England, solely or mainly for the sake of canvassing, conducting registration, diffusing literature, getting up courses of lectures, holding meetings and passing resolutions, has little or no power. . . . But when an organization which the party is in the habit of obeying, chooses a party candidate, it exerts power, power often of the highest import. . . .

Decentralization of the functions of nominating and promoting the election of members of the Congress is reflected in a lack of cohesion on important policy matters within the "parliamentary" parties—within the party in either House and between the party in one chamber and "the same" party in the other—and in fairly frequent rejection of the legislative leadership of "the party's" President when it "controls" the White House. It is too easy to underestimate the influence of party affiliation upon legislative voting and to ignore the evidence that it is more reliably predictive of such behavior than any other factor so far identified. But on controverted issues of prime significance the leaders of the "parliamentary" parties not infrequently find themselves in the minority among their nominal following or split into two opposing wings, and the Administration may have to count on appreciable support from a segment of the "opposition" in Congress for the enactment of a basic portion of its legislative program, often despite extraordinary efforts by a popular President through public appeals and pronouncements, efforts which depend for effectiveness upon their infrequent use.

This state of affairs leads to criticism of the party system and demands for party "responsibility" by those who desire central place among the functions of party for the formation of a more coherent and enforceable program. Of such criticisms the recent report of the American Political Science Association's Committee on Political Parties may be taken as representative. A common shortcoming of such appeals, illustrated in the committee's proposals, is that in their enthusiasm for programmatic elegance they tend to underestimate the significance of the decentralized nominating function. It seems unlikely that any amount of policy talk in local meetings or of platform writing by interstate bodies will increase discipline within the congressional parties or cohesion within the Administration as a whole, unless they are preceded by a centralization of the risks and sanctions associated with the selection of candidates for seats in the legislature. It may be doubted, in fact, whether in any party system dominated by two major aggregations, even in a country less extensive and socially less complex than the United States, cohesion is provided primarily by the programmatic element rather than by a central leadership whose policy tendencies are but vaguely known and whose displeasure with a parliamentary follower is enforceable at the nominating stage. If the legislator's risks are localized, he will look in that direction when making difficult choices on matters of public policy.

III

The American party system thus tends to be characterized by decentralization of power with respect to its most crucial function, by structural confederation, and by a lack of coherence in matters of major policy. What have the facts of federalism to do with this? To what extent is this an inescapable consequence of the federal system itself? Federalism, by the constitutional protection of constituent governments, creates at least the possibility, as Herbert Wechsler has argued, that the states will control the composition and influence materially the legislative processes of the national entity. If, as Arthur Holcombe suggests, the national political party is the principal agent for restricting these tendencies, its effectiveness in the United States has been something less than complete. Is the molding force of the federal system itself such that a party system op-

erating within it must inevitably show the characteristics of political organizations in the United States?

This is a question of considerable importance for an understanding of the American experience and for an estimate of its potentialities in the future. It is a question which the Committee on Political Parties tends to avoid by treating party organization as a matter dissociated from that of governmental sructure. Thus it asserts that: "In the case of the American party system, the real issue is not over the federal form of organization but over the right balance of forces within this type of organization."

The basic political fact of federalism is that it creates separate, self-sustaining centers of power, privilege, and profit which may be sought and defended as desirable in themselves, as means of leverage upon elements in the political structure above and below, and as bases from which individuals may move to places of greater influence and prestige in and out of government. This does not mean simply that a socio-economic interest group, dominant within a state or, more typically perhaps, a group of contiguous states, will utilize state powers to protect itself from assault both from within the area and from the national center. This is true enough; it merely restates the facts underlying the original choice of a federal rather than a unitary structure for the second American constitution, and it points to the familiar fact of sectional politics present through most of our history and recurrent with each wave of state creation.

The separate political existence of the states in the days of the nation's industrial and political maturity, on the other hand, provides effective access to the whole governmental structure for interest groups whose tactics may be local or sectional but whose scope is national. Separatism, whether within the federal system or in the form of a specious demand for making a governmental activity "independent of politics" at whatever level of the structure, has frequently been a refuge for interests bent on defensive or evasive action, and the "states' rights" argument has often had about it an air more of expediency than of principle. This is not new. But it is the fact of federalism which permits an interest group or other enterprise of national scope, in alliance with lesser interests which may be primarily local or sectional, to prevent or negate action on the national level and to insure inaction or indulgence in the states. It was not merely Yankee stubbornness and dedication to local self-government which in the thirties prevented federal action to foster integrated development of the Connecticut River Valley. Such sentiments may have been more than mere expedient romanticism, and they might alone have affected the outcome of the proposal and the fortunes of elected state officials and members of Congress, but they received significant support and direction from private utility interests whose reach was nationwide. Nor were the interests exclusively local or sectional, though such were allied at least peripherally, which induced the Congress to alter in favor of state action a Supreme Court decision asserting or permitting national control of insurance. These illustrations are not cited by way of indictment but merely of illustration. In the maturity of the federal system the existence of the states as self-contained centers of power permits the use of them and associated party units by interests which are state or local only in a tactical sense. This is not equivalent to the separatism of a geographically defined interest, though it appears in the same garb and owes its significance as a technique to the continued existence of the states as power centers. Its effects on the party system are conducive to neither centralization nor cohesion at the national level.

In viewing the states as channels of access for interest groups, however, it is easy to forget that elective positions within the states, especially the governorships, are prizes in themselves and that the political "game" may be merely a means from the viewpoint of the interest group leader but is likely to be an end in itself for many of the more active partisans. It is perhaps a commentary on the instrumental, almost a-political attitudes of many academic observers of politics that they lay such stress upon the American parties as alliances of socio-economic interest groups. They are of course, alliances of groups, but parties are not distinguishable exclusively or even primarily in terms of their socio-economic policy content. In varying but important measure they are purely political, focused upon securing and holding power for their leading elements as an end in itself. The grand patterns of sectional and perhaps class alliances which have successively dominated our presidential politics for periods lasting up to several decades can in the large view perhaps be explained most meaningfully in terms of socio-economic interest. But at shorter range the detailed patterns take on a more exclusively political appearance. There is here no intended implication of petty place-seeking but rather suggestion that to aspire to be among those who govern and to associate for that objective as an end in itself is both normal and honorable. The evidence which indicate that enduring attachment to a party is for many voters a loyalty independent of though not dissociated from, socio economic interest supports the assumption that similar attachments to party, clique and faction exist among the more active elements in political organizations.

The significance of this point in the present context is that, given the multitude of elective positions in the system (only partially a consequence of federalism) and given the absence of a clearly defined and recognized path from one position to another in the loose hierarchy of political careers (a consequence more of a decentralized party system than directly of federalism itself), conflicting but interdependent clusters of loyalty and aspiration build up around various positions in the governmental structure. Thus, within a given "party," the career aspirations and prospects of a state governor, a United States Senator, and a member of the House of Representatives are likely to be ambiguous to one another or to others in the political structure with whom they must deal. Each may want one of the other offices; the governor and Senator may both have presidential ambitions which are mutually exclusive; the Senator or the Representative, though occupying a "national" office, may hope to move to the governorship and is likely to be far more closely dependent upon the state governor, from considerations either of preference or of expediency, than upon the leaders of the "parliamentary" party or upon a President bearing the same party designation. This is a simplified and hypothetical example, but it illustrates the role played by the offices established in the federal structure, and especially the state governor, in fractionating and decentralizing the party system, in encouraging the development of largely independent, hostile, and internally cohesive factional groupings.

The connection between these tendencies and the existence of federalism should not, of course, be overstated. The basic phenomenon of clique and personal rivalry is familiar enough in all organizations, including political parties. The point of significance here is the extent to which the federal structure tends to give these free rein. It is symptomatic of the function in the party system of state political positions, especially the governorship, that of the forty-three major candidates in the twenty presidential elections from 1876 through 1952 (counting three candidates in the elections of 1912, 1924, and 1948), only seven, excluding the thirteen incumbent Presidents, came to the nomination directly from a national political position, such as a seat in the Congress or a cabinet post; five were nominated from non-political positions of national or regional importance, and the remaining eighteen were drawn from state political roles, mostly governorships. Such nominations are, of course, available under normal conditions only to

governors of the large doubtful states, but the disruptive potentialities of the governorships are not confined to presidential races. The governor who merely seeks to retain his office through an effective organization covering major sections of the state is in a position to influence the fortunes and the choices of members of Congress, and a Senator or Representative who is aiming at the governorship is likely to be peculiarly solicitous of interests located in his home state.

These three factors derived from the existence of the states as separate and largely self-sustaining power centers — channeling the claims of local socio-economic interest groups, inviting their use as leverage against federal action by interests which are only tactically local, and providing for competing and frequently incompatible nuclei of decentralized intra-party conflict — are, of course, interrelated. In various combinations they go a long way toward indicating that there is something inherent in federalism which induces decentralization and lack of coherence in a party system.

But it is not sufficient merely to show that federalism has had some effect upon the nature of the party system. The important question of how much effect it has remains unanswered and to a precise degree unanswerable. It can easily be pointed out that decentralization and lack of cohesion frequently are apparent within the state parties, where factors other than federalism are influential. Could the like of these account in considerable measure for the peculiarities of the system as a whole? Would the American party system have developed essentially its present characteristics if the Founding Fathers had established a unitary constitution? The question is hypothetical but not irrelevant.

v

It seems clear that the structural fact of federalism is not alone sufficient to account for the peculiar characteristics of the

American party system, though it may be fundamental. Additional influences must be identified and accounted for. Yet any effort to identify the additional forces in the American experience and to assess their relative importance is, in a sense, likely to be artificial. It sets the analyst to the unenviable task of cutting apart what is a seamless web of multivariant and interdependent factors with the prospect that he will end up with a set of separate elements whose chief significance lies in their interaction. . . .

If the present analysis is sound, it is not the partial constitutional isolation of executive from legislative functions or the accompanying system of checks and balances that is of chief interest. Attempts to encourage or to develop means for improving communication and collaboration between the White House and the Congress are, in this context, essentially palliatives, though commendably constructive ones of considerable potential significance. It is the separate election of chief executives at both levels, and perhaps all three, which seems relevant here. Governors have often succeeded in imposing their leadership upon state legislators and presidents have with varying degrees of success bridged the long mile from Capitol Hill to 1600 Pennsylvania Avenue. Nevertheless the separate election of chief executives has multiplied and thereby rendered ambiguous the lines of succession within the governmental structure, and ambiguity of this sort seems almost certain to encourage independence and parallelism in party structures rather than coherence and centralization. As long as Presidents may be recruited from Congress, from the governorships, or from the cabinet (as well as from outside of political life), and as long as men in any of these positions may reasonably aspire to any of the others, decentralization and lack of coherence are likely to appear in many subtle but significant ways. The hypothesis is rhetorical, but if gubernatorial aspirants could be recruited only from within the state legislature or only from among the principal executive

positions and if presidents were drawn exclusively from the Senate, or, in Jeffersonian fashion, from the hierarchy of the cabinet, the reasons for independent and poorly articulated party structures would be reduced.

But if the separation of powers is relevant, it is not sufficient. Such elements of structure would not alone be controlling, particularly in face of the kinds of factors which originally produced a federal scheme and which give it vitality today. Looking broadly at such factors over the sweep of the years, one gets the impression that with one great exception, our politics has been carried on at relatively low temperatures. Except for the conflicts leading up to the Civil War, the issues generally have been of moderate intensity or, when heated or persistent, have been considerably tempered by a timely improvement in prices or in the level of industrial and commercial activity. Operating in the context of a large domestic market and a rapidly expanding economy, unrestricted by the kinds of factors which stoked the fires of conflict in Australia, our politics has been occupied with parceling slices of a pie that has had way of expanding when awkward choices were imminent, not only over the relative sizes of the portions, but over who might partake and who must go without. Until very recently, moveover, our controversies have been for the most part domestic.

Our domestic, low-temperature quarrels have taken full cognizance of the geographically defined diversities which are still reality within the country. In fact, the system has frequently exaggerated them; in viable polity, and the survival value of the American scheme need not be argued, cleavages along local or sectional lines are not likely to dominate the scene in the presence of intersecting issues of great significance, especially if the latter have their origin on the international plane. In the absence of such issues, and occasionally in default of a recognition of their importance, Americans have been able to engage in locally or regionally based disputes which have not infrequently had the appearance of political luxury. The argument is not that all these geographically defined issues have been without substance, although some of them clearly have, but rather that their prominence is in part owing to the absence of more intense, intersecting issues and that collectively their impact on the party system has been decentralizing and disintegrative. These conditions, if this estimate is valid, may help account for tendencies toward a decentralized politics within many of the states as well as in the nation as a whole.

In no respect is the quality of American politics . . . more clearly indicated than in the labor movement. No substantial proportion of American wage earners has ever developed strong class attitudes. Given our characteristically uninhibited methods of settling and exploiting a rich and virgin continent, the steadily expanding economy, and the resulting high social mobility, the dominant values of the society have been "middle-class" and individualistic. So thoroughly have these values been accepted by the wage-earning population that the labor movement throughout its history has been haunted by the problem of cohesion. For decades this problem was dealt with in the organized sector of labor more by a reliance on differences within the working-class population than on cleavages between class groupings. From the "plain people" movements of the eighteen-sixties to the industrial unionism of the nineteen-thirties and nineteen-forties, American workers have been more likely to divide along sectional, commodity, even ethnic and religious lines—all essentially decentralized—than to consolidate along the shadowy boundary of social class. For good or ill, the American political system has not been faced with the intersecting issues churned up by a class-conscious labor movement.

A further consequence of the low-temperature, domestic quality of American politics is the high visibility of the organized interest groups which have developed around the lines of cleavage and specialization in a complex, industrialized society. Many of these are local or sectional only in a tactical sense, as noted earlier, but all of them are on occasion highly significant, in the absence of other sorts of controversies, as elements in the calculations surrounding the nomination function, even though they may not be overtly active in this respect. Moreover, even when, in partial consequence of their own characteristically federal structures, they have been rent by divisive controversy, their local or state components are no less likely to be influential in the facilitation or disruption of political careers and in the determination of legislative action at state and national levels.

In this connection it is worth while to point out that a considerable element of localism has inevitably been injected into American politics, regardless of constitutional structure, by such factors as the patterns of immigration from Europe. Immigration itself has rarely provided a controversy of national scope, and nativist movements have been conspicuous on occasion but of no lasting significance. Ethnic issues as such, perhaps excluding the Negro question, have not had the impact on national politics that they have had, for example, in Canada. But with the tendency for individual nationality groupings to concentrate in particular areas, especially in the cities, and to find in their common rootlessness and frequently in the experience of discrimination and exploitation a basis in addition to national origin for cohesion and interdependence, they have constituted a means to power and influence for locally oriented political organizations outside and inside their own ranks.

It is these geographically defined factors, accentuated by a low-temperature, domestic politics, which give major force and relevance to the possibility of state control over the composition of the national governing bodies, through the electoral college and related means, which Herbert Wechsler points out in his chapter. Structural elements in the system—some, it is argued here, inherent in federalism—alone encourage an irreducible minimum of decentralization and disruption in the party system. But it is as these reflect the underlying pace of the political process and as they are harnessed to regionally differentiated issues and clusters of organization that they find their most impelling dynamic.

As in other national systems, moreover, there are additional governmental arrangements which support and in some instances reflect the decentralizing tendencies apparent in the process as a whole. Not the least important of these is the practice of frequent elections specified by the calendar and the related constitutional provision for unequal terms of office. Decentralizing in intent, they have operated to accentuate localized concerns, especially in the midterm primaries and elections at the national level. But in a system in which any election may be relevant to all others in an area, whether they are held simultaneously or not, the very frequency of elections and campaigns can accentuate and exploit local and transitory animosities and consolidate localized patterns of control. This point has never been more dramatically illustrated than it was in the tragic years leading up to the Civil War. During the decade of the eighteen-fifties "the baneful influence of elections almost continuously in progress, of campaigns never over," accentuated local and sectional hostilities. Aided by the fact that at that time elections to the Congress were not held at a uniform date throughout the nation, the upthrust of localism further crippled already imperfect efforts to forestall a fatal break. In Nichols' words, "The incessant procession of artificially ordered election conflicts frequently meant nothing more than the routine return of pleasurable electioneering excitement; but in the 1850's it had become dangerous." "It was," he points out, "harder for the statesman at the capital city to calm the emotions stirred in these countless local contests when their representatives brought them to Washington."

The difference between this fateful dec-ade and the more normal course of our politics is one of degree, the more so as a multiplicity of local elections may support a professionalized corps of politicians whose organized relationships within the area can be utilized to resist an effort at centralization.

A representative and significant response to such an effort is provided by the Hatch Act of 1939. Stimulated by Franklin Roosevelt's awkward and ill-fated attempt at a "purge" of rebellious Representatives and Senators in the Democratic primaries of 1938, a bipartisan combination in the Congress took steps to forestall the possibility that a centralized party leadership could be built upon presidential patronage, through the device of a statutory prohibition against political campaign activity by federal employees below the policy-forming level, whether they are in the classified civil service or not. This was an effort at insurance against an extremely remote contingency, since the requirement of senatorial confirmation and the practice of senatorial courtesy have made patronage a comparatively feeble instrument of centralized leadership except in the opening months of an Administration or for purposes of securing renomination for an incumbent President. It is impossible to estimate precisely the effects of this restriction or of the comparable provision in the 1940 legislation restricting the annual expenditures of national committees, but at minimum their enactment testifies to the strength of the decentralizing tendencies.

VI

In a federal system decentralization and lack of cohesion in the party system are based on the structural fact of federalism, but, it has been argued here, the degree to which these become the dominant characteristics of the distribution of power within the political parties is a function of a variety of other governmental and social factors which are independent of the federal structure or are merely supportive of its endencies. Within the American structure there clearly are limits beyond which centralization and coherence in the parties may not go. Nevertheless, accepting the argument that the national political party is the most responsive instrument of restraint upon federalism's centrifugal tendencies, it may be appropriate briefly to inquire into the circumstances which might produce a gradual shift in the locus of power within the American parties.

It seems clear that the prospects for such a shift must rest fundamentally upon the emergence or intensification of a dominant and persistent set of interests and issues which will tend to cut through rather than to unify constituencies, especially the states, and which demand standardized national solutions. These would imply a more intense and urgent, perhaps a more explosive, politics; that would seem to be the price of change. Here is not the place to attempt a detailed examination of any such issues, but it seems entirely possible that their most likely source would lie in the problems of an increasingly urbanized and industrialized society, as Arthur Holcombe suggested more than twenty years ago in his anticipation of the replacement of sectional by class politics. Another complex of such issues may emerge or may be in process of emerging out of the problems besetting the new American leadership on the international scene.

Neither of these complexes of issues appears to hold much promise of startling immediate developments within the party realm. In the unlikely event of an increasingly even industrialization of all the states, it is by no means certain that an expanding economy will not so check the importance of intersecting issues of full employment, social security, and the like, that the demands of commodity and of section will still be dominant. Nor in such circumstances is it at all sure that leadership forces will not prefer the occasional inconveniences of a decentralized politics to the less manageable potentialities of an opposite trend. And in the realm of foreign policy it is by no means clear that an emerging consensus on direction and general posture will not leave the center of the stage free for geographically defined issues of pace and of precise application.

These obstacles aside, the dominance of issues capable of dividing major constituencies internally presupposes their emergence or evocation in sections now monopolized by a single party and the development of a vigorous and genuine bipartisan pattern. This result is not likely to be the work of a single day and not only because of the stubborn disinclination of voters to alter partisan attachments once they have been formed, though this is a factor of no inconsiderable importance. Rather, as V. O. Key has amply demonstrated in his study of the South, a single-party monopoly based on the assertion or defense of a dominant sectional interest tends to inhibit the identification and expression of intersecting national issues. It induces a fluid factionalism along personal and clique lines incapable of the organization necessary to sustained expression of such issues from within and to effective response to their assertion from without. Moreover, the purely political advantages of a one-party monopoly are considerable and not to be surrendered without resistance. Only the most intense conflict over persistent issues is likely to prevail over efforts by an invigorated majority party to capture the leadership of an emerging opposition and to hamstring its efforts with all the statutory and polemic resources at the command of an entrenched group.

The federal structure itself imposes no insuperable obstacles to a shift in the locus of power within the party system, but it seems improbable that the country will soon dispense with the talents of the politician skilled in the manipulation and reconciliation of decentralized and recalcitrant power blocs.

*Bernard B. Hennessy*

# DOLLARS FOR DEMOCRATS, 1959

CRITICAL IMPORTANCE OF STATE PARTY
LEADERS

The highly personal nature of the American party system was demonstrated again in the Dollars for Democrats Drive of 1959. Participation, whether nominal or real, depended very largely on the personal views of a few leaders in each state.

In most of the states the chairman was, generally speaking, the key figure in the decision to participate or not to participate. This was true wherever the organizational factors of the state and its history with regard to previous Dollars for Democrats Drives gave him the practical opportunity to make a choice. Roger Kent in California, for instance, could hardly have made the choice by himself; neither he nor Neil Staebler in Michigan could have refused to participate without invoking a serious crisis among their state and county leaders who looked forward to the drive. On the other hand, the chairmen of the southern states probably could not have led a successful drive had they wanted to—in fact, it appears that Florida Chairman James Milligan, with the most modern party organization in the South, made a serious but on the whole not very successful effort in the drive. In most of the other states, the chairmen had wide latitude in making the decision.

At the risk of overgeneralization, we may say that only those states participated where one or more of the following factors obtained:

(1) Earlier drives had demonstrated the potential of Dollars for Democrats. The state chairmen (and/or other key figures) in Oregon, Washington, West Virginia, Ohio and Arkansas seemed to have endorsed the drive because of its proven money raising possibilities. Also, in all of these states there were enthusiastic Dollars for Democrats supporters who pushed the state chairmen into participation.

(2) Some state leaders felt that this was a project in which they wanted to cooperate with the National Committee. Some felt they could do so without damaging their intrastate positions, and in this way offset the charge that they were not sufficiently supporting the National Committee activities. A number of southern states particularly—Virginia, Georgia, and Texas for example—seem to have given support to the drive for this reason in part.

Other state leaders made the Dollars for Democrats Drive at the insistence of National Committee officers and staff because it seemed, quite simply, the path of least resistance. The state chairman in Indiana, Charles Skillen, agreed to the drive only after strong representations from Paul Butler himself (with whom Skillen had not been on the most friendly terms) and from John Doran, one of the National Committee's regional representatives and a young politician from South Bend. Texas, Missouri, and New Mexico established Dollars organizations under the strong urging and helpful assistance of another National Committee regional representative, Harold Jinks of Arkansas. It seems that the Utah state leadership supported nominal drive activ-

From *Cases on Party Organization*, ed. Paul Tillett (New York, 1963), pp. 166–172, 176–178. Reprinted by permission of The Eagleton Institute of Politics.

ity largely for the sake of appearing to go along with the national program; Calvin Rawlings, the National Committeeman, had been a close ally of Butler and prominent in the National Committee for many years.

(3) In some states certain party leaders, for personal reasons, attached themselves to the Dollars for Democrats Drive and worked in it with considerable enthusiasm. The drive chairmen in Wyoming (Raymond Whitaker) and in Colorado (Dr. Will Irwin) seem to have found their assignments useful in getting known around their respective states; both, it was said, intended to run for public office.

In northern California and Washington, Mrs. Alanson and Mrs. Cochrane seem to have won places as state Dollars chairmen entirely through their dedication to the principle of small gift fund raising and their ability to organize this kind of project.

In Pennsylvania the treasurer of the National Committee, Matt McCloskey, assumed personal responsibility for the job. There seem to have been several reason for his decision, but one of them was no doubt to demonstrate his loyalty (which had been questioned) to the National Committee's administration under Butler.

Whatever the historical, institutional, or personal factors obtaining in a given state, the decision to participate in Dollars for Democrats—and if to participate, with what degree of activity—was made in almost every instance by a handful of party leaders, often by only one or two persons. In Arizona, Montana, Illinois, New York and Oklahoma, it appears that no more than three persons in each state (in two states only one person) were effectively involved in making the decision not to participate in the 1959 drive. Perhaps other non-participating states involved many persons and used group decision-making procedures in establishing state policy on the 1959 drive, but to my knowledge only one state, North Dakota, took the matter to a representative party body which decided against participation.

## VARIOUS PATTERNS OF RELATIONSHIPS

A great variety of relationships was worked out among national, state, and local levels of operation in the 1959 Dollars for Democrats Drive (DFD). A total of 29 states had some kind of DFD life. A few states showed vigorous activity in every county, with heavy accent on coverage by many solicitors. At the other end of the list, in a few states, the materials apparently never trickled down past the state Dollars chairman.

In California (both north and south), Michigan, Colorado, and Wisconsin, the Dollars for Democrats Drive was self-initiated and run with enthusiasm. Northern California had the equivalent of three full-time people on DFD. Bernard Tietlebaum, a Citizenship Clearing House Intern working with the northern California state Democratic headquarters, assisted Mrs. Ann Alanson all summer in setting up county and city organization for the drive. Mrs. Nancy Swadesh, Executive Secretary of the northern California state committee, gave many days and weeks to DFD work. And Mrs. Kris McClusky coordinated public relations and edited a Dollars for Democrats newsletter.

In a letter to the Democratic National Committee early in the drive preparations, Mrs. Swadesh described the northern California strategy and their plans to mesh "D-Day" (the Californians' term for the drive) with the building of precinct organization.

We consider D-Day one of four activities or obligations a precinct worker undertakes: (1) registration; (2) D-Day; (3) precinct work during the campaign; (4) getting out the vote on election day. It has been a long hard pull to make people accept the idea that this is their civic duty. . . . We have no patronage to speak of and workers are out there for love of God and country. And before they will move they must know the answers to many questions—where does the money go? what is it used for? what is the National Committee and what does it do? what are we going to do about southern control of the Senate? *etc. etc.* . . .

The California Dollars for Democrats newsletter (mimeographed) was issued weekly from June to September and then daily for the thirty days just preceding the drive. It went to all state and county officials and to the workers at every level who had been recruited for specific drive jobs. Tips for finding and using new workers and how-to-do-it advice on the handling of mailing lists and drive materials alternated in the newsletter with articles of exhortation from national and state Democrats (Senators Kennedy and Johnson, Governor Pat Brown) and stories of success by former Dollars for Democrats workers "just like you."

Besides the newsletter, northern California put D-Day organizational manuals and publicity manuals into the hands of their local leaders and workers. Both these mimeographed pieces were models of their kind: extremely detailed, yet simple and clearly written.

Colorado, another state in which the drive was self-initiated, activated Dollars organizations and established quotas in each of the counties. (County or precinct quotas were also established in Wisconsin, Michigan, Vermont, and Montgomery County, Maryland). State chairman Robert Crites, a full-time salaried party official in Colorado, and Dr. Will Irwin, Colorado State University political scientist and state Dollars for Democrats chairman, toured the state organizing the drive and recruiting leaders.

Irwin described the Colorado operation as follows:

Our organization was exceedingly simple. We have 18 judicial districts in the state covering 63 counties. A judicial district dollars chairman was chosen in each who, in turn, chose and encouraged county dollars chairmen. I, myself, actually visited 42 counties covering approximately 5,000

miles in my car. Personal contact has always proven the most effective means of gaining support. . . .

A massive, unseasonable snowfall hit Colorado during the drive week, but despite this the hard work in Colorado paid off with gross receipts of over $19,000.

In Wisconsin the state chairman, Pat Lucey, personally led the drive. The former congressional candidates, James Megallis and Norman Clapp, were staff fieldworkers for the Democratic party of Wisconsin; they devoted much time in the late summer and early fall to the Dollars drive. Lucey, Megallis and Clapp, and Bruno Bitker, state Dollars chairman and Milwaukee lawyer attempted to secure the participation of party leaders in all 71 counties. Their state goal of $30,000 was not met, but an estimated gross of $10,000 made the drive worthwhile.

Some other states—Florida, Michigan and Vermont—were enthusiastic about the 1959 drive and needed no urging from the National Committee. Kansas, too, showed initial interest and carried through well with occasional encouragement from the National Committee's regional representative, Harold Jinks.

On the other hand, Iowa, Maine, Minnesota, Nebraska, New Hampshire, and South Dakota all had internal problems with regard to the drive. The Iowa state chairman, Donald Norberg, and finance director Chris Mulkey, both paid officials of the party, were concentrating on a new sustaining membership plan in the summer and fall of 1959; they felt a strong Dollars for Democrats Drive at that time would only divide their own energies and confuse the party supporters upon whom the sustaining membership plan depended. Out of loyalty to the national program they established a token drive in Iowa. Minnesota, Nebraska, and South Dakota had similar difficulties which resulted in minimum drives in each state. Maine, as a result of death and disaffection in the leadership ranks, was reestablishing party equilibrium in the summer of 1959, and although Edwin Pert, state assemblyman and party executive secretary, gave considerable attention to the drive, little was accomplished. In New Hampshire the party was being remade by an insurgent group of leaders: Bernard Boutin, former Mayor of Laconia and 1958 gubernatorial candidate; Murray Devine, Manchester lawyer and new state chairman; James Farley, editor of a small town newspaper; and Charlotte Morrison, Lawrence Radway, Richard Sterling, and others from the Dartmouth community. Allen Foster, former high school teacher, was appointed executive secretary of the state party in midsummer. Despite his best efforts, those of Mrs. Luther of the National Committee's Women's Division and of the New England regional representative, Bill Dunfey, the drive in New Hampshire met only limited success.

Among the other states, seventeen had at least minimal state participation. Minimal participation, it will be recalled, means only that an official state Dollars for Democrats chairman was appointed. Washington and Wyoming, for reasons which have been presented in part, were vigorous in their drive. Georgia, at the end of the drive, sent what can only be described as a conscience check of $100. Hawaii organized late, with indifferent and undetermined results. Indiana, as we have seen, was dragooned into the drive, participated fitfully, and contributed to the National Committee only reluctantly. The New Mexico drive appears to have been stillborn, although the National Committeewoman and Dollars chairman, Mrs. U. D. Sawyer, made efforts to save it. West Virginia looked good out of the starting gate, but never seemed to be in the race thereafter; on the late summer backstretch, West Virginia returned half of its certificate books (the only state to admit, frankly, that it over ordered), and ended far back in the pack.

Oregon presented an interesting national-state relationship. Oregon—especially Multnomah County (Portland)—had participated in earlier drives with some en-

thusiasm. But in early summer of 1959, and before he had designated a Dollars for Democrats chairman, state chairman David Epps died. Because of the uncertainty over his successor, and because we were temporarily without a regional representative for the west coast, our communications with Oregon broke down in the critical midsummer months.

Toward the end of August, national drive headquarters received a wire from the chairman of the Multnomah County central committee inquiring about Dollars for Democrats supplies. Since the stock was entirely committed by that time, we responded by suggesting that northern California or Washington might have drive material to spare. Northern California, it turned out, did. But as soon as this was done—perhaps a week or ten days later—Chairman Butler received a letter from Mrs. Beulah Hand, Oregon state vice chairman and by then acting chairman, complaining in strong and heated terms that we at the National Committee were dealing directly with the county committees, ignoring not only the state committees, but sacred principles of sound organization and party loyalty. For the chairman, I drafted a response explaining the case in some detail. I also took the occasion to write Mrs. Hand a short personal note. But the damage had been done, and no amount of explanation or apology in this case could have completely wiped out this misunderstanding caused by a rupture in the always-thin lines of communication between state and national committees.

Ohio had been a front-running state in the 1958 drive. It was assumed that the 1959 drive would be a success because it would be directed by state chairman William Coleman and his Dollars for Democrats chairman Joe Waterman, an able young lawyer and Young Democratic club leader. For a number of reasons, related both to ambitious precinct organization work and some intraparty friction over Governor DiSalle's legislative program, the Dollars drive was organized late in Ohio. Waterman headed the drive, but it was postponed nearly two months, until mid-November. No money came to the National Committee from Ohio in 1959, but on January 26, 1960, the National Committee received $5,000 from the drive in that state.

The state and national-state relations in the 1959 Texas drive were unique. Harold Jinks, the National Committee's regional representative for the southwest, laid the groundwork for the Texas operation. He first spent several days in and around Austin talking to Texas party officials — and at one point had a summit meeting with Sam Rayburn himself. "I talked to those boys as one Texan to another," Texas born Jinks said in describing these negotiations. As a result of these discussions, in which Democratic loyalty was much played up and Paul Butler much played down, Texas allowed the drive to go forward in those counties where local leaders desired it. Under this arrangement the state committee was to waive its third of the take and the National Committee to get at least half and frequently two-thirds (in some counties all) of the gross. The Texas State Committee was to supply a state level "coordinator" for those counties which wished to participate; the coordinator, John Wildenthal, Jr., of Austin, served very ably as the clearinghouse officer for supplies and information for the 37 Texas counties which participated.

The Texas case illustrates, again, the highly personal and *ad hoc* nature of national-state relations. The situation agreed upon was one of almost pure expediency, offering a national program to some of the liberal anti-Johnson elements in the Texas political scene, while at the same time preserving for the state organization a show of being willing to cooperate, of demonstrating loyalty, and a painless way of paying part of the Texas quota of the National Committee budget.

The 1959 showing in Virginia, despite lip-service from the Byrd organization, was almost wholly a result of hard work in the two-party Ninth Congressional District, and especially that of Congressman Jennings' able and effervescent assistant, Miss Kitty Clark. While activity was slight at the state level in Virginia, it was, as far as we could tell, non-existent in Delaware. Rhode Island, too, was disappointing despite the most optimistic hopes of state chairman Frank Rao, old style politician and wealthy beer distributor.

But some other states raised fairly large amounts of money, with Pennsylvania and Arkansas among the leaders. Neither Pennsylvania nor Arkansas followed the textbook rules for door-to-door, face-to-face fund raising. Many of Pennsylvania's 23,000 certificate books were mailed out in scattergun fashion; Arkansas earmarked part of the receipts from a fund raising dinner for Dollars for Democrats. And it seems probable that some pressure to contribute was put on state employees — a practice with a long, if not unexceptionable, history in both states.

The Democratic Committee in a number of important states did not participate at all. New York and Illinois are cases in point. In both states a strong, confident, and relatively affluent Democratic party can maintain its internal strength in safe jurisdictions almost regardless of national party fortunes. It is no secret that *any* effort to strengthen national party organization and influence is apt to be received coldly by New York City and Cook County, Illinois, Democratic leaders. The situation in 1959 was especially exacerbated by the personal dislike which Carmine De Sapio, New York's national committeeman, and Jacob Arvey, Illinois national committeeman, had for Paul Butler; they considered Indiana Butler a sharp-tongued, puritanical, country boy.

In this situation we were more displeased than surprised when the treasurer of the New York State Democratic Central Committee wrote a short letter indicating that the state would not conduct a 1959 Dollars for Democrats Drive because their earlier experience with the Dollars drive had not been successful — in fact, had

ended in the red. Our impression was that
they had made no effort in 1958, and that
their 1959 excuse was merely that, an excuse. A few of the New York City "reform"
clubs conducted independent drives in
1958; one, the Riverside Democratic Club,
had an indifferent campaign in 1959, from
which the National Committee received
*eight* dollars. In Illinois, State Chairman
William Ronan informed the National Committee's regional representative, John Doran, that the Illinois committee would not
conduct a Dollars drive in 1959, but he had
no objection to an option system under
which some county committees might
sponsor drives. Materials were sent by the
National Committee to two Illinois counties, but as of May 25, 1960, no returns had
been made to Washington. . . .

GETTING THE RETURNS IN

As we expected (because it had been true
in earlier years), the states were slow in
getting their money collected, divided and
posted to the National Committee.

Two states—southern California and
Colorado—made contributions to the National Committee in the financially critical
weeks just before the drive; but it was understood that this constituted an advance
on Dollars for Democrats returns, and that
these states would in a sense repay themselves from the national share of drive receipts.

Returns from the actual drive started
coming into the Washington office on October 7. The drive had been delayed some
places (Ohio, Montgomery County) and
extended in other states (Colorado, Michigan), but those states which had reported
neither money nor reasons for delay were
sent a mild dunning letter by the chairman
in mid-October. The letter recounted the
strained condition of the National Committee's finances, reminded the state leaders that the watches to be given as national
prizes could not be awarded until all reports were in, and urged the winding up of
the drive and the bookkeeping not later

than November 1. This "deadline" was
later extended to November 15, then December 15; then January 1. The watches,
finally, were awarded about March 1. In the
meantime, Dennis Jensen, Birkhead's successor as finance director, and I had made
many calls and sent many letters to the lag-
gard chairmen, exercising moral suasion
with indifferent results.

When a final accounting was made on
May 25, 1960, five states had returned
nothing at all to the National Committee.
Of these five states, only South Dakota—
which paid all its national quota in 1959,
one of less than six states to do so—had
told us in advance that, for reasons peculiar
to their organizational situation at the time,
their participation in 1959 would be only
nominal. We had been led to believe that
the other four states would support the
drive in good faith and as energetically as
they could. Either they raised some money
and reported nothing or, just as likely, no
drive at all was organized by the state
Dollars for Democrats chairmen.

We had hoped that all of the money collected in the Dollars for Democrats drive
would come in fairly large sums through
the regular state or county organization.
The requirements of the Hatch Act for
recording and receipting each contribution
result in the channeling of many National
Committee man-hours into the functions of
the comptroller's office. Mrs. Mary Salisbury, with the Democratic National Committee since 1928, and the most know-
ledgeable staff member on money
housekeeping, agreed to give us periodic
running totals on the drive returns. As it
turned out, we got a number of individual,
direct, drive contributions, but most of the
money came through the state committees
and none of the anticipated bookkeeping
problems arose.

On the basis of experience with earlier
drives we had reason to suspect that some
state and local committees would "fudge"
on their returns in the Dollars for Democrats drive. There had been frequent failure
to turn over the full two-thirds of the re-

ceipts from the county to the state, or the full one-third from the state to the National Committee. Besides being the victim, so to speak, of this cumulative fudging, the National Committee also had to pay its expenses out of its diminished third, while usually the local committees subtracted their expenses before making the three-way division, and the state committee subtracted expenses before making the two-way division.

This tendency to withhold was especially common during election years when understandably local collectors believed the money could be spent more usefully on state and local contests. Nevertheless, this natural stickiness in the money pipelines was a matter of much concern to the Democratic National Committee; no effective way of reducing it has been found.

The Dollars for Democrats money raised in a state was accredited at the National Committee to paying off that state's quota (amount set by the Committee as the state's reasonable share of the National Committee's annual operating expenses); but this "recognition," like the moral suasion mentioned previously, can easily be passed up for more tangible or immediate reasons.

In the face of this history of rather sys-

TABLE I

| State or County | Books Sent | Return by 5/25/60 | Returns per Book Sent |
|---|---|---|---|
| Alaska | 250 | $   3,300.00 | 13.20 |
| Arkansas | 2,750 | 16,500.00 | 6.00 |
| Northern California | 20,000 | 8,417.06 | .42 |
| Southern California | 20,000 | 13,903.15 | .70 |
| Colorado | 3,500 | 6,969.81 | 1.99 |
| District of Columbia | 400 | 2,989.00 | 7.47 |
| Florida | 2,000 | 425.95 | .21 |
| Georgia | 1,000 | 100.00 | .10 |
| Indiana | 6,075 | 1,036.68 | .17 |
| Iowa | 1,000 | 167.50 | .17 |
| Kansas | 3,000 | 1,822.50 | .61 |
| Maine | 500 | 5.00 | .01 |
| Montgomery County, Md. | 1,000 | 2,002.00 | 2.00 |
| Michigan | 8,500 | 10,095.53 | 1.19 |
| Minnesota | 4,000 | 1,290.79 | .32 |
| Missouri | 4,000 | 127.00 | .03 |
| New Hampshire | 500 | 238.55 | .48 |
| Ohio | 20,000 | 5,000.00 | .25 |
| Oregon (sent from n. California) | | 389.63 | — |
| Pennsylvania | 23,000 | 11,885.01 | .52 |
| Rhode Island | 1,000 | 670.00 | .67 |
| Texas | 1,000[1] | 9,483.31 | 9.48 |
| Vermont | 800 | 1,333.33 | 1.67 |
| Virginia | 1,000 | 2,525.16 | 2.53 |
| Washington | 9,000 | 4,011.00 | .45 |
| West Virginia | 3,000[2] | 1,108.66 | .37 |
| Wisconsin | 5,500 | 2,674.70 | .49 |
| Wyoming | 600 | 1,408.62 | 2.35 |
| Miscellaneous | | 31.00[3] | |
| Total | | $109,910.94 | .77[4] |

[1]Approximately.
[2]6,000 books were sent, but 3,000 were returned before the drive.
[3]Returns from scattered Democrats who contributed to the drive in states that did not participate. The money in these cases was sent directly to the National Committee by the contributors.
[4]On the basis of the 143,375 books sent to the states returning money. If *all* books sent is the basis for computation the returns per book drop to $.74.

:ematic fudging on the part of state and
ocal committees, we were tempted to keep
money sent directly to us from individual
:ollectors in states conducting drives. This
we refused to do, both for ethical reasons
and because we might, by being discovered in a $10 withholding from a state,
oring upon ourselves a $100 withholding
*by* that state.

In 1959, at the national level accounting
problems arose in cases where the state
committees or other officials either did not
specify the source of purpose of money
sent to National, or attempted to get double-duty out of such contributions. One
$5,000 Dollars for Democrats check in late
1959 was credited simply to the entry
"State Committee," rather than any specific
project heading (Sustaining Membership,
750 Club, Dollars for Democrats, etc.), in
Mrs. Salisbury's ledger; it was later established that it had actually been Dollars
money, but smaller mis-entries were apt to
go undetected.

An illustration of the attempt to get double-duty from contributions to the National

Committee was the practice of buying
$110-a-plate tickets to the annual Washing-
ton fund raising dinner with state money
which would come to the National Committee anyway. One person in a position to
know said, in early 1960, "look around you
at the dinner this year; some of the Dollars
for Democrats money from _____ will
be there in the form of $100 tickets." Other
double-duty contributions took the form of
Sustaining Memberships, *Democratic Digest*
subscriptions and the purchase of supplies
directly from the National Committee's
printer.

PAY OFF

As of May 25, 1960, $109,910.84 had been
received in Washington as the National
Committee's share of the 1959 Dollars for
Democrats drive. The sources of this total,
by states, are shown in the following table.
The total number of $35 certificate books,
and the national returns per certificate
book, as one measure of the effectiveness of
the states' drives, are also indicated.

THE VIEW FROM THE STATES

Among the many problems in understanding how American federalism
works is the system's prismatic character, which causes it to reflect different
images when examined from different perspectives. Thus programs and functions which look highly centralized when viewed from the national perspective
turn out to be parts of a coherent "package" at the state or local level, actually
controlled within the state or locally through a combination of political and
administrative devices. The "view from the states," then, adds another dimension to our understanding of the system, a particularly important one since the
states remain the keystones in the American governmental arch — the primary
governments in matters domestic. The view from the states reveals what the
national view conceals — that the federal system at its best is not a hierarchy of
levels, stacked one atop the other, nor simply a marble cake of diffused functions that effectively obliterate all meaningful structural differences, but a
multi-dimensional matrix through which authority and power are dispersed in
such a way as to prevent the formation of any simple chain of command for the
issuance of orders. In this matrix, different planes of government take different

roles at different times. If the federal government is the senior partner in the field of foreign relations, the states are the senior partners in the highway field and the localities in the field of law enforcement, and so it goes. . . .

Federal grants-in-aid remain the major vehicles for intergovernmental collaboration. In "Federal Grants," the Advisory Commission on Intergovernmental Relations briefly traces the purposes, scope, history, and overall impact of the grant system. Written in 1964, this selection does not reflect the changes introduced by "Great Society" legislation. Though the number of grant programs has expanded radically since then—the Commission estimated 379 separate authorizations in 1967—the essential details of the grant system have not been altered.

By the same token, the studies of the impact of federal programs on the individual states undertaken for the Kestnbaum Commission in the early 1950's, remain as valid today as they were then. Reading them, we are not only given some sense of the way in which each state assimilates federal aid in its own way but an understanding of how the same problems of impact regularly recur. Studies of two states, different in size, culture, complexity, location, and attitude toward federal aid, are included here: Virginia, the foremost exponent of states' rights, southern style; and Illinois, the nation's crossroads state where virtually every social current and political pattern in the country is represented. The limitations of the general outline given the authors of these studies force them into a rather formal mold which tends to obscure the political dynamics that reduce the federal impact even more than the studies themselves reveal. In some cases, changes in state or federal organization affecting specific grant programs have occurred since 1955, when these studies were published; for example, Congress has altered the public health grant program to provide for block grants in place of categorical ones, thus increasing the states' policy-making role in that field. Also, the number of programs has expanded radically in the past decade. Nevertheless, the overall picture presented in these studies has not changed.

One of the major findings in the "impact" studies is that federal grants have tended to strengthen specific state agencies at the expense of the governors and legislatures. This, indeed, has been one of the ways in which state control over the grants has been enhanced. Thomas J. Anton's "State Planning, Gubernatorial Leadership, and Federal Funds: Three Case Studies" shows how the governors can make use of the same devices to enhance their own positions and strengthen the general government institutions of their states in the process. Notice how he uses the word "federal" to mean both "shared-by-all-governments" and "national." Since the original publication of his article, state planning activities have greatly increased—as a direct result of new federal programs.

# FEDERAL GRANTS

The Federal grant-in-aid has developed into an important instrument for carrying out the essential partnership of the States and the National Government in a federal system. It reconciles State and local administration of public services with Federal financial support in programs of national concern. In the century in which it has been used, the Federal grant has been forged into a tool capable of doing many types of jobs both small and big. Its strength has been its flexibility and adaptability.

Present Federal grants-in-aid illustrate the variety of provisions that have been developed to meet the specific requirements of a large number of programs in which the Nation and the States with their localities work together to furnish public services. At one extreme are grant programs in which the Federal Government finances all or almost all of the program costs; at the other, those in which the Federal share is a small part of program outlays. A grant is used to assure a nationwide interstate highway system by allocating earmarked gasoline and other automotive taxes levied uniformly across the nation to cover the major part of its cost of construction. The grant is being used to demonstrate new techniques for providing health services for the aged and the chronically ill and to train professional personnel in short supply. It is being used to encourage planning for the reconstruction of our cities, to stimulate innovation, and to help in a substantial way to carry out a public welfare program. The grant is being applied increasingly to meet the problems of the cities with their extra cost burdens originating in that group of public services required for metropolitan living. . . .

THE AMOUNT OF FEDERAL GRANTS

Federal annual expenditures for aid to State and local governments have increased sizeably since the Second War and in the *Budget of the United States Government* for fiscal year 1965 are estimated at $10.6 billion. At the beginning of the 1930's, they aggregated only about $200 million a year. The increases have generally come in spurts, reflecting the emergence of national problems for which solutions were sought through cooperative Federal, State, and local action. Depression programs and social security legislation raised them above the one billion dollar level, from which they declined before and during the Second War to less than $1 billion. Most of the growth was thus concentrated in the postwar years, when new programs were enacted and existing programs expanded. (table 1).

From $855 million in 1946, total Federal payments to State and local governments rose to $2.6 billion in 1952, $3.3 billion in 1956, and $7.9 billion in 1962. Excluding shared revenues and other nongrant payments, the 1962 total for grants-in-aid to States or localities was $7.0 billion. Part of the increase is accounted for by the interstate highway program, enacted in 1956, under which substantial sums have been paid to the States annually since 1957. Excluding that program, Federal aid amounted to about $6 billion in 1962, or seven times the 1946 total.

Statistics on the amount of Federal aid payments differ depending upon the inclusiveness of the definition of such aid, that is, whether shared revenues and contractual payments, as well as grants-in-aid, are included. Moreover, grants-in-aid may also

From *The Role of Equalization in Federal Courts* (Washington, D.C.: Advisory Commission on Intergovernmental Relations, 1955), pp. 12–24.

TABLE 1.: TRENDS IN FEDERAL AID RELATIVE TO GENERAL REVENUE OF STATE AND LOCAL GOVERNMENTS AND TO FEDERAL GENERAL EXPENDITURE, 1902–1962

(DOLLAR AMOUNTS, EXCEPT PER CAPITAS, IN MILLIONS)

| Fiscal year | State and local general revenue | | | | Federal general expenditure | | Federal aid as a percent of | | | Federal aid as percent of GNP |
| | Amount | | Per capita | | | | | Federal general expenditure | | |
| | Total | Federal aid[1] | Total | Federal aid[1] | Total | For civil functions[2] | State & local general revenue | Total | For civil functions | |
|---|---|---|---|---|---|---|---|---|---|---|
| 1962 | $58,214 | $7,857 | $313.28 | $42.28 | $96,689 | $29,871 | 14 | 8 | 26 | 1.4 |
| 1960 | 50,505 | 6,974 | 280.61 | 38.75 | 83,719 | 23,562 | 14 | 8 | 30 | 1.4 |
| 1958 | 41,219 | 4,865 | 237.80 | 28.07 | 75,689 | 19,066 | 12 | 6 | 26 | 1.1 |
| 1956 | 34,667 | 3,335 | 207.26 | 19.94 | 68,792 | 16,854 | 10 | 5 | 20 | 0.8 |
| 1954 | 29,012 | 2,966 | 178.63 | 18.26 | 72,631 | 14,598 | 10 | 4 | 20 | 0.8 |
| 1952 | 25,181 | 2,566 | 160.34 | 16.34 | 67,778 | 12,001 | 10 | 4 | 21 | 0.7 |
| 1950 | 20,911 | 2,486 | 137.86 | 16.39 | 40,285 | 13,890 | 12 | 6 | 18 | 0.9 |
| 1948 | 17,250 | 1,861 | 117.34 | 12.39 | 34,175 | 9,839 | 11 | 5 | 19 | 0.7 |
| 1946 | 12,356 | 855 | 87.39 | 6.05 | 65,448 | 8,340 | 7 | 1 | 10 | 0.4 |
| 1944 | 10,908 | 954 | 78.87 | 6.89 | 100,032 | 11,749 | 9 | 1 | 8 | 0.5 |
| 1942 | 10,418 | 858 | 77.25 | 6.36 | 35,180 | 7,035 | 8 | 2 | 12 | 0.5 |
| 1940 | 9,609 | 945 | 72.73 | 7.15 | 9,780 | 6,704 | 10 | 10 | 14 | 0.9 |
| 1938 | 9,228 | 800 | 71.08 | 6.16 | 8,278 | 5,732 | 9 | 10 | 14 | 0.9 |
| 1936 | 8,395 | 948 | 65.56 | 7.40 | 9,099 | 5,686 | 11 | 10 | 17 | 1.1 |
| 1934 | 7,678 | 1,016 | 60.76 | 8.04 | 5,881 | 4,029 | 13 | 17 | 25 | 1.6 |
| 1932 | 7,267 | 232 | 58.21 | 1.86 | 4,215 | 1,878 | 3 | 6 | 12 | 0.4 |
| 1922 | 4,781 | 108 | 43.44 | 0.98 | 3,754 | 1,378 | 2 | 3 | 8 | n.a. |
| 1913 | 1,912 | 12 | 19.66 | 1.12 | 970 | 508 | 1 | 1 | 2 | n.a. |
| 1902 | 986 | 7 | 12.46 | 0.09 | 572 | 226 | 1 | 1 | 3 | n.a. |

n.a. – Not available.

[1] Includes amounts received from the Federal Government for contractual services and shared revenues, as well as Federal grants-in-aid.

[2] Excluding national defense, international affairs and finance, space technology, veterans' benefits and services (except education), and interest on debt.

Source: United States Bureau of the Census. Historical Summary of Governmental Finances in the United States, 1957 Census of Governments, Vol. IV, No. 3; and Governmental Finances in 1962, October 1963.

be differently defined. Amounts paid to non-profit institutions (including public agencies) for example, may be included or excluded. Even for the identical item, the amount may be counted at different phases of the disbursement cycle—the time received by the recipient governments. Some of the grants appear in Federal Government records as trust account expenditures; others as part of the administrative budget. These factors explain in part also differences between the amount of grant expenditures reported by Federal agencies and the amount of grant receipts reported by State and local governments. These differences are not unfamiliar to those working with business accounts; they are complicated in governmental accounting by the wide variation among programs in classes of eligible recipients, sometimes government agencies, sometimes non-profit institutions including government agencies, and sometimes individuals employed by eligible institutions. The amounts recorded as grants-in-aid, accordingly, differ depending upon the source of the data and definitions employed.

While the count of grant-in-aid dollars differs from source to source, there is even wider variation possible in the count of the number of grant-in-aid programs. Within many of the grants there are separate allocations of funds, or an earmarking of a part of a grant for a specialized purpose. The grant may be considered as one grant or as a composite of a number of separate grant programs. As with the expenditure amounts, moreover, the count may be limited to those programs in which payments are made only to States and local governments, or it may include also programs under which some payments are made to States and localities from funds available to other classes of eligible recipients as well, for example, non-profit institutions. In this report we have followed the classification regularly employed in the *Annual Report*(s) of the Secretary of the Treasury, and included as a single grant those items of

expenditure shown as a composite grant outlay in the Treasury *Report*.

In fiscal year 1962, the last year for which closed accounts are available, the Secretary of the Treasury's *Report* listed about 70 separate grant programs aggregating $7.9 billion. This includes, however, distributions in kind (commodities and services), distributions limited to selected governmental jurisdictions (District of Columbia, territories, and possessions), payments for contractual services, and shared revenues, which have little direct relevance for equalization and can be disregarded. Excluding these groups, there were 60 Federal grant-in-aid programs in 1962. Of these 60 programs, 37 had been enacted since the Second War, including such important grants as those for urban renewal, education aid to Federally impacted areas, national defense education, hospital and medical facilities, airports, sewage facilities, and public works acceleration. Eleven new programs were enacted by the 87th Congress, many of them small demonstration or experimental programs. The 87th Congress, however, enacted also the grants for public works acceleration and the area redevelopment grants for construction of public facilities. Of greater importance in terms of dollar expenditures were the amendments to the public assistance programs enacted in 1962 which authorized Federal matching up to 75 percent in the costs of rehabilitative services and training for those receiving public aid, as well as other basic changes in those programs. . . .

As table 1 makes clear, Federal aid to State and local governments has remained a fairly stable share of the Federal Government's total resources devoted to civilian government purposes. This—programs undertaken cooperatively with State and local governments—is the form the Federal Government's civilian expenditures often take. The percentage of Federal general expenditure for purposes other than defense, international affairs, space, veterans, and interest costs, represented by grants-in-aid has ranged between 20 and 26 percent most years since 1948, never falling below 18 percent nor rising above 30 percent. The 1962 calculation is 26 percent.

Moreover, the increases in Federal aid are small in comparison with the growth in State and local expenditures. During the fifteen year period from 1948 through 1962, when Federal aid expenditures rose by $6 billion, State and local expenditures increased by $49 billion. In considering the growth in Federal aid, it is essential to keep in view that the Interstate Highway System, which accounts for $1.9 billion of the Federal aid total, is in some respects a national rather than a State program financed from earmarked Federal taxes levied for these specific purposes, and shaped in the form of grant programs for tactical reasons.

IMPACT ON STATE AND LOCAL FINANCES

Federal assistance has assumed an increasingly important role in financing State and local governments since the turn of the century. State and local governments' receipts in the form of Federal aid amounted to nine cents per capita in 1902, less than one percent of their general revenues. The relative importance of Federal aid reached a peak at the height of the Depression, fell somewhat during the war years, and rose again in the postwar years (table 1).

In 1962 State and local governments collected $58.2 billion from taxes, charges for current services, and other general revenue. Of that total, $7.9 billion, or 13.5 percent, came from the Federal Government, mainly in the form of grants-in-aid, but including also shared revenues and contractual payments for scientific research and other public services. The proportion of State and local government revenue represented by Federal grants and other Federal payments has been increasing since 1946 when it was only 6.9 percent.

There is considerable interstate variation in the Federal contribution to State and local revenues. In 1962 it ranged in individ-

ual States from less than 10 percent of State and local general revenue in three eastern industrial States to more than 25 percent in two Western and one New England State (table 2). In general, the States with the lowest per capita incomes also have the largest proportion of revenue from the Federal Government relative to their total general revenues. Thus, Federal aid averaged 17.4 percent of general revenue in the South.

It is estimated that State and local governments provided $3 billion to match the $7 billion Federal grants-in-aid distributed in 1962. In the aggregate, this was 7.6 percent of all State and local tax collections. The 12 lowest per capita income States provided from 9.7 to 17.9 percent of their tax collections to match Federal grant funds. By contrast, the percentage in nine of the 12 highest income States was less than 7.6 percent. It was only 4.3 percent in New Jersey and 5.1 percent in New York (table 3).

The required State and local matching under existing grant programs generally takes a larger fraction of fiscal resources in the poorer States than in those with relatively high per capita income. For example, Delaware devotes $4.54 per $1,000 of its personal income to match Federal grant offerings while Mississippi devoted more than three times as much, or $14.78 per $1,000 of personal income (table 4). It is for this reason that the highest proportion of their spending for the major federally-aided functions — highways, public welfare, health and hospitals, and education — goes in the low income States to meet matching requirements (table 3).

Since 1916, when the first highway aid program was enacted, and the Depression years, when the social security programs were initiated, highways and public welfare have dominated the Federal aid picture. Federal intergovernmental expenditure for highways and public welfare has not fallen below 50 percent of the total since 1922 and in some years reached four-fifths of total Federal intergovernmental expenditure. In 1962 about two-thirds of

TABLE 2.-FEDERAL AID IN RELATION TO TOTAL GENERAL REVENUE OF STATE AND LOCAL GOVERNMENTS, BY STATE, 1962

| State & Region | Amount (in millions) | | Per capita | | Revenue from Federal Government as % of total general revenue |
|---|---|---|---|---|---|
| | Total general revenue | Revenue from Federal Government | Total general revenue | Revenue from Federal Government | |
| United States | $58,214 | $7,857 | $313 | $ 42 | 13.5 |
| New England and Mideast | 16,825 | 1,647 | 334 | 33 | 3.8 |
| Maine | 277 | 41 | 284 | 42 | 14.7 |
| New Hampshire | 178 | 32 | 287 | 51 | 11.8 |
| Vermont | 144 | 42 | 372 | 109 | 29.8 |
| Massachusetts | 1,798 | 200 | 346 | 39 | 11.1 |
| Rhode Island | 247 | 34 | 281 | 38 | 13.6 |
| Connecticut | 881 | 95 | 336 | 36 | 10.7 |
| New York | 6,837 | 484 | 391 | 28 | 7.1 |
| New Jersey | 1,922 | 168 | 302 | 26 | 8.7 |
| Pennsylvania | 3,116 | 340 | 274 | 30 | 10.9 |
| Delaware | 157 | 15 | 337 | 33 | 9.8 |
| Maryland | 977 | 118 | 302 | 36 | 12.0 |
| District of Columbia | 291 | 78 | 369 | 99 | 26.8 |
| Midwest | 16,085 | 2,013 | 307 | 38 | 12.5 |
| Michigan | 2,604 | 289 | 324 | 36 | 11.1 |
| Ohio | 2,818 | 359 | 281 | 36 | 12.7 |
| Indiana | 1,314 | 142 | 282 | 30 | 10.8 |
| Illinois | 3,189 | 357 | 316 | 35 | 11.2 |
| Wisconsin | 1,300 | 146 | 324 | 36 | 11.2 |
| Minnesota | 1,222 | 149 | 353 | 43 | 12.2 |
| Iowa | 882 | 108 | 318 | 39 | 12.3 |
| Missouri | 1,163 | 210 | 269 | 49 | 18.0 |
| North Dakota | 232 | 37 | 367 | 58 | 15.8 |
| South Dakota | 244 | 59 | 339 | 81 | 24.0 |
| Nebraska | 400 | 62 | 277 | 43 | 15.4 |
| Kansas | 716 | 94 | 323 | 42 | 13.1 |
| South | 14,143 | 2,464 | 256 | 45 | 17.4 |
| Virginia | 944 | 154 | 222 | 36 | 16.3 |
| West Virginia | 454 | 87 | 253 | 48 | 19.1 |
| Kentucky | 730 | 148 | 237 | 48 | 20.2 |
| Tennessee | 810 | 164 | 222 | 45 | 20.3 |
| North Carolina | 1,071 | 162 | 228 | 35 | 15.2 |
| South Carolina | 511 | 90 | 209 | 37 | 17.5 |
| Georgia | 1,003 | 196 | 246 | 48 | 19.5 |
| Florida | 1,541 | 166 | 284 | 31 | 10.8 |
| Alabama | 753 | 181 | 227 | 55 | 24.1 |
| Mississippi | 510 | 105 | 226 | 47 | 20.7 |
| Louisiana | 1,065 | 213 | 316 | 63 | 20.0 |
| Arkansas | 421 | 101 | 229 | 55 | 24.0 |
| Oklahoma | 752 | 162 | 307 | 66 | 21.6 |
| Texas | 2,734 | 375 | 270 | 37 | 13.7 |
| New Mexico | 345 | 77 | 346 | 78 | 22.4 |
| Arizona | 498 | 82 | 335 | 55 | 16.4 |
| West | 11,160 | 1,739 | 403 | 63 | 15.6 |
| Montana | 253 | 53 | 363 | 76 | 20.9 |
| Idaho | 253 | 47 | 306 | 67 | 21.8 |
| Wyoming | 160 | 50 | 483 | 151 | 31.1 |
| Colorado | 716 | 114 | 378 | 60 | 15.9 |
| Utah | 306 | 61 | 320 | 64 | 20.0 |
| Washington | 1,157 | 163 | 384 | 54 | 14.1 |
| Oregon | 654 | 124 | 362 | 69 | 18.9 |
| Nevada | 152 | 28 | 435 | 81 | 18.5 |
| California | 7,142 | 1,000 | 419 | 59 | 14.0 |
| Alaska | 135 | 46 | 557 | 190 | 34.0 |
| Hawaii | 271 | 52 | 391 | 76 | 19.4 |

Source: U.S. Bureau of the Census, *Governmental Finances in 1962*, October 1963.

II. Federalism in Action: Some Cases in Point

TABLE 3.: Required State and Local Matching of Federal Grants-In-Aid
in Relation To State and Local Tax Revenue and General Expenditure
from Own Sources for Selected Functions

12 Highest and 12 Lowest Income States, 1962

| States (ranked from highest to lowest 1962 per capita income) | Required matching as % of tax revenue | Required matching as percent of general expenditure from own sources[1] | | | | |
|---|---|---|---|---|---|---|
| | | Total | Education | Highways | Public welfare | Health and hospitals |
| U. S. average | 7.6% | 6.1% | 1.9% | 12.8% | 48.0% | 2.6% |
| *12 Highest Per Capita Income States* | | | | | | |
| Nevada | 7.2 | 5.1 | 1.6 | 6.8 | 52.9 | 8.0 |
| Delaware | 5.9 | 4.7 | 1.8 | 3.6 | 25.0 | 16.5 |
| Connecticut | 5.3 | 4.1 | 1.3 | 7.4 | 29.3 | 1.2 |
| New York | 5.1 | 4.3 | 1.4 | 8.1 | 42.5 | 0.9 |
| New Jersey | 4.3 | 3.7 | 1.4 | 9.1 | 33.7 | 1.8 |
| California | 5.6 | 4.6 | 1.1 | 8.3 | 44.0 | 2.0 |
| Illinois | 6.6 | 5.7 | 1.7 | 14.0 | 34.9 | 2.2 |
| Massachusetts | 7.5 | 6.7 | 2.0 | 13.3 | 44.6 | 1.1 |
| Maryland | 5.6 | 4.4 | 1.7 | 9.5 | 48.7 | 1.5 |
| Alaska | 10.0 | 5.9 | 2.7 | 4.1 | 37.9 | 6.7 |
| Washington | 7.9 | 6.0 | 1.5 | 13.6 | 48.2 | 3.0 |
| Michigan | 6.7 | 5.1 | 1.6 | 10.5 | 41.9 | 2.0 |
| *12 Lowest Per Capita Income States* | | | | | | |
| Oklahoma | 16.0 | 12.9 | 2.6 | 20.3 | 69.4 | 5.0 |
| West Virginia | 11.0 | 9.3 | 3.2 | 9.9 | 86.4 | 5.4 |
| New Mexico | 11.2 | 8.4 | 2.1 | 16.5 | 68.0 | 7.9 |
| Louisiana | 13.2 | 9.5 | 2.4 | 14.1 | 79.9 | 4.0 |
| Georgia | 12.9 | 9.4 | 3.4 | 18.0 | [2] | 4.3 |
| North Carolina | 9.7 | 7.9 | 3.1 | 14.8 | 90.0 | 5.1 |
| Kentucky | 12.1 | 7.4 | 2.6 | 12.1 | 74.4 | 6.8 |
| Tennessee | 11.5 | 8.6 | 3.4 | 14.2 | 69.1 | 4.3 |
| Alabama | 16.7 | 11.6 | 3.0 | 23.3 | 96.3 | 5.1 |
| Arkansas | 17.9 | 15.1 | 5.3 | 29.9 | 96.3 | 7.7 |
| South Carolina | 10.9 | 8.9 | 3.5 | 25.9 | 72.1 | 6.5 |
| Mississippi | 13.5 | 9.4 | 3.1 | 17.6 | 54.6 | 6.5 |

[1] The expenditure categories are as defined by the Bureau of the Census and include substantial amounts for activities for which there are no Federal grant programs. "General expenditure from own sources" is defined as total general expenditure less amounts received from the Federal Government..
[2] Approximately 100%.

TABLE 4. — REQUIRED MATCHING UNDER EXISTING FEDERAL GRANT PROGRAMS
PER $1,000 OF PERSONAL INCOME, BY STATE, 1962

| States ranked in order of per capita personal income (high to low) | Required matching | States ranked in order of per capita personal income (high to low) | Required matching |
|---|---|---|---|
| Delaware | $ 4.54 | Kansas | $ 9.53 |
| Nevada | 6.29 | Iowa | 8.70 |
| Connecticut | 4.74 | Arizona | 6.07 |
| New York | 5.45 | Montana | 12.71 |
| California | 5.88 | Florida | 5.66 |
| Alaska | 7.92 | Texas | 7.67 |
| New Jersey | 3.57 | Utah | 7.23 |
| Illinois | 5.61 | Vermont | 16.66 |
| Massachusetts | 7.37 | Virginia | 6.47 |
| Maryland | 4.70 | Oklahoma | 15.68 |
| Washington | 8.05 | Maine | 8.95 |
| Ohio | 6.36 | New Mexico | 11.20 |
| Michigan | 6.55 | Idaho | 11.04 |
| Hawaii | 8.60 | South Dakota | 11.61 |
| Wyoming | 12.91 | West Virginia | 10.53 |
| Colorado | 10.50 | North Dakota | 13.18 |
| Pennsylvania | 5.78 | Louisiana | 15.21 |
| Oregon | 7.97 | Georgia | 11.09 |
| Missouri | 9.27 | North Carolina | 8.79 |
| Rhode Island | 7.65 | Kentucky | 10.64 |
| Indiana | 5.82 | Tennessee | 9.80 |
| Wisconsin | 6.51 | Alabama | 13.89 |
| Nebraska | 9.22 | South Carolina | 9.62 |
| New Hampshire | 8.11 | Arkansas | 16.84 |
| Minnesota | 8.33 | Mississippi | 14.78 |

TABLE 5. — FEDERAL INTERGOVERNMENTAL EXPENDITURE, BY FUNCTION, SELECTED YEARS, 1913-1962
(INCLUDES FEDERAL PAYMENTS TO STATES OTHER THAN GRANTS)

| Year | Amount in Millions | | | | | Percent distribution | | | |
|---|---|---|---|---|---|---|---|---|---|
| | Total | Edu-cation | High-ways | Public welfare | Other | Edu-cation | High-ways | Public welfare | Other |
| 1962 | $7,735 | $1,169 | $2,748 | $2,448 | $1,370 | 15.1 | 35.5 | 31.6 | 17.7 |
| 1957 | 3,873 | 604 | 944 | 1,557 | 768 | 15.6 | 24.4 | 40.2 | 19.8 |
| 1951 | 2,585 | 436 | 415 | 1,181 | 551 | 16.9 | 16.1 | 45.7 | 21.3 |
| 1946 | 894 | 149 | 79 | 429 | 242 | 16.7 | 8.8 | 47.4 | 27.1 |
| 1944 | 1,072 | 193 | 147 | 420 | 312 | 18.0 | 13.7 | 39.2 | 29.1 |
| 1942 | 887 | 76 | 164 | 383 | 264 | 8.6 | 18.5 | 43.2 | 29.8 |
| 1940 | 884 | 154 | 195 | 278 | 257 | 17.4 | 22.1 | 31.4 | 29.1 |
| 1938 | 762 | 112 | 264 | 218 | 168 | 14.7 | 34.6 | 28.6 | 22.0 |
| 1936 | 908 | 147 | 285 | 290 | 186 | 16.2 | 31.4 | 31.9 | 20.5 |
| 1934 | 976 | 61 | 279 | 495 | 141 | 6.3 | 28.6 | 50.7 | 14.4 |
| 1932 | 232 | 12 | 191 | 1 | 28 | 5.2 | 82.3 | 0.4 | 12.1 |
| 1922 | 118 | 7 | 92 | 1 | 18 | 5.9 | 78.0 | 0.8 | 15.3 |
| 1913 | 12 | 3 | — | 2 | 7 | 25.0 | — | 16.7 | 58.3 |

Source: U. S. Bureau of the Census, Historical Summary of Governmental Finances in the United States, 1957 Census of Governments, 1959, Vol. IV, No. 3; Governmental Finances in 1962, October 1963.

all Federal intergovernmental expenditure was for highways and public welfare—$2.7 billion, or 35.5 percent for the former and $2.4 billion, or 31.6 percent for the latter (table 5). Because highway aid is dominated by the Interstate Program, which is largely Federally financed, more matching funds are provided by the States and localities for public welfare than for highways. Thus, it is estimated that the $2.4 billion of public welfare grants called for $1.3 billion of State and local matching funds. Most low income States spend little more for public welfare from their own resources than can be matched by Federal grants under matching requirements, while high income States spend for this purpose considerably more from their own resources than is matched by the Federal Government (table 3).

*Spencer D. Albright and Jess H. Walters*

# VIRGINIA

### GENERAL FINANCIAL ASPECTS

[D]irect Federal expenditures within the State [Virginia] are far more important to the economy than are grants. Thousands of Virginia residents work in Washington for the Federal Government, and many more thousands are employed in agencies on the Virginia side of the Potomac River, the most notable of which is the sprawling Pentagon. Moreover, there are numerous military installations throughout the State. Although the estimates vary, it would appear justifiable to assume that the Virginia economy receives from $500 million to $1,000 million from Federal Government operations in the State. A 10 percent cut in Federal grants could be absorbed rather easily but a 10 percent reduction of other Federal expenditures would have profound and far-reaching effects. . . .

### IMPACT ON THE OFFICE OF GOVERNOR AND ON STATE ADMINISTRATION

Because of the reorganization of the State government under Gov. Harry F. Byrd, 1926–30, and the earlier introduction of the executive budget system, the Governor of Virginia occupies a very strong position.

The organization of the operating departments has further enhanced executive leadership. While some departments are under a board or commission, there is a single administrative head in almost every case. The chairmen of such boards or commissions serve as the executive officers of the agencies; they are usually appointed and removed by the Governor, the other members serving largely in an advisory capacity. This pattern holds true for the Departments of Health, Highways, Education and Welfare—the principal grant administering agencies examined in this study.

Under such a setup, it is difficult to discern any impact of Federal grants on the office of Governor. There has been no change of legal power and little change of informal powers as a result of Federal aid. The political regime has authority from administrative integration and from efficient government.

All the State administrative officers are within the political system dominated by the Governor and the senior United States Senator. This does not mean that all officers play politics with administration. Good administration is the rule among State agencies, and the reputation enjoyed by Virginia for its insistence on integrity

From *The Impact of Federal Grants-in-Aid on the Structure and Functions of State and Local Governments* (Washington, D. C.: Advisory Commission on Intergovernmental Relations, 1955), pp. 462-473.

among high officials is well earned and carefully guarded.

The Governor's control over State agencies administering federally aided programs is the same as for agencies without such programs. There is an indirect difference in procedures, not because of the character of Federal aid but because of the character of special funds. Since special funds are acknowledged to receive less critical review by the Governor and legislature than the general funds do, and since Federal aid programs all come under special funds, they are given less attention. Yet all appropriations are viewed from the standpoint of State needs.

The impact of Federal grants on the office of the Governor of Virginia cannot be explained solely in terms of formal powers and procedures. It is more intangible and lies in the Governor's balancing of two forces in Federal-aid relationships. He must respect the traditional concept of independence—a concept that leads to the popularly held notion that Federal aid is undesirable, if not an outright evil—and he must respect attitudes among departments using Federal funds. The notion of Virginia's complete independence and the accompanying corollary that the State is vastly more efficiently administered than almost any feature of the Federal Government are advanced for popular consumption. The other factor rests with operating departments which maintain cordial relations with agencies in Washington with whom they work. Virginia administrators handling Federal aid programs state quite frankly that they respect their Washington colleagues; that they do not experience any dictation from Washington; that they have faith in the programs in which they are engaged; that they do not believe that money, either State or Federal, is improperly spent; or that Washington has displaced, or has tried to displace, State administration. On the contrary, they believe that federally aided functions are the responsibility of the States to administer, that the relations between State and Federal administrations

are maintained with mutual respect, and that differences are examined professionally and resolved without any attack on the rights of the States.

The Governor has been and is a part of the dominant political regime in Virginia. Every Governor has lived within this orbit and has risen to power by understanding the purposes and workings of the dominant regime. Learning to work with seemingly contradictory forces, he is bound to know the ambivalence which besets his office with regard to Federal aid. In blunter language, the ambivalence can be illustrated by the remark of an explosive individual who sat in the Governor's chair some years ago and who is alleged to have said, "I'll blast h—— out of the federal aid program, but over in your department take every nickel you can get for state needs."

This quotation should not be taken to mean that the Governor will so arrange his budget as to get all the Federal money which is available. Marvin H. Sutherland, Assistant Director of the Budget, who is also Clerk of the House Appropriations Committee, put it as follows: "Whatever funds we can get without undue restrictions we shall take if we think they are spent usefully." This point is illustrated by the following letter of executive disallowance from Governor Stanley from which the introductory paragraph has been omitted.

June 18, 1954.

Dr. H. N. Young, *Director*,
    *Virginia Agricultural Experiment Station,
    Blacksburg, Va.*

Dear Dr. Young:

. . . I am fully aware of the great contribution research has made toward the improvement of agricultural practices and its attendant benefits to the social and economic life of Virginia farm people. Undoubtedly, there are many new fields in which research would bring beneficial results, but inevitably we must approach a point of diminishing returns at which the benefits will not justify the cost. At that point we must be selective in adopting the program from which the most good will result for the invested dollar.

Our Federal government's history of deficit spending indicates that greater care should be exercised over selection of subjects for expenditure. The study of "Adult Control Over Children" in my judgment, would not possess potentialities for benefit to Virginia agriculture in as great a degree as would the other projects.

Therefore I do not feel that I can authorize acceptance of $4,000 in Federal funds for this purpose. You, however, are authorized to accept an increase of $105,530.60 in Federal funds for the other research items set forth in your letter of June 12.

The authorization is granted with the understanding that acceptance of such funds under no way obligates the Commonwealth to expenditures of funds other than those already available for matching purposes.

Sincerely yours,

Thomas B. Stanley,
*Governor.*

There is no doubt that the effective budget system places the Governor in a strong position with respect to the administrative agencies and also with respect to the legislature. The Division of the Budget is within the Executive Office of the Governor. The Governor is legally the chief budget officer and may appoint a Director of the Budget to assist him. The Director represents the Governor at legislative hearings on budgetary matters. Although the Director seldom speaks at such hearings and then only to answer questions, the financial proposals of the Governor carry great weight with the legislature.

Turning from the general impact of grants on the office of Governor, a word should be said about the effect on State personnel and practice. It was agreed that Federal grants have stimulated professionalism in the departments concerned. There is evidence of this among many administrative officers who maintain high standards of competence and demand the same of their subordinates. However, none of those interviewed felt that professionalism had led to the development of "Federal loyalties" to the detriment of overall State interests. The thought is repugnant to Virginians and the administrative and budgetary controls of the Governor are such as to discourage any "treason."

Standards are set after consultation among Federal and State administrators concerned with a given program. Changes which affect Virginia are made through such consultation, except for an occasional sudden curtailment by the Federal Government. One suggestion was that any Federal downward revision ought to be worked out systematically between Federal and State officers, thus giving time to rearrange State programs with proper regard for all involved. Other comments will appear in the following discussion of the impact of Federal grants on the Departments of Education, Health, Highways and Welfare.

*Education*

Federal aid programs for education are as follows: (1) Vocational education with its four occupational fields—agriculture, home economics, trade and industry, and distributive occupations; (2) vocational rehabilitation; (3) veterans' training; (4) school lunches; and (5) aid to federally affected areas. . . .

Government projects and military installations have added to the demands on local government, especially as the result of bringing in large numbers of school children without corresponding increase in local tax revenues. Federally affected areas include Arlington and Fairfax Counties near the District of Columbia; the cities of Norfolk, Portsmouth, and other Hampton Roads urban areas having naval personnel and large industrial centers engaged in vast shipbuilding contracts for the Federal Government; and various military installations at Fort Lee, Fort Eustis, Langley Field, Quantico Marine Training Base and elsewhere. In Norfolk, the local school budget receives about $1,500,000 in Federal funds.

The school lunch program used $1,693,843 of Federal money for the fiscal year 1952–53 and the local units are responsible for meeting Federal matching requirements. The State contribution is small, being only $87,047 for administration. All officials interviewed in the offices of the Governor, the Director of the Budget and the Department of Education expressed the belief that, if Federal aid for school lunches were withdrawn, it is highly unlikely that the legislature would carry the program through State appropriations. Other activities, such as vocational and veterans' programs, have considerable support in Virginia and would probably be continued with State financial support if Federal grants were cut off.

On the whole, high officials in the State Department of Education feel that there is an absence of dictation from the Federal Government. Plans involving Federal aid are worked out in consultation between State and Federal personnel. The Federal Government always works through the State government, all funds for local authorities being channeled through State authorities. Federal-State relations are cordial; in fact, it was said of the Federal representatives that "They lean over too far." Federal inspectors receive clearance from State education officials; Federal officials show a determination to comply with State standards. There are many educational plans for the distribution of Federal aid which contain no mention of content of courses to be given, teaching methods or the hiring of teachers. There has never been any indication that the Federal Office of Education has tried to direct general education.

*Health*

The Department of Health receives Federal funds under eight categories of grants — tuberculosis, venereal disease, heart disease, cancer, general health, maternal and child health, crippled children and hospital surveys. The program of hospital construction is carried on under the Department but is separately administered.

In formulating its budget, the Health Department prepares its requests with both Federal funds and the needs of a sound State health program in mind. It is gener-

ally expected on the part of State health officials that the General Assembly will appropriate the difference between the amount of Federal grants received and the total expenditures anticipated.

Dr. Mack I. Shanholtz, State Health Commissioner, related an experience which he had had with the budget estimates in 1953–54. In the summer of 1953, he anticipated a cut of 26 percent in Federal aid for tuberculosis control. His request for State funds to make up the expected reduction was approved in the executive budget hearings. Subsequently, the President's address to Congress indicated that there would be a cut of 60 percent in Virginia's share of money for tuberculosis control. The General Assembly upon request approved an increased appropriation to offset the larger expected reduction in Federal aid. However, Congress later exceeded the President's request and Virginia received more money for tuberculosis control than was counted on. The extra funds made it possible for the Department to expand its case detection work.

In reply to a question put by the Virginia State Chamber of Commerce, John H. Bradford, Director of the Budget, said that Federal aid under the public health program had been refused on one occasion. His explanation was that the money was turned down "because of lack of office space in which to conduct the activity . . . (but that) this was not a significant amount in relation to the total."

With reference to the administration of Federal aid funds, the Health Department told the State Chamber of Commerce that:

Insofar as public health is concerned, there is no evidence that federal funds are expended more freely or more wastefully than state or local funds. In fact, there is no evidence that any funds from any source are expended freely or wastefully.

However, a frank admission was made by the Department that, whenever possible, "federal money is spent first and state money is spent second." If all funds are not expended by the close of the fiscal year, the State's unexpended balances are usually larger than the balances for the Federal aid funds. This seems to be a conscious policy on the part of the Department and probably holds true of other departments.

Beyond the earmarking of funds for particular programs required by congressional legislation, the Federal officials do not interfere or attempt to interfere with State control. The United States Public Health Service is reasonable and there is no dictation. With respect to Federal standards, Dr. Shanholtz pointed out that many of these follow the recommendations of the American Medical Association and the American Hospital Association but added, "We write our own programs. Virginia's standards always exceed the minimum prescribed by the Public Health Service." There may be differences between State and Federal officials but these are of a professional nature and are never a conflict between jurisdictions. They are ironed out amicably and on a professional basis. Inspections and observations by personnel of the United States Public Health Service are made only after permission is sought from the State Health Commissioner's office. This is a matter of courtesy and contributes to the pleasant relations between the Federal and State health authorities.

*Highways*

The Virginia highway program began in 1906. A primary highway system was set up in 1918 with approximately 4,000 miles of road. In 1932 most of the State's secondary road system was taken over from the counties under the provisions of the Byrd Road Act. Two counties, largely urban in character (Henrico and Arlington) have not come into the State system and maintain their own secondary roads. All highways within cities are municipally maintained. Federal aid for highways began in 1916. All Federal funds, whether for primary, secondary, interstate or urban roads are handled through the State Highway Department even for money allotted to cities.

Virginia politics, in the best sense, definitely has been concerned with highways. Harry F. Byrd acquired his first prominence through campaigning for a "pay-as-you-go" highway system in 1923–25. The reorganization of the Highway Department in 1922 and Byrd's administration as Governor from 1926 to 1930 laid the foundation for a progressive highway system. The Byrd Road Act of 1932 created the integrated system of primary and secondary highways throughout the State. It is an accepted principle among Virginia leaders that road-building is to be financed through taxation rather than through borrowing although the State has resorted to "revenue bonds" for the purchase and construction of toll bridges and more recently for the toll road authorities.

The Highway Department's estimates are not questioned by the Governor in his budget hearings or in the legislative hearings. This is not a matter of political domination; it results from implicit confidence in the accuracy and integrity of the highway administrators. Virginia's highways are a source of pride and represent one sphere of government where the Old Dominion has exhibited great initiative and foresight.

The relations between the Federal and State highway officials are excellent. In an address made to the League of Virginia Counties on November 19, 1951, Gen. James A. Anderson, State Highway Commissioner said:

In my opinion, the greatest exponent of States' rights on highway matters in all Washington is Commissioner MacDonald of Public Roads. For more than 30 years he has steadfastly refused to bypass the States or to deal directly with local political subdivisions. He has set the example for State highway departments in their dealings with counties, cities, and towns. He firmly believes in strong State government; if we are true to our salt, we believe just as firmly in maintaining and upholding strong local government.

*Welfare*

Welfare occupies a peculiar status within the government of Virginia. Unlike health, certain aspects of welfare are critically viewed, perhaps even regarded with hostility by many people. Herbert Spencer's notion that the State has no responsibility for the relief of the poor and afflicted has some advocates in the Commonwealth.

The legislature supports various welfare programs costing more than $20 million annually, of which more than 11 millions are from Federal aid. Local funds are also involved. . . .

Like those in other departments, the administrative officers in the Welfare Department are a remarkably competent body of public servants. Yet it is clear that welfare programs are not as well accepted as are the activities of the Health and Highway Departments. To what extent they would be retained if Federal aid were withdrawn is problematical. The counties are not prepared to take over and the State legislature would not readily provide the additional State appropriations needed. Meanwhile State welfare officials agree that their Washington counterparts are cooperative and reasonable.

IMPACT ON THE LEGISLATURE

. . . As previously noted, special funds receive less consideration from the legislature than do general funds; Federal aid programs fall within the special funds category. In an interview, Jesse W. Dillon, State Treasurer, candidly stated that Federal projects receive somewhat briefer consideration than do nonaided projects. It is generally agreed among Welfare Department officials that the legislature is more drastic in cutting general relief requests, which are not federally aided, than welfare projects which have such assistance.

Members of the legislature are not concerned with Federal aid as such; the overall impact of grants has never been examined by any committee of that body. The first and foremost interest of legislators is in solving State problems and hence Federal aid is incidental to State interest. A member of the House of Delegates from Richmond, Edward E. Lane said, "The first test is the question, 'Is a specific proposal a matter of local concern and can it be met through the resources of the locality?'" He further stated that each Federal grant should be examined on its merits. While expressing strong disapproval of Federal aid in general, he felt that generalized statements are often not justified. He personally approved of certain programs, particularly for highways and for conducting nationally important research in the field of public health.

Grants have had no serious effect on the balance of power within the legislature other than the well-recognized tug-of-war in a conservative State between ultraconservatives and moderately liberal conservatives, both groups being largely within the Democratic Party. Groups most critical of Federal aid are the conservative press and certain politicians, especially of the ultra-states rights philosophy. In the 1954 legislative session, the resistance to the established leadership was over appropriations. The ultraconservative forces wanted lower and the moderately liberal forces higher appropriations. The struggle involved State solutions for State problems and was only incidentally related to Federal aid.

Over the past three decades, there has been a shift of State policies toward programs favored by Federal aid, especially in highways, health, education and welfare. Some of these doubtless would have been launched without Federal funds. Other, such as welfare and school lunches, would not have been initiated by State action if they had not been federally promoted.

Numerous programs have affected various groups and "have whetted the popular appetite for government services." All the welfare and assistance programs are of this character. Nevertheless, an ambivalent attitude toward Federal grants still exists among a considerable number of Virginia citizens. As a newspaper reporter put it, "People will talk for or against Federal aid according to whether it benefits them or not." The Richmond newspapers have had numerous editorials condemning Federal aid and yet these same newspapers vigorously supported the plan to build the Richmond Memorial Hospital with the help of Hill-Burton funds from the Federal Government.

IMPACT ON STATE-LOCAL RELATIONS AND ON LOCAL GOVERNMENT

There are some unusual features in Virginia's local government system. The 30 first-class cities are governmentally separate from and independent of the 98 counties, and stand on an equal plane with them. Furthermore, local school districts coincide with the various cities and counties. This means, then, that there are relatively few local units in the State and a comparative absence of overlapping jurisdictions. . . .

In spite of Virginia's position on States rights and frequent assertions of Jeffersonian attachment to local institutions, there has been little trend toward strengthening local government powers. To be sure, some cities have modernized their governments and some counties have either the county-manager or the country-executive forms of government. Nevertheless, there has been a definite tendency toward State centralization during the past quarter century, with the local communities, particularly the counties, becoming more and more dependent upon the State. Evidences of this are the Byrd Road Act of 1932 which transferred the secondary road system from the counties to the State, the assumption by the State in 1942 of the financing of the trial justice system, and more recently the bearing by the State of a large portion of school construction costs. Therefore, as a result of the inability or unwillingness of local governments to meet increasing demands, or the desire to achieve uniform administration and action, the State of Virginia has gained in power at the expense of its local governments.

While Federal aid was not the most important factor in this centralization, it did have an influence. Col. R. W. Copeland, Director of the Department of Welfare and Institutions said, "Federal aid to welfare led to the creation of welfare agencies in every county and independent city of Virginia. This was a requirement of the Federal law. Without this overall plan, some counties probably would never have set up welfare agencies." The Welfare Department believes that the local boards have much authority within the standards which must be met to secure Federal and State funds.

The Federal grant program in the field of public health which probably has the greatest effect on State-local relations is the Hill-Burton program for hospital construction. All the money for this program is channeled through the State Health Department, and the State itself participates in it through appropriating additional funds. The State Board of Health decides what types of projects will be supported, where they will be located, and what the priorities shall be. Certain minimum standards have been set by the Federal Government but these are reasonable while those of the State are more stringent. The amount of money for which a local unit can qualify under this grant is determined by a formula established by the State Department of Health. This formula changes from year to year with the increase or decrease of Federal funds available. When the program began, the locality put up 45 percent of the funds and 55 percent came from the State and Federal Government. After a sharp reduction in Federal appropriations, the ratio was changed to 66 percent local and 34 percent Federal-State. In 1954, when Congress again voted more Hill-Burton funds, the formula was changed to 50 percent local and 50 percent Federal-State. This clearly demonstrates what impact a Federal grant can have on both State and local government.

## CONCLUSIONS

This study has led to the following conclusions:

1. The importance of Federal grants-in-aid in Virginia is much less than direct Federal expenditures within the State. The aid represents approximately 3 to 6 percent of the amount of money coming into the Virginia economy from other Federal activities.

2. The working relationships of State agencies and their Federal counterparts are on a professional basis and are characterized by mutual respect and cordiality.

3. Among the grant-administering departments of the State government, there is general acceptance of the principles of Federal aid. Now and then there is a strong expression of approval. There is also an occasional remark, "I don't believe in Federal aid in principle, but I am wholeheartedly in support of this particular program."

4. There is evidence in Virginia of the coexistence of a public philosophy suggestive of Jeffersonian individualism and an administrative philosophy stressing cooperative federalism.

5. In the legislature, there is general debate over appropriations from the general fund, but the attention given to special funds is often perfunctory and Federal grants are included among the special funds. Therefore, the less critical examination which the Federal aid programs may receive results primarily from their character as special funds rather than because they receive money as grants-in-aid.

6. Some programs initiated by Federal grants are, or will be, continued through State appropriations even after Federal aid is withdrawn or decreased. Others, however, are likely to face curtailment or elimination if Federal aid ceases. Those, such as highways, which are firmly established will be continued regardless of what actions are taken by the Federal Government. Others which are not so secure, such as public welfare, would probably suffer from any reduction in Federal participation.

7. There are wide differences of attitude among Virginians with reference to public responsibility for various social programs: (a) Some define need in terms consistent with Virginia's traditional conservative outlook, (b) others disavow all public (i. e., government) responsibility, and (c) still others, among them some State officials, feel that the State is not doing all that it can and should do. Other State officials contend that the State is taking, and will continue to take, responsibility for meeting the needs of its citizens.

8. There is a faith among many people that, if the tax resources were shifted from the Federal Government to the States, the State could then do the work more efficiently and effectively. Others, including some State officials, maintain that this would not necessarily be the case, and that in fact the opposite might be true.

9. There is such a strong assumption that some Federal aid programs will be continued that they are carried in the executive budget as recommendations almost automatically. Others do not have such assurance (e. g., the school lunch program) and are made entirely contingent upon the appropriation of Federal funds for their continuance.

10. The older grant-in-aid programs, such as highways, are now widely accepted and supported. On the other hand, some of the recent programs are highly controversial.

11. Many pronouncements against Federal grants-in-aid on philosophical grounds (or in accordance with a "firm belief in principle!") are probably rationalizations of more practical objections. For example, a staunch States-righter's primary opposition may be to the national leadership of the Democratic Party, but this becomes vocalized as opposition to grants-in-aid.

12. If respected conservative leaders were to speak favorably of a given grant-in-aid program, it is more than likely that Virginians would consider such a program with more cordiality than would be true if the program were offered by a liberal.

13. The fear of dictation from Washington is not justified according to the top administrative officials in the operating departments of Virginia's State government. Although they do acknowledge that such a possibility might exist, they are prompt to point out that from their experience they have seen no evidence, in the past or present, to suggest dictation on the part of any agencies in Washington. Furthermore, they do not foresee any trends toward the development of such a situation.

14. The basic problem of government is how can people best serve their own needs. In the 20th century there is a trend toward various social solutions which employ intergovernmental relationships, and which also are characterized by cooperation between public and private enterprise.

*Phillip Monypenny*

# ILLINOIS

## IMPACT ON THE OFFICE OF GOVERNOR AND ON STATE ADMINISTRATION

Political and administrative leadership has been relatively highly concentrated in Illinois ever since the reorganization of the State administration in 1917 on the lines developed in the Report of the Efficiency and Economy Commission. There are 13 major departments into which most State administrative activities are concentrated, with significant exceptions. The Constitution provides five elective officials in addition to the Governor and Lieutenant Governor. There are several important independent commissions, the Commerce Commission, the Civil Service Commission, the Public Aid Commission, and the 3 boards for institutions of higher education set up by statute, of which 2 are appointive, and 1 elective, the Board of Trustees of the University of Illinois. There are, of course, other lesser agencies.

The Governor of Illinois, therefore, has in his hands the appointment of the heads of nearly all the significant departments comprising the bulk of State employment and activity. This power is largely statutory. He has in addition important constitutional powers. He holds office for 4 years and is eligible for reelection. He gives the General Assembly an account of the State at the beginning of each session, he may call the General Assembly into special session specifying the purpose for which they are convened, he may adjourn the houses if they disagree on a time of adjournment, he may remove any appointive officer; he grants reprieves and pardons, commands the State militia, and has a veto of bills which can be overridden by two-thirds of the members of each house and includes items of appropriation bills. The legislature must approve appointments made by the Governor, but it is rare for an appointment to be rejected although in the last administration the President of the Civil Service Commission, holding an interim appointment, was rejected by the Senate.

Of the elective officers other than the Governor, the Superintendent of Public Instruction, the Secretary of State and the Auditor head relatively large organizations. The Secretary of State administers the motor vehicle licensing laws and the driver's license law, the corporation and security issuance laws, and has the usual archival and authenticating functions. The Auditor, in addition to the function implied in that title, administers the laws regulating banks

---

From *The Impact of Federal Grants-in-Aid on the Structure and Functions of State and Local Governments* (Washington, D. C.: Advisory Commission on Intergovernmental Relations, 1955), pp. 140–158.

and other credit institutions. The Attorney General is of course an important figure in the State administration, but is usually less of a possible rival to the Governor than the other two. The Superintendent of Public Instruction administers the extensive regulatory system over public schools including the distribution of the tremendous State grants. Individual holders of these offices have shown their ability to win election to them when their party was not able to capture the gubernatorial office.

Of the agencies organized as commissions, the only one with large routine administrative responsibilities is the Public Aid Commission which administers the four categorical public assistance programs and allocates State funds to local units for general assistance. Some commissions are grouped within departments for housekeeping purposes, such as the Industrial Commission within the Department of Labor. The Civil Service Commission is a nominally independent administrative unit with most of the usual civil service functions. There is an extensive use of advisory boards and commissions in connection with particular operations.

With three exceptions, the grant-in-aid supported activities are found within the departments under the Governor. Highways are handled by a division within the State Department of Public Works and Buildings. The Divisions of Unemployment Compensation and the State Employment Service are within the Department of Labor. Both of these activities dwarf their parent departments. Public Assistance as noted is the responsibility of the Public Aid Commission, which has had a considerable continuity of membership through changes of administration. Vocational Rehabilitation and Vocational Education are nominally governed by the Board of Vocational Education, but are administratively operated as units under the Director of Public Welfare and the Superintendent of Public Instruction, respectively. Crippled Childrens Services is administered by a division of the University of Illinois. With

minor qualifications for the Public Aid Commission, therefore, and with the exception of the Vocational Education and Crippled Childrens Services grants, it may be said that the Governor can influence the administration of the various Federal aid programs through his major appointees.

The existence of Federal aid has not prevented an extensive experimentation with the overhead administration of several programs. Old-Age Assistance was first administered by the Department of Public Welfare at a time when the Illinois Emergency Relief Commission administered unemployment relief. As that activity came to an end, Old-Age Assistance, Blind Assistance and Aid to Dependent Children were shifted in 1943 to the Public Aid Commission as the successor to Illinois Emergency Relief Commission. The mental health funds spent by the Department of Public Welfare were first received through the Department of Public Health, though they have been channeled directly since 1951, which had been possible under Federal legislation since 1946. Vocational Rehabilitation has only recently been shifted into the administrative control of Welfare, previously having a semiautonomous status. There has been a State Department of Aeronautics to receive Federal grants to airports only since 1945. In the purely State programs, a new Department of Public Safety was created by taking over the penal and correctional institutions from Welfare and adding to it the Highway Police.

It is of some interest in this connection that the Director of Public Health is now serving in his third administration, and that the Director of Aeronautics is serving in his second. The heads in immediate charge of other grant-in-aid programs within the departments have usually been career people who have not changed with changes of administration. This has been true of Vocational Rehabilitation, Vocational Education, Unemployment Compensation and the Employment Service, the Executive Secretary of the Public Aid Commission and the Chief Highway Engineer.

77

Such stability of tenure of important administrative officers is not limited to the grant-in-aid programs but in any case it does raise questions as to the relationships of such a semi-permanent administrative group to the current political heads of the State administration. In the current work of the Commission on State Personnel Administration (a legislative interim commission), questions have been raised about the exemption of policy making positions from civil service similar to those raised in the Federal administration.

It cannot be said, therefore, that Federal grants-in-aid in Illinois have had much effect on the general administrative structure which has been shaped by other considerations.

### The Governor and the Budget.

The Governor of Illinois has the advantage not only of a rather compact administrative organization under his appointive control, but he has extensive powers over expenditure. These are exercised through the Department of Finance which not only makes up the budget, but keeps administrative accounts, operates a preaudit to enforce expenditure controls, and controls purchasing. The Budget Director, who is also assistant to the head of the Department, has held office for 11 years and there is a nucleus of able and experienced fiscal administrators in the Department which has relatively few personnel changes with changes of administration. All State expenditures and receipts, including Federal grants, are now budgeted and appropriated, though budget control over the elective officers and over Federal funds is obviously nominal.

Budget making is carried on actively from September into the early months of the legislative session; and the Governor plays a key role in budgetary decisions, especially with respect to the total expenditure allowable, changes in the tax system necessary to finance the total, and shifts in

expenditure to accommodate desired new programs. The State is constitutionally required to operate within its revenues and budgeting is for a 2-year period, which makes these decisions especially significant.

There is legislative participation in budget making through the Budgetary Commission which includes the Governor, the Chairmen of the House and of the Senate Appropriations Committees, and two other members of each house, one of whom must be from the minority party. The Commission has no staff of its own, operates largely through oral testimony, and it is no clear what influence it has on budget making other than to give the Appropriations Committees a more intimate acquaintance with expenditure requests previous to the submission of appropriation bills. Generally speaking, changes in the Governor's budget by the legislature are fairly minor and he can control unwanted increases by an item veto, which is used extensively. As in most budget making, the emphasis seems to be on justifying increases and finding funds for those activities which are particular administration projects.

The general position of the Governor within the State administration is thus apparent. The principal limit on his control is the relative independence of the elective officers, of whom the Secretary of State and the Auditor are likely to be his rivals. They are in excellent positions to build up support both through the services they provide and the relatively large patronage of their offices which are not under the State civil service system.

As far as the administering officers in the grant-in-aid programs go, they seem to be amenable to the Governor's direction in matters of day-by-day administration. However, Federal requirements impose limitations on the use of positions in these agencies for patronage purposes, even though they do not entirely bar it. Federal oversight also tends to insure that in the administration of programs the intent of

State laws written to meet Federal requirements is respected. When there is some doubt as to whether a proposal calls into question compliance with Federal requirements, there is a tendency to plead the Federal requirements as a defense rather than to put the matter squarely on the ground of what is desirable policy. If the Governor's office wants to avoid the course of action suggested, it is possible to use the same excuse, which tends to save face all round.

As noted, the officers immediately in charge of the grant-in-aid activities are removed, for better or worse, from active participation in party politics. Some of them are active in the public relations of their particular programs, negotiating new programs and winning support. It would not seem that any of them can be aloof, however, when there is a specific intervention from the Governor's office and support from the office is sought wherever possible.

Strong professional organizations and standards exist in many of the grant-in-aid fields—highway engineering, public health, and the various program and professional specialties within it, public welfare administration, social work, mental health, education, employment security. These are sometimes a-governmental as in the medical specialties, and often interstate rather than Federal in their orientation. The more able administrators are likely to be especially active in these professional associations and to win considerable recognition outside their State. This is true, however, of fields in which there are no Federal grants. The worst noticeable failing is a tendency in some programs to rely on Federal support, both financial and professional, to make possible a State program, rather than seeking to build up that support within the State government and among the interested public within the State.

As far as can be seen, there have been no particular difficulties in coordination of State administration occasioned by grants-in-aid relationships. To some extent, coordination is deliberately promoted by grant-administering agencies to ensure a more effective program and the conservation of funds. Plans submitted for maternal and child health grants and crippled children's services must include a reference to related services and provision for coordinating with them. There is extensive coordination in vocational rehabilitation. Apart from finance, however, and a few narrow aspects of personnel policy, there are relatively few instances in which statewide coordination is attempted. The coordination that does grow up is *ad hoc* between departments and units within departments and it is often the work of the nonpolitical staff rather than of political heads.

There are some organizational anomalies in the welfare field arising from the separation of child welfare and other direct services to families and individuals from public assistance, both of which receive Federal aid, but it is State policy that produces the split in organization and there has been an effort to coordinate these services in the field through the regional offices. Federal policy in part was responsible for producing a duplication of industrial hygiene activities in the Health and in the Labor Departments, one receiving aid and one not. This was eliminated by the transfer of the industrial hygiene unit in Health to Labor, on the Governor's order, with a consequent loss of the Federal grant.

There seems to be no particular criticism directed to the possible tendency of individual departments to negotiate new policies with Federal agencies without adequate notice to the Governor's office or other interested State agencies. Except for appropriation action, which is somewhat unpredictable, new Federal policies are negotiated with agencies representing the State units receiving funds and there is ample time for clearance with higher political authority within the State. Probably the principal coordinating instrument is the State budget since most policy changes will require expenditure shifts and the consequences of these will be examined in some fashion at that point. State officers of general responsibility emphasize the cooperativeness of Federal agencies in adapting their procedures to the peculiarities of State administrative practices.

On the whole in Illinois, the grant-in-aid program which provides increased support for some very popular State services probably enhances the position of the Governor rather than diminishes it. With the exception of restrictions on patronage, it is hard to conceive of any policy likely to be advocated by a Governor which would run directly counter to the requirements of grant-in-aid programs. This is not to say that these programs do not definitely limit the directions State policy in the abstract might take, limits which would bar changes which are advocated by some groups within the State. On the other hand, a Governor is not likely to advocate policies which would be supported only by groups of relatively extreme sentiment and limited strength. Illinois being related to the Nation as it is, those sentiments which are extreme within it, are not likely to find a majority of Congress in its favor. On the other hand, what a majority of Congress does is likely to find considerable support within the State, even though it does have vociferous critics.

The increased services which State government provides tend to magnify the importance of those who immediately control them, as more groups within the State are in active contact with some phase of State government and even patronage, which is smaller percentagewise, may be larger numerically. Furthermore, the grant-in-aid program gives State officers a stake in the development of national policy and an occasion for speaking with reference to it. The enlarged scope of State government provides a better introduction to problems and issues that are national in scope. The significant role of the Republican Governors at the last Republican National Convention is a case in point as is the nomination of Governor Stevenson by the Democrats.

The reaction of the States to the opportunities and limits of the grant-in-aid program has produced new intensity of activity among State officials, including Governors. The Governors' Conference addresses itself to a common stand among Governors on the grant-in-aid programs. Associations of State officers administering grants participate in the development of policies in the fields which they administer. They sponsor legislative changes in the governing statutes of these programs. They become actively acquainted with the officers of Federal administration responsible for the programs in which they have an interest.

The Governor's relationships with the legislature would not seem to be affected in any significant way by the grant-in-aid programs. In Illinois the Governor very definitely sets up the legislative program even when his party controls only one, or neither, of the houses. The legislative leaders of his party are in weekly meetings with him during the legislative session and action on important measures is worked out at that time. On most issues strict party lines are not drawn, although the Governor can apply considerable discipline to the legislative members of his party if the occasion calls for it. The legislative measures affecting grant-in-aid activities have been minor, though fairly numerous during the last two sessions. The custom is for departmental bills to be introduced through the majority leader of the two houses so that he can act as a coordinating point. There is full opportunity for the matters affecting the Governor's program to be brought to his attention through this device. In addition the Governor has a virtually absolute veto both because of the extreme difficulty of a two-thirds vote of members to override, and because the legislature is out of session when most bills are signed.

Although there is no specific information available on the Governor's relationship to members of the Illinois congressional delegation, there is no reason for believing that it is affected by the grant-in-aid program. The operation of such activities as drought relief or the placement of defense contracts in depressed areas offer examples of the Governor's interest in securing Federal action to benefit his State and of appeals to the congressional delegation to that end. There is an inevitable rivalry between the Governor and a Senator of the opposite party which is likely to be minimized, at least in public, when the Governor and the Senator or Senators are of the same party.

## IMPACT ON THE LEGISLATURE

. . . The party division is close in the House of Representatives because of the system of cumulative voting by which 3 representatives are elected from each of 51 senatorial districts and each voter may use 3 votes as he pleases, all for 1 candidate or distributed between 2 or 3. The result is to provide one minority member in most districts of the State. . . . By and large the result of the districting system and of the close division between parties is to give a large degree of influence to those legislators who come from districts where party organization is tight with consequently less critical review of their action outside the inner party organization. The most difficult questions ordinarily are those which present differences between upstate and downstate interests, or rural and urban groups. These are apt to be most pronounced in matters affecting the burden of State taxes, the distribution of State expenditures, as on schools and highways, the organization of local government, some welfare policies and some regulatory issues. The most notable characteristic of the Illinois Legislature would seem to be its great respect for well-disciplined groups, whatever their political objective, and its unwillingness to be caught in the middle of a struggle between such groups, which often causes a stalemate unless the groups are able to come to some adjustment between themselves.

On the other hand, the influence of the Governor as noted above is very considerable. If he wishes to take a strong position, he can state the issues on which the legislators must be counted, and if he has a well thought-out program and can show support for it, it is likely to be adopted. One of his most important weapons is the veto by which the projects of concern to individual members or rather small groups, which are the grist of the legislative mill, can be stopped. The Governor therefore must be counted upon in any legislative policy making.

### The Legislative Process

The part-time character of legislative action which puts individual members in a position of great dependence on their leaders for guidance on most issues, leads to a considerable concentration of responsibility for shaping policy in the hands of these leaders, and, as we have seen, this leadership includes the Governor. Individual members are acquainted with relatively few bills, they follow the word of others, particularly the minority and majority leaders and the chairmen of the committees that the proper consultations and calculations have been made, unless they themselves are spokesmen for some particular group on some issue. Committees are important as screening devices and few bills which they disapprove are passed. On the other hand, important measures coming up late in the session may never be referred to committee, bills are freely transferred from one committee to another, or called from committee without a report, and the committee memberships are assigned pretty much at discretion by the Speaker of the House and President pro tem of the Senate for the majority, and the minority leaders for the minority. Reference of bills to committees is largely in the Speaker's hands. The calling up of bills for floor action is mainly controlled by the leaders of the two houses and the floor leaders.

Bills affecting Federal grant-in-aid programs would seem to get the same handling that others do. In the unemployment compensation programs, there is an elaborate system of negotiation between employer and labor representatives which parallels similar negotiations in workmen's compensation and industrial safety legislation. The initial adoption of the Aid to Dependent Children program was the result of a concerted drive to overcome the opposition of the county officers administering the previous "mothers' pension" legislation. In 1951 a bill to recreate the industrial hygiene unit in health was the object of an unsuccessful drive by the Illinois Manufacturers' Association supported by the Illinois Medical Association. Most recent measures, however, seem to have aroused no such controversy and those which passed were largely departmental bills.

Their way was made that much easier by the assertion that they were needed to assure the continuance of Federal grants, just as other proposals, which may have had much or little support, were easily killed by the information that they raised questions of conformity with Federal requirements. In other words, the standard machinery enabled the proposals affecting Federal aid to be handled with little fuss or bother. The Democratic (minority) Senate leader expressed some discontent with this situation though he had no particular proposals in mind which would have departed from Federal requirements and it might be inferred that some of his specific concerns were matters for administrative rather than legislative action.

There has been no general review of Federal grants-in-aid by the State legislature except for a staff study prepared by the Commission to Study State Government in 1949. Apart from recent public discussions, there has been little awareness in State political circles of the grant programs as a distinct entity affecting State policy or shaping State expenditure.

There have been no occasions to observe the groups lobbying for or against grant-in-aid programs in recent years. The only extensive legislative campaign concerning the acceptance of grants seems to have been over the substitution of the federally sponsored Aid to Dependent Children program for the indigenous Mothers' Pensions, and the campaign for unemployment compensation. The issues that arise currently are mostly with respect to expenditure, particularly the conservation of funds by more meticulous administration, and adjustments in the unemployment compensation scheme.

The assistance programs have been marked by the extension of family responsibility, more complete provisions for recovery from estates or relatives and the development of a work test. In unemployment compensation, the policy developments have been increases in benefit amount and duration in return for more stringent disqualifications including a more severe work test. The extension of the act to employers of four or more will cause no furor. There has been little opposition to the recent changes in the assistance code which have been immediately introduced by the administrative agency, which has associated with it an advisory committee on legislation from the General Assembly. As noted later, an elaborate bargaining system has developed in unemployment compensation between employers and employees, taken over from the earlier experience with workmen's compensation. Within each side there are uneasy shifts, but formal unity is usually maintained.

The only express criticism of grant-in-aid has come from organizations representing business, the State Chamber of Commerce and the Manufacturers' Association. These argue the issue of State-Federal relations, disclaiming any desire to review individual programs. There is really nothing that distinguishes group activity on grants-in-aid from political activity on other issues, except that Federal requirements and the availability of Federal funds condition the discussion. In a way these are only other aspects of a Federal structure that limits State legislation action in nearly all the more general fields of political conflict.

With respect to the balance of power among groups within the legislative membership, it would be hard to make any statements. Legislators, except on party issues and issues intimately affecting their own districts, are usually brokers of influence rather than spokesmen on a continuing basis for particular groups or proponents of particular governmental policies. By and large, the grant-in-aid program has not been a party issue, though measures affecting it, such as highway finance, or the volume of road construction have become administration programs. Similarly only by inference is it possible to construct downstate-upstate patterns since these do not show in voting on grant-in-aid issues, or in the sponsorship of bills. Perhaps the most vigorous proponents of lessened eligibility requirements for old age assistance are downstate Democrats from rural districts. On the other hand, the Aid to Dependent Children program, which has a relatively larger recipient group in Chicago than downstate, and which has a particularly large proportion of Negro recipients, is probably more acceptable to many urban than to many rural representatives, except those who have been educated, as some have been, by their contact with welfare problems. The drive to secure that program was spearheaded by an educated white middle class leadership, with an active contingent of women, carefully organized to secure downstate and suburban as well as metropolitan participation. It was anything but a group of welfare recipients raiding the public treasury. There is little evidence of that sort of move in Illinois politics. The principal opposition to that program came from the local officials who had control of the old Mothers' Pension provisions.

It is probably true that the Federal requirements have tended to make it harder for taxpayer groups to secure administrative arrangements and standards that lower levels of assistance to individual cases. On the other hand, property taxpayers, whose interests always have strong legislative representation, generally benefited by the shift of various programs from the property tax to the State sales tax which came with the increased scope of State responsibility. The benefits to the labor point of view on unemployment have been noted above, though over the years many concessions have been made to employers so that the proportion of wage which is now covered by unemployment compensation benefits is less than it was when the program began, average wages having risen much faster than benefit rates.

## Federal Grants and State Policy

The general impact on State policy may be inferred from what has been said about group participation in legislative policy. Illinois had already moved far toward the acceptance of State rather than local responsibility for the indigent as the depression deepened. What the Social Security Act did provide in these respects was a more systematic welfare program, both in the denotation of categories for particularly sympathetic attention, and in standards of support and of administration. Some of these, such as careful investigation of need, and a budgetary standard for determining assistance, had already been hammered out by State experience, but they were now to be applied on a statewide basis. The new categories have been added with little reluctance, except as noted. It is the statewide unity of standards and administration that is probably the principal result of Federal intervention.

In health and education, the effect of grants has been to stimulate particular programs rather than to create new areas of State responsibility. The State has been very alert to the needs of the blind and the handicapped, particularly children, and vocational rehabilitation and crippled children's service only complement this tendency of State policy.

In highways, Federal support has primarily resulted in a better integration of the State highway network into a Federal system than might have occurred otherwise. There is great latitude for State decision as to the use of Federal funds and there is little evidence of dictation. The general tendency of highway policy has been the same as the Federal, to provide high quality roads between principal population centers, though State expenditure has been spread over more mileage than some critics would think wise. The great battles within the State have been over highway finance, and here the Federal agency has played no part, except indirectly through the existence of the Federal gasoline tax.

In airports, the Federal program led to a program of developing aviation within the State. There seems to have been general agreement on the policy of spending available funds largely on scheduled airline stops, and on those places which would become stops if improvements were made. With the spending of the war accumulated surplus, State appropriations have ceased but local funds are sufficient to maintain the program. The same may be said of hospital construction, which has had wide acceptance, and for which State appropriations have also stopped.

In public housing, the State has not had a positive program, and a single appropriation to support local housing programs has not been repeated. In civil defence, there is some friction between State and Federal authorities. There is little State support, a minimum program is being carried on, and there is criticism of lack of leadership from the higher levels of government in the formulation of a workable program.

It would not appear that any neglected areas of policy development owe their existence to the uneven impact of Federal grants. The State is wealthy enough to meet its own needs as it sees them, and priorities would seem to be determined in a very limited degree by Federal grants. A similar comment can be made of tax policy. The principal earmarked taxes are those for highways, and very elaborate organization and equilibrium among those interested in

highway development buttresses this arrangement.

### IMPACT ON CITIZENS, PARTIES, AND ORGANIZED GROUPS

It is hard to offer anything other than hypotheses with respect to citizen participation as affected by the grant-in-aid programs. The programs are by no means removed from control by legislative and executive officers and these in turn are as much subject to control as they ever were. Legislative and gubernatorial control over the budget is strong, and there is no hesitation to drop State support, as in airports and hospitals, when these programs have a lower priority than others.

The Hatch Act and the merit system requirements of the Social Security Act are deliberate efforts to prevent expanded State activities from being used as the means whereby officeholders can be maintained in power indefinitely by a loyal army of political officeholders and aid recipients. If the Federal requirements have been less stringent than they seem, being notably ineffective in the matter of provisional appointments, tendencies in the State have worked in the same direction, and the public assistance program, perhaps the most fruitful of such possibilities, by common consent has been operated without any subordination to partisan purposes.

The only new organizations which have arisen in State politics directly as a result of grant-in-aid programs seem to be organizations of the aged which have had no dangerous influence on the programs. . . . The principal association is most active in Chicago though there are Townsend clubs all over the State. The influence of the latter seems to be small.

About the only observable impact of Federal grants on the party system has been in patronage. Although Illinois has had a civil service law for several decades, the extent to which it has excluded positions from patronage has varied. Of late the tendency has been sharply toward certified status. The principal means whereby patronage has been available, apart from the exclusion of positions, as in the elective offices, and in the maintenance staff of the highway department, has been by not scheduling examinations or scheduling them infrequently. Persons on provisional appointment in most cases secure their positions after nomination by county committees, and are often expected to contribute regularly to the party treasury. and to perform services in local organizations on call. Federal oversight has tended to keep down the number of provisionals in aided programs. In the county Departments of Public Welfare, examinations have been held with great regularity through the Merit System Council, which is the Civil Service Commission, acting through a separate staff and under a separate act. Some State political leaders believe that a reasonable amount of patronage is necessary to the maintenance of an effective party organization. Others regard it chiefly as an inescapable burden which they would be glad to minimize. It is doubtful whether Federal requirements have reduced patronage to the point where either party is embarrassed, since considerable patronage is available through local government.

With respect to professional organizations as opposed to political, the general tendency of the Federal aid programs, so far as it has increased the stability of staffs, and raised professional standards, is to further the participation of State employees in professional organizations. None of these organizations has been notably active on a State basis with respect to grant-in-aid programs. The usual nongovernmental professional organizations have an interest in State activities that affect their specialties and have been active in cooperating with some programs, as in health and welfare. As far as is known to this observer, none of them have taken a definite stand upon questions arising out of the Federal relationship.

In health, the greatest efforts have been made by the State Department of Public Health and the United States Public Health Service to secure the cooperation of all important professional groups both in legislative programs and in administrative regulations and practices. If anything this tendency to professional participation has probably grown because of the increased activity in certain fields which Federal aids may have promoted. Otherwise there would seem to be no difference between State activities federally aided, and those not federally aided, with respect to political activity or participation.

The demand for increased services, which is always present, is checked by opposition to tax increases, which is also always present and Federal aid programs would seem to be no different in this respect than others. Where no State funds are spent (as in the centers for the care of premature babies, supported almost entirely by Federal grants), the service is not growing. Demand does not seem to be related to Federal initiative, but to otherwise existing interests in certain kinds of service.

There is no indication as to attitudes with respect to State and local self-government, including local home rule. There is little of the latter in Illinois in the sense that local government is extensively controlled by statute and has a limited range of discretion on most issues, particularly in taxation. Certainly there is considerable interest in State politics and there is probably more citizen attention, in diverse ways, to the conduct of State and local government, and more intelligent and unintelligent criticism, than there was in the 19th century before Federal grants started.

The principal question which can be raised is the effect of Hatch Act restrictions. They have been the occasion for some questioning during the session of the present legislative Commission on State Personnel Administration. Legislators do at least formally believe in political participation, and the Hatch Act goes far beyond State restrictions on political activity. Federal and State employees are a large group and their exclusion from participation in party affairs, other things being equal, is probably not a good influence on the political life of the State. The contrary considerations have been stated above, and there is some doubt as to whether the participation of employees in political life under a patronage system is free and spontaneous.

IMPACT ON STATE-LOCAL RELATIONS AND
ON LOCAL GOVERNMENT

Centralization in Illinois both in the transfer of functions from smaller to larger units and in the increased supervision of activities of smaller units by larger has gone on apace in Illinois and many would like to see it go further. Except in a few counties, Illinois has the township system, and, though the townships are increasingly residual, they are probably not good administrative units for the functions they do have.

Federal grants in welfare have interacted with an established tendency. In schools there has been a substantial consolidation, motivated by State aid requirements, and extensive supervision. In highways the county highway department is an important unit under considerable supervision from the State highway department, which sets personnel standards for county highway engineers, and township road work is partly under county supervision. In property tax assessment there is county supervision of township assessors. In welfare, public assistance, except for general assistance, is entirely State administered, through "county" departments of welfare, which are really units of the State administration. There is no local contribution to categorical public assistance. With this has gone increasing State support to local units, particularly for road and school purposes. In Illinois substantial financial assistance to local units has always been accompanied by increased control.

Federal aid has been a neutral factor in reorganization of local government. Schools represent the largest change in local organization presumably for the better. The legislature has provided a number of options to permit the reorganization of services through larger units on an *ad hoc* basis, but they have complicated the general pattern rather than relieved it. The low constitutional taxing power of Illinois counties limits their assumption of functions. It has tended to multiply local units and is perhaps the principal reason for continued township financing and administration of general relief.

Local government officials are an important lobby, especially county and township officials, and they defend their existing prerogatives with great zeal and effectiveness. Federal aid has scarcely affected this, though it has indirectly cost them parts of the welfare function. If anything, the Federal programs which are channeled to local officials largely through State departments have provided them new opportunities for activity and a source of new ideas and methods. In certain programs as in hospital and construction and airports where the State has withdrawn from fiscal support, they are forced to use considerable initiative to finance the improvements they desire. Some have probably found in the new stimuli opportunities for more creative activity; others may resent what they consider to be "controls." Most are probably relatively little affected, other than by the general tendencies of American life.

Limitations of time have precluded a look at direct Federal local relations except in the aid to schools in federally affected areas, in which cooperation with the State Department of Education seems to have been close. In airport construction, local contracts are handled in Illinois through the State Department of Aeronautics to the apparent satisfaction of all three parties. In civil defense, there has been some annoyance on the part of State officials at the willingness of regional officers of the Federal Civil Defense Agency to enter into direct relations with local civil defense officials to the detriment of State policy and planning. There are many informal relationships between local officials and officials in grant-administering agencies, but they do not seem to cause either political or administrative difficulties to State officers.

## IMPACT ON OTHER INTERGOVERNMENTAL RELATIONS

As to the relationship of the State and its officers to other States, the net result of the Federal programs is probably to increase interstate cooperation both administrative and political. The existence of Federal programs provides a common legislative object for associations of State officials to add to the fellowship and exchange of information which otherwise might have been the principal occasion of their association. In some programs as unemployment compensation, there is a Federal requirement of State cooperation to protect the covered wage earner.

There are cooperative research and demonstration projects sponsored by the Federal regional staffs, particularly the United States Public Health Service and the Children's Bureau. Interstate cooperation is facilitated by the communications function of these Federal staffs and the exchange of experience is probably greater than it might otherwise be. Similarly cooperative relationships between local governments are sponsored in the highway program (in the Chicago metropolitan area especially), in health, child welfare, and mental hygiene, especially through the efforts of State staffs. These are probably a small influence on all the varied activity of local government but they do show a tendency in many aid programs to use its resources wherever possible.

## CONCLUSIONS

A concluding remark may be in order. The atmosphere of administration in the Federal grant programs has changed very greatly since 1936. The State officials are sure of themselves and they have confidence in their own staffs and in political support for their programs. The procedures

have been mastered so that operations go forward with relative smoothness. Basic policies have been established and are not currently in question. There is not that dependence on Federal representatives that there was when so many things were new. No longer do young ladies representing Federal bureaus sit down with State legislative committees to plan legislation. The Federal representatives no longer work under such tight restrictions. Control systems are more relaxed, and there are few things other than basic plans and budgets which require advance approval. Representatives of Federal agencies know the State staffs and have confidence in them. They are very much aware that political forces within the State can be exerted through Washington channels and they are chary of intruding on political decisions. They respect the administrative integrity of the State administrative organizations and provide a consultant service on demand, rather than operate a higher headquarters.

Over the years there has been a mutual accommodation of State and Federal policies, sometimes embodied in legislative action, sometimes only in administrative understanding. On the Federal side there is probably some disillusionment with the means which are open to effect compliance when a State does decide to go off the reservation. Impressions about Federal-State relations gained during the formative period under the Social Security Act are inappropriate to the present. The Children's Bureau acts more like the Bureau of Public Roads, and less like its old self. The Public Health Service is even more discreet and less demanding. There are few direct political contacts by Federal representatives. Their oversight of State legislation is accomplished through the cooperation of the State agencies, and their comments are transmitted to them. It is up to the State agencies and the State administration to decide what course of action to take with respect to the issues raised. There are also far fewer matters taken to Washington; there is more staff in the field, and they have more independence of action. Any review of the impact of Federal grants on State administrative responsibility would be incomplete which did not take account of these changes and they go far to dispel the fears about Federal dominance which at one time seemed partially founded. . . .

*Thomas J. Anton*

## STATE PLANNING, GUBERNATORIAL LEADERSHIP, AND FEDERAL FUNDS: THREE CASES

### THE DEVELOPMENT OF STATE PLANNING IN THE UNITED STATES

What is now known as state planning (including comprehensive physical planning, resource and economic development planning, capital programming and budgeting) may be said to have developed in roughly three stages. During the decade of the 1920's interest in state reorganization, the developing concern of both state and national governments in resource conservation and management, and the emergence of the so-called metropolitan problem created an intellectual ferment that produced the first statement of the state planning concept. New York State led the way with the 1926 report of its Commission on Housing and Regional Planning, which cited the need for a central state planning agency. In the same year, Governor Alfred E. Smith proposed a general plan for state reorganization to the legislature which included the following statement:

With the development of our great water power resources, our port facilities, and the tremendous growth of private industry, we feel the pressure of considering plans for the whole State that will relate all these activities effectively to one another. . . . I have no doubt that in the reorganization of the Government, regional planning will be provided in such a manner as to keep in close contact with the executive branch of the Government, making use of the special knowledge of the department heads concerned and also of outside expert assistance.

The United States Congress had, in acts of 1923, 1925, and 1927, authorized the collection of data relating to river basin development on a watershed basis. These data provided the groundwork for later efforts at regional planning and significant programs of river basin construction. At the local level, increasing recognition of the problems developing in metropolitan areas stimulated the creation of county and regional planning commissions in Los Angeles in 1922, Allegheny County (Pittsburgh) in 1923, and the voluntary Regional Plan Association of New York in 1922. Similar organizations were soon established in other metropolitan areas, such as Philadelphia, Chicago, and Boston. By the early 1930's, several states, including New Jersey, Wisconsin, and Illinois, had created state planning and development agencies to provide a coherent framework for local, metropolitan, and state development.

These modest efforts to implement state planning programs had scarcely begun before the depression of the 1930's forced a radical revision of their magnitude and focus. Shortly after President Roosevelt took office, the National Planning Board (later the National Resources Planning Board) was created to prepare a national public works program within the framework of a national plan. In order to implement this program, the national planning agency sought to "cultivate and stimulate" a network of state planning organizations re-

From Thomas J. Anton, *Office of the Governor* (Urbana, 1963), pp. 65–79. Reprinted by permission of the University of Illinois Press.

lated to the national relief and recovery activities. This "cultivation" made use of both the carrot and the stick: states were reminded that state planning could be financed through national emergency relief grants while at the same time they were told that national approval of public works projects would require prior clearance by a state planning agency. Almost immediately, the states (except for Delaware) responded by creating official planning agencies, either by legislative action or by executive order.

The expansion of state planning during the 1930's was accompanied by a rather severe restriction of focus. Whereas earlier planning approaches had tended to emphasize comprehensiveness and coordination, state planning during this period laid heavy emphasis on public works programming in order to take advantage of national aid. By tailoring their planning work so closely to a national program, the states were able to achieve impressive results in public works construction. The cost of this success, however, was heavy reliance on the national government and a concurrent failure to establish a basis for continuing state planning programs. In the period 1934–1939, for example, the states contributed only one-fifth of a total of $11.5 million spent for state planning purposes. And at the end of 1937, some 82 per cent of state planning agency employees were being furnished by the Works Progress Administration. When the national government cut back its public works construction program at the end of the 1930's, state planning agencies lost the principal reason for their existence. By the end of World War II, more than thirty of the former centralized state planning agencies had disappeared.

Since 1945 the state planning function, as such, has been relatively dormant. Although a few state planning agencies have continued to exist, their activities have been greatly overshadowed by widespread state concern for economic and industrial development. A good case can be made that these concerns will ultimately have to be joined together, but, as yet, attempts to do so have produced no consistent and widely accepted pattern of integration. Within the past eight years, however, there has been a noticeable rebirth of interest in strengthening the state planning function by assigning it increased responsibility in a number of important problem areas, including that of economic development. A large part of this renaissance can be traced to efforts to deal with the "metropolitan problem." And once again, the national government has provided "cultivation and stimulation."

The major vehicle for national stimulation here has been the public housing legislation initiated by the Congress in the early 1930's. Originally the purpose of this legislation was the elimination of slums in urban areas and their replacement by more adequate housing facilities financed and managed by public agencies. The Housing Act of 1949, however, introduced the concept of "urban redevelopment," which provided for the replacement of slum areas, not solely by public housing projects, but by other more profitable activities in accordance with locally made decisions as to the proper future use of the land cleared. And, in 1954, the national government introduced the concept of "urban renewal," which made it possible to attempt slum *prevention* as well as slum clearance.

In these programs (and others which subsequently came into being), the basic inducement offered by the national government was money. The national government offered to bear the largest part of the costs of various housing and renewal projects in urban areas. Before such projects could be approved in Washington, local governments were required by the 1954 legislation to submit a "Workable Program," which included a "comprehensive community plan." To facilitate such planning, section 701 of the 1954 Housing Act empowered the national government to bear up to one-half of the cost of such planning work performed in smaller communities (under 25,000) or by state, metropolitan, or regional planning agencies.

As large numbers of urban communities rushed to take advantage of these national aid programs, a pattern of interaction developed which, in the absence of strong state planning agencies, appeared to be strictly national-local in character. Yet it is worth noting that none of this national legislation was designed to bypass the states, if only because it could not. The early public housing legislation was designed "to provide financial assistance to the states and political subdivisions thereof." In promoting urban redevelopment and renewal, national legislation sought to

. . . encourage the operations of such local public agencies as are established on a State, or regional (within a State), or unified metropolitan basis or as are established on such other basis as permits such agencies to contribute effectively toward the solution of community development or redevelopment problems on a State, or regional (within a State), or unified metropolitan basis.

And, while section 701 of the 1954 Housing Act authorizes direct national grants to metropolitan or regional planning agencies, planning grants to smaller communities are dependent upon the existence of a state planning agency. Indeed, such grants are made ". . . to State planning agencies for the provision of planning assistance . . ." to smaller communities.

Far from attempting to bypass the states in planning then, it is apparent that national housing and renewal legislation has assumed significant participation by the states. It is equally apparent that experience in the operation of these programs has led the national government to give increasing emphasis to state planning. Since 1959, 701 grants have been available to "State planning agencies for State and interstate comprehensive planning . . . and for research and coordination activity related thereto." Once again, the national government has

gone into the business of stimulating state planning through grants of money, this time in response to what is viewed as a local or metropolitan—rather than a national—emergency.

Several conclusions can be drawn if this historical sketch is viewed from the perspective of a state governor. It is clear, to begin with, that state planning has never been, and is not now, an exclusive concern of the state government. To the extent that governors have become involved in this activity, they have been participants in a program involving both national and local interests, justifications, and means of support. Precisely because this activity has never been exactly defined or exclusively delegated to a single governmental level, governors who choose to involve themselves in it are free to exercise considerable imagination in shaping it to their own needs or aspirations. Furthermore, this can be done at relatively small monetary cost, since the national government has agreed to bear most of the expense. How, then, have various governors used this opportunity? To give a partial answer to this question, we turn now to an examination of state planning in three states.

### STATE PLANNING IN NEW JERSEY

Although New Jersey has had a state planning agency since the early 1930's, the first twenty years of its existence were characterized by a negligible level of financial support, inadequate staffing, and a consequently poor record of significant accomplishment. With the election of Robert B. Meyner as governor in 1953, and his later appointment of Joseph E. McLean, then a Princeton University professor, as Commissioner of Conservation and Economic Development, a movement to revitalize the state planning function was launched. In 1954, Dr. Coleman Woodbury, a planning and renewal specialist, was asked to advise the state on steps that could be taken to develop and improve the state planning function. Dr. Woodbury's recommendations called for elevation of the organizational status of the state planning agency from "section" to "Bureau" in the Department of Conservation and Economic Development, securing a top-notch professional to head the new Bureau, and a functional organization of the Bureau into state, local, and metropolitan planning units. More significantly, Dr. Woodbury advised the state to take advantage of the newly-enacted section 701 of the 1954 Housing Act to enlarge and improve those parts of the state's program to which section 701 was applicable. New Jersey, he argued, should seek at least $40,000 from the national government on a matching basis for planning assistance to small communities.

In 1955 an administrative order by Commissioner McLean created the State Planning Bureau and in the same year a special appropriation of $50,000 was included in the governor's budget for an "Expanded State and Regional Planning Program." This money enabled the Planning Bureau to apply to Washington for a matching grant under the 701 program. By February, 1956, this application was approved and, when a bureau chief was hired two months later, the Bureau was in a position to begin systematic expansion of its staff.

At this point, the Planning Bureau's staff included just eight persons, only three of whom were professional planners. The $100,000 in state and national funds available to the Bureau was obviously sufficient to support considerable staff expansion, but how was this expansion to be accomplished? 701 money was designed to provide planning assistance to local communities, yet this was a *state* planning agency, with responsibilities for *state* planning as well as local assistance. National funds could not legally be used for state planning work, but if they were not so used, the state agency ran the risk of becoming simply an administrative "middle-man" between the national government and local communities.

This dilemma was resolved by the Planning Bureau's decision to work directly with a number of municipalities in preparing their master plans. Instead of simply distributing state and national money to local communities to pay for planning work done by private consultants, the state agency determined that it would act as planning consultant to selected municipalities, utilizing members of its staff to assist local planning agencies. This decision ". . . removed the Bureau from the realm of merely an administrative agency and . . . provided an additional incentive to build and maintain a professional staff." Moreover, by carefully selecting the municipalities in which there would be direct Bureau participation, the state agency was able to gather detailed information about various portions of the state which provided a solid foundation for later work on a statewide planning program.

Use of the initial 701 grant to build up a professional staff for the Bureau provided a firm organizational base within state government for this agency, based upon the widespread popularity of the new planning assistance program. The *state* planning function, however, still suffered from inattention. By March, 1957, when the second application for 701 funds—three and one half times the amount of the first grant—was submitted, the Planning Bureau had made another decision designed to give more emphasis to state planning. Where possible, local communities were encouraged to bear the full 50 per cent state share of the cost of local planning work. The willingness of most communities to use local funds for this purpose had two results: (1) the total of state-local resources available for planning work was increased, thereby permitting a request for even larger amounts from the national government on a matching basis; and (2) the State Planning Board was able to use a larger portion of the steadily increasing state appropriation for state and regional planning work.

The success of these strategic decisions was apparent in the expanded responsibilities of the Planning Bureau. By January of 1959 more than 100 New Jersey municipalities (out of 567) were participating in the planning assistance program, a regional development agency had been created in the northeastern part of the state, a demonstration study was underway financed by the national government, and state planning studies were increasing. The variety and success of such activities persuaded Bureau staff members that a review of over-all planning objectives and organization was essential in order to provide greater coordination within the framework of state development objectives. In June of 1959 the Bureau issued a report emphasizing the need for state coordination of all local, county, and regional planning and the equally important need to bring about greater coordination of the activities of all state agencies. The report did not seek to draw sharp distinctions between "local" or "regional" or "state" planning. Rather it took the position that all planning accomplished within the state had a single purpose, the orderly development of state resources, and was thus necessarily a part of "state" planning. It argued, furthermore, that only if the state government coordinated its activities could it hope to bring about orderly development within the localities and regions of the state.

After cabinet consideration and endorsement of this report, Governor Meyner created the Interdepartmental Committee on State Planning in November, 1959. Composed of representatives of each cabinet-level department, and staffed by the State Planning Agency, this group meets periodically to review capital improvement needs of the various state agencies, to discuss planning proposals, and to coordinate departmental plans in terms of state development trends and resources. Following this official endorsement of the concept of a coordinated state planning program, the state planning function increased in importance. In July of 1960 the national government approved a grant of $50,000 for state planning in New Jersey under the amended section 701 of the 1959 Housing Act. And the 1961 New Jersey Legislature once again upgraded the status of the state planning agency by constituting it as a major division within the Department of Conservation and Economic Development. Today, the Division of State and Regional Planning enjoys an annual budget of $544,000 and has a staff of some 60 persons.

Clearly, the present status of the state planning agency could not have been achieved without strong support from Governor Meyner during his eight-year tenure. It seems fair to conclude that Meyner, whose reputation for able administration was one of his chief assets while he was in the State House, viewed the development of a state planning bureaucracy as a useful device for achieving greater administrative coordination and control of state government. Since a large portion of the financial support for this bureaucracy was borne by the national government, the governor was in a position to buy a potentially powerful device at relatively little cost to the state treasury. If Meyner did not attempt to use his bureaucracy to enhance his own political prestige—and it appears that he did not—it is nevertheless true that the very act of creating an organization engaged in planning on a statewide basis has resulted in widespread public support for the organization's activities. Thus, New Jersey voters recently approved a $63 million bond issue program designed to enable the state to set aside vast areas of open space for future recreational use. Both the bureaucracy and the public support it has engendered have now been passed on to Meyner's successor, Governor Richard J. Hughes. Hughes has already expressed a strong interest in dealing with New Jersey's development problems through the state planning agency. Whatever success he has will be due in no small measure to the legacy left him by his predecessor.

STATE PLANNING IN WISCONSIN

Like New Jersey, Wisconsin has had a state planning agency in continuous existence since the early 1930's. As the national public works program lost momentum toward the end of the depression period, however, the state planning agency became less and less active. Small state appropriations through the 1940's and 1950's permitted it to administer the state planning legislation and to occasionally serve as a clearing house for information relevant to local planning agencies. But through the postwar period the very concept of planning, whether state or local, clearly was given a very low priority. Indeed, for five years after the enactment of section 701 of the 1954 Housing Act, the state refused to accept any national grants for local planning assistance.

A signal for change in this environment was given in 1958, when State Senator Gaylord A. Nelson campaigned for election as governor. During his tenure in the Senate, Nelson had become known as a strong "conservationist" and had developed a strong interest in planning as a technique for achieving greater coordination of state government activities. It was during this period, too, that Nelson developed a close relationship with David Carley, then holding a research position with the State Chamber of Commerce while completing his doctorate in political science at the University of Wisconsin. Carley had been an assistant city manager at one time and possessed what he termed a "strong urban bias." Working closely together in the campaign for the governorship, both men realized that the problems of resource conservation and urban deterioration were closely related. Accordingly, Nelson promised that if he were elected, he would create a new department in state government to deal with them on a unified basis.

Nelson's subsequent victory was followed closely by the creation of a new Department of Resource Development in 1959, and by the appointment of Carley as its first director. The new department was made up of two divisions, State Planning and Industrial Development, and was assigned broad powers in the fields of recre-

ational and natural resource development, state, regional, and local planning, and economic development. In addition, the department was authorized ". . . to apply for, accept, administer and expend grants from the federal government . . ." for planning purposes. To further complement these powers, Nelson secured amendments to the 1955 Wisconsin Regional Planning Law which assigned broad authority to the governor to become involved in the creation and operation of regional planning commissions.

Quick enactment of these measures had the twin effects of expanding the planning powers available to the governor and of consolidating them in an essentially staff agency. The use that would be made of these powers, however, was still uncertain. Nelson was intellectually committed to a strong planning and development program, but was hesitant to involve himself in a large-scale effort, partly because of what appeared to be widespread apathy toward the planning concept, and partly because of administrative hostility on the part of various state agencies. Carley, on the other hand, urged the governor to recognize the political potential of the local planning assistance program. At little or no cost, he argued, the governor could stimulate the creation of local and regional planning agencies throughout the state which would provide constituencies to support him and his program. Furthermore, he argued, an intelligent recreational development program would be impossible unless some overall priorities were established through planning.

The only way to decide the issue was to test public reaction. In several speeches made in various areas of the state, Carley put forward the concept of local and regional planning within the framework of a state plan. Public and newspaper response was immediately favorable, and the issue was resolved. "I just took the press clippings into the Governor," Carley said later, "and he began to count the votes." An application for a 701 grant was filed and

93

quickly approved. Beginning in early 1960, Nelson and Carley literally "stumped the state," visiting more than 60 communities in an effort to persuade them to create local or regional planning agencies with state and national assistance. By late 1961, after having been re-elected, Nelson was able to report that

. . . over 50 per cent of Wisconsin's entire population lives in areas that are either now actively a part of a regional planning area or have petitioned me under state statutory procedure to become so! It is clear that the public recognizes the necessity for regional planning and is fully ready to accept leadership by the state.

In the meantime Nelson was moving to secure these constituencies for himself through the medium of a ten-year, $50 million outdoor recreation and resource development program. Where other states (New York, New Jersey, and California, for example) had initiated such programs only after referendum approval of borrowing money for this purpose, Nelson proposed to finance his program from state operating revenue. Accordingly, he asked the 1961 Wisconsin Legislature to approve a cigarette tax increase to be used to finance his recreation program. Opposition was plentiful, but the legislation was carefully drawn to provide something for every portion of the state from the proposed $50 million expenditure. Constituency pressure thus built into the legislation itself was more than enough to ensure success. Despite some close victories in committees, the program was finally approved by a near unanimous vote in both houses.

The considerable success Governor Nelson has achieved in building much of his political position around the issue of state planning and development has implied continued expansion of the state planning function. In addition to the relatively huge amount that is supporting energetic work on the recreational program, $750,000 (two-thirds of which is supplied by the national government) has been obtained to

expand the local planning assistance program, and to develop a state plan and a variety of other projects related to state or regional planning, or both. Moreover, an indirect result of all this activity has been a general tightening up of the state administration. Under Nelson's direction various state departments have been called upon to contribute their expertise to various aspects of the planning work. This has resulted not only in greater inter-departmental coordination, but it has also permitted the state to count already budgeted state programs and personnel as the matching portion of national 701 grants.

In Wisconsin the opportunities inherent in the "federal" character of state planning have been used to build a political constituency for the governor, as well as a planning bureaucracy. The beauty of this approach, according to Director Carley, is that "it hasn't cost the State one penny." Furthermore, it has worked. Governor Nelson has become a politically powerful state governor. He has also become a national spokesman for more and better state planning. In a widely quoted speech before the American Institute of Planners, Nelson argued persuasively that only action by the states could solve the problem of "increased congestion accompanied by a steadily diminishing resource base." "Doing something about it," he continued, "is no longer a matter of more research and contemplation but a matter of action. Political leadership in our states can solve the problem." He later added this thought:

Much has been said over the years about the lack of federal government coordination with the states in programs of resource development. I am in full agreement with the critics of the federal government on this point. Federal policy decisions in the transportation, water and recreation fields have bypassed state considerations in most instances. However, we can only exert more influence on federal policy in these areas if we know what we want. And we cannot know what we want if our states do not prepare development plans on which to establish the bases for future social, economic and resource use decision.

## STATE PLANNING IN ILLINOIS

State planning was initially stimulated in Illinois by the State Chamber of Commerce, which undertook to survey the state's resources in 1929. Two years later the governor was authorized to appoint a State Planning Commission, but not until 1935 was an appropriation made to this agency. Utilizing staff made available through state participation in national public works programs, the Commission was able to produce a number of moderately significant planning studies, in addition to public works programming. With the termination of the national WPA projects in 1942, the Commission ceased to function and issued its Final Report in 1943. In 1944, concern over the likelihood of mass unemployment following the end of the war prompted the creation of the Post War Planning Commission. Again, the principal focus was public works programming. When the expected unemployment crisis failed to materialize, this Commission was terminated in 1949.

From 1949 to 1959 no statewide comprehensive planning agency existed in Illinois. In the latter year, the State Housing Board was given responsibility for statewide planning. Although the Housing Board sponsored two potentially important studies, it never undertook to formulate a comprehensive state planning program. The activities of this agency stand in sharp contrast to its counterparts in New Jersey and Wisconsin, especially in regard to local planning assistance. While statewide responsibility was assigned the Board in 1959, it had been the designated state agency for administration of the 701 local planning assistance program since 1955. Between 1955 and 1961, some 54 Illinois communities received national funds for local planning work. Instead of building a staff of its own to handle this program, however, the Board "farmed out" its responsibility to the Bureau of Community Planning of the University of Illinois. Working on a severely limited budget and utilizing only the part-time services of one staff member, the Bureau performed creditably, but it was clearly impossible to do much more than "administer" the funds available from the national government.

At the same time that the Housing Board was conducting its program of limited local planning assistance, the Illinois Legislature was itself developing a concern for dealing with the "metropolitan problem" in the Chicago area. In 1955 the Legislature created the Northeastern Illinois Metropolitan Area Local Governmental Services Commission and charged it with broad responsibilities for investigating and recommending changes in the activities of Chicago-area local governments. In its investigations the Commission discovered that the Chicago metropolitan area ". . . appears to have been unprepared for the service problems that have come to the area as a result of its growth." As a first step in meeting this problem the Commission recommended that an area-wide planning agency be established. With support from both the governor and the mayor of Chicago, this proposal was given legislative approval and, in 1957, the Northeastern Illinois Metropolitan Area Planning Commission came into being.

## THE LOCAL PERSPECTIVE

The development of state planning functions is directly tied to the increased urbanization of America and the growing importance of urban communities in every state. In fact, most of the new departures in intergovernmental relations have developed in an effort to respond to the problems of urban areas, including direct federal grants to localities, the use of lending devices to stimulate local governmental action, and grants for specific projects rather than for overall programs with heavy emphasis on federal approval of project details. "Local Government in Intergovernmental Perspective" identifies the various roles of local government in a system of pervasive intergovernmental cooperation. Local leaders utilize these roles to integrate outside aid into some kind of package at the local—and sometimes at the state—level. Morton Grodzins indicates how this is possible in "Local Strength in the American Federal System: The Mobilization of Public-Private Influence." The ability of the localities to become what this author has called "civil communities," combining a congeries of public and private forces to serve locally determined ends, offers us yet another view through the prism that is American federalism.

*Daniel J. Elazar*

## LOCAL GOVERNMENT IN INTERGOVERNMENTAL PERSPECTIVE

### THE AMERICAN FEDERAL SYSTEM

Local governments—rural, urban, and suburban—are part and parcel of the American federal system. As such, they and their services are inseparably linked not only with each other, but with the state and federal governments as well. Frequently a specific local governmental unit has stronger connections with its state and federal counterparts than with other adjacent local governments. Even within the same local government, a local housing authority, for example, will often be in constant contact with state and federal housing agencies and only in rare instances be in contact with the parks and recreation department located in the same building. In Illinois, most municipal departments have little to do with either the federal government or with their county governments, while the city's special agencies have usually been created for purposes of intergovernmental cooperation and have little contact with the municipal departments. . . .

As a focal point in the federal system,

local government serves in five major capacities: as acquirer of outside aid for local needs; as adapter of government functions and services to local conditions; as experimenter with new functions and services (or new twists for traditional ones); as initiator of governmental programs that spread across state and nation; and underlying them all, as a means by which a local community can pay the "ante" necessary to "sit in the game" (i.e., secure an effective voice in governmental decisions that affect it).

Though not a "state" planning agency, this Commission serves a six-county area which includes more than half of the state's population and is therefore based upon significant state participation. Eight of nineteen commission members are appointed by the governor, with the remaining places filled by the mayor of Chicago and the County Boards of Lake, Cook, Will, DuPage, Kane, and McHenry counties. The Commission is financed in part by the state and in part by contributions from local governments in the six-county area. Moreover, the Commission has authority to assist localities in their planning needs.

From Daniel J. Elazar, *Illinois Local Government* (Urbana, 1961), pp. 24–28. Reprinted by permission of the University of Illinois Press.

Thus, while not officially involved in "state" planning, the activities of the Commission are obviously relevant to the state planning function and can be influenced through action by the governor. In the period since its creation, NIMAPC has carried on a data-gathering-and-dissemination program, stimulated cooperation between local governments in the Chicago area, and promoted research in such areas as the distribution of storm water drainage basins.

By 1961 the increasingly serious problems of "depressed" areas and technological unemployment in Illinois, coupled with the availability of national aid for such areas through the new Area Redevelopment legislation, added further stimulation to state interest in planning. Significantly enough, these developments were coincident with the election of a new governor, whose campaign statements had indicated an awareness of these problems and an intention to re-structure the relationships between the several state agencies that had been created to deal with them. Adopting the view that state planning was closely related to the problem of economic growth, the new administration created a new Board of Economic Development, with broad powers to promote the economic welfare of the state and to coordinate water resource development. In addition, the new Board was designated as the official state planning agency and the responsibilities of the Housing Board were transferred to the new agency. The new Board consolidated the industrial development functions of the old Division of Industrial Development with the planning responsibilities of the Housing Board, and thus left only two agencies involved in state planning activities: the Board of Economic Development and the Northeastern Illinois Metropolitan Area Planning Commission.

The new state planning agency assumed its responsibilities in September, 1961, and began immediately to move ahead on two fronts. First, the local planning assistance program was stepped up. Within a year the number of communities applying for 701 funds was doubled. Utilizing the additional financial resources thus made available, the original skeleton staff was also doubled. Second, an application for a $1.3 million 701 grant for state planning was prepared in consultation with other state agencies and the University of Illinois. This application has now been submitted and, if approved, will permit the state to advance its planning activities in several areas, including population-economic studies, public works planning and development trends, and an all important water resources development plan. While the support of the Governor was obviously necessary to implement this activity, it is much too early to draw any conclusions regarding the uses to which it will be put.

CONCLUSION: STATE PLANNING IN FEDERAL PERSPECTIVE

The above discussion provides documentation for the proposition that the "federal" character of state planning provides a number of opportunities for the state governor who is aware of them. The chief opportunity, obviously, is money. Use of the national grant-in-aid device can enable a governor to take significant action in areas closed off to him by a shortage of state funds. Even if state funds are available, state action can be enlarged through use of the "matching" provisions of national legislation. Another, and perhaps more important, opportunity built into the federal system is the opportunity to exercise imaginative leadership. Contrary to much popular opinion, national grants-in-aid are rarely so precisely defined as to prohibit a variety of different uses in different political environments. Governors can, and do, tailor such grants to fit their own purposes.

In New Jersey, for example, Governor Meyner at first played a relatively passive role while a state planning bureaucracy was being built. When the bureaucracy achieved a sufficient amount of strength, he was able to use it to bring about greater administrative coordination within the state government. This administrative use of a planning bureaucracy should not be under-emphasized, for a wise governor can claim a good deal of credit through its use, not only within the state environment, but on a national basis as well. Thus a good deal of national legislation is stimulated by state bureaucracies working in concert with their counterparts in other states. The decision to channel 701 planning assistance through state agencies, for example, was based upon the experience of several states which had already built up strong state planning organizations.

In Wisconsin, on the other hand, Governor Nelson used the very same national planning legislation as one means of building a political constituency for himself throughout his state. Nelson's conviction that there were "votes" in the planning and development issue has been borne out. Moreover, the feedback from his political success has pushed his state planning program into areas of proposed action previously unheard of in planning circles: *state* zoning at highway interchanges and *state* design and aesthetic controls, for example. Perhaps the moral suggested by the Wisconsin experience is that, at the highest levels, "good planning" can become equated with "good politics."

The Illinois experiment in state planning, which is still very new, can move in either of these directions, or perhaps in another, completely different, direction. At the moment, Illinois has done little more than begin construction of a planning bureaucracy—a not insignificant step. Further steps will necessarily depend partly upon what the public will support, as the Wisconsin experiment demonstrates. They will depend even more, however, on the manner in which the governor chooses to act, or not act, as both the New Jersey and Wisconsin experiments demonstrate. In acting, it

seems clear that the governor of Illinois will have to work out some consistent basis of coordination between the two important agencies involved in state planning activities. Whether or not gubernatorial powers are affected depends upon the governor himself, and his use of the "federal" opportunities that are present.

### Local Government As Acquirer

The most fundamental "proof" of the noncentralized nature of American collaborative federalism lies in the role which local governments must play in order to benefit from most forms of federal and state aid. Even where such outside aid is available, the local governments must actively seek their communities' shares from the limited amount to be distributed. This means that the local governments must initiate and develop specific projects (or at the very least cooperate fully with the local initiators and developers); prepare the requisite governmental facilities; set and maintain the proper standards; and, in many cases, utilize the "multiple crack" system to campaign for their requested share at the state and federal levels.

### Local Government As Adapter

Perhaps the best example of the power of local government to adapt or modify existing programs to meet local situations is furnished by the great grant-in-aid programs. Grant programs are established to utilize the greater ability of the general government to harness the nation's wealth for public purposes, to develop a means for sharing our national wealth with some degree of nationwide equity, and to establish certain minimum nationwide standards for specific governmental services. (The same goals can be seen in state-local grant programs on a reduced scale.) What is commonly considered to be federal supervision of these programs is largely national supervision by a process of mutual accommodation. Leading state and local officials, acting primarily through their professional organizations, are in great measure responsible for formulating the very standards that federal officials then try to implement.

In addition, there exist areas of varying scope in which local officials can take discretionary action in line with local conditions, subsequent to professional formulation of nationwide standards.

If a specific situation demands adjustment and all else fails, local governments can turn to locally elected congressmen and legislators, who are, almost without exception, more responsive to local interests than central directives. The very nature of the electoral and party systems makes this so. Loose national party coalitions of state political organizations and state party dependence on locally elected representatives give local interests powerful leverage within the system. As a result, national political leaders serve as spokesmen and "watchdogs" for local (as well as state, constituent, and group) interests not only in matters concerning the grant programs, but also in fields of so-called "exclusive" federal jurisdictions—including foreign affairs. (This is generally true in state-local relations also, although it seems that the local governments have somewhat less influence, perhaps because it is a relationship within a unitary state.)

## Local Government As Initiator

This access to both federal and state governments through elected representatives and professional associations also gives local governments the power to initiate new programs and services. This power is often unused, but when an aggressive community faces a problem for which no readily available solution is apparent, it is likely to use the aforementioned connections, first to find common ground with other communities facing similar problems and, ultimately, to secure state or federal-state assistance. Probably a majority of the fed-

erally aided domestic programs, ranging from agricultural extension to urban renewal, were first conceived or originated by local governments or local government officials in much this way.

## Local Government As Experimenter

Often a program of service conceived locally is also first tested locally before larger units of government adopt it and foster it in other communities. In recent years, improved educational methods and services have been and are being developed for statewide and nationwide use after experimentation in local school systems. Many other programs in agriculture, commerce, public improvements, and public welfare, among others, have taken similar roads. The role of local government as experimenter has traditionally been an important one in the maintenance of a viable political pluralism in the United States.

## Local Government As a Means of Participating in the Governmental Process

This function of local governments within the context of American federalism underlies all the others. Although not often recognized as such, there have always been two major reasons behind the establishment of new governments in the United States. One is a desire for the greater or lesser degree of autonomy that accompanies any organized government. In local government this may mean the power to levy taxes in a special district; the power to set educational, as well as taxation, policies in a school district; municipal powers in a city, and so forth. The other is a desire to have a base of operations, a focal point, within the American governmental complex. Developing a formal base of operations is the best and easiest way for a community to gain and maintain support, money, aid, recognition, representation, or whatever its political goals might be within the system. In the language of poker, this is the way a community pays the ante required to sit in the game.

### LOCAL GOVERNMENT AND THE STATES

Although there are major formal and informal differences between federal-state-local and federal-local relations on the one hand and state-local and interlocal relations on the other, the intergovernmental questions that are raised in all four categories can be examined as questions of focus of power, acquisition of aid, adaptation of program, initiation and experimentation with services, and "ante." The major differences are that federal relations with local governments are rarely direct and even less often backed by operative coercive powers. The federal government must rely upon persuasion, contract, and, only as a last resort, withdrawal of support. The state government, on the other hand, has very definite powers of coercion since local governments are, without exception, creatures of their state, "home rule" notwithstanding.

The state government is the source and central authority for all the local governments within its boundaries (even when it comes to soil conservation districts and the like, created by the state virtually at the behest of the federal government). The legislature serves as the constituent assembly for the state's local governments, creating and defining them, limiting or extending their powers, even delimiting the possible forms of government they may adopt. In order to amend the local "constitution," it is often necessary to go to the state capital—unless the legislature has already provided for options which can be exercised locally, as in the choice of municipal governmental forms. The state even functions as a local legislature and executive in a wide variety of fields, sometimes retaining exclusive powers and sometimes sharing them with the city council or county board.

The sum of a state's constitutional and political powers within its boundaries and its constitutional position and political role within the federal system as a whole places the states at the keystone in the governmental arch. In its central position, the state serves as a stimulator of local government activities and as mediator between its local governments and Washington and, where necessary, between its local governments and other states. It is significant that this does not hold true for Chicago and cities like it. When a state government fails to fulfill its role as mediator, in this sense, the resulting vacuum leads to a serious weakening of the system. Often the states have refused to accept their role vis-à-vis the large (and not-so-large) metropolitan centers within their boundaries. The first consequences of this have been effectively to deny these great urban centers their due in terms of national concern, aid, and support. The second consequence is for these cities to develop channels of direct communication with the federal government and, insofar as is possible, to bypass their state governments. As yet this latter course has succeeded in limited areas only, but pressures are building up that may lead to radical changes in the federal system.

The problems of intergovernmental collaboration to provide public services are fundamental in a democratic federal system. They have always existed in the American federal system in substantially the same form, and certain general institutions and techniques for dealing with them have been developed in the experience of 170 years. Local governments must accommodate themselves to dealing with these problems in somewhat different ways, depending on the structural division operative in specific cases: federal-state-local (or federal-local) collaboration, state-local relationships, or interlocal accommodations.

As population pressures increase and government on all levels becomes more complex, the basic problem of intergovernmental relations is not to try to limit interaction but to transform it into the most effective collaboration possible. "Effective" in this sense means the provision of necessary services in a manner calculated to strengthen the political institutions deemed valuable in our society.

## LOCAL GOVERNMENTS IN THE FEDERAL SYSTEM

How do the local communities view this collaborative system? With a few exceptions, they do not view it with hostility. For example, local communities seek federal aid in many ways and for many purposes. City officials seek expert advice on building a jail, developing a park, or disposing of their citizens' garbage. Local businessmen seek funds for airport improvements, transfer of an old military installation for industrial development, or grants of fire-fighting equipment under the civil defense program. Civic "improvers" seek grants for urban renewal, FHA loans for community conservation, or FBI instructors to improve the quality of their local police force. It is a massive task just to list the federal aids and services available to local government—from plumbing codes to marina design to disaster relief. These federal activities in their community are not viewed locally as the forcible intrusion of a distant central government but, almost invariably, as the successful consequences of local efforts to secure federal benefits to serve local ends. These benefits are considered to be good for community and nation both. Generally, the same holds true in state-local relations.

This local view, developed over time through concrete experience rather than by abstract logic, is historically the correct one. If the system appears on the surface to be mildly chaotic, this does not mean that some order does not exist within its bounds. While every governmental plane may be involved in all governmental activities, each has its own locus of power and control that jointly provide focal points for the organization of the system.

*Morton Grodzins*

# LOCAL STRENGTH IN THE AMERICAN FEDERAL SYSTEM

### THE MIXTURE OF PUBLIC AND PRIVATE BUSINESS

Local and state governments have great strength in the American federal system. Constitutional arrangements are one source of that strength. The distribution of power within political parties is an even more important source. Measures of centralization which are constitutionally possible are politically impossible. Decisions made by the central government—to establish a federal airport program, for example—may be decentralizing decisions: the principal gainers in power are state and local, not national, institutions.

The importance and influence of the central government have vastly increased in consequence of the nation's new importance in world politics. National defense expenditures for goods and services averaged more than $43 billion annually between 1956 and 1960, some 11 per cent of the gross national product and almost 90 per cent of all federal expenditures for goods and services. Outside the defense area, national influence has blossomed as a result of Supreme Court decisions, particularly those concerning school desegregation and the apportionment of seats in the state legislatures. The size of the defense budget and the decisions of the Supreme Court are

From Morton Grodzins, "Local Strength in the American Federal System," in *Continuing Crisis in American Politics*, Marian D. Irish, ed., © 1964, pp. 132–151. Reprinted by permission of Prentice-Hall, Inc., Englewood Cliffs, New Jersey.

precisely those areas of governance farthest removed from the influence of domestic politics. But where political forces are free to act, the fear of the federal octopus is not supported by the facts. To give only one example, federal expenditures for civilian functions, expressed as a percentage of the gross national product, have *decreased* by more than 50 per cent in the last thirty years. State-local expenditures have remained almost constant (though they also show a slight decline) by this measure. And state-local expenditures for civilian functions during the recent years have been roughly six times central government expenditures for those purposes.

This essay is concerned with one facet of state-local strength in the federal system: the mobilization of public-private influence at the local level for the purpose of influencing national programs. Interest group theory, in the literature of political science, assigns an important role to voluntary groups. The aggregate of group interests, it is argued, becomes national policy and, indeed, the national interest. But voluntary groups do not only influence governments for their own private interests. The literature largely overlooks the fact that they also work on behalf of governments.

It should come as no surprise that private and public purposes often become completely intertwined; or that a public function in one place may be private in another; or that in a given community there may be an easy substitution of public and private responsibilities. Not more than four centuries ago in Europe even tax collecting and the armed forces were in private hands. Within the memory of living men, aid for the indigent in the United States was thought of as almost exclusively a matter of charity, a private virtue and a private responsibility.

Some confusion exists in distinguishing the public from the private sphere even for central portions of both. But a determination is in most cases possible. The manufacturer of steel who has important govern- ment contracts, for example, may convince both himself and others that his first concern is the national defense. In some larger sense, especially during crises which threaten the fate of the nation, the public concern of the industrialist can be taken at its face value. Nevertheless, for most of the group in noncrisis periods (and for some even in crisis), private ends have primacy. Profits, dividends to stockholders, and responsibilities to employees are paramount values. Similarly, officers of the Department of Defense have many obligations to the private sector of the economy. Their programs are carried out with the advice of business advisory groups, and they must always be sensitive, for economic as well as political reasons, to the need for balancing defense purchases among large and small businesses and among the various regions of the nation. But their primary business is the public business of maintaining the nation's armed strength. The mixture of the public and private in these "pure" cases suggests that the distinction becomes greatly blurred in cases that are not so pure. This is so. At the local level, private groups perform public functions, and public offices are used for private purposes.

PRIVATE GROUPS DOING PUBLIC BUSINESS

The mixture of public and private spheres can be seen with great clarity on the local scene. Local influence on national programs is exercised by bringing to bear on national officers the combined weight of the public and private sectors. Where the public-private linkage is strong and where its strength is utilized, local influence over federal activities on the local scene is maximized.

Private groups are involved, and often play a dominant role, in a wide assortment of public, local activities. Private schools, including parochial schools, are an obvious example of the substitution of private for public services. Here public and private facilities exist in parallel, performing roughly identical tasks. In other cases, private contributions are used to initiate, enlarge, or enrich the public program. The recreation program of a small Arizona town exemplifies this relationship. The Rotary Club was the principal force behind a drive to secure federal land for a large mountain park, and Rotary funds were used in payment for the land conveyed to the city. The city swimming pool was secured through the joint efforts of the Lions, Rotary, and other civic groups, and the same cooperation was responsible for building a Scout Lodge on city-owned land.[1]

In still other cases there are complete amalgams of the public and private spheres. The private groups retain their separate, legal identities but become institutionalized as a unified arm of the government. Many health and welfare departments take this form. To cite only one example, a number of Michigan counties operate public health services through city-county Visiting Nurse Association departments. The Visiting Nurse Association is a private organization deriving its income from private donations and the Community Chest. It maintains its private character, but it has become an integral part of the official health department. Similar amalgamations can be found over a wide range of activities. Fire departments in many small towns are operated by private volunteer organizations, with equipment frequently furnished out of public funds. Hospitals in the largest cities provide services to indigent patients through a combination of public funds, medical association cooperation, private university staffing, aid from women's clubs, and do-

nations of time and skill by private practitioners. Local libraries, museums, and parks often represent the same combination of public and private resources.

In many cases the private groups make important public decisions, later ratified by public bodies. An observer in an Arkansas town remarked that the local Chamber of Commerce handled "virtually all new projects" for the city. "Anything that must be tested before the city council will formally risk committing itself is handled through the Chamber." Once a program is proved worthy of official city acceptance, it is taken off the Chamber's hands. Paul Ylvisaker has said that in Mankato, Minnesota (the largest community in Blue Earth County), the Chamber of Commerce, the Junior Chamber, the Builders' Exchange, and the Manufacturers and Wholesalers Association constituted an "economic legislature." "Here are staged the preliminary, and in many cases the decisive, debates on such issues as whether the commercial zone of the city is to extend more than a block and a half up from Front Street, whether and at what expense the state's postwar planning council should be invited to conduct a local economic survey, whether certain business practices are to be condoned. . . ."

In a number of areas private organizations performing public services directly assume important intergovernmental responsibilities. Welfare activities of veterans' organizations provide a case in point. Each of the veterans' groups maintains a nationwide network of "service officers" whose function is to aid veterans to qualify for federal and state benefits. Where the veterans' groups are strongly organized, their service officers are very active indeed. Under these circumstances an officer of a private club in effect acts as the local representative of a vast federal (and a more modest state) welfare program, and simultaneously represents local constituents in pressing their claims before federal and state administrators. This is an important

The examples could be multiplied indefinitely. In many places individual businessmen have an important role in recreational programs. In a Georgia city the basketball leagues are sponsored by one of the largest businesses; Little League baseball groups by the local bank, a mill, and the Rotary Club; teenage baseball by the Veterans of Foreign Wars, and teenage dances by the Women's Club, utilizing the American Legion clubhouse. The town stadium was built by an ad hoc group drawing membership from many civic and business groups. The town square and the courthouse yard were landscaped and maintained by the Women's Club, and plans for new parks in the city were made by a private utility company.

adjunct to the more widely publicized lobbying activities of the veterans' groups.

For example, the American Legion service officer of a small town in DuBois County, Indiana, has done this work for more than twelve years. He is a specialist in veterans' benefits, a private public servant of experience and competence. His aim is to be certain that veterans in his community make maximum use of the special services available to them. These have included a state bonus and federal pension, disability compensation, aid to widows and orphans, and funds for hospitalization, medical appliances, educational training, insurance, and burial. The officer does not consider it desirable to forward claims for every veteran who comes to him for aid. He feels free on the basis of his experience to tell inquirers that their claims will not be allowed and to advise them not to prepare formal applications. In so doing he exercises greater discretion than many government field officials usually do.

The service officer estimates that he spends a minimum of ten hours a week on his social welfare activities. He has in a decade's work processed more than 2300 claims and interviewed more than 3000 veterans or their widows—an impressive record of services rendered. A considerable private bureaucracy at central points is needed to handle business of this volume, and the Indiana Department of the American Legion has fifteen full-time people in the Indianapolis office working on veterans' benefit problems. Moreover, the Legion places its own personnel in the Washington office of the Veterans Administration to act as expediters and as liaison persons between the public and the private bureaucracies.

The other veterans' organizations maintain parallel national networks for the private administration of the public welfare services. In DuBois County the Veterans of Foreign Wars and the Disabled American Veterans are active. The effectiveness of American Legion service officers in the county has led the other groups to refer their "cases" to the Legion. In difficult matters, nevertheless, the VFW service officer will take an active role in soliciting aid from the local congressman. In other places the rivalry of the service organizations in the public welfare field precludes this sort of cooperation.

The collaboration in DuBois County among the private organizations engaged in veterans' welfare work is matched by collaboration between private and public officers. No local government in the county has any official responsibility for veterans' affairs despite the fact that Indiana, like many other states, makes it possible to spend county funds for a veterans' service officer. The post has not been filled in DuBois County, partly because of the efficiency of the Legion services and partly because cooperation between the private veterans' groups does not extend to an agreement on who should be named to the official post. The county, therefore, does not duplicate Legion veterans' activities. But the Legion service officer and county welfare workers nevertheless find themselves working on many common problems. The exchange of information, and referral of persons by one service to the other, is continuous, easy, and informal. The cooperative circle extends beyond the specialized boundaries of welfare activities. For example, the mayor of one of the towns in the county, acting as municipal judge, became irked at the continued necessity of sending a mentally deficient veteran to the county jail (usually at the request of the veteran's wife). The mayor-judge requested that the veterans' service office find some way to help. Once an application to the Veterans Administration was filed by the service officer on behalf of the veteran, the mayor continued his good offices by writing to the local congressman to insure, as he put it, that the application received "fast and fair treatment."[2]

[2]Discussion of the welfare activities of the veterans' organizations in DuBois County is based upon the field notes of Douglas St. Angelo. See his unpublished doctoral dissertation, *Local Impact Upon Federal Programs*, University of Chicago, Department of Political Science, 1960.

PUBLIC BUSINESS FOR PRIVATE GAIN

In many cases where private groups perform public business, private advantage is apparent. The service functions of the American Legion are clearly aimed at bringing advantages to Legion members and, by no means incidentally, at strengthening the Legion itself. Sponsorship by the Farm Bureau of extension service activities is a well known example of a similar amalgamation of public and private purposes. And when a Chamber of Commerce assumes leadership for a local function, it is often possible to see in the short or long run some special advantage to the business groups concerned. Nevertheless it is important to distinguish these cases from those in which private business firms perform public services directly for private gain. Here the profit is immediate and the result of contractual obligations assumed by the local government in return for service received.

All localities at one time or another must take advantage of the special skills and competences of engineering and legal firms, planning and survey organizations, and private specialists in public finance and other fields. In the larger local governments — New York and Chicago, for example — the scale of operations is large, specialization is possible, and experts are employed within the government on a full-time basis. Specialists under contract are utilized as an adjunct to the official administrative group.

For the smaller local governments many special competences are not available at all within the official staffs. This personnel gap is often filled by professional associations of government workers. Organizations such as the American Municipal Association, the International Association of City Managers, and the Federation of Tax Administrators are an important source of technical assistance and advice over a wide range of activities. Private nationwide organizations, such as the National Board of Fire Underwriters, may play the same role.[3]

And in all states, official state agencies supply technical aid to localities over a variety of fields. The University of Arkansas, for example, serves as a technical advisor to localities applying to the federal government for urban planning grants. The University also provides personnel for utilizing grants once they are received by local governments. In a number of states — North Carolina, Tennessee, New Jersey, and New York are good examples — a considerable range of services is offered local governments by state agencies. In a very large number of cases, however, localities turn to private organizations for technical services, another incidental demonstration of the easy substitution of the private for the public. Frequently private firms do not simply furnish an adjunct to local skills; rather, they constitute the local government's total specialized staff.

A convenient example is provided by Casa Grande, Arizona, a desert town of fewer than 10,000 population, on one of the main highways between Phoenix and Tucson. In Casa Grande a private engineering firm has in effect become the city's planning and construction agency and simultaneously one of its chief avenues of influence in shaping national and state programs to local purposes. The process by which Casa Grande secured its sewage treatment plant illustrates how this relationship operates. Casa Grande built a badly needed sewage plant by obtaining a construction grant from the United States Public Health Service and by receiving a loan, covered by a special bond issue, from the Housing and Home Finance Agency. The private engineering firm was responsible for negotiating both the grant and the loan.

The possibility in the first place that Casa Grande was eligible for this federal aid was made known to city officials by a leading

[3]The National Board of Fire Underwriters is a unique private organization doing public business. Through its activities in establishing fire insurance rates, it is in effect a tax levying body. Later publications of the University of Chicago's Federalism Workshop will analyze the various roles of voluntary professional associations in the American government.

engineering firm. In its original contract with the city the engineering company agreed to perform necessary field surveys; prepare plans, specifications, bidding and contract documents; provide a complete inspection for all work done under the project; and, most important, prepare a project application for the proposed work for submittal to the state Department of Health and the United States Public Health Service. Once the contract was approved by the mayor and city council of Casa Grande, the entire task of securing the sewage disposal plant for the city was in the hands of the private company, although city officers were kept fully informed and were called upon occasionally for aid.

The engineering firm was in direct contact with the state and federal agencies concerned. It submitted directly to the State Department of Health the elaborate federal form justifying the grant-in-aid to the city. The state agency had only to certify that the project was constructed in accordance with state approved plans and specifications, and transmit the application to the regional office of the United States Public Health Service. After state approval of the application was secured, the firm continued direct negotiation with the officers of the Public Health Service. Well before official word concerning the grant was received by the city, an officer of the company was able to inform the city manager that he had been advised unofficially that the federal grant had been approved.[4]

The Public Health Service grant could not be completed until arrangements were made for financing the city's share of the sewage plant's cost. While managing the grant application for the sewage plant itself, officers of the engineering firm simultaneously steered the local money-raising effort. They did this by securing aid from another federal program, administered by the Housing and Home Finance Agency, and by mobilizing further private assistance for the city. This assistance was provided by an investment securities firm which acted as fiscal agents of the city in the issuance of the sewage approvement bonds, and by a law firm which gave the necessary legal advice for the proposed bond elections. The engineering company recommended both the legal and the investment companies to city officers.

Just as the private engineering firm had previously taken full responsibility for justifying the Public Health grant, so it supplied all technical information to the Housing and Home Finance Agency. The city's only role was to have the mayor fix his signature to the loan application form. A technical assessment of the city's financial ability to service the loan was at the same time provided the federal agency by the investment securities firm. Once the preliminary loan application had been approved by the Housing and Home Finance Agency, the engineering firm completed the final application and sent it directly to the federal agency, a copy being sent to Casa Grande. This was a technical document, more than forty pages in length. Officers of the engineering and investment firms visited the Housing and Home Finance Agency in order to work out an arrangement for the bond purchase. When officers of the engineering firm were informally given notice that the Public Health Service had approved the basic grant, they pushed hard by wire and telephone for quick approval of the bond arrangement so that there would be no possibility of the grant being lost because of delays in the bond financing.

The private firms were also active on the local scene, managing all arrangements for the necessary special bond election. For example, the investment securities firm supplied the city with all the needed forms including poll lists, tally lists, challeng

---

[4]Federal officials were scrupulous in dealing with the city through the State Department of Health. When a medical officer of the Public Health Service, for example, desired further information on the sewage disposal plant, he sent his inquiry to the State Health Department, which submitted it to the city manager of Casa Grande, who in turn transmitted the inquiry to the engineering firm. The firm was less formal. It replied directly to the state, keeping the city informed through a carbon copy of the response. Officers of the engineering firm followed this up by a direct visit to the field office of the federal agency.

lists, and signs warning that electioneering could not take place too near the polling place. The attorneys supplied the city council with the actual text of the bond resolution and provided the mayor with the text for his official announcement of the bond election. When the special election issue was approved, the bond attorneys (in cooperation with the engineering firm) provided all the technical information needed to support the offering and call for bids; and the engineering firm (in cooperation with the investment company) drafted the city ordinance establishing a sewer-rate schedule to provide income for the repayment of the bonds. Finally the investment security firm supplied the Housing and Home Finance Agency with all the relevant technical information needed by that agency before it could approve purchase of the city's bonds; and the private firms collaboratively then produced a long list of documents that were required by the Housing Agency before the actual purchase of the bonds could take place.[5]

This sort of service to localities by private firms is exceedingly widespread, although existing data do not make it possible to provide exact calculations of its importance in comparison with projects managed by localities themselves. The engineering firm which handled Casa Grande's affairs was one of the largest in Arizona, and a major fraction of its business was with state and local governments. Similar firms exist in other states, some highly specialized in school or road matters, some having wider scope. In Chicago a private engineering and consulting firm has had primary responsibility for constructing the mammoth airport facilities at O'Hare Field. In Arkansas, private organizations give cities and towns precisely the same sort of services described for Casa Grande in Arizona.

A number of private engineering and construction firms have departments whose sole responsibility is to encourage local governments to take advantage of existing state and national programs. In some places this service extends to bringing together citizens for the formation of special ad hoc governments to improve electrical, road, drainage, irrigation or other services. The private firms are then able to solicit funds and perform work for the very governments they helped to establish.

PUBLIC OFFICERS AND THE PUBLIC-PRIVATE
MIXTURE

Private, quasi-governmental, and governmental areas shade so imperceptibly into each other that even public officials cannot distinguish among them. Local officers believe they are serving public purposes when promoting private interests. At least they find it convenient to act as if they did; and in many cases they would not be returned to office if they tried to draw sharp lines of separation.

Simple cases of public support for private and quasi-public activities are those in which public funds are involved. The budget of a county or a city, for example, may contain appropriations for a humane society, a children's aid group, a tourist association, a Chamber of Commerce, a 4-H Club, a soldiers' burial fund, a family operated museum, a poultry society, and an agricultural fair.[6] A step removed from the cases of outright donations are those in which departments of a local government (or officers of those departments) are enrolled as active members of private or quasi-private organizations. Chambers of Commerce benefit frequently from this type of relationship.

The activities of locally elected officers, like the "case work" of congressmen and senators, often illustrate the public-private

[5]In effect, the Housing and Home Finance Agency asked the city (through its private consultants) to supply justification for the sewage disposal plant very much like the original justification that was necessary for the Public Health Service. In addition there was required a classification of laborers and mechanics, their minimum hourly rates, certification by trade unions that the prevailing wage rates were being met, complete plans and contract documents for construction, and the actual forms for contract advertisements, instruction to bidders, forms of the contract, forms of the bid bond, forms of performance and payment bond, and a long list of additional technical data.

[6]State budgets, as well as the federal government's, are used for analogous purposes.

107

mixture. The mayor of Chicago traveled to Washington in February 1959 with a pocketful of problems to present to federal officers. He wanted increased aid for public housing, and he wanted the federal government to provide insurance on home mortgages for persons displaced by slum clearance projects. But his primary aim was to seek from defense department officials top priority for new defense contracts for the Ford Motor Company's aircraft engine factory in Chicago. The mayor explained that he wanted to obtain additional work for the Ford plant because layoffs there had resulted from cutbacks in defense spending. His concern was not with what the cutbacks were doing to the nation's defense, over which he could have no comprehensive view, but rather with the unfortunate effects they were having on employment in Chicago.

Similarly, local prosperity and not national defense was the primary issue when Mayor George Christopher of San Francisco was charged by a political rival with having lost a valuable naval installation for the city. The mayor, his critic said, was "at fault for not sending a lobbyist to Washington, D.C., as we asked him to do. . . ." The mayor's response was to indicate that he would be his own lobbyist. He released a letter he had written to the senior senator from California in which he asked for a conference with "the highest officials of the Department of Defense" to discuss the city's future as a defense center. He said he would try to work out "a formula for the equitable distribution of shipbuilding and ship repair, along with other defense facilities, in this highly important strategic area."[7]

These are typical examples of public officers laboring for mixed public-private purposes. In such circumstances the private interests concerned, of course, collaborate. Energies are merged for a common end that can be designated either public or private, depending only upon the perspective from which it is viewed. For example, when it became known in Borger, Texas, shortly before World War II, that the federal government was expanding facilities to produce synthetic rubber, city officials and the managers of the city's largest industries were at one in believing that it would be wholly desirable to locate a new rubber manufacturing plant near Borger. The city was in an advantageous position because it was located close to a deposit of natural gas, a principal ingredient of synthetic rubber, and because a basic industrial complex, including large refineries, was already located nearby. Yet a number of other oil and natural gas centers were competing for the synthetic rubber factories, and it was by no means certain that one would be located in or near Borger. Officials of the city, civic club leaders, and businessmen joined forces to fight for the plant. In the words of the city manager, "all of us worked like the devil, and [Senator] Tom Connally worked right along with us." The city manager, in company with officers of the petroleum corporation which would operate the plant, made a number of trips to Washington. City officials realized that their work benefited the petroleum company. Then and afterward, they were also sure that success in locating the plant near their town was of first civic importance. "It brought us some problems, but it also brought us a lot of new residences and a lot of our prosperity."

The extreme case of the public-private mixture occurs when a single person cannot tell at a given moment whether he performs a public or a private service. In Texas a number of cities have official Boards of City Development. Board members in Borger were appointed automatically by the city council on the nomination of the local Chamber of Commerce, and the secretary of the Chamber was automatically named manager of the Board of City Development. In this way fifteen leading businessmen of the city were given official advisory posts

[7]*San Francisco Chronicle*, January 13, 1959. But on February 4, 1959, it was announced that San Francisco was sending a full-time lobbyist to Washington, D.C.

in the city government. Moreover, the Chamber of Commerce in 1958 received half its total budget by a direct subvention from the city in the form of an appropriation to the official Board of Development. It was hard to say whether the city paid the Chamber to do the city's work, whether the city paid for the private activities of the Chamber, or whether the Chamber made a contribution of labor and time to the city for public purposes.

All three were true, and they were true of many individual actions by many persons. The Chamber, for example, was responsible through its paid staff for developing the sidewalk and sewer programs of the city. Sidewalks were built only if 50 per cent of the homeowners on a given block agreed to pay the cost, at which time all owners could be assessed. Chamber staff members drummed up the needed support. Even more significantly, a given individual simultaneously represented the private Chamber of Commerce and the public Development Board in matters involving the state and federal governments. Representations were made (before federal agencies) to increase postal services and to extend airline services and (before state agencies) to build a colosseum just outside the city limits. In all such matters, a community spokesman truthfully could say that he represented both the Chamber and the city; if pressed, he could not distinguish one role from the other. It was even impossible to determine at any given moment whether a representative of Borger was spending private or public funds. The Chamber secretary and Development Board manager explained:

I go to Washington to testify before the Civil Aeronautics Board as a representative of this city. I don't know until I come back whether my trip will be charged to Chamber [private] or Development Board [public] funds. What difference does it make? They are used for the same purpose. I see which of the funds has more liquid cash in it. Then I charge my trip to the one that can take the item most easily.

## THE PUBLIC ROLE OF PRIVATE GROUPS

The dependence of local governments upon civic organizations for the performance of public functions is in some cases the simple result of official caution or official ineptitude.[8] And the incentive of private firms is clear: it is profit. What is less simple and less clear is more important for understanding the operation of the American system of government.

*First*, the sponsorship of public activities by civic and social groups provides the local community the means for trying out politically what otherwise might not be tried at all. If private sponsorship proves successful, the public body often assumes responsibility with minimum risk of political penalty.

*Second*, private civic sponsorship also gives the people of a community a sense of molding activities to their own specifications. This is particularly true in large national programs, like that of veterans' welfare services: one can go to his friend at the grocery store or the freight office and there find personal aid in matters involving complicated forms and distant Washington offices. The services of government are thus translated into very human and very personal terms.

*Third*, the network of public services maintained by private groups represents in some measure savings to public treasuries. A clear case is the failure of DuBois County to appoint an official veterans' service officer. It is true for many other private-public services. The Community Chest budget of any large city may include *lagniappe* items such as summer camps that might be deemed inappropriate for public treasuries in some (but not all) local communities. But such private budgets contain many items — hospital and welfare services, for example — that would undoubtedly become

[8]This accounts for the important role played by the Community Club in the upstate New York community of Springdale, according to Arthur J. Vidich and Joseph Bensman, *Small Town in Mass Society* (Princeton: Princeton University Press, 1958), pp. 130–31.

charges against a public budget if they were not supported by privately-collected funds.[9]

*Fourth*, from the private side, the public-private mixture plays an important legitimating role. For civic groups it provides purpose and status. For individuals it rectifies what in other circumstances might be deemed improper. A businessman seeking special consideration from a federal agency may have less need for aggressiveness when he can in truth say he is also performing a public service. But if he must be demanding, he can be so with relative impunity when accompanied by city officials who argue that what the businessman wants is what the city needs.

*Fifth*, the firms for profit supply the expertise and sophistication needed for the planning and execution of large and complex governmental programs. They are a supplementary arm of local governments — like state agencies in some programs, like professional associations in others — that make it possible for localities to deal expertly and aggressively with the state and federal governments. "What the engineering firm did for us on the sewage disposal system," said the city manager of Casa Grande, "We could not possibly have done for ourselves." From this point of view the private firms are substitutes for the civil servants and other professional workers of larger governments. They aid in balancing the scale of power, particularly the power of knowledge and of specialization, between small and large local governments and between units of the federal system.

*Sixth*, the specialized knowledge is also utilized as a means of communication. The *Federal Contributions* manual of the Civil Defense Administration is a large and cumbersome set of regulations, resembling a big-city phone book in size, and reads partly like a legal, partly like an engineering text. City officials, especially those in smaller places, have neither the time nor the skill to make full use of it. Salesmen for electronic manufacturing firms are of first importance in bringing possible federal contributions to the notice of local officers.[10] The private engineering firm serving Casa Grande was assiduous in pointing out forms of federal and state aid to local officers in Arizona. Municipal officials of Casa Grande were informed in the first place by that firm of the existence and availability of a number of federal grants from which the city has profited. Other firms in other fields in other states perform the same communications function.

*Seventh*, knowledge and specialization, given impetus by the desire for profit, are powers of persuasion. The typical contract provides no payment to the private firm unless the grant applied for is received, the bonds are sold, or the facility is built. Considerable investments, especially investments of time, are made in the early stages of any federal contract, and these investments have to be protected by a high percentage of successes. This is a strong spur to the private firm to render rapid and professionally competent work that will stand the scrutiny of federal inspection. It also enlists the private firms in campaigns for winning approval of local proposals. The process is a simple and natural one. It is abetted by the easy professional ties that exist between federal and private lawyers, engineers, school specialists, and financial experts. They talk the same language. A phone call or a cocktail conversation can settle in a few moments a problem that

[10]A city manager of a small midwestern town told an interviewer that he had received a two-way radio system from the CAA "by courtesy of the General Electric Company." The manager said that "the GE salesman told me about the program and filled in all the forms." The interviewer noticed that the radio was made by the Motorola Company. "Sure," said the manager, "that poor GE fellow did all the work and was then underbid by Motorola. But it was still his idea." During World War II the Office of Price Administration carried on an elaborate information program to keep butchers informed of rationing and price changes. But a study revealed that butchers hardly ever utilized the official publications. They acted upon information received from their wholesalers.

[9]It may be true that the total *social* cost would be less for the same services if they were entirely supported by public funds and entirely administered by public officials. This might, for example, reduce costs of duplicating personnel for both fund raising and administration. Assuming this to be true does not negate the point made in the text. Year to year budgetary savings for public bodies are not inconsistent with larger total public-private costs.

might go unsolved for months if it followed the official channel from federal to state to local officer to private consultant and then back up the chain.

Finally and most importantly, the civic groups, local officials and firms-for-profit come together at this point of persuasion. Working as a single unit for a single purpose they utilize all possible avenues for fostering the local program. They can speak with the voice of the Chamber of Commerce at one moment, the Rotary at another, the City Council at a third, the expert engineer at a fourth. They can present their cause at a congressional hearing, a public meeting, or an administrative conference; and although the cause is one, the local voices are varied for maximum effectiveness. If a congressman needs persuading, a friend of the congressman will phone or wire him. If a conference in a senator's office will expedite matters, someone in the nexus of public-civic-private relationships can be found to make such a conference possible and effective.

In sum, the public activities of civic groups and business firms strengthen the position of local governments, especially small local governments, *vis-à-vis* the state and federal governments. As the local government's equivalent of a professional, specialized civil service, the firms-for-profit play the principal role. As a powerful lobbying aid at all administrative and legislative points, the civic and social groups are most prominent.

THE STRENGTH OF THE MOBILIZED COMMUNITY
FRONT

The mobilized locality is very strong indeed. A single small city can win significant concessions from both state and federal officials in establishing personnel standards for the administration of public assistance programs. Local insistence not only maintained in office a person formally without qualifications for his job; it also led to the alteration of state merit standards in order to qualify the unqualified local in-

cumbent, as well as to the approval of this change by federal officials.

When a federal agency decided for economy reasons to close a field office in a city of 49,000, local officials and businessmen mobilized in protest. They were able to bring together for a final conference an assistant secretary of one of the great federal departments, four congressmen and spokesmen for three others, and spokesmen for two senators. The decision was made to keep the office open. When it was announced that a link of the national highway system was to run through Hillcrest, an unincorporated suburb of Binghamton in upper New York State, residents of the community first asked themselves in despair, "What chance do we have against the State Department of Public Works and the United States Bureau of Public Roads?" They discovered that their chances were very good indeed. The local citizens established a protest group that included representatives of the Rotary and the Kiwanis, a number of churches, the American Legion, the PTA, the Town Board, the Board of Education, the Children's Home, several garden clubs, and a general community association. Leaders of this group were soon in touch with the local congressmen, the state senator, the appropriate state and district engineering officers, civil defense authorities, local planning boards, and other officials. "We kept Albany and the Washington Bureau of Public Roads and our legislators at all levels apprised of what we were doing." When their request that the highway be built at another place was initially rejected, the group simply redoubled its efforts. An impartial expert was employed, the local congressmen and both New York senators were again contacted, and over a thousand signatures, telegrams, and letters appealed to Governor Harriman. The state senator arranged a meeting between community leaders and the Superintendent of the State Department of Public Works. Subsequently, a new routing of the highway was established.

Many more examples could be given. The

mobilized community—in which the private and public spheres act as one—is potent far beyond numbers. It takes full advantage of the openness of the political system, operating through diverse channels and hitting many points of the legislative-administrative process. In short, it makes use of what I have called the "multiple crack." The mobilized community capitalizes on the regard of the legislative member for the local constituency, a regard that must be maintained if the legislator is to remain in office. It can be obdurate and badger an administrative official, knowing that the local congressmen are watchdogs of any administrative affront to local interests.

VARIATIONS IN LOCAL INFLUENCE

Evidence of the strength of the mobilized locality in influencing state and federal programs is of course no evidence of absolute local control over those programs. Full consideration of limitations on, and variations in, local power would have to consider that local strength in national affairs varies markedly from program to program. Local control over the many projects of the United States Army Corps of Engineers is maximized by virtue of the Corps' definition of its mission, its relationship to Congress, and its procedures for determining what to do. Though local influence is not inconsiderable with respect to foreign policy, the nature and extent of that influence is of a different and lesser order than is true with respect to most domestic areas. Furthermore, some localities have greater power than others in state and federal legislatures (here rural local governments have an advantage); some places have greater influence than others in the election of chief executives (the big cities are at a relative advantage in affecting the presidency, and urban areas in general are becoming more powerful in governors' offices); and certain kinds of cities have natural alliances with national interest groups (for example, the NAACP and Chi-

cago's mayor are not likely to take opposite stands on any major issue). The effectiveness of any particular city in promoting or opposing a given federal action is likely to be affected by such larger considerations.

On the other hand, the issue of party is not likely to be controlling. A mobilized community, by definition, is one in which public-private proponents from both parties are involved. Aid from congressmen and senators follows as a matter of course. If the community majority and a crucial congressman or senator are of the same party (and faction), the city's cause may be aided. But party congruence is by no means necessary. A congressman is likely to work very hard for a community in which he does not have a majority of votes; he sees an opportunity to win new friends. So partisanship gives way before community programs that cut across party lines, a process made easier by the relative lack of definition in party lines.

The degree of community mobilization produces the chief variations in local influence on federal programs. Where local leaders are skillful in producing community consensus, where they understand the political resources of the united public-private front, where they can exploit the sensitivity to local demands by national legislators and administrators, localities have maximum power. Success is easier where there is substantial social and political homogeneity. Again, this gives advantage to the smaller and more rural places where, if actual homogeneity does not exist, dissidents at least are not likely to be noisy. Larger urban places suffer in this game because of their lack of consensus (the urban masses, it turns out, are not a mass but a highly differentiated social structure). When a community loses in a contest of strength with a federal agency, it often turns out, on closer inspection, that the community is splintered. Such a situation not only decreases its strength but gives federal officials an opportunity to reward friendly factions and punish unfriendly ones. An apparent local defeat is, therefore, often a victory for one local group. Where local groups are united and determined, defeat is unlikely.

## CONCLUSIONS

This essay has attempted to show some of the many overlaps between public and private spheres at the local level and demonstrate the importance of the public-private linkage in giving strength to local governments in their relationships with the federal government. There are three concluding observations.

First, the power of the mobilized community (or group of communities) is the power of those who feel strongly about a given matter and are willing to work for it. Yet the widespread understanding among localities that the system may operate to their special advantage cuts in two directions. On the one hand, acting upon that understanding often gives them what they want. On the other hand, it sets up numerous competing influence sources. If every individual locality, and every group of localities, and every group of officers serving localities were well organized to exercise influence on national programs, the influence of any single place or group would thereby be diminished. Special privileges are readily available only if the knowledge and skill necessary to achieve them are relatively limited. Widespread sensitivity to what localities may accomplish with respect to federal programs means, in effect, that the special influence of one locality or one group of localities is continuously checked by the influence of others. The wealth of the nation is such that accommodations to many special requests are possible. At the very least, attempts to satisfy competing special interests have the effect of freeing the hands of those who have broader views. The competition of special interests makes it easier to assert and implement a more general interest.

Second, local communities, even assuming maximum skill in mobilizing the public-private spheres, do not always win. But they are full and powerful partners in the process of decision-making. In most programs at most times some group of localities (or a single one) exercises a substantial influence. The fact of local influence has more meaning to the local leaders concerned than the fact of federal financing or general federal rule-making. From this perspective many federal programs may be considered local programs. The sense of substantial participation and the fact of substantial influence are everywhere apparent.

Finally, the data illustrate the falsity of the rhetoric of local-federal conflict. Though local communities gird themselves to mold federal programs to their desires, federal agencies are themselves organized to make this process an easy one. The two planes of government are not adversaries. They serve the same people for the same ends. If local advantage occasionally means national disadvantage, the congruence of advantages is far more frequent. (There is even a national interest in the pork barrel.) "Victory" for the locality, among those most concerned, is rarely conceived as national "defeat." The Public Health Service did not grant funds grudgingly to Casa Grande for a sewage disposal plant. National and local officers toasted each other when Chicago's application for a large urban renewal program was approved by the Housing and Home Finance Agency.

The traditionally described three-level American government is in fact telescoped on the community. From the point of view of the local consumer of governmental products, the American system of government is not a pyramid, but a range of services sometimes supplementary and sometimes duplicative but rarely alternative. No logic can distinguish between the local character of government's services and the non-local character of another's. The federal government has built city halls for many cities and has paid for tearing down slums in others. It provides for the health of new mothers. It draws plans for the best land use for a poor farmer and supplies funds for the construction of a vast manufacturing plant to a multimillion-dollar corporation. It constructs schools here and libraries there. It aids one community in drawing up a city plan, supplies a second with funds to build a sewer, gives a park to a third, and provides expert advice to the police chief of a fourth when the hardware store is robbed. Federal activities of this sort are as close to the citizen as any activities of the states and localities, however closeness may be defined. They are also close to local citizens because, by the process of public-private mobilization, they are substantially controlled by those citizens. The typical situation is one in which all governments participate in given activities. To deny the local character of federal activities one would be forced to deny the local character of local governments. Closeness to the citizen is an attribute of all American governments. Local is as local does.

## CIVIL RIGHTS

The structures and processes of intergovernmental cooperation are brought together in the solution of governmental problems and in the implementation of governmental programs. In the last analysis a political system is judged by whether it can meet problems and provide the programs which its sovereign demands. In the American system, where the people are sovereign and, at the very least, judge of their governors, the test of governmental effectiveness is rarely based on theoretical principles of governmental organization, but rather on the practical consequences of efforts to execute public policy. Because of the pervasiveness of federalism, every program undertaken by government in the United States could be examined as a problem in federalism. Here, we can only examine the variations in intergovernmental collaboration in three fields: civil rights, education, and water resource development.

The first field, civil rights, is one which has been consistently and perennially marked by hostility rather than cooperation; it is the one area in which the sharing system is not generally recognized. The deep divisions between the South and the other sections of the country on this issue have been translated, on several occasions in American history, into a conflict between the nation and the states. The South, as the embattled section, has consequently relied upon the existence of the states to legitimize and promote a policy of segregation while the overwhelming majority of northerners and westerners have turned to the federal government with equal consistency to legitimize and promote a legal policy of equal rights for all citizens.

Despite the obvious element of conflict generated by the civil rights issue, there still is a marked degree of partnership in handling civil rights problems. In the first place, there is a clear record of partnership between the federal government and the states of the North and the West where there are essentially similar policy commitments involved. In the second place, where the federal government has reached out to touch the states of the South to alter their behavior, every effort has been made to do so not by coercion but by obtaining local implementation of the national goals. The pace of federal action is heavily influenced by a realization that force is not the ultimate answer to the civil rights issue but, rather, that a change of mind must be effected among those who are immediately affected by new civil rights policies. While the nation has agreed that this change of mind can be greatly helped by laws and legal action to enforce those laws, the very existence of federalism makes the responsible leaders on both sides recognize that second thoughts are necessary and consensus is the most desirable end.

All this can be seen in the enactment and enforcement of the Civil Rights Act of 1964—the great landmark of our times in civil rights legislation. The Act itself can be legitimately described as a treaty among the states that opened the door to greater federal action wherever the states fail to act in a field where state police powers are preeminent. This "treaty" was a product of complex negotiations involving the efforts of private and public nongovernmental agencies as much as representatives of government or electoral units. Moreover, the groups lobbying for the bill were those which evoked the deepest moral instincts of the American people, so that the measure represented a rare combination of both moral concern and political negotiation. The passage of the act represents a comprehensive victory for the position dominant in the states of the North and West. Indeed, while the civil rights issue is all too often conceived to be one in which progressiveness is a monopoly of the federal government while the states are the embodiment of reaction, one may well argue that, until 1964, the situation was just the reverse. A clear majority of the states had enacted significant civil rights legislation while the national government, necessarily reflecting all the currents in the country, had not.

Perhaps the central feature of the Civil Rights Act of 1964 is Title VI, which requires desegregation in all state and local programs receiving federal aid. The implementation of its provisions has been the most important aspect of the enforcement of the Act to date. The first step in that direction was the promulgation of federal guidelines to cover the appropriate programs. In reading those guidelines, the hand of moderation is immediately apparent.

Limitations on the budget and personnel of the federal enforcing agency clearly meant that most actions to detect violators of the guidelines would have to come from private parties who were victims of segregation. Consequently, several private agencies interested in civil rights issued manuals designed to explain the provisions of Title VI and suggest plans for community action under it. Selections from the manual of the Potomac Institute are presented here. They not only tell us something specific about the enforcement of federal civil rights legislation but provide important insights into cooperative programs generally. Perhaps the most important of these is that the enactment of federal legislation is just a license for beginning negotiations and the outcome of those negotiations depends upon the actions of many parties, public and private.

While federal enforcement of the act was conducted with moderation and local compliance was widespread in the South, efforts by federal officials to broaden their arena of activity led to sharp reactions in some corners. One example was the attempt by the Office of Education to deny federal funds to the Chicago school district for allowing *de facto* segregation. This attempt immediately evoked heavy state and local pressure against the Washington authorities, who pulled back but did not entirely abandon the field. Congressional response to this and similar efforts was strong and sharp, as the item

115

from the *New York Times* indicates. Although the end result of their efforts to weaken Title VI was ambiguous, the Office of Education has since relaxed its pressures somewhat.

What are we to conclude from all this? The existence of federalism does complicate the civil rights struggle. At the same time, the commitment to partnership has led to substantial compliance with the Civil Rights Act of 1964 (and the others) in almost all of its provisions, while the possibility for influencing the mode of enforcement of its provisions is enhanced through use of the mechanisms of federalism. This, in turn, has worked to lessen federal enforcement pressures even in those areas where the character of the compliance has been questioned.

---

## STATE FAIR EMPLOYMENT LAWS AND THE CIVIL RIGHTS BILL

A major feature of the Senate version of the civil rights bill (HR 7152) is a provision granting states a large role in handling complaints of employment discrimination before the Federal Government acts.

The proposal, which was part of the bipartisan leadership substitute to the House bill, was in large part offered to meet charges by opponents of the legislation that the bill would grant the Federal Government too much power in an area that should be reserved to the states. It also was designed to protect employers from unnecessary duplication of federal and state action.

FEDERAL FAIR EMPLOYMENT LAWS

*Title VII Amendments*

As passed by the House, Title VII of HR 7152 established a five-member Equal Employment Opportunity Commission (EEOC). Upon receipt of a sworn complaint or a written charge by a member of the Commission, the EEOC was authorized to investigate instances of alleged discrimination and to seek compliance with fair employment practices through conciliation and persuasion. If these efforts were unsuccessful, the Commission could sue in federal court for an injunction to enforce compliance.

The leadership amendments to Title VII were included in a "clean bill" adopted June 17 as a substitute for the pending measure. They provided, in part, that where there was a state or local fair employment law, an individual could file a charge with the EEOC only after the local agency had had 60 days to settle the complaint, or 120 days in the first year of a new law. The same reference to local agencies and waiting period would be required when the charges were filed by a member of the federal Commission.

Following the filing of a complaint with the EEOC, the Commission would have a maximum of 60 days to seek voluntary compliance with the law. Should its efforts fail, the individual could then bring suit. Without waiting for state action, the Attorney General could also bring suit where he had "reasonable cause to believe" that a pattern or practice of discrimination existed with intent to deny equal employment opportunities. (Weekly Report p. 987, 1032)

*Earlier Federal Action*

The first federal law prohibiting employment discrimination in activities of the

---

From *The Congressional Quarterly Guide to Current American Government*, Fall, 1964 (Washington, D.C.: Congressional Quarterly, Inc.), pp. 41–42, 2509.

Federal Government or by private contractors conducting business with the Government was the Unemployment Relief Act, passed in 1933. It provided that "in employing citizens for the purposes of this Act no discrimination shall be made on account of race, color or creed." Similar nondiscrimination provisions were included in the Hatch Act and the Civilian Pilot Training Act, both passed in 1939, the Selective Training and Service Act of 1940, and the Nurses Training Act of 1943.

In 1941, President Roosevelt issued Executive Order 8802 which created the Fair Employment Practices Committee (FEPC). This five-man group, largely advisory in character, was to seek an end to discrimination in hiring by the Federal Government and by companies with defense contracts, and in vocational and training programs administered by federal agencies. The Committee's operations ceased in 1943, when it was replaced by a new group that lasted until 1946.

Additional executive orders issued by Presidents Roosevelt, Truman, Eisenhower and Kennedy established a series of committees to deal with discriminatory hiring by the Federal Government and by companies holding Government contracts.

## STATE FAIR EMPLOYMENT LAWS

Twenty-five Eastern, Midwestern and Western states have mandatory fair employment practice laws. The National Assn. for the Advancement of Colored People estimates that these states contain 41 per cent of the Negro population of the United States. (See chart)

In four other states — West Virginia in the East, Nevada in the West, and Kentucky and Oklahoma in the South — commissions have been appointed to consider the adoption of antidiscrimination laws covering employment as well as other areas.

Supporters of HR 7152 are hopeful that passage of the bill might act as a spur to increase the effectiveness of state FEPC laws by providing recourse to the federal courts when discriminatory hiring practices cannot be successfully challenged at the state level. Herbert Hill, Labor Secretary of the NAACP, April 26 released a study of state FEPC laws which expressed the view that the statutes for the most part had been less than fully effective. In Hill's words, the state laws "have proved unable to cope with the problem of changing the Negro occupational pattern and . . . do not provide a solution to structural unemployment problems." Hill called both for more forceful application of state fair employment laws and for passage of a strong federal law.

Majority Whip Hubert H. Humphrey (D Minn.) June 3 said that adoption of the leadership amendments to Title VII of the civil rights bill would be a "concession . . . and that, in a sense, we have weakened the bill." He said the title had been rewritten in the belief "that the prime responsibility for action and enforcement is at the state and local level. . . ."

\*      \*      \*

## FEDERAL RACE GUIDELINES

Attorney General Nicholas deB. Katzenbach Dec. 27 issued "Guidelines for Enforcement of Title VI," referring to that title of the Civil Rights Act of 1964 which required desegregation of federally aided facilities and programs.

Copies of the Guidelines were sent to heads of 21 departments and agencies having enforcement responsibilities under Title VI, and Katzenbach said a training program for agency compliance officers would begin within 45 to 60 days.

In a letter accompanying the Guidelines, the Attorney General said: "There should be no mistaking the clear intent and effect of the Guidelines — Title VI must and will be enforced. Assistance will be refused or terminated to noncomplying recipients and applicants who are not amenable to other sanctions."

The Guidelines placed a strong emphasis

on voluntary compliance, and urged federal officials to exhaust all possibilities of obtaining voluntary compliance before resorting to the "ultimate sanctions" of the law—terminating or withholding federal funds because of the failure of the state or local agency to meet the desegregation requirements.

The Guidelines noted that under Section 602 of the Title, the "ultimate sanctions" could not be invoked until the federal agency concerned determined that

voluntary compliance could not be obtained, failed in alternative methods of carrying out the assistance programs, afforded the applicant a hearing and completed other procedures, including notifying the appropriate Congressional committee 30 days before cutting off funds. The last two requirements were added to the Act in floor amendments in the House. . . .

As alternative methods of obtaining enforcement, the Guidelines mentioned court

STATE FAIR EMPLOYMENT PRACTICE LAWS AND HR 7152

| State | Enacted | Applicable to State Political Subdivisions | Extends to Labor Unions and Employment Agencies | Minimum Employees for Coverage | Exceptions for Special Groups[5] | Enforcement |
|---|---|---|---|---|---|---|
| Alaska | 1953[1] | No | Yes | None | Yes | Punishable as misdemeanor. |
| California | 1959 | Yes | Yes | 5 | Yes | Punishable as misdemeanor. |
| Colorado | 1957 | Yes | Yes | 6 | No | Cease and desist orders, injunctions. |
| Connecticut | 1947 | Yes | Yes | 5 | No | Cease and desist orders, fines. |
| Delaware | 1960 | No | No | None | No | Criminal sanctions. |
| Hawaii | 1963 | No | Yes | None | Yes | Fine ($500 maximum), imprisonment (90 day maximum) or both. |
| Idaho | 1961 | No | No | None | No | Punishable as misdemeanor. |
| Illinois | 1961 | Yes | Yes | 50 | Yes | Punishable as contempt of court. |
| Indiana | 1945[2] | Yes | Yes | 6 | Yes | Administrative enforcement. |
| Iowa | 1963 | Yes | Yes | None | No | Fine ($100 maximum) or imprisonment (30 day maximum). |
| Kansas | 1961 | Yes | Yes | 8 | Yes | Criminal sanctions. |
| Massachusetts | 1946 | Yes | Yes | 6 | Yes | Criminal sanctions. |
| Michigan | 1955 | Yes | Yes | 8 | No | Criminal sanctions. |

STATE FAIR EMPLOYMENT PRACTICE LAWS AND HR 7152, cont'd.

| State | Enacted | Applicable to State Political Subdivisions | Extends to Labor Unions and Employment Agencies | Minimum Employees for Coverage | Exceptions for Special Groups[5] | Enforcement |
|---|---|---|---|---|---|---|
| Minnesota | 1955 | Yes | No | 8 | No | Criminal sanctions. |
| Missouri | 1961 | Yes | Yes | 50 | No | Punishable as misdemeanor. |
| New Jersey | 1945 | No | Yes | 6 | Yes | Punishable as misdemeanor. |
| New Mexico | 1949 | Yes | Yes | 4 | Yes | Cease and desist orders. |
| New York | 1945 | No | Yes | 6 | Yes | Punishable as contempt of court. |
| Ohio | 1959 | Yes | Yes | None | No | Punishable as contempt of court. |
| Oregon | 1949[3] | No | Yes | 6 | Yes | Judicial enforcement. |
| Pennsylvania | 1955 | Yes | Yes | 12 | Yes | Criminal sanctions. |
| Rhode Island | 1949 | No | Yes | 4 | Yes | Administrative enforcement. |
| Vermont | 1963 | No | Yes | None | Yes | Fine ($500 maximum). |
| Washington | 1949 | Yes | Yes | 8 | Yes | Administrative enforcement. |
| Wisconsin | 1957 | No | No | None | Yes | Judicial enforcement. |
| HR 7152 | | No | Yes | 25[4] | Yes | Punishable as contempt of court. |

1. Law already on books when Alaska became a state in 1959.
2. Amended in 1963.
3. Amended in 1963.
4. Beginning fifth year after enactment.
5. Such as nonprofit social, religious, charitable and educational organizations.

enforcement (of federal property rights, other sections of the Act or other laws, for example); administrative action through other federal or state agencies or by by-passing the "recalcitrant" state agency; and prompt and clear efforts to obtain voluntary compliance at the outset of every non-compliance situation.

On new applications for federal aid, the Guidelines said that when the required assurance of nondiscrimination in the program was not filed by the applicant, action "should" be deferred until Section 602 pro-cedures were completed. If the federal agency had grounds to believe that the as-surance was untrue or was not being hon-ored, the agency head "may" defer action on the pending application until comple-tion of Section 602 procedures, the Guide-lines said.

In the case of a new application for a long-term program, the Guidelines said, deferral was "less appropriate because of the opportunity to secure full compliance during the life of the assistance program." Under such circumstances, the Guidelines suggested paying out funds to the applicant "for short periods only, with no long-term commitment of assistance given."

For applications for continuation or renewal of long-term, existing programs, the Guidelines also found deferral of funds inappropriate until Section 602 procedures were completed. Again, however, the device of short-term, periodic payments combined with insistence on compliance could be used. The Guidelines suggested, too, that, in cases of short-term, special projects, agency heads suspend normal procedures and attempt to gain rapid compliance, including notifying the Justice Department for possible use of court proceedings.

The Guidelines said that the same procedures applied for any subgrantees of federal funds; normally these were state agencies which received and in turn disbursed federal funds. The federal agency involved had responsibility for informing the subgrantee of its responsibilities, the Guidelines said.

The Guidelines said that the Justice Department should be notified "in advance" of applications on which action was to be deferred, hearings scheduled or refusals or termination of federal aid contemplated. The Department also was to be kept advised of other enforcement actions, the Guidelines said.

## THE CIVIL RIGHTS ACT OF 1964

*Sec. 601.* No person in the United States shall, on the ground of race, color, or national origin, be excluded from participation in, be denied the benefits of, or be subjected to discrimination under any program or activity receiving Federal financial assistance.

*Sec. 602.* Each Federal department and agency which is empowered to extend Federal financial assistance to any program or activity, by way of grant, loan, or contract other than a contract of insurance or guaranty, is authorized and directed to effectuate the provisions of section 601 with respect to such program or activity by issuing rules, regulations, or orders of general applicability which shall be consistent with achievement of the objectives of the statute authorizing the financial assistance in connection with which the action is taken. No such rule, regulation, or order shall become effective unless and until approved by the President. Compliance with any requirement adopted pursuant to this section may be effected (1) by the termination of or refusal to grant or to continue assistance under such program or activity to any recipient as to whom there has been an express finding on the record, after opportunity for

hearing, of a failure to comply with such requirement, but such termination or refusal shall be limited to the particular political entity, or part thereof, or other recipient as to whom such a finding has been made and, shall be limited in its effect to the particular program, or part thereof, in which such noncompliance has been so found, or (2) by any other means authorized by law: *Provided, however,* That no such action shall be taken until the department or agency concerned has advised the appropriate person or persons of the failure to comply with the requirement and has determined that compliance cannot be secured by voluntary means. In the case of any action terminating, or refusing to grant or continue, assistance because of failure to comply with a requirement imposed pursuant to this section, the head of the Federal department or agency shall file with the committees of the House and Senate having legislative jurisdiction over the program or activity involved a full written report of the circumstances and the grounds for such action. No such action shall become effective until thirty days have elapsed after the filing of such report.

*Sec. 603* Any department or agency action

taken pursuant to section 602 shall be subject to such judicial review as may otherwise be provided by law for similar action taken by such department or agency on other grounds. In the case of action, not otherwise subject to judicial review, terminating or refusing to grant or to continue financial assistance upon a finding of failure to comply with any requirement imposed pursuant to section 602, any person aggrieved (including any State or political subdivision thereof and any agency of either) may obtain judicial review of such action in accordance with section 10 of the Administrative Procedure Act, and such action shall not be deemed committed to unreviewable agency discretion within the meaning of that section.

*Sec. 604.* Nothing contained in this title shall be construed to authorize action under this title by any department or agency with respect to any employment practice of any employer, employment agency, or labor organization except where a primary objective of the Federal financial assistance is to provide employment.

*Sec. 605.* Nothing in this title shall add to or detract from any existing authority with respect to any program or activity under which Federal financial assistance is extended by way of a contract of insurance or guaranty.

# A GUIDE TO COMMUNITY ACTION UNDER TITLE VI

"Title VI" is a phrase which will be heard increasingly in the months ahead, as new government programs are begun and old ones are reviewed. This section of the Civil Rights Act of 1964 has a clear aim: federal assistance shall not be given any program that discriminates against any individual on the ground of race or national origin.

Entitled "Nondiscrimination In Federally Assisted Programs," Title VI says that *"no person shall, on the ground of race, color, or national origin, be excluded from participation in, be denied the benefit of, or be subjected to discrimination under any program or activity receiving Federal financial assistance."*

This is among the most far-reaching of all the provisions of the historic law by which Americans now seek to end discrimination in every aspect of our national, state, and local life.

The law is the culmination of years of work by many citizens and their organizations. The same drive which led to the law's enactment must now be turned to its enforcement. The law will not work automatically. The efforts of Americans can now best be mobilized, not in a negative manner to punish, but in a positive thrust to achieve the equality of opportunity that is the nation's goal.

*Public Help Vital*

Nowhere is the aid of the public needed more than in enforcement of Title VI. However, Title VI is so comprehensive (190 federal programs are covered by it) that the layman might be disheartened at the prospect of trying to keep track of what it does, and how it does it. Moreover, its enforcement essentially is left to the agencies and bureaus of government, federal and state, rather than to the courts. This involves regulations and procedures not familiar to the general public.

But Title VI is not an impenetrable mystery. And, like the rest of the law, it does require the understanding of the general public, both in a broad way for general support and in more detailed, technical ways for active help in achieving its ends. This is important because it is different

From *The Federal Dollar and Nondiscrimination: A Guide to Community Action Under Title VI, Civil Rights Act of 1964* (Washington, D.C.: Potomac Institute, 1965), pp. 3-11.

from the other parts of the law, less simple and obvious, and because, properly functioning, it can accomplish so much.

## How Title VI Works

At the heart of all the regulations and procedures for making it function properly is the provision for complaints from private individuals and organizations.

In the simplest terms, Title VI says that no one may be denied participation or be subjected to discrimination while participating in any program which receives federal money or other assistance.

The programs in our national life that receive federal money or other assistance are many and varied, and they include some of the most basic institutions and activities of our society. Education, employment, agriculture, business, housing, health care, and welfare are a few of these. In all, the Federal Government spent approximately $15 billion in 1964 on the kind of assistance covered by Title VI.

Many of these programs receive federal aid in the form of grants to state agencies. The state agencies, in turn, administer the federal money, often combined with state funds, through a number of smaller units that are frequently—as is the case with schools—parts of a county or city government. In 1963, federal money averaged 14 per cent of the total revenue of all the states of the union, and as much as 32 per cent of the total revenue of some states.

Some kinds of federal aid often are unseen. The programs and institutions are run by state governments, or by county and city governments, as in the case of vocational education or of welfare departments. They include such things as hospitals, state mental health programs, employment security offices, agricultural extension services, and construction of highways and airports. There are also federal programs which give specialized aid to institutions largely supported by state funds—like research grants

to state universities. And there are programs where the Federal Government deals directly with the city or county government—as in urban renewal, public housing, and airports—or even with private groups—as in the economic opportunity ("antipoverty") program.

An important distinction written into the law is that compliance is required only of the recipients of federal aid who are conducting programs for the benefit of others. A "recipient" does not include the individual who ultimately receives the financial aid or other benefit under the program. For example, an individual receiving unemployment compensation is not a "recipient," but the state unemployment insurance office is, and must not discriminate against applicants for assistance. A farmer receiving federal aid is not required to adopt nondiscriminatory practices in operating his farm, nor are individuals receiving veterans' pensions or social security payments covered by Title VI.

## Federal-State Cooperation

In the situations covered by Title VI, the federal agencies in charge of dispensing funds or aid are charged with seeing to it that recipient state and local agencies or institutions comply with Title VI. If, acting as middle men, these state and local agencies administer funds to smaller units under them, they are supposed to see to it that these smaller units comply.

There is a long background and tradition for this interaction of the Federal Government with state agencies in administering funds designed to benefit all American citizens. The process has its roots deep in the nation's historical efforts to achieve a working balance between state and federal power. Title VI, in its language and in the regulations drawn up to implement it, faithfully follows this tradition. Emphasis throughout the administrative procedures for enforcement is on helping the state and local agencies and institutions make necessary adjustments smoothly and voluntarily.

Only where there is evidenced open intention or action not to comply does coercion come into the process. The sanction is the obvious one in such a situation—the federal agency may withhold funds, or sue for specific performance. But even when this is deemed necessary, the regulations allow ample room and time for negotiation and persuasion.

In short, the idea is not to cut off funds, not to punish anyone, but to gain compliance with the working operation of the law. The cutting off of funds is an ultimate weapon, not to be used lightly, but the provision for it gives teeth to Title VI.

All of this is consistent with the main thought behind the title—which is that federal spending is for the benefit of all, and this purpose is defeated when some of those whom it is designed to help are cut off from the benefits, or are given them in different, diluted form. The intent is to include everybody who should be included, on an equal basis.

## Statements of Assurance or Compliance

The regulations call for statements of assurance or compliance, which are legal contractual agreements that state or local agencies and the units under them are or will immediately begin complying. Obviously, if there is refusal to make these statements of good faith, the withholding of funds is mandatory on the part of the federal agency administering the program. So far, there seems to be little tendency toward outright refusal to cooperate. Compliance by school districts, for example, seems to have the potential of accomplishing more desegregation than years of litigation under the 1954 Supreme Court school decision.

Enforcement may become complicated after the statements of assurance or compliance have been signed. Segregation and discrimination are deep-rooted and far reaching; often they exist almost without notice. Signs may come down in waiting rooms, but people may continue exerting pressure for the old, customary arrangements. Policies may be adopted and regulations read to employees, but practices may continue as they always have.

In such situations, the complaint procedure and the work of private individuals and organizations could make the difference between whether Title VI is a fiction of form or a true rendering of the national will. In all instances, such work is a necessary part of a very large cooperative effort between the federal and state governments, and their citizens.

## Compliance Reviews

The regulations call for regular reports to federal departments from state and local agencies and institutions to show the extent of compliance. These are to be confirmed by agents from the federal departments making visits, called "compliance reviews," to the local agencies and their units. The tremendous number of such visits that will have to be made and the time this will take is another indication of the need for private surveillance and checks in the meantime. There is also, of course, the importance of the viewpoint of people who are detached from the routine of governmental organization.

## Complaint Mechanism

Complaints may come from a person with a particular grievance, from someone who observes what appears to be an act or pattern of discrimination under one of the programs, or from people or organizations that set out systematically to check on the various programs in a city or rural area. It will be a continuing process. It will involve a determined and conscientious effort to root out the stubborn remnants of outlawed customs, and a patient effort to help those less sensitive to such things to see violations of Title VI and remedy them.

## II. Federalism in Action: Some Cases in Point

### New Opportunities

In cities, where such work toward equality of opportunity has been done in the past and where organizations specifically equipped for it exist, Title VI will mean new opportunities to solve many old problems. In small towns and rural areas, where local minority leadership may be timid or intimidated, and where organization is lacking, enforcement of Title VI will be most difficult. Here, perhaps, is a new opportunity for organizations from the cities to strengthen leadership in these small town and rural areas to take advantage of the new opportunities opened up by Title VI.

Title VI has created many such new opportunities. In an age when people often complain that government is remote and inaccessible, here is an open invitation for citizens to work with their governments to achieve something that the nation wants. With the help of the people, Title VI can be one of the most significant achievements of our democratic process.

#### WHAT DOES TITLE VI COVER?

To determine which local programs and institutions are receiving federal benefits covered by Title VI requirements, a community inventory may be organized under the following headings:

1. *Construction Projects:* Those that are financed or receive partial financing, equipment, or land from the Federal Government are covered by Title VI. While construction is being planned and while it is being carried out, checks can be made and complaints registered where there are violations of the nondiscrimination requirements. After construction is completed, the facility itself is subject to continuing Title VI compliance.

Such construction projects may include: Airports, College Facilities and Dormitories, Dams, Defense Projects, Government Buildings, Highways, Lakes, Parks, Urban Renewal Projects.

All new construction proposals in your area sponsored by local and state government should be examined for Title VI coverage.

2. *Public and Private Institutions*: Those that receive any kind of federal aid for their operation and maintenance are covered by Title VI.

These may include: Conservation Projects, Colleges, Defense Installations, Health Centers, Hospitals, Libraries, Medical Schools, Mental Institutions, Nurses Training Schools, Public Housing Projects, Schools.

3. *Government Services*: Such services are covered by Title VI, even though operated by state, county, or city governments, or special boards, if they receive all or part of their support or other aid from the Federal Government.

Examples of such services are: Agricultural Extension Programs, Aids To Businesses, Apprenticeship and Manpower Training, Area Redevelopment, Disaster Relief, Economic Opportunity ("anti-poverty") Programs, Forest Protection, Mental Health, Public Health and Welfare, Research Grants, Rural Electrification, School Lunches, State Employment Services, Student Loans and Graduate Fellowships, Teacher Training, TVA, Vocational Rehabilitation. . . .

### Excluded Activities

Three categories of federal programs are excluded from the requirements of Title VI:

1. Federal contracts of insurance, and federal contracts of guaranty. These include federally-insured bank loans and guarantees for mortgage loan repayment under some federal housing (FHA) programs.

2. Direct grants or loans, such as loans made directly to farmers by the Farmers Home Administration, or veterans' pensions, or social security payments.

3. Employment, except where the purpose of the federal program is to provide employment, as in Area Redevelopment projects and Economic Opportunity

("anti-poverty") programs. Title VII of the Civil Rights Law covers equal employment opportunity.

It should be noted, however, that a section of the regulations under Title VI has been interpreted as involving, in some cases, employment practices. In examining programs and institutions, a report on whether or not employment is desegregated should be included in complaints about other matters, as well as in complaints about segregated employment alone. It would then be up to the federal agency involved to determine whether the employment question is covered for this particular program by the administrative regulations under Title VI.

## Inventory of Local Programs

A systematic examination of Title VI coverage would involve drawing up a list of all the different activities in your community that are federally benefited. Your own sources of information and knowledge of the area will tell you some of these programs. A check with the various local offices of each of the federal agencies (listed in your telephone book) will add activities to your list, as will inquiries to state agencies. . . .

To help you begin your local inventory, there follows an illustrative list of the most commonly found programs benefited by federal assistance. It will also suggest appropriate inquiries about specific local institutions. For example, if a hospital receives neither Hill-Burton aid nor federal research grants, it still may be covered because it receives federal funds through the local public welfare agency for care of indigent patients.

### Executive Office of the President

Office of Emergency Planning
  Disaster Relief and Repairs
Office of Economic Opportunity ("anti-poverty" program)
  Youth Programs (Job Corps, Work-Training, Work-Study)
  Community Action Programs (Slum Clearance,

Remedial Education, Adult Education, Voluntary Aid to Needy Children)
Programs to Combat Poverty in Rural Areas (Loans to Rural Families, Programs for Migrant Farmworkers, Indemnity Payments to Farmers)
Employment and Investment Incentives (Loans to Small Business)
Work-Experience Programs (For Needy Persons Receiving Public Assistance)
Assignment of Volunteers in Service to America (VISTA)

### Department of Agriculture

Agricultural Marketing Services
  Agriculture Commodity Distribution
  School Lunch and Milk Program
Farmers Home Administration Services
Soil Conservation Services
Federal Extension Services
Rural Electrification and Telephone Programs
Price Support Programs
Cooperative State Research Programs
Food Stamp Program
Agricultural Experiment Stations
Research Assistance to Educational and Other Institutions

### Department of Commerce

Area Redevelopment Programs
  Public Works Acceleration
  Aid to Small Businesses
Highway Construction
Assistance to Support Mobile Trade Fairs
Research Assistance to Educational and Other Institutions

### Department of Defense

National Guard (Army and Air Force)
Loan of Surplus Property
Civil Defense Activities
Civil Air Patrol
Research Assistance to Educational and Other Institutions

### Department of Health, Education, and Welfare

Office of Education Programs
  Vocational Education
  Land-grant Colleges
  Higher Education Facilities Construction
  Student Loans at Institutions of Higher Education
  Graduate Fellowships, Traineeships, and Institutes
  Public School Construction and Maintenance in Federally Impacted Areas
  Library Services and Construction
  Donation of Surplus Properties for Education, Public Health, and Civil Defense

Public Health Services
  Community and Environmental Health Activities
  Community Health Practice, including Clinics and Research
  Hospital and Medical Facilities Construction, Technical Assistance, Research and Demonstrations (Hill-Burton Program)
  Nurse Training and Nursing Research
National Institutes of Health Programs
Vocational Rehabilitation Programs
Welfare Services
  Public Assistance
  Child-Welfare Services
  Maternal and Child Health Services
  Other Health and Welfare Programs
Research Assistance to Educational and Other Institutions

*Department of the Interior*

Indian Affairs
Payments for School and Road Assistance in Counties with Federal Land
Granting of Leases and Other Privileges on Federal Land
Disposition of Land at less than Market Value
Other Activities Related to the Use of Federal Lands, including Parks, Territories, Wildlife Refuges, Fish and Game Preserves, Etc.

*Department of Labor*

Manpower, Apprenticeship, and Training Activities
State Employment Services
Unemployment Compensation
Work-Training Programs
Research Assistance to Educational and Other Institutions

*Department of State*

Cultural Exchange Programs
Assistance to Refugees
Donations of Foreign Language Tapes and Other Educational Materials
Agency for International Development Grants to Organizations and Institutions

*Department of the Treasury*

Coast Guard
  Leases, Permits, Licenses, Easements, and Other Uses of Coast Guard Property
  Maritime Instruction and Training and Other Utilization of Coast Guard Personnel
  Disposal of Materials to Sea Scouts, Coast Guard Auxiliary, and Non-Profit Organizations
  Research Assistance to Educational and Other Institutions

*Atomic Energy Commission*

Atomic Energy Research, Training, and Equipment in Universities and Hospitals
Payments to State and Local Governments in Lieu of Property Taxes

*Civil Aeronautics Board*

Compensations to Air Carriers

*Federal Aviation Agency*

Acquisition of Land for Airports
Airport Construction

*General Services Administration*

Transfer of Surplus Property for Airport, Park or Recreation, Historic Monument, Wildlife Conservation, or Street Widening Purposes
Loan of Machine Tools to Non-Profit Institutions or Training Schools
Donation of Personal Properties to Charitable Institutions, the American Red Cross, and Public Bodies
Allotment of Space to Federal Credit Unions
Grants for Compiling and Publishing Historic Documents
Disposal of Property for Education or Public Health
Provision of Free Space for Vending Stands Operated by Blind Persons

*Housing and Home Finance Agency*

Urban Renewal Projects
Public Housing Projects
College Dormitory Construction Loans
Senior Citizen Housing
Municipal Gas Works
Public Sewer Systems

*National Aeronautics and Space Administration*

Research Grants and Contracts to Universities and Other Organizations

*National Science Foundation*

Scientific Research Grants and Science Teacher Training in Universities and Hospitals
Donation of Equipment to Public Schools

*Small Business Administration*

Small Business Development Company Loans
Small Business Studies, Research, and Counseling

*Tennessee Valley Authority*

Transfers, Leases, and Licenses of Property to

Public Agencies for Development for Public Recreation
Cooperative Resource Development Programs
Test Demonstration Farms for Fertilizer Experiments

*Veterans Administration*

Payment to State Homes
State Home Facilities for Furnishing Nursing Care

\*   \*   \*

WHAT TO DO ABOUT NONCOMPLIANCE

Private citizens and voluntary organizations enter into the administrative procedures for enforcing Title VI by filing complaints that some institution or activity covered by the regulations is practicing discrimination.

A typical regulation covering this vital phase says: *"Any person who believes himself or any specific class of individuals to be subjected to discrimination prohibited by the regulations in this part may by himself or by an authorized representative file with the Secretary or any Agency a written complaint. A complaint must be filed not later than 90 days from the date of the alleged discrimination, unless the time for filing is extended by the Agency or the Secretary."*

In preparing a complaint, the following should be noted:

1. The complaint must be in written form. This could be a simple telling of the act or pattern of discrimination: what happened, when, where, by whom, and to whom. The information derived from the preceding check list may be used as a basis for reporting the complaint. It should, of course, be signed.

2. The complaint may be submitted not only by a person who feels he has been discriminated against, but also by someone who knows about the discrimination, or by someone (including an organization) who is an authorized representative of either.

3. The complaint must be filed not later than 90 days after the act of discrimination occurred, unless the time is extended, as set out in the regulations.

4. As the most direct, and likely most effective approach, it is suggested that the complaint be sent to the chief officer of the federal department or agency administering the particular program—the Secretary of Agriculture, the Director of the National Science Foundation, etc. Normally, you probably will wish to send a copy to the local or state official in charge of the program.

It is recommended that a copy of each complaint be sent also to the U. S. Commission on Civil Rights, which will follow through with inquiries about its progress.

*The Complaint Procedure*

The complaint procedure was established to enable citizens to start the administrative process that could end in the cutting off of federal funds to the offending agency or activity, but which preferably would result in an end to the discrimination.

An investigation of the complaint is conducted ("promptly," say the regulations) by the concerned federal agency. If it fails to substantiate the complaint, the complainant must be notified in writing. If it substantiates the complaint, efforts are made informally to end the discrimination. If these fail, a hearing is scheduled. The accused unit is given adequate time to prepare for the hearing.

The hearing is conducted by officials of the federal agency. If the local unit is found to have violated Title VI, it may appeal this finding to the head of the federal agency. If he upholds the finding, he orders the funds to the particular unit cut off. This order would apply only to the offending unit—a school district, for example, not the entire school system; a single hospital, not all the hospitals in the state.

The funds cut-off order does not go into effect until 30 days after appropriate committees of Congress are notified that such a determination has been made. In the meantime, the local unit may appeal the finding in federal court.

The regulations require that as far as

127

possible identity of complainants and witnesses will be protected. Any threats, intimidations, coercions, or reprisals are prohibited by Title VI. The regulations also require that information about Title VI procedures be made available by the federal agencies and local beneficiaries to the general public.

Exact procedures in this process will probably vary from department to department of the Federal Government. Private citizens and organizations should not be content merely with making a complaint. There should be follow-up inquiries about progress of the complaint.

It should be obvious that complaints must be soundly based and reflect a legitimate and well-documented case. The most useful complaints are those that establish a pattern of discrimination.

## CONGRESS ERODING INTEGRATION LAW

There is concern within the Administration that the most far-reaching desegregation law — Title VI of the Civil Rights Act of 1964 — is in danger of repeal.

Bit by bit, both houses of Congress have been chipping away at Title VI, which is intended to prohibit racial discrimination in any federally assisted program. This has had an adverse effect on enforcement.

"Now when we call on Southern school officials for compliance, they just laugh at us," an official in the Office of Education said. "They feel they have the rest of the country on their side now."

On Thursday, the House voted, 220 to 116, to require a hearing in advance of any Office of Education move to delay Federal funds to any school district suspected of practicing discrimination.

Earlier, the Senate had voted by a substantial margin to let physicians decide whether a patient should be assigned to a segregated hospital room for his health or well-being.

Both houses agreed to cut the appropriation for civil rights enforcement by the Department of Health, Education and Welfare by $927,000. These actions are subject to approval in conference committee.

In addition, the department and the Commissioner of Education, Harold Howe 2d, have been under fire by members of Congress from both the South and the North, who say the administrators are going beyond the law in the enforcement of Title VI.

Some officials within the department believe that damage to Title VI so far is more psychological than substantive.

The House Amendment on schools, for instance, could be harder on the school districts than on the Federal Government. The Government would have to terminate funds sooner for noncomplying districts rather than to delay funds and work with the districts to achieve compliance.

But some Administration officials believe Congress is not yet through with Title VI.

"We believe there will be more attempts to weaken it," one official said. "A lot of people would like to see it repealed or gradually eroded away."

New opposition to Title VI, as heard almost daily on Capitol Hill, is making a difficult enforcement task even harder, a spokesman for the Department of Health, Education and Welfare said.

Title VI has been called the atomic bomb of civil rights. If it were invoked in regard to every Federal dollar, as it could be in all but a few cases, it could be felt in almost every fabric of the society.

For various reasons, the Administration has attempted to enforce it only in selected programs, chiefly schools, hospitals, and the Federal agencies.

Further, Title VI is not popular in the bureaucracy. Because it carries the power to withhold funds, it gets in the way of agencies that are trying to pursue their goals by making Federal grants.

### OFFICIALS CITE DISTRACTIONS

Many officials say privately they wish it did not exist. It involves them in the emotional area of race relations that they would rather avoid. And it distracts them from what they consider to be their major concerns.

The Office of Education is committed to integrated education as one of its goals. But there are those in the office who feel that civil rights problems have interfered with its major job of building quality schools, whatever the racial balance.

This week, Commissioner Howe proposed before the House Rules Committee that enforcement of Title VI in school desegregation be delegated to the states. He said this could be incorporated into general state administration of Federal education programs, if the states wished to assume that responsibility.

The Federal standards and guidelines would have to be maintained, Mr. Howe said, and it is presumed that most Southern states would decline to take on the desegregation role. Nevertheless, some of the complaints about Federal control would be removed.

### ENFORCED ONLY IN SOUTH

Title VI has been enforced only in the South and border states, which have a history of segregation by law or official pronouncement. The Office of Education has made no attempt to enforce Title VI outside the South since last year, when it deferred funds to Chicago and was overruled by the White House.

The reason for the general assault on Title VI is that Southerners have mounted a campaign against it, and many Northerners are sympathetic for the first time.

Constituents voice complaints of "Federal control," and Congressmen are sensitive to increased white resistance to attacks on neighborhood schools.

The main charge is that the Department of Health, Education and Welfare is intent on achieving racial balance, while the law is aimed only at removing racial barriers.

EDUCATION

Intergovernmental collaboration in the field of education dates back to the earliest days of the Republic. Indeed, the first federal grant program, authorized in 1785, involved the transfer of lands, in every township of every public land state, to state or local government for the establishment of common schools and the development of universities. The selections included here reflect the various aspects of a very complex system of intergovernmental and public-private cooperation that fuels the American education system.

Charles A. Quattlebaum outlines the federal role in higher education both historically and in terms of contemporary responsibilities, showing how an apparently untidy process has served to create the greatest system of higher education the world has yet known. Sidney C. Sufrin provides us with a study of the schoolmen's reaction to one particular aid measure, the National Defense Education Act, which has had ramifications at all levels of education and for all

129

levels of government. In examining the responses of state and local school officials to this program, Sufrin exposes many of the perennial problems of cooperative programs as well as the specific problems associated with the sensitive area of aid to education. The NDE Act is an excellent example of how an external catalyst sets the wheels of government in motion on all levels. Note, in particular, the fundamental question of whether the federal government should provide general assistance or categorical assistance to the states and localities, a question that is attracting renewed interest in many fields today. Sufrin's analysis is based on studies conducted during the first three years of the program's operation.

The growing costs of education force state and local officials and educators to seek federal assistance even as they jealously guard their autonomy. One of the best ways of obtaining noncategorical assistance from Washington is through the program of federal aid for federally impacted school districts. This money is channeled from the U.S. Office of Education to those local school districts which can demonstrate that their programs are affected by some federal activity nearby that increases their enrollment. Strictly speaking, the states need not play any role in such a program, but as I.M. Labovitz points out in "Aid for Federally Affected Schools," they do carve a role for themselves in this program, partly by virtue of their central position in the federal system (in this case in their capacity as creators of local school districts) and partly because state educators consciously seek a role. In fact, as Labovitz points out, the state role in this program is not dependent upon state expenditures. This program documents what is almost invariably true, that the states are the only ones able to involve themselves in intergovernmental activities without paying a proportionate share of the cost, simply because of their constitutional power over local governments and the primary responsibility which they bear under the Constitution for virtually all domestic government activities.

The development of new federal aid programs has led to suggestions that the "impacted areas" device be abandoned as no longer necessary. As the selection from *The Reporter* indicates, the local desire for this form of federal aid regardless of theoretical quibbles remains as strong as ever. To date, efforts to eliminate that program have met with no success—nor are they likely to.

While the states' constitutional responsibility for education is clear, they are nevertheless worried about the increasing involvement of the federal government in the regular support of educational activities. This worry has two dimensions. First is the sheer question of who is to retain control of educational policy-making among the various levels of government. At the same time, the generalists in state government, the governor and the legislators, have discovered that federal grants often strengthen the specialists, enabling them to develop independent sources of money and power. In the education field, the almost sacrosanct position which educators have forged for themselves vis-à-vis the public has already substantially emancipated them from the control of governmental generalists. In order to overcome some of this estrangement between generalists and specialists and reassert the role of the former as elected representatives of the public, to firmly tie down the states' primary role in education, and to raise nationwide educational standards as both wish, the governors of the 50 states have gotten together to create an Interstate Compact on Education. Next, the development of this compact is examined, beginning with James B. Conant's original proposal and following with the compact itself and a description of its purposes. (A sufficient number of states adhered to the Compact by 1966 to enable it to begin functioning with headquarters in Denver, Colorado.)

---

*Charles A. Quattlebaum*

# FEDERAL POLICIES AND PRACTICES IN HIGHER EDUCATION

## ORIGIN OF FEDERAL POLICY

Probably most adult Americans know that historically and under the Constitution education in the United States has developed mainly as a function of state and local governments and of non-governmental organizations and agencies. It is less known that in its infancy the federal government initiated two educational policies: (1) operating educational programs of its own, and (2) aiding the states and territories in financing and otherwise promoting education. Both policies antedate the Constitution, and have, almost from the beginning, included higher and lower education.

The federal government's own educational pursuits can be traced back to instruction in the military service which as early as 1777 included schooling in mathematics. Federal educational programs now cover practically all subjects, at all levels, carried out throughout the United States and in many other parts of the world. Examples are operation of the service academies at home, and education of dependents of federal personnel abroad.

Federal aid to education for the territo-ries began as early as 1785, and later for the states. An ordinance adopted in that year by the Congress of the Confederation for the disposal of public lands in the Western Territory set aside one section in every township for the endowment of schools within that township. In the Ordinance of 1787, providing for the government of the Northwest Territory, the Congress made the clear declaration of policy that "religion, morality and knowledge being necessary to good government and the happiness of mankind, schools and the means of education shall forever be encouraged."

The policy-making importance of the Ordinance of 1787 was recognized by Daniel Webster:

I doubt whether one single law or any lawgiver, ancient or modern, has produced effects of more distinct, marked, and lasting character than the Ordinance of 1787. . . . It set forth and declared it to be a high and binding duty of Government to support schools and the means of education.

## CONSTITUTIONAL BACKGROUND

. . . Inasmuch as the tenth amendment to the Constitution provided that powers

---

not delegated to the federal government
were reserved to the states, public education at all levels, as it slowly developed
during the nineteenth century, came generally under their jurisdiction. Thus the
United States, instead of developing a national system of education such as exists in
a number of other countries, has developed
many systems. The concept of state responsibility for public education at all levels has
accompanied the growth of publicly controlled, nonsectarian education.

At the same time certain provisions of
the Constitution have furnished support
for a great variety of federal educational
programs. Outstanding among such provisions is the general welfare clause. Exercising its constitutional powers to tax and appropriate for the general welfare, the
Congress has from time to time provided
for federal contributions to the financing of
education, as in the case of the land-grant
colleges.

Besides the general welfare clause,
among Constitutional provisions which
have afforded bases for federal educational
programs are those giving the federal government various powers to exercise exclusive jurisdiction over the seat of government of the United States and over certain
other areas, and the implied power to govern outlying possessions of the United
States. In 1931, the National Advisory Committee on education, appointed by President Herbert Hoover, reported finding in
the Constitution a total of fourteen war-
rants for federal activities in education.

However, in the enabling Acts of Congress providing for the admission of at
least ten of the states, exclusive authority
over public education was reserved to
them. In some other Acts the Congress has
prohibited federal control over education in
the states. In the National Defense Education Act of 1958 the Congress reaffirmed
this principle, declaring that the states and
local communities have and must retain
control over, and primary responsibility
for, public education. . . .

EARLY FEDERAL GRANTS POLICY

In 1802 the Congress of the United States
took definite action in continuation of the
general support of education initiated seventeen years earlier by the Congress of the
Confederation. With the admission of Ohio
to the Union in 1802, Congress began designating lands for school support at the
time of admission of a state.

Under a provision of the Ordinance of
1787 for a grant of two townships for "a
literary institution, to be applied to the
intended object by the legislature of the
State," a contract was arranged with the
Ohio Company which assured to the State
of Ohio two townships of land for the support of a university. The land was used to
endow the State University at Athens,
known as the Ohio University. Other new
states also received lands for the endowment of universities. Each State admitted to
the Union after 1802, except Maine, Texas,
and West Virginia, received two or more
townships of land for the purpose of en-
dowing a university. Occasionally since
1803 federal lands have been granted to
specifically designated educational institutions. During the first half of the nineteenth century the Congress also made
certain monetary grants to states which
were used in many cases to support education.

Except for the few grants to specific institutions, the early land and monetary
grants were without specification as to the
kind of education to receive aid. The Congress pursued a policy of giving financial
support to education without attempting to
influence the services of the school systems
and educational institutions receiving support.

In his history of school finance in the
United States, Fletcher Harper Swift has
pointed out that the funds created out of
the federal land grants were the first stable
support for free public education in more
than half the states. Undoubtedly the
grants strengthened public as related to

private education at all levels and set a precedent for other forms of federal aid to education.

## EDUCATION IN SPECIAL FEDERAL JURISDICTIONS

The federal government early assumed responsibility for the education of persons residing in areas under its special jurisdiction. Formerly the largest of these were the territories, where education at all levels was offered. Areas of special federal jurisdiction now include the District of Columbia, reservations such as military posts, Indian reservations and national parks, and the outlying possessions.

In 1804 an Act of Congress approved the administration of education in the District of Columbia by established authorities; subsequent acts delegated the administration to these authorities. The organic act of 1906 for the educational system in the District of Columbia and other legislation has made clear the continuing policy of Congress to maintain in the District a complete system of education as that term is commonly understood in the United States — including higher education, at least to the extent of operation of a teacher-training institution.

Provisions of the Constitution, treaties, legislative acts and court decisions have contributed to the education of Indians living on reservations. The Office of Indian Affairs, which since its creation has administered educational services for Indians, was established in 1824. Lodged in the Department of the Interior since 1849, the Office has provided for the education of Indians through day schools and boarding schools and federal payments to states.

As a responsibility incidental to the building of the Panama Canal, the government in 1905 took steps to establish a system of public education in the Canal Zone. Besides elementary and secondary schools, there is now a junior college.

The varying conditions on federal reservations have led from time to time to different federal provisions for education in these areas. It is noteworthy that the policy has been expressed in recent actions. Acts of Congress within the last decade have established general policies for education on federal properties.

## CONTRACTS WITH COLLEGES FOR RESEARCH

As early as 1830 the Secretary of the Treasury entered into a contractual arrangement with the Franklin Institute of Philadelphia for an investigation of the causes of explosion of steam boilers. During World War I the federal government began large-scale contractual agreements with colleges and universities for research activities connected with national defense. Some such arrangements were continued after the war. The scope of such research and the number of fields of investigation were greatly increased during World War II.

Within the last several years a considerable portion of the large expenditures for the research programs of the federal government has been going to colleges and universities through grants and contracts. The federal government has developed a broad utilization of the facilities of colleges and universities for research purposes.

There has been much disagreement concerning the extent, if any, to which government research contracts have generally given financial aid to the institutions. Some investigators have said that these "practical" research projects, predominantly in the natural sciences, have created problems for the institutions. Cited problems have included the development of an imbalance between the teaching and research functions, and impairment of the need for the colleges and universities to advance the frontiers of knowledge through theoretical research.

The government contracts have given important, if indirect, financial aid to many students in the form of opportunities for employment in research, often with credit toward advanced degrees. Altogether the contracts have had effects upon higher education so extensive that they must be considered in a following chapter.

### LAND-GRANT COLLEGES AND ASSOCIATED SERVICES

With the passage of the Morrill Act of 1862 the Congress began giving aid to the states for higher education in certain specified fields. Agricultural and industrial expansion had emphasized the need for more and better education in the natural sciences. The Congress took action to insure the development in each state of at least one college adapted to the needs of agriculture and industry.

*The Colleges*

The Act provided a grant of federal lands or land scrip to each state in the amount of 30,000 acres for each senator and representative in Congress from that state. It gave scrip to the states in which there were not sufficient federal lands to make up their allotments. The proceeds of the sales of these grants were to be used for the endowment and support of colleges "to teach such branches of learning as are related to agriculture and the mechanic arts, in such manner as the legislatures of the states may respectively prescribe." The Act also required the teaching of military science.

Congress later enacted the Second Morrill Act (1890) and other loans for continuing annual appropriations to these institutions. They now number 68. Commonly called the land-grant colleges and universities they have also sometimes been referred to as "democracy's colleges," because of the impetus they gave to the expansion of public higher education.

In the second Morrill Act, the Congress introduced the policy of federal money grants for instruction in certain branches of higher education. The Act specified subjects, required annual reports to a federal agency, and provided for withholding of

federal funds under certain conditions. It set a pattern for subvention programs not only in education but also in other fields.

The federal grants for these institutions have markedly influenced the course of higher education in the United States, by contributing significantly to its expansion, and by stimulating state support of education in agriculture, engineering and the natural sciences.

*The Experiment Stations and Extension Service*

With the Hatch Act of 1887 the Congress initiated the granting of funds to each land-grant college for the establishment and maintenance of an agricultural experiment station. This was the first Act giving funds to the states for "practical" research. Continuing annual appropriations for this purpose were increased by several subsequent acts. The Department of Agriculture has administered the federal funds for the experiment stations, which have helped provide a scientific basis for agricultural education at all levels.

Through the Smith-Lever Act of 1914, the Congress formulated cooperation with the states in extension work in agriculture and home economics. Pursuant to the intent of Congress, this program has been carried out in connection with the land-grant colleges. Subsequent acts have further developed the basic federal policy and provided additional funds for this work, with the requirement of "matching" by state, college, or local funds for participation in the program. The Secretary of Agriculture has the responsibility for administering the federal funds.

Acts of Congress in 1924 and 1937 authorized certain reforestation activities involving extension work and the land-grant colleges.

In the study of the federal government and higher education made for the Commission on Financing Higher Education, Richard G. Axt named four characteristics of the policy which led to the grants for the land-grant colleges and associated services. In brief these characteristics were:

(1) The federal policy toward higher education was influenced by public land policy and the interests of farmers; (2) it emphasized vocational and professional rather than "liberal" education; (3) it included emphasis on "practical" scientific research; and (4) accented the education of the many rather than a select few.

## THE ROLE OF THE OFFICE OF EDUCATION

In 1866 the National Association of State and City School Superintendents presented a memorial to Congress urging the creation of a federal educational agency. Subsequently, Representative (later President) James A. Garfield introduced a bill for this purpose. The bill, signed by President Johnson in March, 1867, set up a federal "Department of Education" headed by a Commissioner. Since then, Congressional and Executive actions have several times changed both the name of the agency and its position in the federal structure. As the "Office of Education" it has been a constituent of the Department of Health, Education and Welfare since the creation of that Department in 1953.

The primary function of the Office of Education, as set forth in the establishing act, has been to collect such statistics and facts as shall show the conditions and progress of education, to diffuse information to aid the people of the United States in the establishment and maintenance of efficient school systems, and otherwise to promote the cause of education at all levels. Subsequent acts and Executive orders have added responsibilities for administering federal grants-in-aid to education, cooperative research, special programs and studies, and other functions.

The Office of Education has served as the principal agency of the federal government for formulating educational policies and coordinating elementary, secondary and higher educational activities at the national level. In carrying out its work the Office has cooperated with other government agencies, the states and territories, professional groups and institutions, citizen groups and individuals and international agencies.

## Role of the Office in Higher Education

The Act establishing the Office of Education required the commissioner to audit the several grants of land made by Congress to promote education, including those for the land-grant colleges under the Morrill Act of 1862.

Pursuant to the second Morrill Act of 1890 and subsequent delegation of authority by the Secretary of the Interior, the Office of Education has since administered federal grants-in-aid for the further endowment and support of the land-grant institutions.

An Act of Congress in 1928 charged the "Bureau of Education" to make an annual inspection of Howard University.

Among the several emergency programs administered by the Office of Education during World War II was the Engineering, Science and Management War Training Program. In cooperation with degree-granting colleges and universities the Office carried this out for the organization of short courses of college grade designed to meet the shortage of engineers, chemists, physicists and production supervisors.

The Office also administered the Student War Loans, which furnished assistance in designated technical and professional fields, and projects for research in universities.

Through the years, the Division of Higher Education in the Office of Education has been assigned, and now carries out, among other duties, the responsibilities for: (1) formulating plans, policies and procedures for higher education; (2) administering funds appropriated for the land-grant colleges and universities; (3) allocating funds for loans to students in higher education; (4) allocating funds for fellowships in graduate schools; (5) negotiating federal contracts for centers for teaching modern foreign languages, for training to improve the qualifications of counseling and guidance personnel, and for the operation of institutes for advanced training in the use of new teaching methods and instructional materials; and (6) advising the Housing and Home Finance Agency on educational eligibility of institutions seeking loans for college housing.

The Division of Higher Education has been carrying out its work through the College and University Administration Branch, the Higher Education Programs Branch, and the Financial Aid Branch.

*The College and University Administration Branch—* has been promoting improvement in the organization and administration of higher education. It has conducted and published field studies and consulted with representatives of higher education.

*The Higher Education Programs Branch—* has been promoting improvement in the liberal arts and graduate and professional education, with emphasis on social science, as well as on physical sciences and mathematics, teacher education, and engineering. It has worked through conferences, institutes, publications and addresses.

*The Financial Aid Branch—* has been responsible for the administration of the National Defense Education Act of 1958 as it pertains to higher education. The Branch has administered the National Defense Student Loan Program, the National Defense Fellowship Program, and the Language Development Program authorized by the Act. The Branch has also been responsible for the establishment of counseling and guidance training institutes authorized by the Act for the identification and encouragement of able students.

Commenting upon the future role of the Office of Education, in October, 1959, the United States Commission of Education said in part:

The future role of the Office can be readily envisaged as a natural and necessary development of the decades of experience in these areas of activity: (1) statistical and informational services,

(2) surveys and consultative services, and (3) participation in financing educational facilities and programs. Judging from the past history of the Office of Education, the increasing national interest in education can continue to be served by assistance without interference and leadership without domination. The Office of Education was instituted as an integral part of the Nation's total educational enterprise, and the significance of Office activities has been enhanced by the deepening realization that education is intimately related to all major fields of national and international concern.

### VOCATIONAL EDUCATION
### AND REHABILITATION

For many decades the federal government has engaged in the carrying out, financing or otherwise promoting vocational programs for civilians, some in higher education.

*Nautical Education—Merchant Marine*

An 1874 Act of Congress established nautical schools at six designated ports. This Act inaugurated the principle (already mentioned) of "matching" funds. It provided that a state or locality would receive federal funds equal to the amount appropriated by the state or local government. The training in the nautical schools was later consolidated in four institutions, known as state maritime academies. These train Merchant Marine officers, who upon graduation receive the degree of bachelor of science.

In 1938 the Maritime Commission established the Merchant Marine Cadet Corps, which in 1941 began operating the Merchant Marine Academy at Kings Point, Long Island. This became a permanent, degree-granting institution. Kings Point is to the Merchant Marine as West Point is to the Army and Annapolis to the Navy, except that its graduates become employees of steamship companies rather than of the federal government.

*In-Service Training of Government Personnel*

The federal policy of affording and encouraging in-service training of government personnel appears to have had its origin in the form of an apprentice school for engravers, started by the Bureau of Engraving and Printing in 1879. Thirty years later the National Bureau of Standards instituted technical training for employees, which later led to the organization of the National Bureau of Standards Graduate School. The well-known Graduate School of the Department of Agriculture was organized in 1920, principally for advanced training of federal personnel. Its certificates of credit are accepted by graduate schools of a number of colleges and universities.

An Act of Congress approved July 7, 1958, declares that self-education by federal employees shall be supported and extended by government-sponsored programs.

Systems of in-service training in the federal government now vary widely. They comprise many types of courses and instruction, mainly at the secondary level and above.

## Vocational Education Below College Grade

Federal promotion of vocational education below college grade undoubtedly has had important effects upon higher education. By passing the Smith-Hughes Act of 1917, for example, the Congress created a new federal policy in agricultural and industrial education. This Act extended below college grade a stimulus similar to that given at the higher level through the Morrill Act of 1862.

Acts of Congress in 1929, 1934, and 1936 continuing and extending the promotion of vocational education below college grade were superseded by the George-Barden Act of 1946, which added new services. Further extension was made by the 84th Congress, which legislated training for practical nursing, for the fishing industry, and for teaching vocational subjects. The laws have required dollar-for-dollar matching of federal funds with state or local funds, except for instruction in practical nursing during the years 1957 and 1958.

## Vocational Rehabilitation

In the Smith-Bankhead Act of 1920 the Congress began to provide federal funds for cooperation with the states in the vocational rehabilitation of persons disabled in industry. A number of subsequent acts, including the Social Security Act as amended in 1939, have changed the federal provisions for this program, which utilizes education at all levels. About 20 percent of the total federal funds for vocational rehabilitation is used for education of disabled persons.

## Aeronautical Education

Pursuant to the Civilian Pilot Training Act of 1939 the Civil Aeronautics Administration organized a program of civilian pilot training in cooperation with colleges throughout the country. The program was discontinued five years later.

The Federal Aviation Agency, which succeeded the Civil Aeronautics Administration in January, 1959, currently aids and encourages the development of aviation education by furnishing technical assistance and guidance to schools, colleges and educational bodies.

### EDUCATION FOR VETERANS

Vocational rehabilitation training for veterans dates from World War I. The Vocational Rehabilitation Act of 1918 provided substantially that any discharged veteran of World War I unable to carry on a gainful occupation should be given such course of rehabilitation as the Federal Board for Vocational Education should furnish. The Act imposed upon the Board the responsibility for facilities, courses and instructors, pay allowances for maintenance and support of trainees, and other things necessary for vocational rehabilitation and placement. Section 3 of the Act provided for training, but not maintenance allowances, for honorably discharged veterans disabled but not seriously handicapped vocationally.

In 1921 Congress established the Veterans Administration and assigned its duties and powers previously exercised by the Federal Board for Vocational Education respecting disabled veterans. Unlike the Federal Board for Vocational Education, the VA did not establish educational institutions of its own although given authority to do so.

The Vocational Rehabilitation Act of 1943, commonly referred to simply as "Public Law 16," afforded vocational rehabilitation training benefits for veterans of World War II like those given disabled veterans of World War I.

The Servicemen's Readjustment Act of 1944 (often referred to simply as Public Law 346) extended education to veterans in unprecedented scope. Most veterans were eligible. Each was free to select his own course of study, his school, college or other training establishment approved by the authorized agency in the state in which the establishment was located. He was allowed time not in excess of one year plus the number of months he was in the service, not in excess of forty-eight.

The law prohibited control or supervision by any federal agency over any state educational agency or any educational or training institution participating in this program.

Except for certain cases under Public Law 346, as amended, both Public Law 16 and Public Law 346 terminated on July 25, 1956. Similar benefits were later extended to veterans of the Korean conflict.

But Public Law 550 modified veterans' educational benefits. Under a simplified system of allowance, the individual veteran became responsible for payments to the educational institution.

In the history of federal policy, the Servicemen's Readjustment Act of 1944 has been called "the twentieth century Morrill Act." It led to enrollment of unprecedented numbers of college students and gave thousands of young people an education they might not have got otherwise.

SURPLUS PROPERTY DISPOSAL

In 1919 Congress passed and the President approved an act authorizing the Secretary of War to sell to educational institutions "at 15 percentum of their cost to trade," World War I surplus machine tools under control of the War Department. Later acts, before World War II, authorized the Armed Forces to donate to educational institutions certain specified surplus equipment needed for vocational educational purposes.

During World War II the government accumulated huge quantities of property which later became surplus, and some of this was made available for education, public health, and civil defense.

*Surplus Personal Property*

The Surplus Property Act of 1944 provided for transfers of personal property to educational and health institutions at discount from fair value, and for donation of personal property to such institutions when the administrative cost of other disposal would exceed the recoverable value. In 1946 the Office of Education began determining the educational need for such property and its allocation among the states and territories.

In 1948 Congress further developed the policy. It authorized the Armed Forces to donate personal property to schools, colleges and universities upon determination by the Commissioner of Education that such property was needed and usable.

The Federal Property and Administrative Services Act of 1949 repealed some of the earlier legislation and made surplus personal property of all executive agencies available by donation to educational institutions. Amendments in 1950 and 1956 made such property also donable for public health and civil defense.

Under existing legislation, the General Services Administrator is authorized, in his discretion, to give surplus federal property which has been determined to be usable and needed for education, health or civil defense to *established state agencies* for distribution to eligible institutions within the respective states. The Secretary of Health, Education and Welfare is expected to decide what surplus federal property is needed for health, educational and civil defense purposes. (He has delegated the responsibility respecting civil defense to the Director of the Office of Civil and Defense Mobilization.) The Secretary is also responsible for equitable allocations of such property to the state agencies, and for establishing minimum standards of operation. The administration of the Secretary's responsibilities is centralized in the Office of Field Administration of his Department.

*Real Property*

The Federal Property and Administrative Services Act of 1949, as amended, established a federal practice of selling or leasing surplus real property for education or public health where need exists. With respect to determination of selling or leasing price the legislation takes into consideration the benefits that have accrued or will accrue to the United States from such use. The responsibilities of the Administrator of General Services and the Secretary of Health, Education and Welfare are essentially the same in the surplus personal property program, already described.

Institutions recipient of federal surplus real property pay for it partly in cash and partly in public benefits accruing through the institutions. Public benefits, which are predetermined by the program use, may justify a full 100 percent discount.

DEPRESSION-PERIOD PROGRAMS AND POLICIES

During the depression of the 1930's the federal government carried out educational activities as aspects of relief. For example, the Civilian Conservation Corps, created by Congress in 1937, offered vocational training as well as employment to youth in need of jobs. The Federal Emergency Relief Administration, established in 1933, worked widely in the states, giving part-time employment to college students and to out-of-work teachers. The emergency agency, first called the Works Progress Administration, and later the Works Projects Administration, supported a large number of projects ranging from literary classes to college education. The National Youth Administration, established in 1935, gave work training to unemployed youth and part-time jobs to needy college students.

The Public Works Administration made numerous grants and loans to states and municipalities for the construction of school and college buildings. The Reconstruction Finance Corporation also made self-liquidating loans to states, municipal authorities and institutions for educational projects. . . .

SCHOLARSHIPS, FELLOWSHIPS, TRAINEESHIPS

. . . The "Regular" NROTC differs markedly from the "Contract" NROTC and from the Army and Air Force ROTC programs. Each year the Navy selects approximately 1,600 high school seniors for four years of college in the "Regular" NROTC. Each person is free to select his field of study and during the academic year receives $50 a month besides tuition, fees, books, instructional equipment and uniforms. Upon graduation, the "Regular" enrollee is obligated to accept a commission in the Regular Navy or Marine Corps and serve at least three years on active duty.

The federal government has also promoted manpower development through other scholarships, fellowships and traineeships, particularly in the sciences. The National Science Foundation Act of 1950 created the National Science Foundation for a number of purposes, including the following related to higher education in the sciences: (1) development and encouragement of a national policy for the promotion of basic research and education; (2) awarding of scholarships and graduate fellowships; and (3) providing a central clearinghouse for information concerning scientific and technical personnel.

In 1952 the Foundation started giving fellowships. Through grants for the support of basic scientific research the Foundation has also indirectly aided a large number of graduate and post-doctoral students performing research services for the grantee agencies or institutions.

Under the provisions of the Atomic Energy Act of 1946 (amended in 1954) the Atomic Energy Commission established small numbers of fellowships in radiological physics in 1948, in industrial medicine in 1949, and in industrial hygiene in 1952.

Federal research fellowships in public health began with the passage of the National Cancer Institute Act of 1937. As other national institutes of health have been activated they have also organized research fellowships or traineeships or both. Related to these was the provision by the 84th Congress of graduate traineeships to increase the supply of public health specialists and the number of professional nurses to teach or supervise other nurses.

With Title IV of the National Defense Education Act of 1958 came appropriation of "such sums as may be necessary" to reduce the shortage of qualified college teachers. The Act took two approaches: giving money to graduate students, and increasing the number and scope of graduate programs. The Office of Education allotted 1,000 fellowships for the first year of operation.

### COLLEGE HOUSING PROGRAMS

Under an extension of the Lanham Act of 1941 the federal government began assistance to college housing on a temporary basis.

The Housing Act of 1950 authorized the Housing Administrator to borrow up to $300 million from the Treasury to support long-term, low-interest-rate loans to colleges and universities for the construction of dormitories and faculty housing. The legislation represented Congressional recognition of a critical, accumulated need for on-campus residential facilities for the fast-growing enrollments of the institutions. However, because of the advent of the Korean conflict the program was suspended in July 1950. Subsequently a program limited to $40 million of borrowing was activated to serve the most acute needs arising from defense or defense-related activities.

By the housing amendments of 1955 federal loans were continued to colleges and universities for dormitories and certain other housing. This authorization was increased to $500 million in 1955 and to $750 million in 1956 ($100 million to be lent for service facilities such as dining rooms and student unions). In the 1957 Housing Act the Congress boosted it to $925 million, including $25 million for housing for student nurses and interns.

The maximum term of a loan has been fifty years. Junior colleges are eligible. Loans are administered by the Housing and Home Finance Agency through direct government-college transactions. The Office of Education provides educational advisory services.

At the close of 1959, loan funds for college housing were exhausted; and it was expected that in 1960 the Congress would consider new college-housing legislation.

\* \* \*

### CONCLUSIONS

From this historical study a number of conclusions emerge, the following among them.

The policies might be classified in several ways. First they might be called either "permanent" or "temporary." Federal support of the land-grant colleges is continuing and presumably permanent, whereas aid to students provided by the National Youth Administration during the depression of the 1930's, and operation of the Army Specialized Training Program during World War II, were temporary. . . .

With respect to underlying purpose the policies might be classified as pertaining to (1) the national defense, (2) the promotion of public health, or (3) other specified purposes. . . .

An outstanding conclusion from this study is that there is no single department or agency which has an overall responsibility or even coordinating authority for carrying out federal policies in higher education. The Office of Education (which might be supposed to have such authority) is only one of a large number of agencies administering programs in this field. From a study for the Commission on Organization of the Executive Branch of the Government, Hollis Allen found that only one percent of federal funds expended for education in the fiscal year 1949 was channeled through the Office of Education. Later studies have shown this percentage continuing very small.

In some instances two or more federal agencies have cooperated in the administration of a particular educational program. There has been, however, no general cooperation of the federal departments and independent agencies in the administration of federal educational activities. Frequently a large educational program has been administered quite independently by a single federal agency.

It is apparent that in education, as well as in some other fields, the nation has not been so much concerned with comprehensive organization as with satisfying special needs or interests. Federal agencies desiring to utilize education or educational institutions for special purposes have obtained diverse authorizations for a variety of higher-educational programs without evident regard for broad federal policy. Some consolidations of administration have been made and others attempted. However, a number of the separate programs in higher education have become deeply rooted historically, and there are strong forces in favor of maintaining their independent administration. Furthermore, the close relationship of many of the programs to the broader functions of the agencies administering them raises serious questions of the feasibility and practicality of consolidating the administration of these educational activities. . . .

There has been no blanket legislation giving all federal agencies similar authority to enter into contracts with colleges and universities for research. Also there has been no overall legislation governing the geographical distribution of such contracts. According to information obtained from some agencies, they have awarded their contracts to institutions judged best equipped to perform the desired services. The question of what other considerations may have influenced the awarding of such contracts is open to further study. Many of the largest federal contracts have been given to some of the nation's largest and most heavily endowed universities. This fact has raised the question of the effects of federal payments to educational institutions upon (1) the stronger and the weaker colleges and universities, and upon (2) the geographical distribution of opportunities for higher education in the United States.

Federal payments to colleges and universities, for whatever purpose, have had important indirect as well as direct effects. The choice of a university by hundreds of veterans, for example, may have been influenced by their knowledge of the existence of superior educational facilities at that institution. These better facilities in turn may have resulted in part from the use of federal funds paid to that institution for purposes other than the education of veterans.

On the other hand, some universities have declared that they have received no financial gains from fulfilling federal contracts. Whether the contracts have, as a whole, tended to make "the rich richer and the poor poorer" among the institutions might be an appropriate question for investigation.

For a number of years higher education

in the United States has been receiving a large measure of its support from federal funds. In the academic year 1958–59 between one-sixth and one-fifth of the income usable for educational and general purposes by institutions of higher education came from federal sources. This does not include transfers of federal surplus property or direct federal appropriations for building purposes. Federal payments to the institutions now consist principally of those for the further endowment and support of the land-grant colleges, and payments made under contracts for research and for the training of federal civilian and military personnel.

Generally the federal programs are for the accomplishment of educational objectives of federal agencies which are promotional to the primary functions of those agencies. This study has revealed little evidence that the primarily non-educational federal agencies administering higher-educational programs have been particularly concerned about the effects of their respective programs on higher education in general, although these effects have been far-reaching.

In this connection it might be pointed out that the many service training programs have considerable general educational value for the nation. They lift its educational level, even though they are designed for specific purposes of the administering agencies.

Following is a brief summary of some of the characteristics of federal policies that have evolved to date:

(1) There has been no general policy governing what the federal government should or should not do in higher education.

(2) Federal activities in this field have generally been subsidiary to (although often also basic to) the performance of other federal functions, such as provision for the national defense, or promotion of public health.

(3) The federal programs have been largely for the higher education of special groups, such as military personnel, veterans, and federal civilian employees.

(4) The federal programs have emphasized the teaching of particular subjects, notably military science, the natural sciences, agriculture and engineering.

(5) Directly through fellowship awards, and indirectly through contracts with institutions for research, federal programs have provided financial aid to a number of graduate students.

(6) Federal policies have advanced "practical" research, particularly in the physical, biological and medical sciences but have given little direct aid to theoretical research in the social sciences or in the humanities.

(7) The federal policies have encouraged vocational and professional rather than liberal education.

(8) Federal policies have produced a great variety of procedures in the administration of federal higher-educational programs, sometimes involving relationships of a primarily non-educational federal agency with hundreds of educational institutions.

(9) Although mainly promoting training for particular groups, federal policies have also encouraged higher education for large numbers of people.

(10) Federal policies have in the main promoted publicly controlled rather than privately controlled education.

*Sidney C. Sufrin*

# THE NATIONAL DEFENSE EDUCATION ACT AND ITS IMPACT

THE ACT — A CATEGORICAL INSTRUMENT

The NDEA is a monumental legislative reaction to the great national concern with education. It follows tradition in at least two ways insofar as elementary and secondary education is concerned. First, in general, it provides funds for certain educational functions. In this sense the federal government gives money to the states with a set of fairly general instructions as to how the money shall be spent and for what purposes. The administration of the funds and the programs is essentially a concern for the states. The funds are not given to the states without strings, however. There is at least the auditing requirement to assure that the purposes of the grant are being accomplished.

The second traditional aspect of NDEA is that the monies are given to the states for special purposes, e.g., education in mathematics, science, and language, or construction of scientific laboratories in secondary schools. Since the money is given for well-defined purposes, the program takes on some slight coloration of the vocational education programs which, as pointed out, have had a long history in the United States. . . .

The provisions of the Act may be divided into three major categories. The first is the assistance to students at the university and collegiate level. Such assistance is given through loans and fellowships (Title II, Loans to Students in Institutions of Higher Learning; Title IV, National Defense Fellowships). Second are the programs for assisting state education at the elementary and secondary levels. These programs include funds for strengthening science, mathematics, and foreign language instruction; funds to strengthen the guidance, counseling and testing programs of schools; and finally area vocational programs (Title III, Financial Assistance for Strengthening Mathematics and Modern Foreign Language Instruction; Title V, Guidance, Counselling, Testing: Identification and Encouragement of Able Students; Title VIII, Area Vocational Programs). The state programs are administratively aided by federal government funds to strengthen the statistical services of state departments of education (Title X, Improvement of Statistical Services of State Departments of Education). The third area of concern of the Act is to assist interested research scholars in finding better ways to teach. This is contained in Title VII (Research and Experimentation in the Effect of the Utilization of Television, Radio, Motion Pictures and Related Media for Educational Purposes).

\* \* \*

SCHOOLMEN VIEW FEDERAL AID

The attitudes of the professional educators at the state and local levels with respect to NDEA can be summarized in a fashion such as this:

Federal aid to elementary and secondary education is probably a necessity. The facts of political life in the several states make it most unlikely that state and local funds will be forthcoming in sufficient additional amounts to raise substantially the education enterprise at the elementary and secondary levels. On the whole, the public

From Sidney C. Sufrin, *Administering the National Defense Education Act* No. 8, pp. 9–10, 11, 46–64 in *The Economics and Politics of Public Education Series*. Copyright © 1963 by Syracuse University Press. Reprinted by permission of Syracuse University Press.

educational system, as presently conceived, has worked fairly well in that when given a chance it has succeeded in making the population literate and has inculcated various social and technical skills. Some of us would go further and assert that the public educational system in the United States is the most effective in the world!

However, the ever-emerging complexity of modern society requires educational changes and adjustments which are expensive because often they are experimental and require new skills of the instructor as well as new, costly devices. Some of these changes are in the sciences and mathematics, others are in the social disciplines, the humanities, or in technical training. Realistically, educational processes cannot remain static in a developing society, for education is an integral and significant part of the changing social situation.

*Taxes*

The position of the schoolmen is that the traditional tax base for education—property—is in many instances overburdened from the viewpoint of the taxpayer. It is not, therefore, meaningful to argue that the taxpayer can afford to pay more taxes because by some objective statistical measure disposable incomes are high. The point that the school administrators generally make is that the taxpayer himself, in many instances, feels that he cannot afford to pay more property taxes for education. Therefore, some indirect method of securing funds is desirable, and this indirect method implies the use of federal funds secured by whatever method the federal government uses to secure funds—largely the personal and corporate income tax, with redistribution to the states.

*Federal Aid*

Federal aid, however, should not be categorical, according to the view of virtually all the schoolmen interviewed. This is to say, the commentators are inclined to argue that categorical aid, aid for particularly defined objectives such as mathematics or language, tends to support aspects of education which the Congress or some national administrative agency in Washington be-

lieves to be significant. What appears to be significant on the national level, however, need not be significant on the local or state level.

One example frequently cited is aid for modern languages. In some sections of the country, state officials believe that additional funds spent on improving foreign language instruction pay less in social dividends than equal funds spent for other purposes, such as technical and vocational training or improvement in mathematics and English. Personal and social needs, from the viewpoint of training and education, are so different in various parts of the country that categorical aid is an ineffective device to solve the range of problems. Yet when categorical aid is offered, either on a matching base or on some other basis, the local and state officials feel reluctant to pass up a chance for "cheap" money, even though it involves matching. Matching, it is sometimes feared, is a means of federal control.

What frequently occurs is that the categorical aid grant is accepted and then the funds are used, in part at least, for other purposes. This, in the language of one state administrator, "makes crooks out of local boards and local principals." In less dramatic form, the argument is that categorical aid tends to create imbalances in the curriculum offerings because of the attractiveness of cheap money, and also tends to induce local school administrators to seek and find questionable accounting techniques and rationalizations for the use of equipment for purposes other than those contemplated by the categorical program.

Yet the improper use of categorical aid is not the major concern which gives rise to criticism. Of great immediate importance is the feeling that the NDEA program involves paper work, both at the local and state levels, far beyond what funds of similar size secured from state sources involve. The growth in size of the Office of Education is often seen as a prelude to more pressure by the expanded bureau.

*Paper Work and Auditing*

The paper work concern is endemic. The whole administrative NDEA process is bathed in the threatening shadow of the General Accounting Office. Federal funds, it is believed, require accounting and auditing care and justification far beyond that normally evinced for state funds. State school administrators who have contact with the Washington federal officials are perhaps more conscious of the GAO spectre than local boards and local school officials. Local officials are less sensitive to "Washington" as a direct threat, since it is a kind of threat by state reference and they are often unimpressed. Consequently state officials constantly fret over the handling of funds by the local boards and local schools, and require more information and records than local boards and schools are willing or perhaps able to provide. The result is a frustration of the state officials, a frustration which they feel to be unnecessary and which might be relieved by appropriate action from Washington.

Similarly, state officials feel their position threatened by the Office of Education. Chapter and verse were not cited to show where the Office of Education had intervened in any markedly untoward sense; nevertheless, state officials are jealous of their own control over curriculum and general administration. They fear that federal funds, even though slight, are a vehicle by which the Office of Education can ride into what has up to now been a state domain; namely, the supervision of elementary and secondary education.

Yet the fear of the Office of Education and, to a certain degree, the fear of federal auditing are paradoxical because state officials understand and support the view that where federal funds are involved the federal government has an obligation to concern itself with how and for what the funds are spent. No one can object to auditing; the only objection can be to unnecessary auditing and record-keeping. The resolution of this paradox—fear of Washington, but a recognition of Washington's responsibility—is not at all clear.

Local and state responsibility for federal funds was not denied by the schoolmen. Accounting for federal funds is necessary. That the accounting be made simpler than it is, and that federal funds be in a sense melded with state funds, were the ideals of the schoolmen interviewed.

In the small but select universe of fifteen state and local school officials who were queried about the administration of NDEA there was general agreement that the accounting, auditing, and purchase order procedures are burdensome and probably irrelevant in that they do not reflect the needs for accountability. Part of this unhappy situation, according to the respondents, is attributable to the administration of NDEA from Washington, and part is due to the uncertainty and insecurity which state officials feel, both with respect to Washington and to their local administrations. A third part is due to the unwillingness (or inability) of the local school agencies to perform properly the functions expected of them.

Examples were adduced to show that local administrators sometimes do not understand that the Act provides for the purchase of new equipment and programs and, having a fondness and respect for existing established programs, local officials try hard to use the federal funds to pay for established programs and their extension. For example, many believe that tape recorders are needed to carry out a program in English. Funds for tape recorders may be secured under the foreign language provisions of the NDEA. The reader can understand, without approving, the subsequent action of the local school principal, who is always short of funds.

Another example of red tape and cumbersome administration is the provision in at least one state that every individual invoice must be filed with and examined by state officials. The administrative care in filing and examination of federal funds is far greater than that of the state funds because of the overriding fear of the U.S. General Accounting Office. In at least one state the accounting practice is to require that each different piece of equipment purchased with federal money virtually have its own order sheet. The filing problem becomes backbreaking. Yet in the examination of the order sheets, little has been learned of any policy violations. At best, it is argued, state officials have picked up unimportant mistakes in arithmetic or other minor clerical errors. Conscious errors also are picked up. For example, through a field investigation one state official discovered that the orders for equipment under one of the National Defense Education programs were being charged at list price, while, in fact, the local school was receiving a discounted price with the difference credited to the school for other purposes. No individual here profited in any profoundly improper sense. The federal government paid more for an item than the school normally would have paid, while the school was the recipient of a credit for the difference between its usual (market) price and the list price. To understand the motive is not to approve the action, but the motive was not one of personal gain; rather it was intended to thwart what was believed a bad practice to gain a good end!

*Size and Efficiency*

It would appear that very large school districts—those with complex accounting and administrative controls and a well-organized purchasing system—find the NDEA requirements not especially excessive. Some large districts, however, have educational programs which are above the average in effectiveness in relation to need, even without NDEA help.

To such districts and to larger cities generally NDEA has probably been more of a boon than to some of the smaller communities. This view was frequently expressed both by state and local officials. Richer (and often larger) communities, it is averred by some school superintendents, have taken more advantage of the NDEA than poorer communities. The NDEA funds, in a sense, were incorporated into the plans that the local schools already had for the extension of their mathematics, language, and science programs. Furthermore, the equipment and remodeling, in many instances, would have occurred perhaps a year or two later without NDEA help. This led one of the state officials to suggest that NDEA aid or, from his viewpoint, more desirable general aid to local school boards should be allocated in accordance with the ability to pay of the local school board, even though this implied different matching fund ratios for different states. Thus a poor state might only match federal funds with 20 per cent of its own funds while a richer state might match federal funds with 70 per cent of its own funds. This keenness of feeling with respect to ability to pay and equalization was apparent in the discussions with the school officials, and there was a strong feeling that these principles of equity were not being met by NDEA.

*Categorical vs. General Aid*

Categorical versus general aid is the one problem to which the discussions with the school administrators always returned. No school administrator interviewed was opposed to the principle of federal aid. No administrator interviewed supported categorical aid as a wise and inclusive policy; all supported general aid. The last sentence, however, requires a qualification. Some administrators argued that the federal government might properly provide funds for bettering teachers' salaries, building schools, or strengthening the training in given fields such as mathematics. While this view, in a sense, supports categorical aid, those school officials who supported this also went on to argue that the expenditure of the funds and the standards required of the local schools should be entirely a matter of state control rather than of federal control.

The views of school administrators with

respect to categorical versus general aid are based on an almost universal philosophical principle that the curriculum and personnel control of education is and should be state oriented. This view is held as a belief or even an assumption, rather than as a rational conclusion, although many arguments of a rational sort are adduced to defend the position of state autonomy.

## The Locus of Power

There was but little attempt on the part of the respondents to consider the wisdom and propriety either of federal standards for education or for more strict local control of education. Insofar as the local school superintendents and state school administrators are concerned, the issue of the location of the central power to control elementary and secondary schools has been determined, and the locus of authority, in the American tradition, is the state. The implication that local administrators lack breadth of vision and that federal administrators are domineering is clear. Thus, by exclusion, state administration remains. On this issue there seems to be little tendency to engage in a great or even a minor debate.

This strong attachment of school administrators to the state as the central agency determining standards, or at least minimal standards, is of more than passing interest because the local boards often tend to believe that determination of policy standards should properly be in the hands of local boards, thus arguing for decentralization as against state centralization. This view was abundantly apparent in contacts with officials of the New York State School Boards Association.

The superintendents of schools in the cities, in their turn, while respecting the function of the state school administrators to determine certain rather general minimal standards and to administer state funds destined for local school districts, were protective of the right and authority of the local school administrative machinery. In general local administrators suggested fis-

cal independence from county or city budget determinations.

It is not at all unlikely in the view of some administrators that should federal aid to education increase (especially on a categorical basis), the growth of federal administration will create a feeling on the part of the federal officials that their role is superior to that of either state officials or local officials. That federal personnel and bureaus will not increase with a larger dollar program is possible, but not very likely. Administration and administrative loyalty are closely tied up with the feeling that the administrative machinery to which one happens to belong is the wisely "chosen instrument" for carrying out a given function.

The division or sharing of authority and power among administrative institutions and administrators is indeed a difficult problem. On several occasions, local superintendents of schools pointed out that the typical superintendent of the moderately large city is more qualified as an educational administrator than state officials. State officials in their turn felt superior to the city school officials.

Another aspect of what may be called administrative parochialism is also apparent. Each administrator not only desires great freedom, he also tends to attach great, often undue, importance to what he is administering. School superintendents and state officials are the objects of various types of lobbying by their subordinates.

Administrative loyalty which results in the administrator's giving undue significance to his area of responsibility is paralleled by teachers with a subject matter loyalty. In paraphrase, one administrator said:

To be sure, each particular discipline, mathematics, social studies, the humanities, and literature, believes that it should receive more of the school monies than it presently receives. If this were not so, the teachers and officials in this area would probably not be sufficiently devoted to their disciplines. It is, however, a function of higher administration to make the determination of how the funds should be distributed among the several disciplines, and this is essentially a less than national task because the viewpoint of public social and individual need from the perspective of Washington is not the same as need from the perspective of the state capital or the local school board.

He might have added that the perspective from the viewpoint of the local school board is much narrower than the perspective from the state capital.

*Aid and Program Imbalance*

All the schoolmen interviewed, without exception, believe that federal aid is necessary, yet they fear federal control. They even fear the sheer technical control over funds by a federal agency because, they argue, technical control over funds can ultimately lead to control of substance. That the one who pays the piper the most calls most of the tunes is forgotten. That state and local governments pay, and for the foreseeable future will continue to pay the major share of the costs is not considered a conclusive argument. There is a great inherent fear of the power of the federal government, a power not defined merely by its share of any money payments.

Providing funds in greater quantity for the sciences, it is feared, can lead to swamping the curricula of individual schools in science. Ultimately, allocating varying sums of money to the several disciplines, it is argued, might control the emphasis which the local schools would have in their curricula. This is but one step from determining the specifics of what is taught or, as one official put it, "Racism or some other improper social doctrine could be literally forced down the throats of the schools." This assertion, while a hyperbolic exaggeration in itself, is indicative of the depth of feeling which this particular schoolman had with respect to categorical aid, a feeling shared by many of his colleagues.

In this general line of argument, one administrator argued that the colleges and universities, in a sense, have been maneuvered into a position of having the federal government determine the directions of teaching and research in the universities. Scholarships, fellowships, and research contracts in such areas as physics and chemistry tend to emphasize these studies, not only in the university curricula but in the whole university thought process and behavior. This, the respondent argued, indirectly puts the educational planning of the university in the hands of the federal government to the extent that the university's responses to federal aid are different from what they would have been had no federal aid been available. This same schoolman expressed belief that categorical aid and increased federal control would lead to an increase in the growth of private schools which stress curricula of a more rounded or more traditional sort than the curricula in the public schools which respond to federal intervention. This he felt was retrogression, for it would place broad humanistic education in the private school sphere and technical education in the mass public school sphere. While his views were probably more strongly expressed than those of his colleagues, they were not antithetical to the views of others.

Another schoolman argued that if NDEA continues for a relatively few years then it (or something like it) must be continued forever because the programs which the schools undertake with NDEA funds are, in a sense, built into the total curriculum and budget. Withdrawal of federal funds would then be disastrous, and Congress, under the pressure from "back home," could not countenance it. His view was that the appropriate role for the federal government in curriculum building should be stimulative rather than shaping. This view was rather widely accepted by the respondents. As some expressed it, the introduction of categorical federal funds tended to reweight the financial claims of the various disciplines. The flow of federal funds to a single preferred discipline then diverts state funds from other disciplines to the discipline in question through the matching funds provision.

*The Office of Education—The Schoolmen's View*

On the relations with the Office of Education, these respondents were crystal clear. They unanimously believe that the Office of Education should not initiate any advice to the state or local school authorities, and state officials felt the Office of Education should not deal with the local school authorities except through state school authorities. On the other hand, all believe that the advice, technical studies, and technical assistance of the Office of Education would be most desirable but only when and as requested. Both state and local officials obviously desire to be administratively independent of Washington, which in this case means the Office of Education.

Two provisions of the NDEA received universal support from the respondents. These provisions dealt with the grants to states for supervisory and related services and administration of state plans (Title III), and improvement of statistical services of state educational agencies (Title X, Section 1009). The respondents in general agree that in these actions the National Defense Education Act strengthens state administrations without causing the states to institute new policies and programs or radically change programs and administrative purposes. Here it is felt that the federal government was supporting an activity which required support, and the policy effects were neutral, while the accomplishment effects were very great.

In all these reactions certain considerations stand out. In the minds of the respondents the field of educational administration seems very often to be a closed universe of discourse in which there are three operating agencies: the local school boards, the state educational agency, and the Office of Education. The feeling is that at the moment state school administrators dominate educational policy and programming within the states. Increasing the flow of funds, especially for categorical aid from the Office of Education, the respondents seem to believe and fear, would increase the power position of the central government.

## THE SCHOOLMEN'S MODEL

In this model the whole United States is broken into fifty compartments. Each compartment contains a cluster of functioning local school boards, the central agency of the state school administration, and a little opening in the compartment through which can flow federal power. The federal power is small compared to that generated within the compartment. Somewhere in the middle of the model, but not part of any compartment, is the Office of Education. At the moment its power (NDEA funds) flows through very small apertures into each one of the state compartments. The feeling is, however, that should the flow of funds, which is the carrier of power, increase, the apertures will prove too small and will be widened, and in widening will break down the compartment walls, thus attaching the educational structure directly to the federal mechanism by the flowing funds. The result will be a diminution in the importance and role of state and local school bodies.

It is thought that as and if the Congress votes more funds, the general government administrative agency—the Office of Education—will increase in size and the flow of funds carrying power will press further upon the local and state school boards. To carry the model further, the ultimate effect would be that the flow of federal funds and power would regiment the state and local bodies in such a fashion that state differences would tend to disappear, with a resulting homogeneous mass whose structure and form is directed from Washington.

This, in part, is the argument made frequently which claims that federal aid to schools of necessity implies some kind of federal control. The model and its presumed operation may or may not be appropriate in analyzing the situation in the United States. Indeed, one would be inclined to argue that it is a static picture in which the boundaries of the universe of discourse are fixed, and the boundaries surrounding the state institutions are made of such flimsy material that a modest increase in federal funds would cause the apertures through which these funds flow to widen and destroy the walls which make up the boundaries of the state administrations.

*An Alternative Model*

A more dynamic model would suggest that as federal funds are distributed to the states, the universe of discourse, the whole area of education, would expand and part of the federal funds would be devoted to widening, deepening, and strengthening the educational enterprise so that the pressures of federal funds would not grow intolerable in compressing state and local activity. If the universe of discourse expands, and if the state compartments expand, what might well happen is that the functions and responsibilities undertaken by local boards, the state school administration, and the central government will all increase. The relative positions of state, local, and federal influence might change, probably giving a greater role to the federal government, but the absolute position of all might increase. More decisions will have to be made at all levels and, if the whole model expands, more important ones, too. The greater role of the federal government would not necessarily be at the expense of other authorities. Increasing federal funds in such a fashion as to call forth more local and state funds might actually increase the responsibilities, activities, and effectiveness of state and local school administrations, and at the same time serve the national interest and the interests of cities and states which presently suffer because of inadequate programs of other states and communities. By and large, large cities and industrial states would benefit if the educational standards of rural areas and states of population emigration were improved.

The conventional and static model seems to assume that federal, state, and local administrations are without imagination or will, that they act merely mechanically. Surely the educational process in the United States must be carried on differently, with different goals, techniques, and aspirations in different parts of the country. With this view so frequently expressed by the schoolmen one can be thoroughly sympathetic. Regional differences need not be destroyed by the expenditure of more money, whatever the source of the money, provided that state and local administrations have a coordinate voice in determining how the money is to be spent. One can easily imagine a situation in which the programing and expenditure of federal funds in either local school districts or through state agencies receives the thorough approval of local and state administrators.

Many intergovernmental activities bear witness to this. There seems to be a tendency on the part of school officials, as well as on the part of others, to assume that the political machinery of the United States and its public administration is hidebound, rigid, and that movement and adjustment take place only after long travail and with arthritic clumsiness. However, in truth, flexibility and imagination are not entirely absent from the American scene. Our national boasting about democratic flexibility and administrative adjustment may not be universally justified, but enough cases can be adduced to show that such action does occur when the needs are great. The establishment of Selective Service prior to World War II, and the implementation and the administration of the Unemployment Compensation Act are but two examples. When the pressures are great the federal government, jointly with the states, does act and react rapidly, and often with remarkable cooperation and good will. Such cooperation and good will in the educational field, as in any other field, can only be achieved after the parties at interest are mutually informed as to each others' needs, desires, and purposes. Schoolmen generally believe that federal aid to education is inevitable and necessary. When inevitability and necessity join, administrative machinery can and will somehow be devised.

The argument on local-state versus national control tends to neglect the non-governmental pressure forces. These too should be part of any discussion of control. In an interesting paper Roald F. Campbell studied the pressures, governmental and non-governmental, on seven secondary schools of varying sizes and in different types of communities. He found that courses, subject matter, and curricula were not only directly and indirectly affected by the action of federal programs but also by the pressures of college entrance board examinations, organizations with particular social views, college scholarship programs, and college entrance requirements. The pressures on schools are numerous, which is understandable and even desirable if the school system is to be responsive to popular will.

## THE OFFICE OF EDUCATION REPLIES

The reactions of officials of the Office of Education to criticisms leveled at the Office and its administration of NDEA must be appraised and weighed. The unofficial but nevertheless thoughtful answers of various staff members of the Office of Education to the complaints and concerns of the state and local schoolmen fall into two categories. First, there is the denial that many of the complaints and fears of state and local officials have any basis in fact and practice. The second reaction is that the expenditure of federal funds necessarily requires an accounting to assure that appropriate care and responsibility are exercised in the expenditure of these funds.

### The Audit Problem

First of all, the Department of Health, Education, and Welfare (as is true of all federal agencies) does not employ the General Accounting Office as an auditing

agency. GAO is a creature and an arm of Congress and not of the administration. Auditing and accounting are done by the department concerned, in this case the officials of the Department of Health, Education, and Welfare assigned for these purposes to the Office of Education. Departmental audits and state and/or local audits are initially the relevant ones. GAO audits are not very likely to be on a continuing basis.

But, the officials of the Office of Education insist, their policy goes even further. The Office of Education and its parent department, HEW, are desirous of building up state responsibility with respect to administrative and substantive matters. Therefore, whenever possible, existing state procedures rather than federal rules are followed in the accounting and auditing of funds. Section 141.7 of the regulations (Sections 301 through 304 of Title III of the Act) concerning financial assistance for strengthening science, mathematics, and modern foreign language instruction, provides that "accounts and supporting documents relating to any program involving federal participation shall be adequate to permit an accurate and expeditious audit of the program." Paragraph (b) of the same section is entitled "Audit of Local Projects" and provides:

All expenditures of local educational agencies claimed for federal participation shall be audited either by the state or by appropriate auditors at the local level. The state plan shall indicate how the project accounts for local educational agencies and other agencies that participate in the state plan will be audited; and, if the audit is to be carried out at the local level, how the state agency will secure information necessary to assure proper use of funds expended under Section 301–304 inclusive, of the Act by such local educational agencies.

It would appear from this paragraph that the state is responsible for the auditing of local projects and that no specific rules are laid down for state accounts other than they "shall be adequate to permit an accurate and expeditious audit of the program."

151

On the face of it, this would indicate that the Office of Education is in fact willing to accept state accounting and auditing forms and methods provided they permit an accurate audit. State officials must first of all have an acceptable audit system. Still, disagreements between federal and state officials may occur as to what is acceptable and accurate. This is, one may assume, what the state officials fear, for their control over local school districts is sometimes less than complete. No cases of state-federal disagreement have emerged from the investigation of this study, although the opportunity for state officials to refer to specific cases of disagreement has of course been available.

This is not to say that disagreements as well as fear of differences are nonexistent. One is left with the feeling that the Office of Education has given a responsibility to the states which they are reluctant to accept. A gift can be very expensive at times. The issue between the state and federal officials may well be one more of communication than of substance.

As is so often the case in controversies regarding administrative procedure, the issues are not clearly drawn. The Office of Education is formally correct in its contention that the federal administration auditing process is in the hands of its own staff. However, this is not the concern of the school administrators. The General Accounting Office is, in truth, a legislative arm, but it has the authority to conduct investigations and audits of federal grants-in-aid. The General Accounting Office, upon learning of the possibility of fraud or chicanery, would doubtless investigate the matter to see whether federal funds were actually being misused. It is this that the school administrators are wary of.

To be sure, no one would knowingly defend the misappropriation of funds. School administrators, however, fear, according to their comment, that what the federal government would consider misappropriation of funds is not what school administration

at the local level might so consider and, furthermore, that state officials cannot control or easily oversee the actions of local bodies.

On the whole, however, it would appear that the concern with the GAO is in a sense a bogeyman. Time and experience alone will fashion a local-state-federal relationship within which each can operate effectively. Audits are an aid to good administration, not a drawback. The cliché about the good administrator being one who knows how to control confusion and make the best of it is, in reality, a wisecrack rather than a guide.

The general discussion of the question of state audits with the respondent officials of the Office of Education led to another consideration—the concern with auditing and accounting of federal funds in the light of state methods. There is a feeling in the Office of Education that the audit systems of some states are neither sufficiently detailed nor well enough administered to permit their use in the accounting of federal expenditures. In such cases, specific invoices, usually the raw material of an audit, become the major substance of the audit. This, it is argued, is not a weakness of federal procedure but rather a weakness of the state auditing systems and service.

Here as before the personal judgments and personal relations of state and federal accounting and administrative officials become the anvil on which the argument must be hammered out. In all this the position of the Office of Education is not a happy one. If it insists upon certain auditing practices and procedures, it is accused of financial dictation. If it agrees to use a state system with the caveat that the system be adequate, the personal judgments of the federal officials become an easy complaint by state officials that whim and caprice rather than rule and regulation are the mainstays of the Office of Education administration. Yet one cannot reasonably argue that state auditing systems should not be accurate and understandable.

*Imbalance and Aid*

It was suggested earlier that a major criticism of the state and local schoolmen is that categorical aid tends to imbalance local and state programs. A corollary of this criticism is that the larger school districts, with a greater number of programs than the smaller school districts, are not so restrained by the categorical aid approach since there is a greater probability that with many programs some can be expanded profitably with the help of federal money. On the latter point, the respondent officials of the Office of Education are in agreement. Their view is that the larger school districts, generally the big city school districts, are likely to have not only many projects to choose from as justifying improvement which would secure federal funds, but also greater administrative and financial sophistication and therefore will make better use of NDEA.

While granting this, however, the officials of the Office of Education are not ready to grant the first part of the criticism—namely that the categorical aid program leads to widespread or serious imbalancing of local projects. There is the obvious argument that the state or local government has the right simply to refuse to allocate any of its funds to a program which does not make sense to it. This, to be sure, would deny the use of federal funds but on the other hand would conserve state funds. Yet the total of federal funds would not be reduced by a state or local district not following one particular categorical line. So long as there are other categories which can be profitably expanded, federal aid would be forthcoming. The limitation is, of course, that other categories must be judged worthy of expansion, and fit under the rubric of the Act.

Such consideration leads some of the officials of the Office of Education personally to favor general aid which would give a wider scope to categorical development within the states, since any aid in the last analysis must go to a particular category, be it science, teaching, salaries, or buildings. Nevertheless the feeling on the part of other Office of Education respondents was that the categories which are destined to receive aid under the Act are generally accepted as so necessary that the imbalance feature is likely to be very small indeed.

It is as if the criticism by the state and local officials against categorical aid, in this context, comes down to the desire of such officials to expand their activities in the realm of English literature, the humanities, social sciences, and other exempted categories. If this interpretation is correct, state and local officials would approve general aid, that is, aid for all categories. In this at least some of the respondent officials of the Office of Education would be sympathetic. But the Congress sets up the categories, not the Office.

*The Fiscal Problem*

Of perhaps greater importance tnan the imbalance concern is the fiscal problem— that dealing with ability to pay as it affects local districts. Some of the schoolmen argue that school districts which need assistance least because of their greater wealth, income, and better tax basis, are likely to be in a preferred position in securing federal help because of their size and administrative sophistication. Therefore, the argument is that the 50–50 matching fund arrangement improves the position of these well-situated school districts as compared to the poorer school districts.

The Office of Education respondents point out, however, that the matching fund provision is on a state basis—that each state, in its turn, can use other than a 50–50 provision at the local level. Only the total contribution of the state must equal the federal grant. Indeed, some states have changed the conditions of local matching. Thus a poor district might receive $7 for every $3 spent on a new, approved project, while a rich district might enjoy the inverse of this ratio, $3 of federal funds for every $7 of local funds spent. The program is entirely a matter of state administration and discretion within the total state matching limitation. The states have not generally provided for variable matching because of internal administrative difficulties or because of other policy considerations. However, the option is open to them.

The essential argument made by the Office of Education respondents is that the purposes of their administrative concern are program and educational excellence rather than money. They realize that federal funds are not great compared to the total expenditure of the states on education, but the persistent Office of Education concern is to assist in improvement of the states' educational enterprises.

### Federal-State Liaison

To gain the ends of their policy, the Office of Education has held frequent meetings to explain to state officials its policy and program and to stress that the accounting and auditing procedures, which officials in the Office of Education expected to be troublesome, were to be determined by the states, with the proviso that they be sufficient to permit an accurate and expeditious audit of the program. That the Office of Education has not been entirely successful in this communication problem seems to be illustrated by the attitudes expressed in an earlier part of this chapter.

### Intergovernmental Relations

The final area of discussion regarding the details of administration deals with the relations between the Office of Education and state and local school bodies. The officials of the Office of Education are emphatic in saying that they do not desire to dictate school curriculum or educational (or any other) policy to state and local school bodies. This is almost a reflex response to any question which even vaguely infringes upon state or local autonomy. In specific,

the Office of Education respondents insist that they come into states only on the request of the states, and even then usually make it a point never to deal with local officials unless state officials are present.

On the question of standards in general and federal standards in particular, the personal view of respondent officials of the Office of Education seems to be that state standards are improved by the upgrading of personnel and by advice and investigation of teaching methods and subject regardless of source. The local school boards, it is felt, are almost impervious to direct impingement by the Office of Education or by general information and advice from universities and research agencies. The local school boards' major contacts with the educational world tend to be with state educational authorities. Therefore the Office of Education respondents believe that the state bodies are the ones with which the Office must work to improve standards. The great national concern with educational excellence cannot, in the opinion of respondent officials of the Office of Education, be secured with any likelihood by federal mandatory action. Persuasion, advice, and cooperative action are the keys to improvement. Even the expenditure of more funds offers no assurance that teaching methods will be improved or that the subject matter taught will be any better. The way to educational excellence is to improve personnel and provide more competent personnel.

The great needs of the educational system, the respondents urged, are research which provides a fund of knowledge and ideas, people to administer the school system and do the teaching, and facilities and tools to accomplish the educational program. Pilot projects are of extreme value. Showing school officials at the local and state levels that improvement can occur because it is occurrring in the pilot operation is held to be an irrefutable argument. State contact with the universities and research agencies on the one hand, and with the Office of Education on the other, are also considered promising paths to excellence.

Although progress may be slow, the states can be helped by federal aid of money and advice. The local boards become the major problem since their awareness, knowledge, and even interest in the educational enterprise are often less than are required. Yet some Office of Education officials feel that wisdom would suggest that the local boards not be skirted and thus isolated from the educational enterprise. On the contrary, the argument is that steps should be taken to strengthen the interest of the local boards in the educational process and enterprise. This can only be done, it is felt, by assisting the states to work with the local boards. The federal government is viewed as an agency outside the state educational system, coming in upon request to assist the state central authority which in turn operates with the local authority.

*I. M. Labowitz*

# THE STATES AND AID FOR FEDERALLY AFFECTED SCHOOLS

### ROLE OF THE STATES

Although public education is generally a state responsibility, it is, . . . a responsibility from which common practice long excluded many categories of federally connected children. To what extent has state action closed the gaps since P.L. 815 and 874 were enacted? What is the role of state educational agencies in these federal programs?

*State Policies toward Federally Connected Children*

Where state assistance to schools is important, state policy toward acceptance or rejection of federal children for the state aid claim ordinarily sets the pattern for local practice in admitting children freely to schools. Generally, a federal connection derived from the parent's workplace is ignored if the pupil lives in a taxable dwelling. Chapter III shows that most states likewise make no distinction when the pupils live on federal property but several exclude these pupils in calculating state aid. In some places, especially where the home and place of work are both on property in exclusive federal jurisdiction, statutory provisions or constitutional interpretations still assign federally connected pupils to the status of nonresidents.

Special state aid is infrequent. An Office of Education survey for 1957–1958 indicated that Illinois and Nebraska retained their long-standing provisions for special payments for pupils from military installations, and Vermont continued to allow a total of $500 a year for children from Fort Ethan Allen. The review indicated also that Wisconsin paid tuition for children whose parents were employed and lived at federal military camps and veterans' hospitals; Minnesota paid on an acreage basis for school districts in which a large proportion of the area was tax-exempt; and Pennsylvania paid tuition for certain Indian children on reservations.

State legislation specifically opening public schools to federally connected children likewise appears to be rare. On the other hand, exclusion policies have persisted. A Michigan state law which denied free public education to children who lived on property in exclusive federal jurisdiction

From I. M. Labowitz, *Aid for Federally Affected Public Schools*, No. 9, pp. 174–185 in *The Economics and Politics of Public Education Series.* Copyright © 1963 by Syracuse University Press.

was modified in 1951 to provide state aid for the children, but the amendment raised technical difficulties by specifying that each board of education might serve as agent of the federal government in providing education if the government paid the full per capita operating cost for each child. The Oregon legislature in 1951 repealed a 1945 statute which authorized free public education of all children living in areas of exclusive federal jurisdiction. These enactments were cited by the Commissioner of Education among state actions contrary to the P.L. 874 objective of relying upon local educational agencies to provide schools for children living on federal properties. He contended that the jurisdiction which the federal government assumed over its real property acquisitions was only in rare instances incompatible with the continuance of state responsibility for education of children living on the property. In the light of the Buck Act of 1940 and court decisions based on it, he considered that the states had concurrent jurisdiction to render all ordinary municipal services and, in fact, were obligated to furnish services on request from the federal government.

A sidelight on state policies is provided by operations under section 6, which permits direct federal arrangements where state or local taxes are not legally available or no local agency is able to make suitable provision for children on federal property. Comparison of operations in 1952 and several years later indicates that responsibility for schooling some or all of these children had been assumed in Alaska, Arizona, Ohio, and Oregon, with the state departments of education indicating approval of their free acceptance in local public schools. In six other states where section 6 operations were necessary in 1952 to provide for children on certain properties, state responsibility still was disclaimed in 1956 and the number of section 6 cases was the same or larger. These were Georgia, Kentucky, Michigan, Missouri, New York, and North Carolina. Similarly, no tendency toward state approval of free enrollments ap-

peared in Virginia, Alabama, and Florida, but the situation in these states was confused by the integration issue.

In Pennsylvania section 6 operations were necessary in 1956 to provide for a dozen children from a Veterans Administration hospital, apparently because a local school board declined to admit them after the state department of education ruled that a board might permit nonresident pupils to attend its schools but was not required to do so. The number of section 6 arrangements in this state rose sharply in 1960 after the Pennsylvania Attorney General advised the Superintendent of Public Instruction that children who lived on property in exclusive federal jurisdiction were not entitled to free public education. The opinion acknowledged that other federally connected children should be considered residents entitled to free public education.

## State Participation in Administration

Since federal payments under P.L. 815 and 874 are made directly to local educational agencies, the state departments of education may, if they choose, perform in a relatively passive role in the administration of these programs. They cannot stay out completely, since local districts will not qualify for payments unless the state agency provides information and certifications. Also, the federal agency is required to consult with state education departments on specific items.

In practice, all state departments of education have had a significant part in the administrative procedures from the outset. The extent of activity varies with the number of school districts involved, the magnitudes of their claims, and in some measure, traditions of educational leadership in the particular state. Several state superintendents or their representatives have testified before congressional committees considering amendments and extensions of the laws.

When school districts seek to establish

eligibility for federal payments, the general policy of the U.S. Office of Education is to refer them to the state department of education as a source of advice, application forms, and instructions. Completed applications are submitted through the state educational agencies, which certify the accuracy of supporting information insofar as this can be determined from official state records.

The chief state school officer in each state has designated one or more representatives to work with local school systems and with regional and field representatives of the U.S. Office of Education. State representatives distribute application forms and other materials issued by the Office of Education. They help school district officials in preparing applications, and if necessary may revise them before certification.

State education departments have an important part in choosing "generally comparable" school districts under P.L. 874. (The concept is not used in P.L. 815.) Either of two methods is accepted—individual selections for comparison with each applicant district or predetermined groupings for the state as a whole. Legal responsibility for the final choice rests with the Commissioner of Education, but the initial decision and any later change has been made ordinarily by the state agency in consultation with representatives of the Office of Education.

Where statewide groupings are used, the state educational agency designates major groups comprising school districts that are in the same legal classification or operate under the same laws. Secondary groupings are made to assure that all districts in any group operate the same grade levels, to avoid extreme differences in size as measured by average daily attendance, and also to avoid substantial differences in degree of urbanization or other factors that might result in material differences in contribution rates and current expense per pupil. The local contribution rate for each group is determined annually by the state agency, again in consultation with representatives

of the Office of Education and in conformity to instructions issued by the Office. Where each applicant lists selected comparable districts as a basis for setting its local contribution rate, the state usually helps in collecting necessary data from the other districts.

P.L. 815 applications from local educational agencies are not approved until the state education department has assured the Commissioner that each proposed project is not inconsistent with state plans for school construction and is coordinated with the state program for education. The state agency also supplies information about school building costs used by the U.S. Office of Education in determining the average cost per pupil on which allotments are based. The Office of Education calculates the average but submits the results to each state education department for concurrence. The law specifies that if the Commissioner finds information for a state inadequate or not sufficiently representative, he shall determine cost on the basis of such information as he has available, but only after consultation with the state agency. State education officials are consulted, also, in determining whether particular school facilities are "minimum facilities" and what their construction cost may be.

The laws require that various other decisions by the Commissioner also be preceded by consultations with the state educational agency. In P.L. 874 this includes decisions to make payments in cases where federal real property acquisitions have significantly reduced the local tax base or where districts claim sudden and substantial attendance increases. A similar requirement applies to the Commissioner's decisions under both laws to provide schools on the ground that no local educational agency is able to provide suitable free public education for federally connected children living on federal property, and decisions to admit to these schools certain children living off the federal property. Under P.L. 815, also, the Commissioner must consult state officials before decid-

157

ing to give construction assistance to school districts which accept substantial numbers of pupils who live on Indian lands outside their boundaries.

A review of major policy issues surrounding P.L. 815 and 874 necessarily includes the question of federal control over local schools. Explicit prohibitions incorporated in both laws are evidence of concern lest the special aids inadvertently carry with them an element of national direction over personnel, curricula, or programs of instruction. Nevertheless, federal control as an issue is surrounded by a kind of mysticism, an ethereal remoteness, unrelated to the administrative procedures by which local, state, and federal school officials operate under these two laws.

Because these are not formula programs, there are no allocations of federal money to any state or to local school districts other than in response to specific, detailed applications filed by school officials or for contractual payments under section 6 of P.L. 874. Consequently, there are no sanctions for compelling observance of prescribed standards or conditions — such sanctions, for example, as the withholding of an allocated amount which sometimes occurs in, say, a highway aid or public assistance program. Officials or a school district presumably file no application if they consider any requirements of P.L. 815 or 874 onerous. This means there is no way to determine whether any qualified school systems have deliberately refrained from applying: eligibility can be ascertained only with an application officially reviewed.

*Survey Reports*

Inquiries about federal controls within these programs usually have taken the form of questions addressed to successful applicants. Invariably the responses have been close to unanimous, to the effect that there has been no federal control. Many replies have included laudatory comments about the laws and the administrative staff in the Office of Education.

Most extensive among such studies was a dissertation completed by Robert I. Sperber in 1957, analyzing "potential control factors" in P.L. 874. He defined control factors as

any administrative decisions, or regulations, or actions arising under this law which directly or indirectly govern the personnel, curriculum, or program of instruction of any school or school system of any local or state educational agency.

In this concept, as in the statutes, "personnel, curriculum, or program of instruction" are identified as the areas to be safeguarded.

Sperber sent questionnaires to one-fourth of all school districts which received P.L. 874 payments in the fiscal year 1955. He reported replies from 500, or 70 per cent, with at least one response from every state. It was the view of 99 per cent of the respondents that the statutory caveat was complied with: they attested that federal control did not accompany federal payments.

Among the few respondents in the other 1 per cent, one or two were "undecided" and a maximum of four said they had experienced "control." This was in reply to a question as to whether field examinations of claims or central review of applications ever resulted in federal control over personnel, curriculum, or instructional program. One of the four mentioned only that he had to make reports and maintain records of federally connected pupils; he added that the curriculum was not affected. Another felt "control" because of uncertainty about the amount to be received. The other two did not explain.

Among 416 school officials who had experience with discretionary powers of the Commissioner of Education (such as waiver of the 3 per cent minimum requirement for small districts and special increases in local contribution rates to allow for unusual geographic factors) none reported any federal control. Almost equally agreed were 490 respondents to the question whether direct federal payments to local school districts resulted in federal control: 489 answered "no." The one affirmative reply was from a superintendent who indicated that some specialist positions were cut from his estimates for an on-base school under section 6.

Nine respondents reported experience with contract-operated schools under section 6. One of these—possibly the one mentioned earlier—saw control in the fact that his staffing proposals were not always approved in full. Another was undecided. The rest said there was no control.

On a separate question as to whether noneducational federal agencies ever exerted control when the Commissioner of Education used their services or facilities, three school officials answered "yes"; 484, "no"; and one, "undecided." Each of the three who said "yes" operated a contract school under section 6 and dealt with the Department of Defense. One indicated that he was required to buy textbooks through Army procedures, and noted, "This increases cost to the Army and hampers our operation."

In a final summary question, Sperber asked whether the subsection prohibiting federal control was complied with by the Commissioner of Education, his representatives, and other federal departments. Of 489 respondents, 484 answered "completely," and three "most of the time." One reported that the section was "often disregarded," explaining that delays in filing field reports held up aid to his district and this caused cancellations of courses of study or orders for necessary supplies.

Similar in effect were responses of Texas school officials who were asked in 1956 to estimate the degree of federal control or interference with local schools that may have resulted from accepting P.L. 815 payments. Among 76 respondents, 65 replied "none" and 10 "little." One said "some." Supplementary comments were typically to this effect: "Just one check to see if money was spent for the purpose." On a related

query as to whether P.L. 815 carried a possible threat to local and state control of education, local officials revealed a trifle more doubt: 72 replied, with 58 saying "none" and eight "little," but two each checked "some," "much," and "undecided." One who replied "much" commented only, "Who knows?"

## Testimony and Debates

From Massachusetts, a spokesman for the state department of education testified in 1958 that at the inception of the program to aid federally affected school districts

there were those in Massachusetts who felt rather strongly that federal assistance of any type would bring with it federal control of the local school systems. The experience of the Massachusetts Department of Education, for what it may be worth, has been that the officials of the Boston regional office of the United States Department of Health, Education, and Welfare have succeeded in making clear the distinction between assistance and advice on the one hand and authoritativeness and outright direction on the other. A very harmonious relationship exists in our state between federal and state officials.

Senator Vance Hartke reported in 1961 that Indiana school officials responded with "a consistent and emphatic 'no'" when he asked whether acceptance of P.L. 815 or 874 grants had resulted in "any federal regulation, specific or implied, with regard to school curriculum, personnel, or administration." He added: "Not a single instance of federal control or regulation was reported."

The Senator had written to executives of all Indiana school districts given aid under either law in recent years. About half had replied when he announced his findings. As a proponent of general federal aid for schools, the Senator said his purpose was to learn whether any federal control over local school autonomy might have resulted from administration of the special programs. Since federal payments under these laws were made directly to local school authorities, he assumed that "the danger of federal control or federal regulation would seem more real to those who conscientiously fear control than in the [general] federal aid to education bill . . . , which, of course, allocates funds to the states for distribution to local school districts." Besides reporting that P.L. 815 and 874 introduced no federal controls, the school officials indicated that the payment generally was a small proportion of the local school budget. At the same time, "they emphasized its importance in no uncertain terms. Without dissent, every one of the respondents voiced their anxious hope that the program would be continued."

In the 1961 debates on general aid, Senator Lee Metcalf and others remarked that congressional committees had made repeated efforts to discover instances of federal controls (other than labor-standard requirements) under P.L. 815 and 874. Said the Senator from Montana:

In the 11 years of this act the opponents of the act and the enemies of federal aid to education have been unable to come forth with one example of dictation so far as curricula is concerned or dictation with respect to textbooks or courses of study.

*"Suitable" Schools*

In the face of nearly universal agreement that operations under P.L. 815 and 874 have conformed to the statutory requirements of no "direction, supervision, or control" over "personnel, curriculum, or program of instruction" of any school or school system, contrary intimations recur from time to time on specific points. These are the "minimum school facilities" requirement in P.L. 815, reviewed earlier in this chapter, and the desegregation requirement tied to the standard of "suitable free public education" for contract schools. The racial issue has aroused most comment.

Objections to direct federal operation of any schools appeared early. The Office of Education adopted from the outset a policy of making "every effort" to arrange schooling for residents of federal property

in schools operated and controlled by local public school systems. Nevertheless, President Eisenhower's decision to stop segregation in schools at military posts was followed by some increase in direct federal operations on the reservations as local school systems either declined or found that they were not permitted by state law to operate desegregated contract schools. In 1953, schools within eight military posts in the continental United States were operated directly by the armed services and two by nearby local educational agencies under contracts. In 1956 the number had risen to 21, with three operated by local agencies and 18 by military departments.

In a study of P.L. 874 operations in Virginia, Louie Reid Davis noted in 1953 that six post schools in that state included two which were operated directly by the military departments—one at the Quantico Marine Base and the other at the Dahlgren Naval Base. Neither installation was so isolated that the local public schools could be considered inaccessible. Conceding that "no Virginia school system could operate a school on federal property on a nonsegregated basis," Dr. Davis continued:

But there would seem to be no excuse for educating children residing at either Dahlgren or Quantico in schools located on federal property. Were these children to be educated in regularly established public schools, children of different race would be educated in accordance with state law.

Education "in accordance with state law" was synonymous with "education in racially segregated schools." Perceiving no relationship between segregation and the standard of "suitable free public education" (indeed, at that time the Office of Education had not indicated that it saw a connection), Davis argued that the federal government was bound to consider local schools "suitable" unless the government proposed to guarantee a higher standard of educational program for children living on federal property than was available to other children in the nearby community. This, he contended, would be "not only contrary to established principles of federal-state relations but . . . a denial of our concept of democracy."

In every other respect, Davis declared, P.L. 874 as applied in Virginia conformed to a set of eight "principles for federal-state relations in education" which he had formulated as part of his study. But the two federally operated schools meant that the program was not "compatible" with one of his precepts which held that the education of children living on federal reservations should be conducted by local public educational agencies even if extensive use of transportation is necessary.

The Department of Defense order for an end to segregation in all schools on military posts impelled Dr. Davis to record again his "considerable conern" over "the extension of federal control, and especially military control, over the post schools of this country." He saw in federal operation of any public schools a threat to the national tradition that education is a state function. Post schools, if desegregated, necessarily would be federally operated, since segregation was required by state law in most of the southern states.

Stronger comment, especially in political quarters, greeted the announcement by the Secretary of Health, Education, and Welfare early in 1962 that, beginning in September, 1963, racially segregated schools would not be considered "suitable" schools for children living on federal property. This action was denounced by Senator Strom Thurmond as "the rankest type of economic blackmail"—a contradiction of previous assurances

that controls, especially integration controls, would not follow the dollar, particularly in federal aid to education. These assurances had been given to win passage of a general federal aid to education bill. Now, however, the control cat is out of the bag, and the administration will be able to lure few, if any, Southern votes.

Critics of the "suitable" schools policy did not charge that it carried any explicit "controls" over personnel, curriculum, or instructional programs. The allegation that economic pressure would be exerted through denial of federal payments to the local school system also was not explained. It was not subject to easy demonstration. Ordinarily a local school district should experience no economic loss from termination or denial of a contract to receive pupils from a nearby military reservation or to operate schools within the reservation. The district might suffer diseconomies from a reduction in the scale of its operations, and it might also be left with surplus facilities if the federally connected pupils had been attending its schools off the base. But the payment under P.L. 874 for children residing on federal property is not calculated to yield to the local school system any excess over expenses required for the federally connected children, and the withdrawal of the pupils and the payment should not impair local school finances. Far more serious in school districts which seek to continue a policy of racial separation is the proximity of a desegregated school operated on federal property by the federal government.

Military operation of post schools is by no means the innovation that Dr. Davis' comment implied. Chapter I records that operation of post schools by the armed services was recognized by Congress at least as early as 1821. P.L. 815 and 874 were, in fact, designed to modify another historic tradition in American public education— the tradition by which pupils living on federal property were excluded from many local public schools. By opening local school doors to these children, the federal payments were supposed to reduce the need for federally operated schools. Already noted is the fact that such schools were almost eliminated by 1953, but their number again increased as the national policy of racial desegregation in the armed services was made more fully effective. If locally operated desegregated public schools continue unavailable to substantial numbers of pupils from the federal posts, there may be a further proliferation of schools operated directly by the military services within these reservations under the authorizations provided by P.L. 815 and 874.

It could turn out to be one of the ironies of United States political and social history that legislation devised to bridge an inter-governmental gap in the structure of public education may provide mechanisms for a continuing division of responsibility in some areas. Where this happens, differences in the patterns of community life off-base and on-base are emphasized, for the federally operated schools on military posts are desegregated schools adjacent to communities where the local schools continue to operate on a segregated basis. The proximity of the two systems might accelerate or it might slow down the general trend toward desegregation in public schools; such effects are speculative. But a clear result of this arrangement is that groups of children again are treated as were earlier generations of federally connected children: as strangers in the states, foreigners to be sequestered in special schools.

## THE IMPACT IMPASSE

*Fe* equals *Ln* times *Nf* over *Nn* minus *Lf* plus *A*. The equation, accompanied by an explanation of its symbols, is one of many that appear in an elaborate two-volume study of the impacted-areas school program prepared for Congress by the Stanford Research Institute. In plain English, the report has concluded that the going formula for granting financial assistance to school districts that are burdened by the presence of Federal government installations "results in wide discrepancies . . . with many districts receiving large windfalls. . . ." And in even plainer English, Congress is now letting it be known that, despite the administration's eagerness to trim back the program on the basis of the Stanford report, the political impact of such a move would be intolerable.

"Maybe we should never have started it in the first place," Senator John O. Pastore (D., Rhode Island) told Secretary of Health, Education and Welfare John W. Gardner at an appropriations hearing recently. "All I am saying is, once you give a lollypop to a child you don't take it away too easily without that child doing a little crying, and we are getting a lot of crying." Senator Norris Cotton (R., New Hampshire) was perhaps plainest of all. The program, which he had opposed at its inception, would be phased out, he told Gardner, "over my dead body."

In a candid aside during the hearing, Cotton recalled that in opposing the original legislation he had foreseen what would come about: intense lobbying efforts to land Federal installations in an area, followed by equally intense efforts to qualify for school aid. There has been a good deal more going on than that, however, as Congress has painted, patched, and enlarged the legislation by amendments over the years. P.L. 81–874, which was enacted in 1950, sought to compensate school districts for an influx of what are known as "Federally connected children"—that is, children whose parents lived and/or worked on Federally owned and therefore untaxable property. Some of that property, however, has been leased to private concerns and is therefore taxable. Moreover, some of the largess is going into relatively well-to-do school districts that could easily afford more local effort. Most important, by process of amendment the act now permits localities to compute the "burden" not simply on the basis of local cost but on the basis of average state and national expenditures for education. Thus, a school district

---

By Meg Greenfield from "The Reporter's Notes," *The Reporter*, Vol. 35 (1966). Reprinted by permission of *The Reporter*.

that actually spends a relatively low sum per pupil may be compensated by the Federal government at a much higher sum based on expenditures for schooling elsewhere in the country. "When educators talk about this among themselves," Gardner said—to the discomfiture of the subcommittee—"they joke about it."

The joke may not be particularly uproarious, but it is apparently widely shared. There are programs of aid to impacted school districts in all fifty states and in 322 of the 435 Congressional districts. These figures, which do not exactly bode well for Congressional action to cut back the program, were mentioned to us in passing by Oscar Rose, superintendent of schools of Midwest City, Oklahoma, where the Tinker Air Force Base is situated—a circumstance that accounts for impacted areas aid flowing into 104 neighboring school districts. Rose is also the chairman of what he describes as a panel and others describe as a lobby of Federally impacted-area school superintendents. "I serve as chairman and get out information on what's going on in every state," he told us, adding that his duties include holding regional meetings of superintendents, advising applicants for aid, keeping abreast of what is going on in Congress, and informing his constituency of the same. While there is no question that much of the Federal aid has been well placed or that districts suddenly threatened by the administration's proposals have reason to protest, it is also apparent that

Rose's panel has done its work well. "I think," Pastore remarked to the Secretary, "I heard from almost every individual in Rhode Island who is interested in it."

What Gardner has in mind to do is to revise criteria of eligibility, methods of computing compensation, and the definition of untaxable Federal property. All this has been proposed by way of amendment to last year's Education Act, and it would probably cut the number of qualified districts by about a fourth and the expenditure by about $260 million. In arguing the inequities of the present program, Gardner made plain that he would like to use the funds for expansion of Title I of the Education Act, which is focused on school districts where economic need is great. To be sure, there is something to the lollypop logic of Senator Pastore, in that an abrupt cancellation of existing local programs could cause great distress in districts that would be obliged to revamp their tax structures overnight; and Pastore's plea for working together with the affected districts on a more gradual, long-range withdrawal of aid had obvious merit. But the rare show of unanimity on the Hill, which has seen Senators Wayne Morse (D., Oregon) and George Murphy (R., California) colloquizing in harmony on the virtues of continuing the program, seems to indicate that there will be no revision at all and that the program has become impacted in the good old-fashioned dental sense of the term.

James B. Conant

# SHAPING EDUCATIONAL POLICY

My thesis this afternoon can be stated very simply. We need to evolve a nationwide educational policy, and this can only be done by the fifty states in partnership with the federal government. The U.S.

Commissioner of Education Francis Keppel in an address delivered in Detroit on October 15 raised some large questions about American education. He said, and I quote: "Today I propose that we ask . . . where

From James B. Conant, "Shaping Educational Policy," *State Government* (Winter, 1965), pp. 34–38. Reprinted by permission of The Council of State Governments and of the author.

we stand now, where we seem to be going, where we should seek to go . . ."

The ultimate answer to these questions, he went on to suggest, "will not and cannot come from Washington, from the Federal Government, but from each of our States . . . and from the new vigor and vitality they bring to our educational enterprises."

Later in the same speech the U.S. Commissioner of Education declared:

"In the long run nothing that we in education can do, whether in Washington or anywhere else, can be more important than strengthening the capacity of our States to respond to the educational needs of our time . . . In education we look to the States not merely as a matter of law or precedent, but as a matter of practical soundness and necessity. In this Nation of 50 States with vast and independent enterprises for education, the Federal Government can help as a partner, but only as a partner . . . and a somewhat junior partner at that."

#### WHY THE STATES ARE BASIC

It is hardly necessary for me to spell out to this audience why what Mr. Keppel said is true. You know that we cannot have a national educational policy in the sense that France, or England or Sweden can have a national policy. Why? The competence of the Federal Government of the United States in educational matters is limited. It cannot establish school districts, open or close schools and colleges (except for special cases such as Indians and the military), hire teachers, or determine curricula. Congress can provide money, and has done so in recent years in ever larger amounts. How the money is spent, however, and where it is spent, depends in the last analysis on the wisdom of state officials who administer funds for schools and colleges.

#### ORGANIZING STATE ADMINISTRATION

We do have fifty state educational policies, some well thought out and well ad-

ministered, some highly unstable and poorly administered. We could have fifty independent but coherent policies looking to the future, each effectively carried out. The sum total would be a nationwide policy which could be in part supported by Congressional appropriations and assisted by executive acts of federal agencies. I shall have a good deal to say in a few moments about a possible scheme for interstate cooperation as regards planning for the future. But before considering this possibility let me repeat what I said in New York two weeks ago to the Council of Chief State School Officers.

That organization has long held the view that there should be in each state a lay board of education, and the board should appoint the chief state school officer. According to the Secretary of the Council, during the sixteen years of its existence, the number of states so organized has increased from eight to twenty-four. To my mind this is progress, but unfortunately some of our most populous states are in the twenty-six which are not properly organized, that is, not properly organized according to my view. There are and have been very competent chief state school officers who have been elected. Nevertheless, the system is not a good one. Therefore, an immediate task in more than one state is to enact laws or amend the state constitution so that the state educational machinery will be made effective. As I see it, the state board of education should be a lay board of considerable size, each member appointed for a period of as long as five or seven years so that no single Governor could by his appointments dominate the board. Experience with boards of trustees of state universities, unless I am much mistaken, shows the importance of this principle. The relation of the chief state school officer to the state board should be similar to that of the president of a university of the board of trustees.

A properly organized state office of education needs a strong civil service staff and an ample budget. Furthermore the state government should be so organized that the special importance of the chief state school officer is fully recognized. Quite apart from the planning and leadership function of the office, the demands placed on each state by the legislation of the last Congress require that each state put its educational house in order as soon as possible. While the amounts of federal money supplied by the new federal legislation are but a small fraction of the total public funds spent within a state for educational purposes, *how* the new money is spent is of great importance. A pattern will be set which will influence future federal-state relations. Therefore in terms of effective use of the taxpayer's dollar, the departments of education in most states need to be greatly strengthened. I cannot believe that anyone here this afternoon will challenge this proposition. To argue further along this line would be to force an open door.

## PLANS FOR HIGHER EDUCATION

In addition to a strong, well organized state department of education, each state needs a master plan for higher education. Again, few of you here would probably disagree with me on this point. You might not agree with me, however, when I emphasize that the plan should be adopted by the legislature as a firm policy for the coming years. There is all the difference in the world between having a master plan adopted by the legislature, as in California, and having a master plan worked out by some committee and left hanging in the air without acceptance by the ultimate source of power—the state legislature. More than one member of a state legislature has told me that for his own protection against local pressures to transfer a local two year college to a four year institution he needed a master plan for the state adopted by the legislature. One can hardly speak of a stable educational policy for higher education in a state unless the legislature has adopted a well thought out plan.

## AN INTERSTATE COMPACT COMMISSION

In developing such a plan a state might well take note of what other states are doing, particularly in the same region. Interstate cooperation in the area of higher education in recent years has become possible through interstate regional compacts or agreements. I am sure you are all aware of the existence of the Southern Regional Education Board, the Western Interstate Commission for Higher Education, and the New England Board of Higher Education. These arrangements have proved their worth. But they are by themselves not sufficient to develop a nationwide coherent policy for higher education and, as far as I am aware, there has been no attempt to extend the area of competence to include education up to and through the twelfth grade. Yet, today the line between high school and college is very fuzzy. The continued expansion of two year colleges and the introduction of college work into the 12th grade in many schools (the advanced placement program) underlines this point. Why not extend the idea of regional pacts both in terms of the area of education to be covered and also in terms of number of states to be included? In short, why not establish by interstate compact an "Interstate Commission for Planning a Nationwide Educational Policy"?

In my recently published book entitled *Shaping Educational Policy* I have answered this question in the affirmative. I suggested that if it were too difficult for all fifty states to enter at once into such an agreement, the scheme might be started if fifteen or twenty of the more populous states entered into such a compact with provision that the other states might later join. The first group need not be in one region, but if the idea proved feasible, one would hope that very shortly all the nation would be covered.

The compact would have to be drawn up by the states and approved by Congress. The document would provide for the membership of the commission and the guidelines for its operation. Each state should be represented on the commission, though a regional group of the less populous states might decide to be represented by one person. The person or persons authorized to represent the state would be determined either directly or indirectly by the state legislature. He should be a layman of the stature of the best members of the boards of trustees of state universities. I assume the United States Commissioner of Education would be a member, indeed it might be provided in the compact that he would be the presiding officer. I leave open for discussion the way this commission, a commission of the representatives of fifty states, would relate its activities to those of the U.S. Office of Education, the National Science Foundation, and other federal agencies.

### STATEWIDE, NATIONWIDE POLICIES

My main point is that, if the American people would only accept the fact that we do not have a national system of education but rather fifty state systems, we could then proceed to debate education with more reason. We would stop flirting with the idea of a national policy and consider how we might develop a nationwide policy. We would then be willing to examine ways of interstate cooperation at least as far as planning is concerned.

Let me make quite plain the fact that I am not talking about states rights. Nor am I advocating that a state should establish an education system run from the state capitol. We cannot and should not abolish local boards; they are a vital and permanent part of our tradition. But we can and must have far more leadership from chief state school officers than is now exercised in some states. We can introduce, with the interest and help of all citizens, better statewide planning in the selection of teachers, curriculum revision, eradication of slum schools and the solution of other critical problems. We can, I believe, develop a mechanism by which the states can know what other states are doing and thus plan together.

### HOW THE COMMISSION COULD WORK

Let me take a few moments of your time to spell out in detail how I think the Interstate Planning Commission might work. You may well say a commission of fifty members is unwieldy and unworkable. I agree. A vital fact of my proposal is the creation of "working parties" appointed by the Interstate Commission and reporting to it. While the members of the Interstate Commission would be laymen, the working parties would certainly include many educators and, in some cases, perhaps be composed exclusively of professors, researchers, teachers, and school and college administrators.

First of all, the Interstate Commission would have to agree on certain basic principles to guide the activities of all the working parties. I have suggested in my book that some six or seven widely accepted premises be officially adopted. These principles would include a statement of the ends of education in preparing youth to function as responsible members of a free society, a statement that the state was committed to free schooling through twelve grades for *all* children, the right of parents to send children to private schools, the responsibility of the state for public education beyond the high school for at least some youth, the support of a state university for advanced scholarly work and research and the guarantee of academic freedom for the teachers in the university.

The declaration of some such set of premises by an Interstate Commission would be the first step in shaping an educational nationwide policy. If each state legislature would pass a resolution accepting such a declaration, we would for the first time as a nation be officially committed to certain basic principles of educational policy. We now *assume* these principles to be valid, but in fact they have never been promulgated by representative assemblies and could not be promulgated by the Congress.

The working parties would be so chosen as to represent a variety of views. Unanimous reports would *not* be expected. The right of dissent would be guaranteed to each member. The reports would be reviewed by the commission and perhaps returned to the working parties for fuller comment. In this way the diversity of state tradition and the differences state-by-state as to the nature of the problems would be reflected in the final report.

To each of these parties would be assigned a particular task. Let me give just two or three examples of the kind of task which might thus be carried out by a working party.

First, there is a question of obtaining a thorough study of the needs of the nation on a state by state basis for people trained for the various vocations. I think it is generally agreed that we do not have yet anything like adequate information. The Assistant Commissioner of Education emphasized this fact at a meeting I attended in Pittsburgh not long ago.

A second matter which might well be considered by a working party would be the "drop-out," again on a state-by-state basis, and here, by the drop-out problem, I mean something far more than the drop-out of high school. I mean the loss of talent between the high school and graduation from a college or university. A document published by the National Science Foundation some years ago brought out some alarming statistics which have not yet been fully appreciated by the American public. I have referred to these in my book, *The Education of American Teachers*, and would merely like to repeat here what I have written in that book. According to estimates in a study by the National Science Foundation, it would appear that of the 30 per cent most able students in the high schools of the country only 38 per cent graduated from college (45 per cent of men, and 31 per cent of women), and even of the

top 10 per cent in terms of ability, only about half complete college work. These data were obtained from the nation as a whole by a sampling procedure. What we need are much more accurate data on a state-by-state basis, for the differences state by state must be considerable. Such data could be obtained by a working party established by the Interstate Commission.

To name another example—with the vast sums of money being spent on research and training research people, I think it is time we had a look on a nationwide basis at the standards for the doctor's degree. There are only 219 institutions awarding this degree. One suspects the standards in some of these are low. We need a study of the whole problem of the doctorate. I think only at this high level would it be practical to consider the matter of degree standards. For the lower degrees the task is too great and the institutional standards too diverse. Before it is too late, however, we should see if we cannot develop a nationwide policy for the doctor's degrees awarded by our universities. I do not propose that the Interstate Planning Commission would attempt to *enforce* any standards. It would have no power, no administrative staff. What I envisage is a report finally agreed to by the commission and transmitted to each of the states. It would then be up to the states to take appropriate action by *state* authorities to accept or reject these standards and, if accepted, to enforce them.

KEY POSITION OF LEGISLATORS

You may well ask why the tasks which I have mentioned and the others I have described in my book could not be as well performed by some committee appointed in Washington. My answer would be that I do not believe a report of a working party whose authority comes from the federal government either on the executive or Congressional level would have the acceptance by state legislators as would the report of a working committee appointed by an interstate commission which would be, in the last analysis, composed of representatives of the legislatures of the fifty states.

Whether we like it or not, the legislature has the last say in the question of money, of the chartering of colleges and universities, and can, unless properly guided, pass legislation which would be a detriment to the progress of American education. A legislature to my mind would be far more ready to listen to the views of a working committee whose report had been carefully analyzed and discussed by an interstate commission, *particularly a report that dealt with state-by-state differences.* Indeed it is the existence of these state-by-state differences of which I think you are all aware, which has persuaded me to make my radical suggestion, as a hope of making progress in developing a nationwide educational policy.

I am sure I do not have to tell you that in asking citizens to be as much concerned with what happens at the state capital as what happens in Washington, I am not making an old-fashioned plea on the basis of states rights. This is a nation operating under a Constitution created by all the people, yet we are not a federation of fifty states. This question was settled one hundred years ago on the battlefields of the Civil War. But unless we were to amend the Constitution the separate states have and will continue to have the responsibility of developing state systems of education. They will differ one from another in important points. It is important that there be a mechanism for the interchange of information and for informing the public, the Congress and executive officers of the fed-

eral government of what the facts are in many a crucial situation.

THE THESIS SUMMARIZED

To sum up, educational policy in the United States has been determined in the past by the more or less haphazard interaction of (1) the leaders of public school teachers, administrators and professors of education, (2) state educational authorities, (3) a multitude of state colleges and universities, (4) private colleges and universities, and (5) the variety of agencies of the federal government, through which vast sums of money have flowed to individual institutions and the states.

It is my thesis that such a jumble of influential private and public bodies does not correspond to the needs of the nation in the 1960s. Some degree of order needs to be brought out of this chaos, primarily for the benefit of the on-coming generations, but also, to achieve a more effective use of public and private moneys.

Each state needs to put its educational planning machinery in good order. This is the first priority in the matter of getting forward with developing a nationwide policy. But, if I am right, in addition we need a new procedure for interstate communication and interstate cooperation. Whether my specific suggestion has merit or not, I feel sure the American people must in some way work out a method by which the states and the federal government together can plan for the future and develop a dynamic policy adequate to meet the challenges of a highly industrialized society in the strongly divided world in which we live.

# THE COMPACT FOR EDUCATION

On the basis of Dr. Conant's idea, Terry Sanford, Governor of North Carolina 1961–1965, wrote governors, educators, associations, and others with concern for education that: "I have felt that we need to do two things.

"First, we need to involve governors and state leadership in the process of improvement of education to a greater degree than they have ever been involved.

"Second we need to have available the best and broadest possible array of suggestions and goals from which the policy makers, state and local, can make the policy decisions which will lead to improvement of schools and other educational institutions. If these goals and suggestions are to result in action, they should be put together in the first place by those who will be in a position to make the state and local policy decisions.

"For widespread advances in the quality and effectiveness of our educational processes it is essential that we have the vigorous leadership of the several governors.

"Involvement of the governors will, with few exceptions, involve the legislative and administrative leadership of the state. It will involve the budget and tax structure of the state. It will involve greater public understanding of what must be done.

"The efforts of the governors, in turn, cannot be productive without the cooperation of their chief state school officers, leaders in higher education, and local school administrators. Unless these two groups, political and educational, are joined by the non-professional educational leaders, the school board members, it will be difficult to achieve the general and popular support which will be necessary for success."

In May, 1965, Governor Sanford called a meeting of representatives of all organizations and associations related to education plus representatives of the National Governors' Conference to seek their advice "on the best method and organizational structure for bringing together the political and educational leadership of the several states for the purpose of studying, planning, suggesting and promoting sounder objectives and goals for the improvement of education in America." They met in Washington and the consensus was that the ideas should be developed.

As a result of the Washington meeting, a Special Planning Committee met in the spring and summer of 1965 to develop tentative proposals for forming the Compact. It consisted of representatives of the Governors' Conference Committee on Human Resources; the American Council on Education; the Association of State Universities and Land Grant Colleges; the Council of Chief State School Officers; the National School Boards Association; the National Association of State Boards of Education; the American Association of School Administrators; and a few advisors, such as John Ivey of the Michigan State University Department of Education, Mitchell Wendell of the Council of State Governments, and Alan Pifer of the Carnegie Corporation as well as Governor Sanford and his staff.

The idea of an Interstate Compact for Education was submitted to the National Governors' Conference in July by the Governors' Conference Committee on Human Relations, chaired by Governor Richard Hughes of New Jersey and Governor Mark Hatfield of Oregon. The Committee said it believed the "proposals are of such a lasting significance and far-reaching importance as to be the subject of a special report to this Conference . . . . It is the belief of this Committee that the leadership in the determination of (educational) policy decisions must remain with the States . . . only by state leadership can our invaluable diversity be maintained . . . there must be a mechanism which will weld the states together into a nationwide organization. We agree with Governor Sanford that only by the vigorous leadership of the governors and the intensification of communications between the states can the desirable end of state pre-eminence in the field of education be preserved." The Governors' Conference adopted unanimously the Committee's special report stating the need for a nationwide alliance for the improvement of education with the active leadership and personal participation of the governors.

In August, the National Legislative Conference recommended "to the legislatures and the governors that they give serious consideration to a proposal for interstate cooperation for the advancement of education."

Presentations of the proposal were also made at the annual meetings of the National School Boards Association, National Association of State Boards of Education, the Western Interstate Commission on Higher Education, the Council of Chief State School Officers, the National Congress of Parents and Teachers, the Midwestern Governors' Conference, the White House Conference on Education, and the Southern Regional Education Board.

On September 29 and 30, 1965 at Kansas City, a general planning conference on the Compact for Education, attended by nineteen governors and representatives from every state, the Commonwealth of Puerto Rico, and the territories of American Samoa and the Virgin Islands, approved the idea and took steps to implement it.

### THE KANSAS CITY CONFERENCE

The Planning Conference for the Compact for Education met in Kansas City in

September, 1965 and took the following action:

1. Approved the idea of interstate cooperation in education and took steps to implement a proposal to establish, through an interstate compact, an Education Commission of the States, consisting of seven members representing each party state, including the governor, two state Legislators and four others appointed by the governor.

2. Approved the Bylaws for the Education Commission of the States.

3. Approved the Compact document, to be transmitted to the states.

4. Approved a schedule of entry fees and state pro-rata contributions to support the Compact organization.

5. Instructed the Steering Committee to seek and hire the best qualified person as Executive Director of the Compact for Education.

6. Authorized a Standing Committee to search out and accept bids from the States for the location of the permanent offices of the Compact organization, making every attempt to locate the site near a university.

7. Set up an Interim Planning, Development and Steering Committee with instructions to:

    (a)   Carry out the intent of the Conference,

    (b)   Accept and expend funds,

    (c)   Hire a director and staff,

    (d)   Select a headquarters site, in consultation with the site-selection committee,

    (e)   Present and explain the Compact to the various governors and state legislatures,

    (f)   Generally assume the task of creating the Compact for Education.

### STATE ACTION

The next steps on the part of each state will be:

1. Adherence to the terms of the Com-

pact by Executive Order by the Governor, and/or

2. Enactment of the Compact and its Enabling Act by the Legislature.

The National Governors' Conference unanimously adopted a resolution endorsing the Compact idea, as did the National Legislative Conference. At the Kansas City Planning Conference, every state, the Commonwealth of Puerto Rico and two territories were represented. Nineteen governors came personally as did fifty State Legislators and over 300 educators from all levels of education and sections of the country. At that time, more than a dozen governors indicated an intention to adhere to the Compact by an immediate Executive Order until their legislatures could do so by Enabling Act at their next Legislative Session.

When sufficient states have adhered by either Executive Order or legislative enactment, the Interim Committee will call a conference of participating states, will dissolve itself, and a permanent Steering Committee, under the terms of the Compact, will be organized to carry forward its purposes.

COMPACT FOR EDUCATION

*Preamble*

WHEREAS, the proper education of all citizens is one of the most important responsibilities of the States to preserve a free and open society in the United States; and,

WHEREAS, the increasing demands of our whole national life for improving and expanding educational services require a broad exchange of research data and information concerning the problems and practices of education; and,

WHEREAS, there is a vital need for strengthening the voices of the States in the formulation of alternative nationwide educational policies,

THE STATES AFFIRM the need for close and continuing consultation among our several States on all matters of education, and do hereby establish this Compact for Education.

*Article I. Purpose and Policy.*

A. It is the purpose of this compact to:

1. Establish and maintain close cooperation and understanding among executive, legislative, professional educational and lay leadership on a nationwide basis at the State and local levels.

2. Provide a forum for the discussion, development, crystalization and recommendation of public policy alternatives in the field of education.

3. Provide a clearing house of information on matters relating to educational problems and how they are being met in different places throughout the Nation, so that the executive and legislative branches of State Government and of local communities may have ready access to the experience and record of the entire country, and so that both lay and professional groups in the field of education may have additional avenues for the sharing of experience and the interchange of ideas in the formation of public policy in education.

4. Facilitate the improvement of State and local educational systems so that all of them will be able to meet adequate and desirable goals in a society which requires continuous qualitative and quantitative advance in educational opportunities, methods and facilities.

B. It is the policy of this compact to encourage and promote local and State initiative in the development, maintenance, improvement and administration of educational systems and institutions in *a manner which will accord with the needs and advantages of diversity among localities and States.*

C. The party States recognize that each of them has an interest in the quality and quantity of education furnished in each of the other States, as well as in the excellence of its own educational systems and institutions, because of the highly mobile character of individuals within the Nation, and because the products and services contributing to the health, welfare and economic advancement of each State are supplied in significant part by persons educated in other States.

*Article II. State Defined.*

As used in this Compact, "State" means a State, territory, or possession of the United States, the District of Columbia, or the Commonwealth of Puerto Rico.

*Article III. The Commission*

A. The Educational Commission of the States, hereinafter called "the Commission", is hereby established. The Commission shall consist of seven members representing each party State. One of such members shall be the Governor; two shall be members of the State legislature selected by its respective houses and serving in such manner as the legislature may determine; and four shall be appointed by and serve at the pleasure of the Governor, unless the laws of the State otherwise provide. If the laws of a State prevent legislators from serving on the Commission, six members shall be appointed and serve at the pleasure of the Governor, unless the laws of the State otherwise provide. In addition to any other principles or requirements which a State may establish for the appointment and service of its members of the Commission, the guiding principle for the composition of the membership on the Commission from each party State shall be that the members representing such State shall, by virtue of their training, experience, knowledge or affiliations be in a position collectively to reflect broadly the interests of the State Government, higher education, the State education system, local education, lay and professional, public and non-public educational leadership. Of those appointees, one shall be the head of a state agency or institution, designated by the Governor, having responsibility for one or more programs of public education. In addition to the members of the Commission representing the party States, there may be not to exceed ten non-voting commissioners selected by the steering committee for terms of one year. Such commissioners shall represent leading national organizations of professional educators or persons concerned with educational administration.

B. The members of the Commission shall be entitled to one vote each on the Commission. No action of the Commission shall be binding unless taken at a meeting at which a majority of the total number of votes on the Commission are cast in favor thereof. Action of the Commission shall be only at a meeting at which a majority of the Commissioners are present. The Commission shall meet at least once a year. In its bylaws, and subject to such directions and imitations as may be contained therein, the Commission may delegate the exercise of any of its powers to the steering committee or the Executive Director, except for the power to approve budgets or requests for appropriations, the power to make policy recommendations pursuant to Article IV and adoption of the annual report pursuant to Article III (j).

C. The Commission shall have a seal.

D. The Commission shall elect annually, from among its members, a chairman, who shall be a Governor, a vice chairman and a treasurer. The Commission shall provide for the appointment of an executive director. Such executive director shall serve at the pleasure of the Commission, and together with the treasurer and such other personnel as the Commission may deem appropriate shall be bonded in such amount as the Commission shall determine. The executive director shall be secretary.

E. Irrespective of the civil service, personnel or other merit system laws of any of the party States, the executive director subject to the approval of the steering committee shall appoint, remove or discharge such personnel as may be necessary for the performance of the functions of the Commission, and shall fix the duties and compensation of such personnel. The Commission in its bylaws shall provide for the personnel policies and programs of the Commission.

F. The Commission may borrow, accept or contract for the services of personnel from any party jurisdiction, the United States, or any subdivision or agency of the aforementioned governments, or from any agency of two or more of the party jurisdictions or their subdivisions.

G. The Commission may accept for any of its purposes and functions under this compact any and all donations, and grants of money, equipment, supplies, materials and services, conditional or otherwise, from any State, the United States, or any other governmental agency, or from any person, firm, association, foundation, or corporation, and may receive, utilize and dispose of the same. Any donation or grant accepted by the Commission pursuant to this paragraph or services borrowed pursuant to paragraph (f) of this Article shall be reported in the annual report of the Commission. Such report shall include the nature, amount and conditions, if any, of the donation, grant, or services borrowed, and the identity of the donor or lender.

H. The Commission may establish and maintain such facilities as may be necessary for the transacting of its business. The Commission may acquire, hold, and convey real and personal property and any interest therein.

I. The Commission shall adopt bylaws for the conduct of its business and shall have the power to amend and rescind these bylaws. The Commission shall publish its bylaws in convenient form and shall file a copy thereof and a copy of any amendment thereto, with the appropriate agency or officer in each of the party States.

J. The Commission annually shall make to the Governor and legislature of each party State a report covering the activities of the Commission for the preceding year. The Commission may make such additional reports as it may deem desirable.

*Article IV. Powers.*

In addition to authority conferred on the Commission by other provisions of the compact, the Commission shall have authority to:

1. Collect, correlate, analyze and interpret information and data concerning educational needs and resources.

2. Encourage and foster research in all aspects of education, but with special reference to the desirable scope of instruction, organization, administration, and instructional methods and standards employed or suitable for employment in public educational systems.

3. Develop proposals for adequate financing of education as a whole and at each of its many levels.

4. Conduct or participate in research of the types referred to in this Article in any instance where the Commission finds that such research is necessary for the advancement of the purposes and policies of this compact, utilizing fully the resources of national associations, regional compact organizations for higher education, and other agencies and institutions, both public and private.

5. Formulate suggested policies and plans for the improvement of public education as a whole, or for any segment thereof, and make recommendations with respect thereto available to the appropriate governmental units, agencies and public officials.

6. Do such other things as may be necessary or incidental to the adminis-

tration of any of its authority or functions pursuant to this compact.

*Article V. Cooperation With Federal Government.*

A. If the laws of the United States specifically so provide, or if administrative provision is made therefor within the Federal Government, the United States may be represented on the Commission by not to exceed ten representatives. Any such representative or representatives of the United States shall be appointed and serve in such manner as may be provided by or pursuant to Federal law, and may be drawn from any one or more branches of the Federal Government, but no such representative shall have a vote on the Commission.

B. The Commission may provide information and make recommendations to any executive or legislative agency or officer of the Federal Government concerning the common educational policies of the States, and may advise with any such agencies or officers concerning any matter of mutual interest.

*Article VI. Committees.*

A. To assist in the expeditious conduct of its business when the full Commission is not meeting, the Commission shall elect a steering committee of thirty members which, subject to the provisions of this compact and consistent with the policies of the Commission, shall be constituted and function as provided in the bylaws of the Commission. One-third of the voting membership of the steering committee shall consist of Governors, and the remainder shall consist of other members of the Commission. A Federal representative on the Commission may serve with the steering committee, but without vote. The voting members of the steering committee shall serve for terms of two years, except that members elected to the first steering committee of the Commission shall be elected as follows: fifteen for one year and fifteen for two years. The chairman, vice chairman, and treasurer of the Commission shall be members of the steering committee and, anything in this paragraph on the contrary notwithstanding, shall serve during their continuance in these offices. Vacancies in the steering committee shall not affect its authority to act, but the Commission at its next regularly ensuing meeting following the occurrence of any vacancy shall fill it for the unexpired term. No person shall serve more than two terms as a member of the steering committee; provided that service for a partial term of one year or less shall not be counted toward the two term limitation.

B. The Commission may establish advisory and technical committees composed of State, local, and Federal officials, and private persons to advise it with respect to any one or more of its functions. Any advisory or technical committee may, on request of the States concerned, be established to consider any matter of special concern to two or more of the party States.

C. The Commission may establish such additional committees as its bylaws may provide.

*Article VII. Finance.*

A. The Commission shall advise the Governor or designated officer or officers of each party State of its budget and estimated expenditures for such period as may be required by the laws of that party State. Each of the Commission's budgets of estimated expenditures shall contain specific recommendations of the amount or amounts to be appropriated by each of the party States.

B. The total amount of appropriation requests under any budget shall be apportioned among the party states. In making such apportionment, the Commission shall devise and employ a formula which takes equitable account of the populations and per capita income levels of the party States.

C. The Commission shall not pledge the credit of any party States. The Commission may meet any of its obligations in whole or in part with funds available to it pursuant to Article III (g) of this compact, provided that the Commission takes specific action setting aside such funds prior to incurring an obligation to be met in whole or in part in such manner. Except where the Commission makes use of funds available to it pursuant to Article III (g) thereof, the Commission shall not incur any obligation prior to the allotment of funds by the party States adequate to meet the same.

D. The Commission shall keep accurate accounts of all receipts and disbursements. The receipts and disbursements of the Commission shall be subject to the audit and accounting procedures established by its bylaws. However, all receipts and disbursements of funds handled by the Commission shall be audited yearly by a qualified public accountant, and the report of the audit shall be included in and become part of the annual reports of the Commission.

E. The accounts of the Commission shall be open at any reasonable time for inspection by duly constituted officers of the party States and by any persons authorized by the Commission.

F. Nothing contained herein shall be construed to prevent Commission compliance with laws relating to audit or inspection of accounts by or on behalf of any government contributing to the support of the Commission.

*Article VIII. Eligible Parties; Entry Into and Withdrawal.*

A. This compact shall have as eligible parties all States, Territories, and Possessions of the United States, the District of Columbia, and the Commonwealth of Puerto Rico. In respect of any such jurisdiction not having a Governor, the term

"Governor," as used in this compact, shall mean the closest equivalent official of such jurisdiction.

B. Any State or other eligible jurisdiction may enter into this compact and it shall become binding thereon when it has adopted the same: provided that in order to enter into initial effect, adoption by at least ten eligible party jurisdictions shall be required.

C. Adoption of the compact may be either by enactment thereof or by adherence thereto by the Governor; provided that in the absence of enactment, adherence by the Governor shall be sufficient to make his State a party only until December 31, 1967. During any period when a State is participating in this compact through gubernatorial action, the Governor shall appoint those persons who, in addition to himself, shall serve as the members of the Commission from his State, and shall provide to the Commission an equitable share of the financial support of the Commission from any source available to him.

D. Except for a withdrawal effective on December 31, 1967 in accordance with paragraph C of this Article, any party State may withdraw from this compact by enacting a statute repealing the same, but no such withdrawal shall take effect until one year after the Governor of the withdrawing State has given notice in writing of the withdrawal to the Governors of all other party States. No withdrawal shall affect any liability already incurred by or chargeable to a party State prior to the time of such withdrawal.

*Article IX. Construction and Severability.*

This compact shall be liberally construed so as to effectuate the purposes thereof. The provisions of this compact shall be severable and if any phrase, clause, sentence or provision of this compact is declared to be contrary to the constitution of any State or of the United States, or the application thereof to any Government, agency, person or circumstance is held invalid, the validity of the remainder of this compact and the applicability thereof to any Government, agency, person or circumstance shall not be affected thereby. If this compact shall be held contrary to the constitution of any State participating therein, the compact shall remain in full force and effect as to the State affected as to all severable matters.

WHAT IT IS NOT

1 The Compact for Education is not a policy-maker . . . it will carry no authority to impose any recommendations . . . nor will it make recommendations without exploring and indicating all avenues and possible courses of action. It will suggest policy *alternatives* . . . leaving to the states — state officials, state legislatures, and trustees of institutions of higher education — which, if any, of the alternatives will be accepted. Its report will not be binding, but will be informational in character.

2 The Compact for Education does not represent a drive for uniformity in American education. It will stimulate diversified answers to the problems in education recognizing the differences between the states. It will encourage dissent.

3 The Compact for Education will not lobby inside the states nor in Washington. It will furnish the educational and political leadership of the states with a vehicle to debate goals and answers.

4 The Compact for Education does not represent an effort to curtail or attack federal aid to education, or federal activity. In fact it makes provisions for Federal cooperation and participation. It is an effort to bring to bear all the resources that the American people have *to improve education* and *to encourage state action* for better schools and schooling.

5 The Compact for Education will not compete with, replace or make obsolete the current voluntary associations or national and regional organizations in the field of education. It will cooperate fully, assuring that there is a minimum of overlap or duplication . . . it will seek the frontiers, where effort is needed and recommendations necessary.

WHAT IT COULD ACCOMPLISH

1 A *partnership* between the educational and political forces for *advancement* of education.

2 A stimulus for *State* action in education.

3 A means of *interchange of information* and ideas and successful programs across state lines and regions for the benefit of the states.

4 A *forum* for discussion and recommendation of various policy *alternatives* for state consideration and decision.

5 A way to collect, correlate, analyze and interpret data for use *by the states*.

6 A way to assemble the best minds and the most experienced opinions into working parties to *explore new ways* for the states to attack the problems and *carry out research* on all aspects of education.

7 A way to encourage the states to *fulfill* their *role* as the *senior partner* in American education.

8 A place for individual states to call on for *specialized help* in evaluating programs and *getting new ideas*.

---

## WATER RESOURCES

Water resource development programs are characterized less by collaboration through formal grants-in-aid than by informal and contractual arrangements between government agencies for projects and services. Cooperation in the water resource development field is promoted by two facts. Legally, there is shared federal and state control of most waterways based on the states' sovereign ownership rights and police powers and the broadly defined constitutional grant of federal powers over navigable waters. Practically, there exists highly developed machinery for exercising local political influence on water resource development activities. While federal agencies such as the Corps of Engineers and the Bureau of Reclamation appear to dominate the field of water resource development in the headlines, their activities are almost invariably products of local political pressure and are frequently financed in part by state or local funds. At the same time, the expansion of water resource development activities into new fields revolving around recreation and conservation of ground water, has led to the increasing involvement of state and local governments as primary agents.

Examination of this particular problem gives us a view of cooperation in its less formal but no less routinized aspects. "TVA and the States" discusses the way in which a federal program, clearly designed by those who proposed and advocated it to be a unilateral one, dominated by federal authorities, was assimilated into the partnership system, partly out of necessity but in great measure by choice of the administrators and elected representatives involved in its formation and actualization. Gordon Clapp's central points are two: cooperation is desirable and the benefits of cooperation have led to a strengthening of state and local government in the Tennessee Valley. His discussion implicitly reflects the credo of those top-level federal administrators who are concerned with promoting cooperation as the best way to achieve their program goals.

---

*Gordon R. Clapp*

## TVA AND THE STATES

### INTRODUCTION

The Tennessee Valley Authority lives and works in a region where the emphasis upon state rights is not of recent origin. Critics outside the region sometimes refer to the Authority as a "superstate," an example of authoritarian power imposed upon helpless states. But people in the region generally laugh off such nonsense; they see in TVA a symbol for a greater Tennessee Valley. And some have even hailed it as the nation's belated compensation for the humiliations imposed upon the South dur-

ing the grim years of the Reconstruction.

TVA emerged from a long history of differing views as to where to rest the responsibilities for resource conservation and development among the federal, state, and local governments. The Act of 1933 is replete with language and ideas recognizing the role of the states in the task of rebuilding the Tennessee Valley. In the light of American history this new method of intergovernmental co-operation may be viewed as an illuminating example of creative federalism.

The idea that conservation of natural re-

---

From Gordon R. Clapp, *The Tennessee Valley Authority*, pp. 71–92. Reprinted by permission.

sources is a matter of public concern goes back to the beginning of our national history. An early concept held that responsibility for conservation could be divided neatly between the federal and state governments, each with a clearly defined part of the task, each keeping out of the way of the other. But natural resources do not arrange themselves to fit such legalistic precision. The more realistic concept of a federal-state partnership in conservation activities and resource development has become established only in the last few decades. This idea was given current expression by President Eisenhower in his State of the Union message in January, 1954: "Part of our Nation's precious heritage is its natural resources. It is the common responsibility of Federal, State, and local governments to improve and develop them, always working in the closest harmony and partnership."

TVA and the states have exemplified this method and sought this goal for twenty years. Jointly they have invented practical arrangements suited to the particular problems which bring them together. The growth and evolution of the methods, the wealth of innovation devoid of doctrinal mental blocks, and the results of co-operative relationships between TVA and the states in and around the Tennessee Valley are the subject of this chapter.

The conservation movement has not always rested on principles of intergovernmental co-operation. Conservation as spearheaded by Theodore Roosevelt at the beginning of the present century was notable for its recognition of the interdependence of our natural resources, that is to say, among water and land and forests. This idea was reflected in comprehensive fashion for the first time, on a large scale at least, in the Tennessee Valley program. But the pioneers of the conservation movement and their successors also asserted a paramount *national* interest in our natural resources. The Federal Water Power Act passed by Congress in 1920, to take a single example, provided for federal retention and control over the development of power sites in the public domain, an idea implied in a veto message by Theodore Roosevelt as early as 1903.

A contrasting insistence on paramount rights of the states was forcibly laid down by the governor of New York, Alfred E. Smith, in 1924: "While it is true that the Federal Water Power Act gave the state the preference, it, nevertheless, attempted to establish as a fundamental principle the belief that the ultimate ownership of [water power sites] rested with the Federal Government. . . . This principle we deny and, I believe, rightly so."

The position taken by Governor Smith was occasioned by debate over development of the St. Lawrence Waterway and led in 1931 to the creation of the New York Power Authority sponsored by another governor of New York, Franklin D. Roosevelt. This action called for *state* control over the development of water resources in the Niagara and St. Lawrence rivers within New York State. This view is not only very much alive in New York State today; it is also backed by financial resources sufficient to apply it with federal capital assistance.

The emergency atmosphere of 1933 seems now, in retrospect, a strange time for a compromise on the federal-state issue regarding natural resources. Highly centralized planning to combat the depression was the keynote of the day. Under the circumstances then prevailing, it is noteworthy, indeed, that the TVA Act in many of its specific provisions called for co-operation among the federal, state, and local governments in the development of natural resources. For the first time an administrative agency was created with instructions to promote actively a federal-state relationship for regional development along lines more recently spoken of as a partnership.

It is also noteworthy that this new federal-state relationship in resource development was to be achieved by regional administrative decentralization. It involved a new kind of decentralization. Regional offices of federal departments usually mark federal responsibility grown too large to be administratively contained in Washington. Regional offices recommend, but headquarters in Washington decide. In the case of TVA, however, the board of directors was placed by law in the region. The decisions of the board were to be made where the work was to be done. This was genuine decentralization. It likewise promoted close co-operation with the states.

Three characteristics of the Tennessee Valley Authority have had considerable bearing upon its relationships to the federal government and the states. It is a multiple-purpose agency, cutting across traditional functional lines of the departments and agencies of the federal government in Washington. Its special responsibilities flow to one region of the nation, effectively discharged only as the regional agency can act without being subjected to veto power vested in federal departments having nation-wide programs. Finally, it is heavily flavored with a large business-type operation, which requires for its success a high degree of managerial flexibility. These three characteristics have been preserved by permitting the Authority to work as an independent agency, under a corporate form, outside the federal departmental structure, deriving its administrative status from a broadly conceived statutory charter. These attributes have given TVA the opportunity to plow new ground in the field of federal-state relationships.

Direct assistance to state agencies by TVA, including financial assistance, has often been found necessary to get a particular activity started, to demonstrate its value, and to lend support to the state or local agency in charge of its administration. As an activity proves its value to the people, and as the state or local agency grows in strength, the scale of direct assistance can generally be reduced.

This process may be illustrated by referring to one small but important activity. When the Authority builds dams, usually in an area remote from large cities, it pays funds to the state or counties to make library and book service available in construction areas. (I assume it is not necessary to explain why it is considered important that employees building a dam should be able to borrow books if they want to—and none is burned intentionally.) As a result of these arrangements a number of regional libraries were organized and operated by the states or counties to serve the construction centers. For the same cost TVA would have incurred by providing the service directly to its employees, the counties reached their own people as well. As dams were finished and workers disbanded, the Authority's financial contribution ended. But library service went right on and expanded, with financial responsibility assumed by the state and local governments. Here is a summary by dollars: In 1943 in the state of Tennessee, $18,000 was spent on regional library services, of which local sources provided $4,000 and TVA $14,000. The state contributed no funds. Ten years later $295,000 went into this same service; $125,000 came from local funds, and the state provided $170,000. The Authority contributed no funds at all.

In a more general way the results of this method of initial stimulation and subsequent withdrawal of financial support are suggested by the following facts: Starting in 1934, TVA's expenditures for resource development activities carried on in co-operation with the seven states in the area gradually increased to reach an all-time high of $7.5 million in 1947. Since that time its expenditures for these activities have declined; [in 1953] they were approximately $3 million. State expenditures for resource development in the seven states were only about $10 million a year in the early period of TVA's operations. By 1947, the high point of TVA's expenditures, annual state expenditures had reached $30 million—almost four dollars by the states for every one dollar from TVA. For 1953 state resource expenditures may be estimated at about $70 million—a ratio of more than twenty to one. These figures reflect growing state responsibility and initiative in the entire field of resource development, built in many instances upon initial financial and technical assistance from the Authority.

One of the first annual reports prepared by TVA recognized that the task of rebuilding the river had been intrusted to it—but that the Valley's future development rested on the co-operative work of many agencies and individuals. To this end, a loose but effective coalition constituting the machinery of regional development has evolved. These relations could be illustrated by reference to many subjects—freight-rate equalization, in which careful joint research with the states gave the southern governors a factual basis for seeking national action; malaria control, where a complex program initiated and led by TVA with state and county agencies participating has almost eliminated malaria throughout the region; and so on through a long list. The partnership with the land-grant colleges, the state agricultural extension services, and experiment stations is also an important chapter in any such recital. But there are other important examples; I have selected three for brief discussion: forestry, regional research, and electric-power distribution.

### FORESTRY

The 14,000,000 acres of forest land in the Tennessee Valley provide the raw material for a $350 million annual business and afford protective cover for more than half of the watershed. This was once the leading hardwood lumber area of the world. After more than a century of agricultural and industrial development, 54 per cent of the land area of the Valley is still forested, and it is estimated that an additional million acres not now in timber production might be reforested to achieve the best land use. Improved management together with reforestation can restore the region to its former importance in the hardwood industry.

Present-day forests of the Valley support thousands of industries—over five thousand sawmills and fifteen hundred other plants using wood as a raw material. The number of sawmills and other wood-using plants has more than doubled since 1935. But, with all its apparent economic productiveness, the forest resource of the Valley is yielding far below its capability. Total wood capital in standing trees could be increased three times. Annual wood growth also could be trebled. If this much wood were available to industry, income from this resource could be increased from $350 million to $1 billion annually.

The Tennessee Valley, like many other forest areas, illustrated the tragic cycle of destructive forest, soil, and water losses which follow "cut-and-run" timber practice. In the early history of TVA, suggestions were made to its board to buy large acreages of forest lands and to seek legislation to introduce some measure of regulation over forest landowners. The board rejected both ideas. It was clear that no one agency or the states alone could stop and reverse this cycle. A program for the Tennessee Valley drainage area as a whole was required. The forestry agencies of the states, the United States Forest Service, and many landowners knew what ought to be done, but they needed help. The Authority provided leadership and joined with them in a four-point program based on these major premises:

1. Increased protection against fire was the first and most obvious need.

2. Better forest management and cutting practices, on farm woodlands as well as on large industrial timber tracts, would improve yields and assure the growth of the future crop.

3. Thousands of acres of eroding, idle lands needed reforestation.

4. Development of wood-using industries and extension of new processes to utilize lower-grade timber would help to make good forest management pay off and provide additional employment.

Within the seven Valley states many public agencies are now working toward these objectives. Those most intimately concerned are the state departments of conservation. Each of these seven state agencies has a definite legislative mandate in the field of forest development. All have joined wholeheartedly in the Valley program. Through the mediation of the Authority, state agricultural extension services also help to promote better forestry practices on farm woodlands. County agents spent only 74 man-days on farm forestry work in 1933 compared to more than 1,000 man-days in 1953. Federal agricultural agencies have lent valuable assistance to the states and counties, especially in reforestation. Central to all, regional in its interest, and using stimulative financial assistance, demonstrations, research projects, and a staff skilled in the art of practical interpretation and persuasion has been TVA's Division of Forestry Relations.

What are the results of this approach thus far?

Forest-fire control has been organized and is being financed through federal, state, and local co-operation. Ninety-seven of the Valley's 125 counties are co-operating financially in this program as compared with 8 counties in 1934. The forest area under organized protection now is 12,500,000 acres, or about 89 per cent of the total forest area.

More than four hundred demonstrations of scientific forest-management practices on a total of some 130,000 acres have been established with landowners. These demonstrations range from small farm woodlands to large industrial forest holdings. More than 200,000 acres have been reforested with 156,000,000 trees provided by TVA since 1933. Some fifteen thousand farmers have demonstrated that serious erosion can be effectively controlled by reforestation. The Valley-wide inventory of the forest resource and the census of wood-using industries, compiled and kept current by the Authority, have helped hundreds of timber operators and industries, large and small, to find the specific kinds of timber stands they needed; new industries have been established; and many communities have been assisted in making plans for industrial development based upon the facts about their timber resources available for the first time in these detailed inventories.

Numerous timber trade associations are joined in this coalition, because forests provide raw material for the industries they represent. Sawmill operators go to school in demonstration meetings to learn how to improve efficiency, reduce wood waste, earn more money, and leave a better forest behind them. Now that forestry is becoming good business, private professional foresters have entered the field, retained by landowners for expert assistance and advice. Many lay groups, banded together by a deep interest in forests or wildlife, are molding public opinion in favor of forest conservation and exerting constructive support toward improvement in the management of natural resources.

These results are but a beginning. The major importance of what has been accomplished is found in the methods by which forest development can be promoted on a voluntary basis. These results have been achieved without the exercise of any power of coercion. There has been no invasion of the property rights of landowners; TVA has not encroached upon the responsibility or functions of the state and local governments. In fact, the state forest agencies are becoming stronger than ever before.

The seven state divisions of forestry, for example—those branches of the state conservation departments charged with forest protection and development—in fiscal year 1935 operated on funds totaling about $500,000. For fiscal year 1952 their expenditures amounted to almost $8 million. Technical personnel increased from 36 to 300. In 1935 these agencies were occupied primarily with forest-fire suppression; 70 per cent of their total funds was spent on fighting fires or getting ready to fight them. Fire suppression is still a big job, but the annual burn is gradually being reduced. And today 80 per cent of the total funds available to the forestry agencies of the seven states goes for positive measures of forest development rather than fire suppression.

The Valley's forests are a better resource now than in 1933, but the job is far from done. Continued progress will depend upon expanding public support for more money and better personnel for the state forestry agencies, with TVA continuing in the background to encourage and assist in the attainment of a regional goal.

REGIONAL RESEARCH

The wise development of natural resources cannot be accomplished without intelligent research. A region needs to build strong agencies for research — agencies whose work will inform the people, broaden the area of their choice, and let regional development proceed on the basis of knowledge and a richer experience. Where research budgets are limited as they are in the Tennessee Valley states, especially in the social sciences, co-operation among research groups can compound the values of information and knowledge and increase the utility of the research dollar.

A few examples in the field of social studies will illustrate a pattern of co-operative research in the Tennessee Valley which extends into a number of fields and includes hundreds of projects. Studies of municipal government and administration were made to provide practical background information for the power-distribution systems of the cities using TVA electricity. The university bureaus of public administration, organized in several instances for the purpose of making these studies, were financed by TVA. Their programs were continued and expanded by the states after completion of the initial co-operative projects. The bureaus of business research in the region have likewise co-operated in the study of regional problems, such as the analysis of county income, in which a new methodology was devised and tried successfully.

In 1944 six state universities joined with TVA in an interstate project which at the time was unique to the region and perhaps anywhere: a study of the administrative organizations and programs of the states relating to natural resources. The research facilities at the several universities were supplemented by a General Education Board grant. Regional meetings of research personnel were held to develop a joint approach suitable for all the participating states. Work conferences compared findings and exchanged ideas. The pattern of co-operation in research thus established carried over into a whole series of joint undertakings. The institutions have formed a continuing organization now known as the Southern Public Administration Research Council. It no longer depends for support upon TVA's financing, although it continues to have the co-operation and participation of the Authority's research personnel.

Another example of co-operative research illustrates the multiple by-products of the regional approach. Each of the Valley states maintains a Negro land-grant college. Until recently these colleges have been concerned mostly with vocational fields of study; research in the social sciences was not an important part of their work, and yet the people they served were passing through a period of great economic and occupational change. Members of the college professional staffs had little contact with each other, with the white land-grant colleges, or with regional development programs. Their isolated existence challenged the theory of a regional partnership for research and education. Here was a relatively unused regional resource which might be strategically equipped to take leadership in studying the needs of an important part of the region's population, largely centered in rural areas but moving rapidly into the cities. And the Authority certainly needed to know the dimensions and nature of this change.

Beginning in 1948 with Tuskegee Institute, TVA has provided modest support for social science research in this group of colleges. The method, developed through the

Conference of Presidents, has encouraged joint projects among the member colleges, under the supervision of a research director, and brought research personnel together in regional meetings from time to time. Through this program the Negro colleges have gained greater recognition by the other colleges. There has also been a tenfold increase in the annual social science research budgets of the seven colleges taking part in the program.

The Tennessee Valley region needs personnel and facilities for more research. Budgets are low, and staffs are generally too small for even the most obvious needs. However, co-operation and the opportunity for joint study have led many institutions to establish better research facilities and to make them useful to their respective states and to the region.

## FEDERAL-LOCAL PARTNERSHIP FOR ELECTRIC SERVICE

A recital of how TVA and the states work together cannot omit what is perhaps the outstanding example of a true partnership — the generation and distribution of electricity serving an area about the size of England and Scotland. This great public power arrangement is sometimes referred to as an example of creeping encroachment by the federal government upon the sovereignty of the states and an attempt to reduce the cities to the status of dejected and helpless captives. Nothing ever said about the Authority could be further from the truth.

[R]eflect upon this example of relationships among governments through the device of a network of contracts, a hundred and fifty in number, which join together, voluntarily, a great body of towns, cities, and rural communities in a complex public service enterprise.

TVA produces large quantities of electric power. The Act provides that this power be used to serve the interests of the people of the Tennessee Valley and the national defense. The board early announced its intention, subject to limited and temporary exceptions, not to engage in the retail distribution of electricity. Its power function, in the main, would be limited to the generation and transmission of electrical energy, with delivery of power at wholesale to the lines of distribution agencies that would in turn serve the ultimate consumers.

In the sale of power the law prescribed that preference be given "to States, counties, municipalities, and cooperative organizations of citizens or farmers not organized or doing business for profit, but primarily for the purpose of supplying electricity to its own citizens or members." The Act also provides that power be sold "at the lowest possible rates . . . to encourage increased domestic and rural use of electricity."

The states in the area enacted special legislation authorizing their cities to establish municipal systems and to enter into power contracts with the Authority. Most of the cities now distributing its power held referendums to decide what course to follow. The legal arrangements developed in Mississippi and Alabama for the rural distribution of electricity through consumer co-operatives set the pattern for state enabling acts which later accommodated rural electric co-operatives in most of rural America. Today TVA electricity is being distributed to consumers over practically all the state of Tennessee and in parts of six neighboring states by 97 separate municipal power systems, 51 rural electric co-operatives, and 2 small, local systems in private ownership.

This bare outline of events gives a deceptively simple picture of the development of a far-flung public power system — the largest single integrated system in the United States. It serves more than 1,300,000 retail consumers, representing a population of 5,000,000 people spread over an area of some 80,000 square miles. In the legal sense TVA's relations with local power distributors are governed by formal contracts by which it becomes the exclusive source of electric-energy supply for resale by distributors at rates agreed upon by both parties. But many, many questions were posed and worked out in the evolution of this public enterprise. The negotiation of each contract, the joint purchase and redivision of former private power-company properties among the Authority and the local power systems, the delineation of retail service areas, the organization of municipal power boards and rural electric co-operatives — these and hundreds of other problems have been the subject of discussion and negotiation. Legislative committees and public utility commissions, state municipal leagues, city councils, county courts, the President of the United States, Congress, and citizen groups in towns and rural areas have all had a hand in shaping the result.

Whenever conflicts arise — as they have and will — compromise must be considered and solution achieved within the broad framework of the public interest in the largest sense of the term. If agreement cannot be reached, the courts are open to either party, a recourse followed only twice in twenty years. And on one important occasion a long study and negotiation among the states, the counties, and TVA produced a plan for revision of the payments the Authority makes to states and counties in lieu of taxes to replace those formerly obtained from reservoir lands and utility properties, and the Act was accordingly amended. The plan for payments in lieu of taxes and the process by which it was developed stand high in the list of examples of how federal, state, and local governments can weigh and resolve equitably local, regional, and national interests.

Here is an illustration, by the way, of the peculiar responsibility of a *regional* agency as it faces in two directions — toward the region and toward the nation. When TVA and the cities and rural electric co-operatives joined to acquire the utility properties of the private companies operating in the region (an acquisition approved by Congress and the President), valuable private property was removed from the tax base of the counties in which several small dams and other electric facilities were located. In a few sparsely populated counties in the mountains the private utility property was the major tax source for county schools. It was recognized that the formula in the original TVA Act for payments in lieu of taxes to states and counties should be changed. But how much?

A careful study was made. With the facts in hand, there were meetings with governors, tax and finance commissioners, and county magistrates to appraise the analysis and to negotiate a proposal to be submitted to the President and Congress as an amendment to Section 13 of the Act.

In these negotiations the counties pressed for the highest possible payments that could be extracted from the power revenues of TVA. The states were interested in the financial needs of the counties, to be sure, but they also had their own budgetary problems — they wanted their share. At the same time both parties were aware of the mounting benefits accruing to the area through the power system. New dams, new employment, new lakes with great recreation possibilities, and new industry were increasing the property value and the tax base within the states and counties. And TVA's revenues are an asset to the federal government, providing a return on the investment made by the nation's taxpayers. The Authority, therefore, had to face two ways — to assure an equitable adjustment between the claims of states and counties and the federal taxpayers' rightful expectation of a return on their investment in the power system.

In the hearings and debates in Congress interesting inconsistencies developed. Some spokesmen from outside the Tennessee Valley urged that TVA be required to pay more to the states and counties in spite of the fact such payments would reduce the amount it would otherwise pay from its power revenues into the general fund of the United States Treasury. Governors and county magistrates were somewhat puzzled by this unexpected concern for their welfare until they realized that the private utilities were trying to load the Authority's payment burden in order to break the wholesale and resale rates for electricity. Others inside and outside the area argued that the new plan would pay too much to the states and counties and thereby reduce cash payments to the federal treasury.

But the amendment as passed incorporated the plan as developed by negotiation and study in the region. The facts and the careful process of negotiation survived an extremely close scrutiny by Congress. The proposal was judged to be fair to electric consumers, states and counties of the region, as well as to the nation's taxpayers.

The understanding and informed relationship between TVA and municipal and co-operative power distributors may be illustrated again by the successful negotiation last year of an upward adjustment of wholesale rates and resale rates for power to industrial customers. Rates for residential and small consumers were not revised. The need for increasing industrial rates had been brought about by the addition of new steam plants to the system, a higher-cost source of power than the dams. These steam plants, available for continuous operation, fit the supply requirements of high-load factor industries, operating around the clock the year round.

Let me cite the following fact as a measure of the true partnership of these arrangements in the Tennessee Valley. In this public power partnership, local distribution agencies through issuance of revenue bonds and use of surplus earnings have invested in their systems about $400 million. This amount is roughly equivalent to that part of TVA's federal investment in generating and transmission properties which serve municipal and co-operative loads, subtracting that portion of the federal investment required to provide power for national defense. . . .

CONCLUSION

The search for effective methods and techniques of co-operation among local,

state, and federal governments must never end. The experience in the Tennessee Valley gives new emphasis to an observation Woodrow Wilson made many years ago:

The question of the relation of the States to the federal government is the cardinal question of our constitutional system. . . . It cannot . . . be settled by the opinion of any one generation, because it is a question of growth, and every successive stage of our political and economic development gives it a new aspect, makes it a new question.

The story of TVA and the states is constantly changing. As a part of the national scene, it is a continuing experiment in the regional decentralization of federal functions. In the light of present national trends the Valley's experience assumes new importance. This governmental partnership in the field of resource development has wide application and is ripe for emulation.

The program to conserve natural resources among the state and local governments in the Tennessee Valley has inspired and encouraged new concepts of stewardship for our natural resources. New activities of government have evolved and found understanding support among local taxpayers; old tasks have been performed more effectively.

For TVA this experience has been both difficult and rewarding, the prospects of the future both sobering and challenging. The methods I have described do not bring quick or dramatic results. There is always a temptation to take short cuts, to by-pass the states when their agencies are understaffed and their staffs underpaid. When people generally seem to be complacent about our disappearing natural resources, a few become impatient with the co-operative process and urge agencies of the federal government to do the job *for* the people, a course that fosters still more complacency on the part of citizens. The purpose of the co-operative processes I have described is to foster interest and action by individuals and communities in conserving and using wisely our natural resources.

A true partnership implies freedom to disagree. It accords the people of a region not only a choice among certain courses of action but the right to reject assistance or, if they choose, to do nothing at all. The partnership between TVA and the region does not exist in an absence of conflict. Successful experience begets understanding and confidence; and as the process of co-operation proceeds from function to function, from program to program, it becomes progressively less difficult. It rests upon tested methods and a proved capacity to reduce potential conflicts of interest and to bring them within reach of agreement in the regional and national interest. The process is not easy; it requires hard work, imagination, and an abiding good will among the participants.

Professor Leonard D. White of the University of Chicago wrote in 1953: "If the states can take the initiative in these hard years to preserve and to strengthen their place in the federal structure, they may have won victories that will stand long in the memory of man." At the heart of this problem lies the need for devices of federal-state co-operation. If TVA, as a national regional agency, is permitted to continue to work in partnership with the states to bring new substance and new processes into the grand scheme of federal-state co-operation, it will have served well our rich heritage of federalism.

# III. *Federalism Today and Tomorrow: Problems and Prospects*

In this section, attention is directed to the large and continuing problem of the maintenance of the American federal partnership. Our particular emphasis will be on three areas of concern: the attempts to "return functions to the states," suggestions for "oiling the squeak points" in the sharing system, and the likely trends in intergovernmental relations in the immediate future.

Beginning with the report of the first Hoover Commission in 1949, the decade of the 1950's saw several governmentally sponsored efforts to turn back functions to the states and localities. The most notable of these attempts were those initiated by President Eisenhower from 1953 through 1957 which culminated in the appointment of a Joint Federal-State Action Committee by the President and Governors' Conference that latter year. The committee worked diligently but unsuccessfully for several years in an effort to carry out its mission. Its failure is particularly significant, not only for what it tells us about the functioning of the federal system, but in that it was the last such attempt before the general acceptance of the partnership idea as the basis for intergovernmental relations.

In his pronouncements about the concentration of power in Washington, President Eisenhower restated the conventional American view of federal-state-local relations in both its weak and strong points. His Williamsburg speech to the Governor's Conference proposing the creation of the Joint Action Committee, sums up the American desire for local control as against centralized power, and private action as against government intervention. It reflects the conventional wisdom as to the original intentions of the formers of the Constitution and what happened to their principles in the previous generation. It also reflects the equally intense American desire for progress which led Eisenhower himself to advocate federal programs which he believed (in light of the conventional wisdom) were in conflict with the values of local control and private action. In this connection, the President repeats the conventional view that the states' failures were responsible for "the march of power to Washington".

Morton Grodzins discusses the results of the Committee's efforts and why those efforts failed. It should be noted that one of the primary recommendations of the committee, the "return" of the vocational education program to the states, was obsolete by the time it was made public. The cry for more governmental aid for vocational education that arose after Sputnik and which was intensified by the recession of the late 1950's, led Congress to expand the federal share of the program in 1963.

The Committee's second report turned away from suggesting federal abandonment of specific functions in favor of a search for ways to improve federal-state collaboration within the framework of shared functions. This new thrust has been the dominant one in the 1960's. Grodzins was one of the first to point out that "oiling the squeak points" (the phrase is his) was the real problem which the components of the partnership had to face. He introduces some suggestions to that end as part of his commentary.

The reasons for the failure of the efforts to strengthen the states and localities by turning functions back to their exclusive jurisdiction are further elucidated in Edward W. Weidner's discussion of "Decision-Making in a Federal System." He shows us the tangled web of sharing from yet another perspective, that of the various interests seeking satisfaction from the system. Weidner's discussion of the real character of conflict within the federal system suggests more appropriate ways of strengthening the states and their subdivisions.

In the final selection, the editor of this volume attempts to point out some likely trends in the continuing experiment in partnership which characterizes the American system of government. Considering the visible problems and possibilities likely to confront the system in the next half generation, he tries to indicate some ways in which the continued existence of federal principles will effect the manner in which Americans will deal with contemporary political issues.

---

*Dwight D. Eisenhower*

## ADDRESS TO THE 1957 GOVERNORS' CONFERENCE

*Governor Stanley, members of the Governors' Conference, my fellow citizens: . . .*

[I]n this historic place, as you and I contemplate our respective responsibilities of leadership, it is but fitting that we should soberly reexamine the changing governmental structure of this Nation, here definitely conceived and partially designed so long ago.

Such an examination is timely—even urgent. For I have felt, as surely you have, that too often we have seen tendencies develop that transgress our most cherished principles of government, and tend to undermine the structure so painstakingly built by those who preceded us.

Of those principles I refer especially to one drawn from the colonists' bitter struggle against tyranny and from man's experiences throughout the ages.

That principle is this: Those who would be and would stay free must stand eternal watch against excessive concentration of power in government.

In faithful application of that principle, governmental power in our newborn Nation was diffused—counterbalanced—checked, hedged about, and restrained—to

Speech delivered in Williamsburg, June 24, 1957.

preclude even the possibility of its abuse. Ever since, that principle and those precautions have been, in our system, the anchor of freedom.

Now over the years, due in part to our decentralized system, we have come to recognize that most problems can be approached in many reasonable ways. Our constitutional checks and balances, our State and Territorial governments, our multiplicity of county and municipal governing bodies, our emphasis upon individual initiative and community responsibility, encourage unlimited experimentation in the solving of America's problems. Through this diversified approach, the effect of errors is restrained, calamitous mistakes are avoided, the general good is more surely determined, and the self-governing genius of our people is perpetually renewed.

Being long accustomed to decentralized authority, we are all too inclined to accept it as a convenient, even ordinary, fact of life, to expect it as our right, and to presume that it will always endure. But in other lands over the centuries millions, helpless before concentrated power, have been born, have lived, and have died all in slavery, or they have lost their lives and their liberty to despots. . . .

Thinking on these things, we, in America, gain renewed determination to hew to the principle of diffusion of power, knowing that only thus will we ourselves forever avoid drifting irretrievably into the grasp of some form of centralized government.

Our governmental system, so carefully checked, so delicately balanced, with power fettered and the people free, has survived longer than any other attempt to conduct group affairs by the authority of the group itself. Yet a distinguished American scholar has only recently counseled us that in the measurable future, if present trends continue, the States are sure to degenerate into powerless satellites of the National Government in Washington.

That this forecast does not suffer from lack of supporting evidence all of us know full well. The irony of the whole thing is accentuated as we recall that the National Government was itself not the parent, but the creature, of the States acting together. Yet today it is often made to appear that the creature, Frankenstein-like, is determined to destroy the creators.

Deliberately I have said "made to appear." The tendency of bureaucracy to grow in size and power does not bear the whole of the blame for the march of political power toward Washington. Never, under our constitutional system, could the National Government have syphoned away State authority without the neglect, acquiescence, or unthinking cooperation of the States themselves.

The Founding Fathers foresaw and attempted to forestall such a contingency. They reserved to the people, and they reserved to the States, all power not specifically bestowed upon the National Government.

But, like nature, people and their governments are intolerant of vacuums. Every State failure to meet a pressing public need has created the opportunity, developed the excuse and fed the temptation for the National Government to poach on the States' preserves. Year by year, responding to transient popular demands, the Congress has increased Federal functions. So, slowly at first, but in recent times more and more rapidly, the pendulum of power has swung from our States toward the central Government.

Four years ago at your Seattle conference I expressed the conviction that unless we preserve the traditional power and responsibilities of State government, with revenues necessary to exercise that power and discharge those responsibilities, then we will not preserve the kind of America we have known; eventually, we will have, instead, another form of government and, therefore, quite another kind of America. . . .

[T]hat same year, I obtained congressional authority to establish a Commission on Intergovernmental Regulations. With the cooperation of State governors, Members of Congress and other leading citizens, the Commission completed the first official survey of our Federal system since the adoption of our Constitution 170 years ago. This study brought long-needed perspective and pointed the way to improvements in areas of mutual concern to the States and the Federal Government. But theory and action are not always the same.

Opposed though I am to needless Federal expansion, since 1953 I have found it necessary to urge Federal action in some areas traditionally reserved to the States. In each instance State inaction, or inadequate action, coupled with undeniable national need, has forced emergency Federal intervention.

The education of our youth is a prime example.

Classroom shortages, in some places no less than critical, are largely the product of depression and wars. These, of course, were national and international, not State or local, both in their origins and in their effects. These classroom shortages have become potentially so dangerous to the entire Nation and have yielded so slowly to local effort as to compel emergency action. Thus was forced a Federal plan of temporary assistance adjusted to the specific needs of States and communities and designed not to supplant but to supplement their own efforts. . . .

Three other basic problems provide simple examples of how "filling the vacuum" tends to constrict State and local responsibility.

These are such problems as slum clearance and urban renewal—problems caused by natural disasters—problems of traffic safety.

As for the first, the lack in the past of energetic State attention to urban needs has spawned a host of Federal activities that are more than difficult to curtail. Today, for help in urban problems, committees of mayors are far more likely to journey to Washington than to their own State capitals.

It always seemed to me that, in such meetings, Federal and municipal authorities have united in a two-pronged assault upon the State echelon of government, attacking simultaneously both from above and from below.

Yet the needs of our cities are glaringly evident. Unless action is prompt and effective, urban problems will soon almost defy solution. Metropolitan areas have ranged far beyond city boundaries, but in every instance the centers and the peripheries are interdependent for survival and growth. As citizens in outer areas clamor for adequate services, too often the cities and the counties avoid responsibilities or are powerless to act as a result of State-imposed restrictions. Those needs must be—and they will be—met. The question I raise before you is this: Which level of government will meet those needs—the city, the county, the State, or the Federal Government? Or, if all must merge their efforts for reasons of mutual interest, how shall we confine each—and especially the powerful Federal Government—to its proper role? . . .

Next, consider for a moment floods, droughts, hurricanes, and tornadoes. Year by year, more and more Federal funds are being requested to meet such disasters which heretofore States, communities, and philanthropic agencies have met themselves.

One of my greatest friends is now head of the American Red Cross. He came to that post when the Red Cross reserve funds had been practically exhausted. The drive for Red Cross funds this year did not realize its full objective. He tells me, from constant travel around this country, the excuse he so often meets is: Why should we donate to the Red Cross? Our taxes through the Federal Government are now taking care of these disasters.

In vain does he explain that the Government steps in only to restore public facilities—roads, bridges, other public facilities, utilities, and so on. The Red Cross meets each person's problem as an individual and as a family.

190

The simple answer is we pay taxes now for disasters and therefore we don't have to donate to the Red Cross. I regard this as one of the great real disasters that threatens to engulf us when we are unready as a nation, as a people, to meet personal disaster by our own cheerful giving. And I think — at least he believes, and he seems to have the evidence to prove it — that part of the reason is this misunderstanding that Government is taking the place even of rescuing the person, the individual, and the family from his natural disasters.

Now, in recent years I have gained some little appreciation of legislative bodies, so I can understand why a governor is tempted to wire Washington for help instead of asking the legislature to act. Now it's easy to send such a wire. But does it not tend to encourage the still greater growth of the distant and impersonal centralized bureaucracy that Jefferson held in such dread and warned us about in such great and intense detail?

In varying degrees, in varying circumstances, Federal Government cooperation with States and communities has been, is now, and will continue to be indispensable. But I would urge that the States insistently contend for the fullest possible responsibility for essentially State problems, well knowing that with responsibility there goes, in the long run, authority.

As for traffic safety, this, happily, is still a State and local responsibility. But day by day the American people are paying an increasingly fearful price for the failure of the States to agree on such safety essentials as standards for licensing of drivers and vehicles and basic rules of the road.

The need could scarcely be more acute. Last year's toll of traffic dead soared beyond 40,000 persons. One and a half million citizens were injured. Many were disabled for life. The estimated cost to the country was 4 billion 750 million dollars.

We simply cannot let this go on. The cost of inaction is prohibitive. Who is going to fill the vacuum? Someone must, and someone will. Are we willing that, once again, it be Washington, D. C.?

I believe deeply in States' rights. I believe that the preservation of our States as vigorous, powerful governmental units is essential to permanent individual freedom and the growth of our national strength. But it is idle to champion States' rights without upholding States' responsibilities as well.

I believe that an objective reappraisal and reallocation of those responsibilities can lighten the hand of central authority, reinforce our State and local governments, and in the process strengthen all America. I believe we owe it to America to undertake that effort.

The alternatives are simple and clear:

Either — by removing barriers to effective and responsive government, by overhauling taxing and fiscal systems, by better cooperation between all echelons of government, the States can regain and preserve their traditional responsibilities and rights.

Or — by inadequate action, or by failure to act, the States can create new vacuums into which the Federal Government will plunge ever more deeply, impelled by popular pressures and transient political expediencies.

I propose that we choose the first alternative, and I propose that here in this historic spot we dedicate ourselves to making it work!

Not in a speech — nor by a collective resolution, no matter how powerfully worded — can we turn back long-established trends. But we can start searching examinations and together lay out, promptly and clearly, a common course toward the ends we seek. I suggest, therefore, that this conference join with the Federal Administration in creating a task force for action — a joint committee charged with three responsibilities:

One — to designate functions which the States are ready and willing to assume and finance that are now performed or financed wholly or in part by the Federal Government;

Two — to recommend the Federal and State revenue adjustments required to enable the States to assume such functions; and

Three—to identify functions and responsibilities likely to require State or Federal attention in the future and to recommend the level of State effort, or Federal effort, or both, that will be needed to assure effective action.

In designating the functions to be reassumed by the States, the Committee should also specify when those functions should be assumed—the amounts by which Federal taxes should be reduced—and increases in State revenues needed to support the transferred functions. As the first step, the Committee might well concentrate on a single function or program and pair it with a specific Federal tax or tax amount. This effort presupposes that Federal taxes would be cut more than State taxes would be raised to support the transferred functions. The elimination of Federal overhead— stopping, in other words, the "freight charges" on money being hauled from the States to Washington and back (a bill, I remind you, that is always collected in full)—would save the American taxpayer a tidy sum.

Obviously, such an effort requires your own thoughtful study as well as Federal analysis. It means reexamining every one of your local and State fiscal policies, including taxation, bonded indebtedness, operating costs, and cash reserves to meet natural disasters and other emergencies. It means realistically relating tax rates and assessed valuations to expanded incomes and real property values.

Once the Committee acts, I have it in mind that all of us would cooperate in securing the necessary action by the Congress and the various State legislative bodies.

I assure you, my friends, that I wouldn't mind being called a lobbyist in working for such a worthy cause.

Regaining lost ground, whether in war or in public affairs, is the most challenging task of all. And because I have seen it done,

I know it can be done by men and women of dedication. This place where we are met abounds with historic examples of the same kind of dedication.

Not one of us questions the governmental concepts so wisely applied by the framers of our Constitution. I have not the slightest doubt that, by mobilizing our collective leadership, we can revitalize the principle of sharing of responsibility, of separation of authority, of diffusion of power, in our free government.

Now I should like to make one point very clear, and that is not only my sincerity, my readiness to cooperate in the kind of effort of which I have been speaking. I realize that you have heard exhortations of this kind time and again. A body such as this I know has talked these things over among its own members. Words are easily said and they can be often repeated. But there is no proof of their validity until action follows. Action is the test and action is what we must take.

In the executive department in Washington, I have begun a searching examination of these things on sort of a unilateral basis. I have a competent man and his assistants trying to identify those things where we believe the Federal Government has improperly invaded the rights and responsibilities of States, where we believe that some adjustments in revenues and functions could be made.

Now I mention this only to show how sincere and serious we in the executive department are about this matter, and to assure you that if you see fit as a body to undertake explorations of the kind I have suggested, in cooperation with the Federal Government, you will find a great deal of work done which should be helpful to the study.

Our broad objectives through this effort should be two:

First, we must see that government remains responsive to the pressing needs of the American people.

Second, we must see that, in meeting

those needs, each level of government performs its proper function—no more, no less.

Thus we will pass on to those who come after us an America free, strong, and durable.

And so, America will continue to be a symbol of courage and of hope for the oppressed millions over the world who, victimized by powerful centralized government, aspire to join us in freedom.

And human freedom, universally recognized and practiced will mean world peace, a just peace, an enduring peace.

Thank you very much.

## Morton Grodzins

# ATTEMPTS TO UNWIND THE FEDERAL SYSTEM

Within the past dozen years there have been four major attempts to reform or reorganize the federal system: the first (1947–49) and second (1953–55) Hoover Commissions on Executive Organization; the Kestnbaum Commission on Intergovernmental Relations (1953–55); and the Joint Federal-State Action Committee (1957–59). All four of these groups have aimed to minimize federal activities. None of them has recognized the sharing of functions as the characteristic way American governments do things. Even when making recommendations for joint action, these official commissions take the view (as expressed in the Kestnbaum report) that "the main tradition of American federalism [is] the tradition of separateness." All four have, in varying degrees, worked to separate functions and tax sources.

The history of the Joint Federal-State Action Committee is especially instructive. The committee was established at the suggestion of President Eisenhower, who charged it, first of all, "to designate functions which the States are ready and willing to assume and finance that are now performed or financed wholly or in part by the Federal Government." He also gave the committee the task of recommending "Federal and State revenue adjustments required to enable the States to assume such functions."[1]

The committee subsequently established seemed most favorably situated to accomplish the task of functional separation. It was composed of distinguished and able men, including among its personnel three leading members of the President's cabinet, the director of the Bureau of the Budget, and ten state governors. It had the full support of the President at every point, and it worked hard and conscientiously. Excellent staff studies were supplied by the Bureau of the Budget, the White House, the Treasury Department, and, from the state side, the Council of State Governments. It had available to it a large mass of research data, including the sixteen recently completed volumes of the Kestnbaum Commission. There existed no disagreements on party lines within the committee and, of course, no constitutional impediments to

\* \* \*

[1] The President's third suggestion was that the committee "identify functions and responsibilities likely to require state or federal attention in the future and . . . recommend the level of state effort, or federal effort, or both, that will be needed to assure effective action." The committee initially devoted little attention to this problem. Upon discovering the difficulty of making separatist recommendations, i.e., for turning over federal functions and taxes to the states, it developed a series of proposals looking to greater effectiveness in intergovernmental collaboration. The committee was succeeded by a legislatively-based, 26-member Advisory Commission on Intergovernmental Relations, established September 29, 1959.

From Morton Grodzins, "The Federal System" in *Goals for Americans* by The American Assembly, Columbia University, New York, © 1960. Reprinted by permission of Prentice-Hall, Inc., Englewood Cliffs, New Jersey.

its mission. The President, his cabinet members, and all the governors (with one possible exception) on the committee completely agreed on the desirability of decentralization-via-separation-of-functions-and-taxes. They were unanimous in wanting to justify the committee's name and to produce action, not just another report.

The committee worked for more than two years. It found exactly two programs to recommend for transfer from federal to state hands. One was the federal grant program for vocational education (including practical-nurse training and aid to fishery trades); the other was federal grants for municipal waste treatment plants. The programs together cost the federal government less than $80 million in 1957, slightly more than two per cent of the total federal grants for that year. To allow the states to pay for these programs, the committee recommended that they be allowed a credit against the federal tax on local telephone calls. Calculations showed that this offset device, plus an equalizing factor, would give every state at least 40 per cent more from the tax than it received from the federal government in vocational education and sewage disposal grants. Some states were "equalized" to receive twice as much.

The recommendations were modest enough, and the generous financing feature seemed calculated to gain state support. The President recommended to Congress that all points of the program be legislated. None of them was, none has been since, and none is likely to be.

*Two kinds of decentralization*

It is easy to specify the conditions under which an ordered separation of functions could take place. What is principally needed is a majority political party, under firm leadership, in control of both Presidency and Congress, and, ideally but not necessarily, also in control of a number of states. The political discontinuities, or the absence of party links, (1) between the governors and their state legislatures, (2) between the President and the governors, and (3) between the President and Congress clearly account for both the picayune recommendations of the Federal-State Action Committee and for the failure of even those recommendations in Congress. If the President had been in control of Congress (that is, consistently able to direct a majority of House and Senate votes), this alone would have made possible some genuine separation and devolution of functions. The failure to decentralize by order is a measure of the decentralization of power in the political parties.

Stated positively, party centralization must precede governmental decentralization by order. But this is a slender reed on which to hang decentralization. It implies the power to centralize. A majority party powerful enough to bring about ordered decentralization is far more likely to choose in favor of ordered centralization. And a society that produced centralized national parties would, by that very fact, be a society prepared to accept centralized government.

\* \* \*

DYNAMICS OF SHARING: THE POLITICS OF THE
FEDERAL SYSTEM

Many causes contribute to dispersed power in the federal system. One is the simple historical fact that the states existed before the nation. A second is in the form of creed, the traditional opinion of Americans that expresses distrust of centralized power and places great value in the strength and vitality of local units of government. Another is pride in locality and state, nurtured by the nation's size and by variations of regional and state history. Still a fourth cause of decentralization is the sheer wealth of the nation. It allows all groups, including state and local governments, to partake of the central government's largesse, supplies room for experimentation and even waste, and makes unnecessary the tight organization of political power that must follow when the support of one program necessarily means the deprivation of another.

In one important respect, the Constitution no longer operates to impede centralized government. The Supreme Court since 1937 has given Congress a relatively free hand. The federal government can build substantive programs in many areas on the taxation and commerce powers. Limitations of such central programs based on the argument, "it's unconstitutional," are no longer possible as long as Congress (in the Court's view) acts reasonably in the interest of the whole nation. The Court is unlikely to reverse this permissive view in the foreseeable future.

Nevertheless, some constitutional restraints on centralization continue to operate. The strong constitutional position of the states—for example, the assignment of two senators to each state, the role given the states in administering even national elections, and the relatively few limitations on their law-making powers—establish the geographical units as natural centers of administrative and political strength. Many clauses of the Constitution are not subject to the same latitude of interpretation as the commerce and tax clauses. The simple, clearly stated, unambiguous phrases—for example, the President "shall hold his office during the term of four years"—are subject to change only through the formal amendment process. Similar provisions exist with respect to the terms of senators and congressmen and the amendment process. All of them have the effect of retarding or restraining centralizing action of the federal government. The fixed terms of the President and members of Congress, for example, greatly impede the development of nation-wide, disciplined political parties that almost certainly would have to precede continuous large-scale expansion of federal functions.

The constitutional restraints on the expansion of national authority are less important and less direct today than they were in 1879 or in 1936. But to say that they are less important is not to say that they are unimportant.

The nation's politics reflect these decentralizing causes and add some of their own. The political parties of the United States are unique. They seldom perform the function that parties traditionally perform in other countries, the function of gathering together diverse strands of power and welding them into one. Except during the period of nominating and electing a president and for the essential but non-substantive business of organizing the houses of Congress, the American parties rarely coalesce power at all. Characteristically they do the reverse, serving as a canopy under which special and local interests are represented with little regard for anything that can be called a party program. National leaders are elected on a party ticket, but in Congress they must seek cross-party support if their leadership is to be effective. It is a rare president during rare periods who can produce legislation without facing the defection of substantial numbers of his own party. (Wilson could do this in the first session of the sixty-third Congress; but Franklin D. Roosevelt could not, even during the famous hundred days of 1933.) Presidents whose parties form the majority of the congressional houses must still count heavily on support from the other party.

The parties provide the pivot on which the entire governmental system swings. Party operations, first of all, produce in legislation the basic division of functions between the federal government, on the one hand, and state and local governments, on the other. The Supreme Court's permissiveness with respect to the expansion of national powers has not in fact produced any considerable extension of exclusive federal functions. The body of federal law in all fields has remained, in the words of Henry M. Hart, Jr. and Herbert Wechsler, "interstitial in its nature," limited in objective and resting upon the principal body of legal relationships defined by state law. It is difficult to find any area of federal legislation that is not significantly affected by state law.

In areas of new or enlarged federal activity, legislation characteristically provides important roles for state and local governments. This is as true of Democratic as of Republican administrations and true even of functions for which arguments of efficiency would produce exclusive federal responsibility. Thus the unemployment compensation program of the New Deal and the airport program of President Truman's administration both provided important responsibilities for state governments. In both cases attempts to eliminate state participation were defeated by a cross-party coalition of pro-state votes and influence. A large fraction of the Senate is usually made up of ex-governors, and the membership of both houses is composed of men who know that their re-election depends less upon national leaders or national party organization than upon support from their home constituencies. State and local officials are key members of these constituencies, often central figures in selecting candidates and in turning out the vote. Under such circumstances, national legislation taking state and local views heavily into account is inevitable.

Second, the undisciplined parties affect the character of the federal system as a result of senatorial and congressional interference in federal administrative programs on behalf of local interests. Many aspects of the legislative involvement in administrative affairs are formalized. The Legislative Reorganization Act of 1946, to take only one example, provided that each of the standing committees "shall exercise continuous watchfulness" over administration of laws within its jurisdiction. But the formal system of controls, extensive as it is, does not compare in importance with the informal and extralegal network of relationships in producing continuous legislative involvement in administrative affairs.

Senators and congressmen spend a major fraction of their time representing problems of their constituents before administrative agencies. An even larger fraction of congressional staff time is devoted to the same task. The total magnitude of such "case work" operations is great. In one five-month period of 1943 the Office of Price Administration received a weekly average of 842 letters from members of Congress. If phone calls and personal contacts are added, each member of Congress on the average presented the OPA with a problem involving one of his constituents twice a day in each five-day work week. Data for less vulnerable agencies during less intensive periods are also impressive. In 1958, to take only one example, the Department of Agriculture estimated (and underestimated) that it received an average of 159 congressional letters per working day. Special congressional liaison staffs have been created to service this mass of business, though all higher officials meet it in one form or another. The Air Force in 1958 had, under the command of a major general, 137 people (55 officers and 82 civilians) working in its liaison office.

The widespread, consistent, and in many ways unpredictable character of legislative interference in administrative affairs has many consequences for the tone and character of American administrative behavior. From the perspective of this paper, the important consequence is the comprehensive, day-to-day, even hour-by-hour, impact of local views on national programs. No point of substance or procedure is immune from congressional scrutiny. A substantial portion of the entire weight of this impact is on behalf of the state and local governments. It is a weight that can alter procedures for screening immigration applications, divert the course of a national highway, change the tone of an international negotiation, and amend a social security law to accommodate local practices or fulfill local desires.

The party system compels administrators to take a political role. This is a third way in which the parties function to decentralize the American system. The administrator must play politics for the same reason that the politician is able to play in administration: the parties are without program and without discipline.

In response to the unprotected position in which the party situation places him, the administrator is forced to seek support where he can find it. One ever-present task is to nurse the Congress of the United States, that crucial constituency which ultimately controls his agency's budget and program. From the administrator's view, a sympathetic consideration of congressional requests (if not downright submission to them) is the surest way to build the political support without which the administrative job could not continue. Even the completely task-oriented administrator must be sensitive to the need for congressional support and to the relationship between case work requests, on one side, and budgetary and legislative support, on the other. "You do a good job handling the personal problems and requests of a Congressman," a White House officer said, "and you have an easier time convincing him to back your program." Thus there is an important link between the nursing of congressional requests, requests that largely concern local matters, and the most comprehensive national programs. The administrator must accommodate to the former as a price of gaining support for the latter.

One result of administrative politics is that the administrative agency may become the captive of the nation-wide interest group it serves or presumably regulates. In such cases no government may come out with effective authority: the winners are the interest groups themselves. But in a very large number of cases, states and localities also win influence. The politics of administration is a process of making peace with legislators who for the most part consider themselves the guardians of local interests. The political role of administrators therefore contributes to the power of states and localities in national programs.

Finally, the way the party system operates gives American politics their over-all distinctive tone. The lack of party discipline produces an openness in the system that allows individuals, groups, and institutions (including state and local governments) to attempt to influence national policy at every step of the legislative-administrative process. This is the "multiple-crack" attribute of the American government. "Crack" has two meanings. It means not only many fissures or access points; it also means, less statically, opportunities for wallops or smacks at government.

If the parties were more disciplined, the result would not be a cessation of the process by which individuals and groups impinge themselves upon the central government. But the present state of the parties clearly allows for a far greater operation of the multiple crack than would be possible under the conditions of centralized party control. American interest groups exploit literally uncountable access points in the legislative-administrative process. If legislative lobbying, from committee stages to the conference committee, does not produce results, a cabinet secretary is called. His immediate associates are petitioned. Bureau chiefs and their aides are hit. Field officers are put under pressure. Campaigns are instituted by which friends of the agency apply a secondary influence on behalf of the interested party. A conference with the President may be urged.

To these multiple points for bringing influence must be added the multiple voices of the influencers. Consider, for example, those in a small town who wish to have a federal action taken. The easy merging of public and private interest at the local level means that the influence attempt is made in the name of the whole community, thus removing it from political partisanship. The Rotary Club as well as the City Council, the Chamber of Commerce and the mayor, eminent citizens and political bosses—all are readily enlisted. If a conference in a senator's office will expedite matters, someone on the local scene can be found to make such a conference possible and effective. If technical information is needed, technicians will supply it. State or national professional organizations of local officials, individual congressmen and senators, and not infrequently whole state delegations will make the local cause their own. Federal field officers, who service localities, often assume local views. So may elected and appointed state officers. Friendships are exploited, and political mortgages called due. Under these circumstances, national policies are molded by local action.

In summary, then, the party system functions to devolve power. The American parties, unlike any other, are highly responsive when directives move from the bottom to the top, highly unresponsive from top to bottom. Congressmen and senators can rarely ignore concerted demands from their home constituencies; but no party leader can expect the same kind of response from those below, whether he be a President asking for congressional support or a congressman seeking aid from local or state leaders.

Any tightening of the party apparatus would have the effect of strengthening the central government. The four characteristics of the system, discussed above, would become less important. If control from the top were strictly applied, these hallmarks of American decentralization might entirely disappear. To be specific, if disciplined and program-oriented parties were achieved: (1) It would make far less likely legislation that takes heavily into account the desires and prejudices of the highly decentralized power groups and institutions of the country, including the state and local governments. (2) It would to a large extent prevent legislators, individually and collectively, from intruding themselves on behalf of non-national interests in national administrative programs. (3) It would put an end to the administrator's search for his own political support, a search that often results in fostering state, local, and other non-national powers. (4) It would dampen the

process by which individuals and groups, including state and local political leaders, take advantage of multiple cracks to steer national legislation and administration in ways congenial to them and the institutions they represent.

Alterations of this sort could only accompany basic changes in the organization and style of politics which, in turn, presuppose fundamental changes at the parties' social base. The sharing of functions is, in fact, the sharing of power. To end this sharing process would mean the destruction of whatever measure of decentralization exists in the United States today.

GOALS FOR THE SYSTEM OF SHARING

*The goal of understanding*

Our structure of government is complex, and the politics operating that structure are mildly chaotic. Circumstances are ever-changing. Old institutions mask intricate procedures. The nation's history can be read with alternative glosses, and what is nearest at hand may be furthest from comprehension. Simply to understand the federal system is therefore a difficult task. Yet without understanding there is little possibility of producing desired changes in the system. Social structures and processes are relatively impervious to purposeful change. They also exhibit intricate interrelationships so that change induced at point "A" often produces unanticipated results at point "Z." Changes introduced into an imperfectly understood system are as likely to produce reverse consequences as the desired ones.

This is counsel of neither futility nor conservatism for those who seek to make our government a better servant of the people. It is only to say that the first goal for those setting goals with respect to the federal system is that of understanding it.

Decentralization by order must be contrasted with the different kind of decentralization that exists today in the United States. It may be called the decentralization of mild chaos. It exists because of the existence of dispersed power centers. This form of decentralization is less visible and less neat. It rests on no discretion of central authorities. It produces at times specific acts that many citizens may consider undesirable or evil. But power sometimes wielded even for evil ends may be desirable power. To those who find value in the dispersion of power, decentralization by mild chaos is infinitely more desirable than decentralization by order. The preservation of mild chaos is an important goal for the American federal system.

*Oiling the squeak points*

In a governmental system of genuinely shared responsibilities, disagreements inevitably occur. Opinions clash over proximate ends, particular ways of doing things become the subject of public debate, innovations are contested. These are not basic defects in the system. Rather, they are the system's energy-reflecting life blood. There can be no permanent "solutions" short of changing the system itself by elevating one partner to absolute supremacy. What can be done is to attempt to produce conditions in which conflict will not fester but be turned to constructive solutions of particular problems.

A long list of specific points of difficulty in the federal system can be easily identified. No adequate congressional or administrative mechanism exists to review the patchwork of grants in terms of national needs. There is no procedure by which to judge, for example, whether the national government is justified in spending so much more for highways than for education. The working force in some states is inadequate for the effective performance of some nation-wide programs, while honest and not-so-honest graft frustrates efficiency in others. Some federal aid programs distort state budgets, and some are so closely supervised as to impede state action in meeting local needs. Grants are given for programs too narrowly defined, and over-

all programs at the state level consequently suffer. Administrative, accounting and auditing difficulties are the consequence of the multiplicity of grant programs. City officials complain that the states are intrusive fifth wheels in housing, urban redevelopment, and airport building programs.

Some differences are so basic that only a demonstration of strength on one side or another can solve them. School desegregation illustrates such an issue. It also illustrates the correct solution (although not the most desirable method of reaching it): in policy conflicts of fundamental importance, touching the nature of democracy itself, the view of the whole nation must prevail. Such basic ends, however, are rarely at issue, and sides are rarely taken with such passion that loggerheads are reached. Modes of settlement can usually be found to lubricate the squeak points of the system.

A pressing and permanent state problem, general in its impact, is the difficulty of raising sufficient revenue without putting local industries at a competitive disadvantage or without an expansion of sales taxes that press hardest on the least wealthy. A possible way of meeting this problem is to establish a state-levied income tax that could be used as an offset for federal taxes. The maximum level of the tax which could be offset would be fixed by federal law. When levied by a state, the state collection would be deducted from federal taxes. But if a state did not levy the tax, the federal government would. An additional fraction of the total tax imposed by the states would be collected directly by the federal government and used as an equalization fund, that is, distributed among the less wealthy states. Such a tax would almost certainly be imposed by all states since not to levy it would give neither political advantage to its public leaders nor financial advantage to its citizens. The net effect would be an increase in the total personal and corporate income tax.

The offset has great promise for strengthening state governments. It would help produce a more economic distribution of industry. It would have obvious financial advantages for the vast majority of states. Since a large fraction of all state income is used to aid political subdivisions, the local governments would also profit, though not equally as long as cities are under-represented in state legislatures. On the other hand, such a scheme will appear disadvantageous to some low-tax states which profit from the in-migration of industry (though it would by no means end all state-by-state tax differentials). It will probably excite the opposition of those concerned over governmental centralization, and they will not be assuaged by methods that suggest themselves for making both state and central governments bear the psychological impact of the tax. Although the offset would probably produce an across-the-board tax increase, wealthier persons, who are affected more by an income tax than by other levies, can be expected to join forces with those whose fear is centralization. (This is a common alliance and, in the nature of things, the philosophical issue rather than financial advantage is kept foremost.)

Those opposing such a tax would gain additional ammunition from the certain knowledge that federal participation in the scheme would lead to some federal standards governing the use of the funds. Yet the political strength of the states would keep these from becoming onerous. Indeed, inauguration of the tax offset as a means of providing funds to the states might be an occasion for dropping some of the specifications for existing federal grants. One federal standard, however, might be possible because of the greater representation of urban areas in the constituency of Congress and the President than in the constituency of state legislatures: Congress might make a state's participation in the offset scheme dependent upon a periodic reapportionment of state legislatures.

The income tax offset is only one of many ideas that can be generated to meet serious problems of closely meshed governments. The fate of all such schemes ultimately rests, as it should, with the politics of a free people. But much can be done if the primary technical effort of those concerned with improving the federal system were directed not at separating its interrelated parts but at making them work together more effectively. Temporary commissions are relatively inefficient in this effort, though they may be useful for making general assessments and for generating new ideas. The professional organizations of government workers do part of the job of continuously scrutinizing programs and ways and means of improving them. A permanent staff, established in the President's office and working closely with state and local officials, could also perform a useful and perhaps important role.

## The strength of the parts

Whatever governmental "strength" or "vitality" may be, it does not consist of independent decision-making in legislation and administration. Federal-state interpenetration here is extensive. Indeed, a judgment of the relative domestic strength of the two planes must take heavily into account the influence of one on the other's decisions. In such an analysis the strength of the states (and localities) does not weigh lightly. The nature of the nation's politics makes federal functions more vulnerable to state influence than state offices are to federal influence. Many states, as the Kestnbaum Commission noted, live with "self-imposed constitutional limitations" that make it difficult for them to "perform all of the services that their citizens require." If this has the result of adding to federal responsibilities, the states' importance in shaping and administering federal programs eliminates much of the sting. . . .

Despite deficiencies of politics and organizations that are unchangeable or slowly changing, it is an error to look at the states as static anachronisms. Some of them — New York, Minnesota, and California, to take three examples spanning the country—have administrative organizations that compare favorably in many ways with the national establishment. Many more in recent years have moved rapidly towards integrated administrative departments, state-wide budgeting, and central leadership. The others have models-in-existence to follow, and active professional organizations (led by the Council of State Governments) promoting their development. Slow as this change may be, the states move in the direction of greater internal effectiveness.

The pace toward more effective performance at the state level is likely to increase. Urban leaders, who generally feel themselves disadvantaged in state affairs, and suburban and rural spokesmen, who are most concerned about national centralization, have a common interest in this task. The urban dwellers want greater equality in state affairs, including a more equitable share of state financial aid; non-urban dwellers are concerned that city dissatisfactions should not be met by exclusive federal, or federal-local, programs. Antagonistic, rather than amiable, cooperation may be the consequence. But it is a cooperation that can be turned to politically effective measures for a desirable upgrading of state institutions.

If one looks closely, there is scant evidence for the fear of the federal octopus, the fear that expansion of central programs and influence threatens to reduce the states and localities to compliant administrative arms of the central government. In fact, state and local governments are touching a larger proportion of the people in more ways than ever before; and they are spending a higher fraction of the total national product than ever before. Federal programs have increased, rather than diminished, the importance of the governors; stimulated professionalism in state agencies; increased citizen interest and participation in government; and, generally, enlarged and made more effective the scope of state action. It may no longer be true in any significant sense that the states and localities are

"closer" than the federal government to the people. It is true that the smaller governments remain active and powerful members of the federal system.

## CENTRAL LEADERSHIP: THE NEED FOR BALANCE

The chaos of party processes makes difficult the task of presidential leadership. It deprives the President of ready-made congressional majorities. It may produce, as in the chairmen of legislative committees, power-holders relatively hidden from public scrutiny and relatively protected from presidential direction. It allows the growth of administrative agencies which sometimes escape control by central officials. These are prices paid for a wide dispersion of political power. The cost is tolerable because the total results of dispersed power are themselves desirable and because, where clear national supremacy is essential, in foreign policy and military affairs, it is easiest to secure.

Moreover, in the balance of strength between the central and peripheral governments, the central government has on its side the whole secular drift towards the concentration of power. It has on its side technical developments that make central decisions easy and sometimes mandatory. It has on its side potent purse powers, the result of superior tax-gathering resources. It has potentially on its side the national leadership capacities of the presidential office. The last factor is the controlling one, and national strength in the federal system has shifted with the leadership desires and capacities of the chief executive. As these have varied, so there has been an almost rhythmic pattern: periods of central strength put to use alternating with periods of central strength dormant. . . .

The American federal system exhibits many evidences of the dispersion of power not only because of formal federalism but more importantly because our politics reflect and reinforce the nation's diversities-within-unity. Those who value the virtues of decentralization, which writ large are virtues of freedom, need not scruple at recognizing the defects of those virtues. The defects are principally the danger that parochial and private interests may not coincide with, or give way to, the nation's interest. The necessary cure for these defects is effective national leadership.

The centrifugal force of domestic politics needs to be balanced by the centripetal force of strong presidential leadership. Si-multaneous strength at center and periphery exhibits the American system at its best, if also at its noisiest. The interests of both find effective spokesmen. States and localities (and private interest groups) do not lose their influence opportunities, but national policy becomes more than the simple consequence of successful, momentary concentrations of non-national pressures: it is guided by national leaders.

*Edward W. Weidner*

## DECISION-MAKING IN A FEDERAL SYSTEM

Federalism has been thought of as the golden mean between excessive centralization and excessive decentralization. It has also been thought of as an inherently imperfect and defective form of government that stymies a positive solution to the pressing governmental problems of the twentieth century. At base, both of these viewpoints picture national-state relations as a give-and-take situation in which there is disagreement and possibly conflict. A common assumption is that in this give-and-take situation the interests of state and national governments are competing or opposed. The one school of thought sees such competition resulting in a highly acceptable compromise, while the other sees it as destroying any possibility of a systematic attack on national domestic problems.

It is a thesis of the present discussion that in the federal system in the United States there are relatively few direct clashes or compromises between state and national governments on large issues of national domestic policy. Furthermore, in the administrative sphere positive cooperation is the pattern rather than aloofness or conflict. The disagreements and conflicts that do arise and that may be encouraged by federalism's structural features are not basically clashes between state and national governments. Instead, they are clashes between much smaller groups of people and the opposing groups are located within a single governmental level as often as not. . . .

A second assumption is implicit in the older view of national-state relations as a give-and-take situation of disagreement and conflict between levels of government as such. A theory of leadership is implied. Political and administrative leaders of national and state governments are thought of as rather forceful and direct. Supposedly they develop and support fairly clear-cut public policies for which they become known. Furthermore, the assumption is that they use all the means at their command to gain acceptance for the public policies they support, including coercive techniques. Given the assumed competing interests of national and state governments, a compromise becomes necessary but only as a last resort. In any event, it is believed that leadership is not based upon the idea of "getting along" with officials of the other level of government at almost any price, nor is a community of interests as-

From *Federalism: Mature and Emergent*, ed. Arthur W. MacMahon (New York, 1955), pp. 363–382 (with omissions). Reprinted by permission of the Trustees of Columbia University in the City of New York.

sumed. A further thesis of the present discussion denies the validity of this view of leadership. . . .

## I

There are countless causes for disagreement and conflict in a federal system. Personalities play a part. So do bothersome procedures, differences in the age and general background of administrators, poor communication, frequency of contact, and so on. However, all these factors are secondary in importance. They are relatively easy to deal with: procedures may be changed, frequency of contact increased, personnel shifted. This is not to say that such variables are never troublesome, for they are very troublesome on occasion. Rather, they are secondary in the sense that they are not of crucial importance to the participants in federal-state relations. The main concern of these participants, and, for that matter, most men, is to have their values implemented to as great an extent as possible. Hence it is not surprising that the fundamental reason for disagreement and conflict in a federal system is that there is a lack of consensus as to what values should be implemented. This is true in both the legislative and administrative spheres.

While differences on public policy or values are to be expected in a country containing as many heterogeneous elements as are to be found in the United States, it does not necessarily follow that officials in the several states will take one policy position and those of the national government another. Indeed, on an *a priori* basis it would seem surprising if this were the case, given the diversity of conditions in the several states and the fact that the union is made up of all states. "States' rights" is only one of numerous values held by state officials, and it is relatively unimportant to many of them. The prime thing that the states have in common is their existence; it is possible that if an issue were presented that threatened the very existence of the states their political officials might be brought to-gether. In actual fact, a major issue of this kind has not been presented. Consequently, usually national government officials can find many of their state counterparts who support national policy objectives and many others who oppose. And among the states, differences in values are the rule.

The framers of the Constitution clearly expected value or policy disagreements among the states as well as between the central government and one or more states. In his famous essay on faction, Madison wrote:

Hence, it clearly appears, that the same advantages which a republic has over a democracy, in controlling the effects of faction, is enjoyed by a large over a small republic,—is enjoyed by the Union over the States composing it. Does the advantage consist in the substitution of representatives whose enlightened views and virtuous sentiments render them superior to local prejudices and to schemes of injustice? It will not be denied that the representation of the Union will be most likely to possess these requisite endowments. Does it consist in the greater security afforded by a greater variety of parties, against the event of any one party being able to outnumber and oppress the rest? In an equal degree does the increased variety of parties comprised within the Union, increase this security. Does it, in fine, consist in the greater obstacles opposed to the concert and accomplishment of the secret wishes of an unjust and interested majority? Here, again, the extent of the Union gives it the most palpable advantage.

The influence of factious leaders may kindle a flame within their particular States, but will be unable to spread a general conflagration through the other States. A religious sect may degenerate into a political faction in a part of the Confederacy; but the variety of sects dispersed over the entire face of it must secure the national councils against any danger from that source. A rage for paper money, for an abolition of debts, for an equal division of property, or for any other improper or wicked project, will be less apt to pervade the whole body of the Union than a particular member of it; in the same proportion as such a malady is more likely to taint a particular county or district, than an entire State.

Thus Madison emphasized that one of the main characteristics of the federal system would be the wide variation in the public policies that would be followed in the several states. To guard against the possible excesses of certain states the central government was given a core of power over matters deemed to be of nationwide concern. The states were expected to disagree among themselves over how the central government exercised its powers, and they were also expected to pursue different policies in matters that were reserved to them for decision. . . .

Given the diverse policy objectives of the several states, it becomes unrealistic and impossible to expect of them any unified approach to important public problems. The United States learned at an early date, under the Articles of Confederation, how true this was. As a result of the experience with the Articles, the framers of the Constitution sought to vest the new central government with effective power over those matters that, in their opinion, required a single, unified policy or that required a minimum standard of performance. Foreign affairs and defense from external attacks were thought to be areas in which a single policy was necessary, while interstate commerce and the preservation of peace in the face of possible internal disturbances were thought to be areas in which minimum standards or assurances were needed.

The experience of 170 years ago is confirmed by contemporary events. The states have been unable to follow a single course even in such comparatively noncontroversial areas as are covered by the so-called uniform state laws. If minimum standards are desired for the nation as a whole in a particular policy area such as health or welfare, it is the central government that must act to assure these ends. To leave the matter exclusively to the states means that there will be a variation in standards from very low to quite high. To set up a system of joint national-state participation means that standards and practices will vary much more than in a system of central action alone. It also means that some disagreement and conflict are inevitable because officials in various states will not all see

eye-to-eye with those of the national government in terms of the objectives of the program.

This is not to blame the states in any way for their actions. Rather it is to recognize that public policy is in large part the result of the values that men hold and that these values vary from individual to individual and group to group. It would be unexpected and surprising if the several states followed identical or even similar courses of action on important public issues. The normal expectancy is that they will differ in greater or lesser degree among themselves in regard to policies they enact and in regard to the policies of the national government.

II

As we have already seen, two broad categories of values are immediately noticeable in a federal system. There are those values that attach to units of government or agencies or individuals within the units, and there are those values that attach to programs or types of substantive policies. The latter may be called principled, programmatic, or organization goals; the former may be called expediency or conservation goals. Programmatic goals are normally those concerned with adequate standards of public service—minimum standards in health and welfare, better public education, a more extensive system of interstate highways, more service to farmers, and so on. Expediency goals refer to the preservation and extension of influence of individuals, agencies, or units of government—for example, the defense of state government against "encroachment" from Washington, the desire of an individual for more power for its own sake, or the protection of an agency from supervision by those deemed unfriendly to it.

It is in the nature of a federal system that there are many occasions when the one set of values conflicts with the other. The states are not creatures of the national government and thus need not accept many of the programmatic or expediency goals that are put forth by those in control nationally. The constitutionally guaranteed semi-independence of the states lends encouragement to the development of strong expediency values relative to them, their leaders, and agencies. At the same time, the trend toward an increase in national-state relations helps strengthen the hold of programmatic values on many state and national administrators. The inevitable result is disagreement and conflict of three kinds: between competing expediency values, between competing programmatic values, and between expediency and programmatic values. The interplay of these goals is such that it is not unusual to find a programmatic value being defended in terms of expediency objectives and vice versa. Thus many who hesitate directly to attack programmatic values such as the so-called welfare state do so indirectly by defending states' rights since they feel that if welfare services were turned over to the states entirely they would be much less extensive and effective. On the other hand a welfare agency may battle for independence from supervision by the governor in order that it may better pursue certain types of welfare policies in cooperation with welfare personnel at the national level.

The net effect of a federal system is not by any means in the direction of increasing value conflict. Rather, while the system results in increasing the likelihood of certain disagreements over goals, it results in decreasing the likelihood of other and often more basic value conflicts. The federal system of the United States has withstood the shocks of wars and depressions and the changing centuries and meanwhile it has provided an organization that has helped weld a strongly unified nation where formerly there were independent states and unorganized territory. This has been an effective demonstration of the ability of a federal system to contribute toward modifying values and reducing value conflict.

The expediency values attached to the several states are not nearly as intensely held as those attached to independent nation-states.

Disagreement or conflict in national-state relations is limited. It is not a matter that normally determines election results or on which there is a clear public opinion. General issues of national-state relations have concerned only a small minority of individuals and groups in recent decades, usually a group of public officials at each level and a few interest groups outside the framework of government. When an important new substantive policy for the national government is under consideration, national-state relations may take on a broader significance, as was the case in welfare and labor policy during the thirties. As a whole, however, interest groups and public opinion have not found states' rights an attractive theme unless by the defense of states' rights they could defend some programmatic value. Nonetheless, for those public officials daily engaged in national-state relations the issues arising therefrom may be crucial.

The values that individuals hold are so diverse that there is no definable "state" point of view in intergovernmental relations as a whole. Even if the . . . governors were considered to be spokesmen for their entire states, there does not emerge a single state approach to intergovernmental relations. Occasionally all the governors will agree on a minor point or two but they have never agreed that a specific general reallocation of activities should take place between national and state governments. This is understandable since some of them are Democrats, some Republicans; some are liberals, others conservatives; some have national political ambitions, others do not; some come from poor states, others from well-to-do areas. These are only a few of the variables that affect the approach governors take on national-state relations. Much of the publicity arising from recent political events, Governors' Conferences, and the Council of

State Governments tends to give the impression that all governors demand that certain functions and tax resources of the national government be turned over to the states. The impression is erroneous. It is true that the governors probably defend states' rights as vigorously as any other group of public officials; they tend to stress expediency values relative to state government. In part this is a function of their role as chief executive and chief party leader. Nevertheless, such a set of values may be subordinate to many other considerations, and consequently consensus is not easily forthcoming.

If the governors as a group cannot produce a state point of view on intergovernmental relations, there is little likelihood that it will be found elsewhere. State legislators or elected state administrators show no more tendency to agree than the governors. Political parties remain rather vague on the subject and public opinion gives no evidence of a state viewpoint. Therefore, the most that can be said is that state political officials who hold elective and/or general executive posts tend to defend state government as such more vigorously than others, but that this expediency value is often secondary to a number of other values these individuals hold.

If an analysis is made of the national government, similar conclusions are reached. Although there is only one unit of government here compared to the forty-eight states, a single approach to national-state relations is never found. Of course, to the extent that the President speaks for the entire government and has a clearly defined policy on relations with the several states, a "national" policy may be referred to. But such a policy is not binding on Congress, and in actual recent practice Congress, the various departments and agencies, and the President have not followed a unified policy on intergovernmental relations. No comprehensive policy has been put forth by the President or the Congress; for the most part a piecemeal approach has prevailed. The reason is not hard to find. A unified policy requires agreement or compromise on basic programmatic and expediency values and such a general agreement is difficult if not impossible to secure even when the President has a large majority in Congress. The major political parties are too diverse in composition, the interest groups too strong relative to special programs, and the determinants of values too varied.

Nevertheless in one way the national situation differs somewhat from that in the states. Since defending the national government per se is usually thought of as centralization and is condemned, the political officials of the nation, at least outwardly, are less oriented toward expediency values than their state counterparts. Within this framework, however, the President is usually more committed to defending the national government than other top officials of his party or of the nation.

To summarize, the states disagree among themselves as to the major public policies they pursue and as to the desirability of particular national policies. They also differ even on smaller issues of national-state relations which may appear to be purely procedural in nature. The explanation is that public policies and even national-state procedures reflect particular values and on these there is lack of agreement. But it is not accurate to speak of the attitudes or policies of the several "states" or "national government." Public policies, and consequent disagreement and conflict, are not the product of entire units of government. Particular individuals, more or less associated in groups and to be found both within a unit of government and without, are the central forces behind the molding of public policy. . . .

III

While it is not possible to speak of a state or a national attitude on intergovernmental relations, there are many interest groups that have rather distinct approaches to the subject. It has already been suggested that as a group state elective and/or general executive officials tend to have more intense expediency values relative to state government as a whole than other groups of officials or employees. As part of its regular program the Council of State Governments tries to further these values; on many occasions its leaders have taken the initiative to get the state governors or other top officials to favor particular provisions in legislation before Congress that emphasize the prerogatives of the states or to encourage the President to appoint certain types of individuals—namely those generally considered pro-states' rights—to commissions or other posts. The Council has probably been more states' rights in its attitude than the recent governors of Minnesota. It would seem a reasonable hypothesis that it has been more states' rights than most state elective officials throughout the nation. Put more accurately, state officials find a large variety of values pressing upon them as they carry out their responsibilities, of which states' rights is usually a minor one. The Council, on the other hand, performs a limited number of functions. In addition to its technical assistance activities, its main emphasis has been placed on states' rights.

The most striking interest groups in national-state relations are those of a professional nature. Formally, these interests are evidenced by the many professional associations that have as members national, state, and often local government employees and occasionally members of the profession who are not employed in government. Professionalism has been introduced into almost all the principal services that state and national governments perform. Education was probably the first, soon after the middle of the nineteenth century. There followed such fields as agricultural extension, public health, highway administration and engineering, and social work, and more recently airport management, employment security, and others. The process of professionalizing has even gone so far that the professional fields have tended to split. Thus, in addition to a general education profession, there are separate groups interested primarily in vocational education, higher education, secondary education, and so on.

As each professional group has its own peculiar way of organizing it is difficult to generalize about the structure and membership of professional associations. For purposes of analysis, considerable clarity may be gained by thinking of a professional interest group as any group, whether formally organized or not, that shares a professional attitude on the basis of which claims are made on others "for the establishment, maintenance, or enhancement of forms of behavior that are implied by the shared attitudes." In observing national-state relations it is immediately noticeable that there is a marked parallel in the behavior of the members of each of the several professions relative to the type of values held, the occurrence of administrative cooperation and conflict, and the decisions made—all this despite the different functions of government involved and the wide differences in formal organization of professional associations.

One of the basic motivations of a professional interest group is the furtherance of programmatic values. If the profession is social work, for example, it will be concerned with high professional standards and conduct in social welfare and the raising of minimum standards of welfare aid. The secondary effect of such goals is of course to promote the well-being of the social work profession—an expediency consideration that is also an agreed-upon goal—but the genuine programmatic interest is clear. From the moment of entrance into schools of social work to the first in-service training and on to regular employment, social workers are placed in an environment where certain programmatic values are accepted without much question. It is partly a matter of conformity but also a matter of mutual interests. Some of the vocational guidance tests are based upon this idea of mutual interest.

Any group, professional or otherwise,

that seeks to implement certain values finds a number of allies in the form of those groups that share some concern for the same goals. Social workers have had ready support on many matters from their clientele, the recipients of welfare services. Liberal and labor groups generally have demanded higher minimum welfare standards and certain segments of the two major parties have indicated their sympathy for action in such a direction. A number of state legislators and congressmen have been favorably disposed, and often the warmest support in legislative bodies will come from those on legislative committees dealing with welfare matters. The position of any one governor or President is less predictable and his policies can be changed more quickly. Also, of all public officials, the chief executives must keep the "general interest" in mind most often.

It is easy to secure the cooperation of those who share the same values. National, state, and local professional officials in social welfare find they see eye-to-eye on most important matters, and consequently their decisions to cooperate reflect basic agreement on welfare programmatic values and agreement on expediency goals relative to their profession. Other values pale in importance to these as far as national-state relations in welfare are concerned. Professional employees do not feel strongly about defending the unit of government for which they work. The states' rights argument is not persuasive, although there may be some expediency values associated with the welfare agency itself. Cooperation not only extends across national, state, and local levels in the administrative work but also includes clientele activities, party and legislative groups, and others who for the moment at least feel that certain welfare programmatic values are especially worthy of their support. The help that the professional welfare group receives from such outside sources is considerable and greatly strengthens its hand.

From the standpoint of social workers, conflicts over social welfare policies are of

three types. There is the ever-present tendency for a large profession to subdivide, particularly under pressure from special clientele interests. Thus child welfare and welfare for the aged tend to be separated (or be kept separate) from a general welfare program. Secondly, at the professional or agency level, welfare values must compete with values associated with the other main substantive services of government such as education, health, and highways. Here the social worker comes in occasional conflict with professionals in other fields. The third and main area of conflict is the political. The citizen and the politician must pick and choose among many expediency and programmatic values of which welfare is only one. To convince citizen and politician that welfare values should have a high priority is the task the social worker assigns to himself.

All three areas of conflict affect national-state relations. In a general way all three have the same effect, namely, to lessen direct national-state conflict and to promote conflict among or within the main substantive services of each level of government. From the standpoint of both political leaders and professional employees, the disagreements within and among the professions are probably less serious than those between the professional and citizen and politician. It is particularly in conflicts of a political type that the very nature of federalism presents a special problem. Under a unitary system, the social worker would be involved in a simple direct clash between professional welfare workers and political leaders, be the latter located in the legislative body, the office of the general executive, or in departmental offices. With federalism the clash occurs at both the state and the national levels, and federalism's structural features make available to the combatants additional goals, tactics, and strategy.

In Minnesota the governor and his staff, the budget officer, and the director of the state welfare agency have traditionally been political officials who have not shared the typical programmatic values of professional social workers. The main division in attitude therefore tends to come between the welfare director and his professional employees rather than between the director and the budget office or governor's staff. In general the political officials feel that professional employees engaged in administering national grant-in-aid programs tend to play off supposedly rigid national standards against state political control they do not like. Since a prime objective of professional employees is to further the governmental service with which they are connected and not necessarily policy control at the state level, they tend to read somewhat more into national minimum standards than is actually there. The professionals are also active in appearing before the state legislature from time to time in an attempt to have legislation modified to anticipate changes in national standards. Often they are optimistic in their forecasts of probable national action. Viewing national standards with a different set of values than the professionals, political officials tend to underestimate the demands of the national agency or overestimate the deleterious effects such restrictions may have on the discretion left for state policy-makers. A similar set of circumstances exists at the national level as to the weight national officials give to state demands—the professionals underestimating them, the political leaders overestimating them. The situation portrayed in welfare is equally true of national-state relations in most other functions.

Considerable empirical data exist to support these conclusions. In a mail questionnaire sent to a cross-section of officials in Minnesota's state government, counties, municipalities, and urban school districts, the following question was asked: "What is your evaluation of the cooperativeness of public officials in the national government with you? (check): no contacts _____, very poor _____, poor _____, fair _____, good _____, very good _____." At the local government level, comparisons were made between the responses of administrative officials and legislative officials and in every one of the three types of local units in the sample, the administrators were markedly more of the opinion that the national officials were cooperative. A comparison of the responses of 302 municipal administrators (engineers, police chiefs, fire chiefs, assessors, and health officers) with those of 280 city councilmen by means of the chi square test indicated that the difference in attitude was very significant beyond the one per cent level; that is, this difference could have occurred by chance less than once in one hundred times. Comparing the responses of 239 county administrators (engineers, superintendents of schools, sheriffs, county agents, assessors, and welfare executives) with those of 199 county governing body members by the same test also yielded a very significant difference beyond the one per cent level. Furthermore no significant difference appeared between the attitude of state administrators and that of county, school district, or municipal administrators. However, county and state administrators felt that the officials of the national government were more cooperative than their school district and municipal counterparts. They are also the officials who have the most contact with the national government. While the questionnaire was not sent to state legislators, a number of interviews indicate that there is every reason for assuming that these officials would have reacted in much the same way as the local legislators did. Seventy-nine per cent of the 275 national administrators queried by questionnaire thought that state cooperation with them could be rated as good or very good. Only about two-and-a-half per cent thought it poor or very poor.

It is difficult to develop a measure of professionalism so that questionnaire and interview data can be classified on the presence or absence of this characteristic. The closest approximation used in the Minnesota study was the breakdown by type of official, together with general education, professional education, age, and various experience breakdowns. All these groups showed a positive orientation to the cooperativeness question; for example, the more education and the more frequent the contacts the more cooperative the national officials were rated.

Since the data from the Minnesota study are being reported at length elsewhere, our present purposes will be served by summarizing the quantitative data in regard to professionalism drawn from about 650 questionnaires and an equal number of interviews of public officials, national, state, and local. The main findings are these:

1. Administrators rate national-state relations as being more cooperative than do legislators, and within the administrative group those who would commonly be thought of as professional rather than amateur or political lean more heavily in the same direction.

2. Administrative officials think that administrators of other governmental levels cooperate best and legislative officials think legislators do.

3. Professional officials at all levels of government tend to favor more centralization and expansion of their own function than of other activities. Here the programmatic values of professional administrators are revealed. At least state and local professional officials seem to value their activity more than their unit of government.

4. Local administrators are much more critical of the extent of control of their departments by the local legislative body and the executive office than are members of the local legislative body or the executive office; the latter groups would like to see their control somewhat increased. This is hardly surprising. Moreover, local administrators see much less danger in the existing extent of state administrative supervision over their departments than the local political officials do, and there is even some tendency on the part of the former group to favor an increase in it. Here again is a

tendency that cannot be explained in terms of expediency values; expediency values would dictate that local administrators should oppose control of their departments both from within and without their units of government. While by far the majority of administrators are satisfied with the existing levels of control both from within and without, four to five times as many want to increase state administrative supervision as want to decrease it. Also, more favor an increase in state administrative supervision than in local control, and more favor a decrease in local control than favor a decrease in state administrative supervision. Chi square analysis indicates very significant differences beyond the one per cent level.

At this point an apparent contradiction arises between national-state and state-local relations. About two-thirds of the state administrators answering questionnaires agreed that the extent of national administrative supervision was about right, but the remainder split about four to one in favor of decreasing it. A number of factors account for this contrast between national-state and state-local relations. In the first place, quite a few state administrators included in the sample have very few relations with the national government, and it was noticeable that the ratio was cut to about two-and-a-half to one in the case of administrators in such departments as education and welfare where contacts are quite frequent. Secondly, state administrators feel less need for national administrative supervision since within their numbers various technical competencies are likely to be found and since there are enough of them in each department to set up a strong defense for professional standards against executive or legislative interference. At the city level a similar tendency is noted in large cities in contrast to the situation in small cities where more administrative supervision is desired by the semi-isolated professionals. Yet neither of these factors explains the entire difference.

States' rights, outwardly at least, are valued more intensively and extensively than local self-government, and here seems to lie some of the explanation. They are valued more partly because of the superior legal position that states hold in their relations with the national government, compared to that held by local governments in their dealings with the states. A subordinate role for local government is accepted much more readily than a similar role for the states. The states, according to the law and theory of federalism, are permanent partners in governance with a set of powers that cannot be taken away except by constitutional amendment. They are the proving grounds where the loyal opposition gains experience and experiments. To subordinate them to the national government is counter to the tenets of federalism and thus runs counter to customary values, and in the eyes of some officials an increase in national administrative supervision appears to lead in this direction.

In fact, however, the difference in national-state and state-local relations is more apparent than real. The difference shows up almost entirely on general questions or issues such as asking a respondent whether he favors an increase in administrative supervision. As actual case studies of intergovernmental relations are examined, the difference all but disappears. In other words, the difference occurs in reacting to general symbols and not to actual events. For example, the enactment of general regulations and their acceptance by officials of lower levels of government is much the same in national-state and state-local relations. So are the processes of audit and review and the possible consequences of finding officials violating regulations. Intergovernmental relations are at base human relations and require some mutual adjustment if they are to be cooperative in nature in the long run. This adjustment takes place in much the same manner in national-state and state-local relations despite the legal differences of federal and unitary systems. In this adjustment, pro-

fessionalism plays an important role because the participants from both state and national governments share many of the same goals.

5. Administrative and legislative officials alike are of the opinion that the main clash of values occurs within a unit of government rather than between units. This is true even in regard to the issues arising from intergovernmental programs. The professional is especially prone to this point of view.

The conclusions outlined so far, based on both quantitative and case study material, have been largely descriptive. They have indicated that the values and identifications of different types of public officials vary widely, and consequently the decisions they make vary. The two most significant values for purposes of this analysis were found to be the expediency values attached to a unit or level of government and held especially by some political officials, and the programmatic values, attached to the performance of certain governmental services and held especially by professional officials. This is not to deny that there are some who defend states' rights or local self-government through a genuine concern for decentralism and not on the basis of expediency. Nor is it to deny that some professionals develop strong expediency values in connection with their own agencies — the Corps of Engineers is a case in point. Indeed the activity of the Corps of Engineers is a good example of intergovernmental action that promotes intragovernmental discord — in this case, within the national government. However, situations where the programmatic values of professional administrators are overridden by their expediency values are not frequent except as professionals develop expediency values in connection with their entire profession rather than a single agency.

Furthermore, problems arising from intergovernmental programs have been described mainly as problems within units of government rather than between levels. Professional administrators are especially prone to perceive the situation in this manner. Yet there are those who perceive the situation in opposite terms—as a national-state conflict—and they may act upon their perceptions. Some political officials, especially a few governors, respond in this manner.

Explanatory conclusions can be drawn as well. As has already been emphasized, professionalism creates a powerful set of programmatic values the existence of which explains much of the behavior of professional and nonprofessional public officials in intergovernmental relations. But there is a larger point. To use the suggestive terminology of John M. Gaus, we are in an era of vastly increased physical and social technology, an era in which the catastrophes of war and depression can strike quickly. As a result, new programmatic values have been emphasized by those who want to take advantage of services that are now available because of the advances in physical and social technology and by those who demand governmental activities designed to lessen or avoid the ravages of wars and depressions. The technicians themselves have become attached to and encourage the creation of programmatic values. In such a situation, the cry of states' rights sounds a hollow note. The stronger the programmatic values, the less states' rights and federalism can become important independent values even for state public officials. States' rights come to be judged by the programmatic values that are implemented by the states and not by a set of independent expediency values.

IV

In a clash of values involving national-state relations some individuals try to affect and succeed in affecting the policies of others. Such political acts are acts of leadership, and leadership plays a central role in decision-making in a federal system. By definition leaders try to influence others; the idea of manipulation is present. But manipulation is not sufficient; some success or influence must result. We have already noted in discussing programmatic and expediency values some of the patterns of leadership in the federal system of the United States and some consequences flowing therefrom. We now turn to an analysis of the methods of leadership and the motives underlying their use.

Leaders, or those who perform acts of leadership frequently, have available to them two general methods, namely, authoritative means and nonauthoritative means. Authority is the formal and effective power "to make decisions which guide the actions of another." This means that the individual affected "sets himself a general rule which permits the communicated decision of another to guide his own choices (i.e., to serve as a premise of those choices) without deliberation on his own part on the expediency of those premises." In contrast, nonauthoritative means do not involve an abdication of choice. "Persuasion and suggestion result in a change in the evidential environment of choice which may, but need not, lead to conviction."

In a unitary system, the political and administrative leaders of the central government are vested with a rather complete set of authoritative means to use in their relations with subordinate units of government. Often there is the power to remove local officials and even appoint others in their place if they do not perform in an acceptable manner; there are powers to issue orders and make general rules that govern the very minute details of local action. Furthermore, the officials at the higher level can substitute, if they wish, direct central legislation and administration. Federalism sets severe limitations on the authority of central government officials in dealing with the lower governmental units. Constitutionally they are forbidden to alter in any way the power of officials in lower units to act. This means they cannot expand or contract such power, and they therefore cannot substitute central administration for local administration on matters that are within the authority of the lower units to perform. Today most national-state relations are based on grants-in-aid or the voluntary exchange of technical information and assistance. Most state-local relations, legally at least, are based upon the state's constitutional unitary authority over local government; there is no formal dependence on local officials accepting state policy decisions voluntarily.

However, when a comparison was made of national-state and state-local relations as observed in the State of Minnesota, no important differences were found in the frequency of use of authoritative and of nonauthoritative means by the two supervisory levels. Both national and state administrators stressed nonauthoritative means. Advice, consultation, technical assistance, information—these were the devices that had an appeal alike to the state and national administrator in charge of state-local or national-state relations, be the program in the field of welfare, education, health, highways, or in some other field. The more authoritative devices went unused, or were used only with the advice and consent of the officials to whom they were to apply, or were used as an unwelcome last resort in one or two rare cases. Occasionally, strong statements and hot words were used by the supervised in describing the supervisors, particularly if one was a professional and the other a nonprofessional official. Almost never was the reciprocal found true.

There are a number of explanations of this phenomenon. "Pulling rank" or flaunting authority are not devices that win many friends, and most individuals with experience in human relations became accustomed to dealing with others in a more friendly, permissive manner. So it is in intergovernmental relations. The more experience an official has, the greater the likelihood that he has cooperative relationships with those of other levels of government. Political and administrative realism lead to other factors of explanation. The success of

a program depends in most instances on the lack of use of authoritative devices in carrying it out. Politically, the superior unit of government is open to attack. If a national administrative official were to offend unduly the administrators from a state, there might be immediate repercussions in the congressional delegation of the state as well as official protest from the governor to the President. State officials have powerful political levers over national action just as local officials have a real check over state administrative supervision through the legislature and governor. These checks are enough of a threat to make frequent use of authoritative means of supervision unlikely. Yet administrators as a group are less concerned with the possibilities of such an attack from the flanks than they are with direct conflict or cooperation with their counterparts on the other governmental level. Here administrative realism enters. No program involving national relations with the forty-eight states is going to be successful if the national officials have to be checking up constantly on the states to see if they are complying with every detail of national standards. Nor is it going to be successful if the national administrators have to make all the important decisions through the use of authoritative methods. A national-state program must be based on the assumption that the great majority of states are going to cooperate to the best of their ability without close supervision, and that therefore the prime role of the national government is to assist the states and to help them carry out the program more effectively. To follow any other course is to increase the cost of administration and decrease its effectiveness. State administrators would rebel against a system that was apparently based on a lack of trust in them, although they do not object to occasional audits to see if their agencies are in accord with national policy. Similar considerations affect state-local relations.

The use of nonauthoritative devices by political and administrative leaders in national-state relations is supplemented by a further practice, namely, the cooperative development of program policy. State and national administrators almost never develop rules and regulations or program changes by themselves without consultation with and participation by local and state officials, respectively. The practice is quite standardized. For example, a prob lem-area arises either in the minds of state or national officials involving a national-state program. Within a short time, the problem finds its way to the agenda of a meeting of state administrators from the several states, a meeting at which national officials will probably be present but withhold much comment. If it is a problem of large proportions, it may be referred to a special committee of state administrators and a report brought in at a subsequent meeting. It will be discussed and debated informally around the country and in regional or state meetings of administrators. Appropriate clientele or other interest groups are likely to be consulted. Finally, the state administrators will recommend a course of action to national officials, usually with prior knowledge that their suggestion will be acted upon without substantial change.

This practice of developing policy from below is based upon much the same line of reasoning as the preference of nonauthoritative devices. In a national-state program, more cooperation will be forthcoming from the several states if their officials have taken an active part in the framing of the regulations and the making of decisions that outline the main course of national policy. State administrative officials must accept part of the responsibility for national policy, and this makes the task of the national official easier when it comes to enforcing minimum standards. It may also place the state administrator in a peculiar position if top state political leaders object to a policy he had a part in developing. In order to defend himself, the state administrator may blame the national government for a policy he helped write.

In thus decentralizing decision-making on public policy, national administrators are acting in accord with rather vague and undefined notions of democracy and therefore receive support from traditional cultural values. At the same time, they are not risking much in terms of lack of control over the direction of public policy because professionalism is prevalent in the states and leads to agreement on many values between national and state officials. To be sure, many of these national-state relations occur essentially between national professional and state political officials, since the heads of state agencies tend to be political rather than professional in orientation. But to a considerable extent the political heads of agencies must rely upon their professional subordinates for advice and help, and consequently the influence of professionalism is not without its effect.

v

. . . Under the conditions that prevail in the United States and in Minnesota, public officials who would be leaders in national-state relations must base their acts on the idea of getting along with officials of the other level of government by using voluntary, nonauthoritative methods. In particular, two theorems are suggested. The more the administrative leaders of the national government use nonauthoritative methods in their dealings with the states and, secondly, the more decision-making related to national-state programs is participated in by state officials, (1) the more cooperative will be the continuing relations, (2) the less chance there will be of the program being seriously curtailed or altered in a direction contrary to the values of the national administrators, and (3) the greater will be the probability that the values of the national administrators will be implemented in the long run. The converse of these propositions is likewise true.

Power as a value and expediency values in general have less hold on those engaged in national-state relations than various programmatic values. The picture of a power-mad individual seeking to strengthen his personal influence over his associates by every means at his command because he values power so highly is a false picture, or at least not a typical one, in national-state relations. This is especially true of administrative leadership in an era of professionalism but the tendency is observable among political officials as well. Program values are the usual goals for which power is sought with expediency values supplemental or subordinate thereto. Perhaps in an era of contracting governmental services expediency and power values would be prized more highly. Since such conditions did not prevail at the time the observations reported here were made the present data do not deny or confirm this possibility.

In conclusion, some comments are ventured on current suggestions for "improving" national-state relations. One of the most popular suggestions is that national-state relations be coordinated by the national government so that a single policy would prevail in all fields. If this idea were followed, national-state relations in highways would follow the same general policy and procedure as national-state relations in welfare, and so on. A second proposal is that the success or failure of intergovernmental relations be judged by the degree of harmony and cooperation that prevails between each set of national and state officials. Thirdly, particularly since the Eisenhower Administration took office, there has been much talk of the desirability of decentralization and a movement "back" to the states.

A common difficulty besets all these suggestions. Coordination, harmony or cooperation, and decentralization or states' rights are not necessarily good or bad in and of themselves. They are usually neutral concepts and are good or bad only in relation to other and more fundamental objectives an individual or group is seeking. To the extent that they are valued in and of themselves, they almost always hold a secondary place in the value framework. A program may be highly successful yet not present a picture of harmony and cooperation between state and nation. This often happens in the early years of a program when program goals remain unanswered or not agreed upon. Complete harmony is simply not possible if there is conflict over program goals. On the other hand, harmony may come at a high price. The professional administrators of national and state governments may have very harmonious relations but this good feeling may be a means of masking their fundamental disagreement with the general political officials of both levels and of suppressing policy issues that the latter would prefer to have brought to light.

As for coordination, all national-state relations cannot be coordinated until policy goals are agreed upon. The important problem is not coordination but coordination *for what*. The President and Congress have found it impossible to give a single answer. The policy and procedures in connection with national-state relations are not coordinated because no one in authority can agree on a single set of goals or objectives. Similarly decentralization. Decentralization for what and with what policy results? Decentralization cannot be considered apart from programmatic values that are affected thereby, particularly with an increase in the nationwide economic and social problems confronting government. Decentralization or states' rights, if applied to a number of activities, would mean virtual elimination of effective governmental action. Decentralization is thus often advocated by those who oppose governmental activity in a particular area and believe that decentralizing it would make action ineffective; it is also frequently supported by those from rich states as opposed to those from poor areas, by those not in political power nationally, and by those voicing a general political philosophy rather than by those confronted with very detailed and practical problems.

The patterns of national-state relations can be changed or "improved." But since these patterns reflect the values of individuals engaged in these relations, any change in the patterns is likely to heighten value conflict, at least temporarily.

*Daniel J. Elazar*

## THE AMERICAN PARTNERSHIP: THE NEXT HALF GENERATION

### THE CYCLE OF GENERATIONS

The great principles and mechanisms of American federalism have remained constant over most of the 177 years since the ratification of the Constitution, to form the basic character of the American political system. Only the manner of their expression in political action has changed. The way in which their expression has been changed follows a pattern which can also be traced through American history; one which helps us understand the way in which they and the governmental institutions they support are likely to change in the future.

The rhythm of social change in America and elsewhere is best measured on a generational basis. Over the course of some 25 to 40 years, men pass through the productive phase of their life cycles then leave the stage of history as new men arise to take their places. While this changing of the guard is a continuous matter, the pattern of human relationship is such that the change is felt cumulatively as a generational one, in the Biblical sense. Each new generation of men to assume the reins of power in society is a product of different influences and is shaped to respond to different problems, heightening the impact of the change and encouraging new political action to assimilate the changes into their lives. The perceptive student of American history will note that the important changes in American politics have come on a generation-by-generation basis with great regularity, beginning at the very beginning of settlement on these shores. If he wishes to get some sense of the "timetable" for future change, he is encouraged to cautiously extrapolate from past generational trends. The accompanying chart outlines the cycle of generations and their relationship to governmental change over the past century and projects both ahead to 1970.

We are presently moving into the last third of a generation which began in the years immediately following World War II (between 1945 and 1948). . . . Our generation, emerging after depression and World War, has had to confront three great problems. We have had to deal with the cold war and the end of colonialism, the problem of integrating the Negroes into American society and the problems attendant on the metropolitanization of the country.

The national response to world problems is and will continue to be a continuous one, varying in intensity from year to year, to be sure, but remaining the primary item on the agenda of the national government. On the domestic front, we are now approaching the end of the concentrated period of national legislation which occurs in every generation. The spurt of legislative activity embodied in the "New Frontier" and the "Great Society" and concentrated in the past four or five years, is similar to the concentrations of national reform legislation that have occurred in each previous generation since the founding of the Republic, concentrations such as the "New Deal," the "Square Deal," or the spurt of

From *Prospective Changes in Society By 1980* (Denver: Designing Education for the Future, 1966), Chapter 6.

domestic reform legislation in the Lincoln administration. As in previous generations, the four or five year period of concentrated legislation at the national level appears to have come to an end, except for isolated pieces of unfinished business and modifications of the new programs which will continue to occupy Congress. Between now and 1980, then, we will have the task as a nation of implementing the new programs established in recent years.

Because of its peculiar nature as the major impediment to the maintenance of traditional American governmental patterns and institutions, the Negro integration problem will no doubt continue to preoccupy Americans nationally as well as on the state and local level until a reasonable solution is attained. However, we may expect the period of intensive national activity that began in 1954 to taper off and be replaced by intensified state and local efforts, so long as the latter maintain their efforts to deal with the problem.

Even with the spate of federal legislation of recent years, meeting the problems of a metropolitan society has remained primarily the province of the states and localities, though with the very important assistance of the national government to stimulate them. National activity in this field, while administratively continuous, becomes important as new activity only at specific points in the generational cycle when new legislation establishing new programs or revising old ones takes the center of the stage and sets the requisite national patterns for subsequent action at the state and local levels nationwide.

By or perhaps before 1980 we should reach the second stage of legislative activity in the generational cycle, the enactment of legislation consolidating the changes initiated during the reform period and opening the doors to activities that will attempt to meet the problems of the generation that will then be just beginning. Our own generation began with just such consolidationist legislation passed between 1946 and 1949. While one cannot say what kind of new legislation will be enacted by 1980, we can assume that it will have to do with the reform of administrative and legislative procedures and will probably pay considerable attention to problems of intergovernmental relations as well.

Politically speaking, the new programs of each generation have been invariably preceded by critical elections through which the reconstituted electorate—which changes from generation to generation as new people attain voting age and old ones die—determines the basic pattern of party voting for the new era, either by reaffirming the majority party's hold on the public by forcing them to accommodate to new demands and then giving them an extended mandate or by rejecting the majority party as unable to meet those demands and elevating the minority party to majority status. These critical elections, which attain their highest visibility in presidential contests, allow voters, blocs, and interests to realign themselves according to the new problems which face them.

Three times in American history the critical elections have elevated the party previously in the minority to majority status. In the series of elections beginning in 1796 and culminating in 1800, the Jeffersonian Democratic-Republicans replaced the Federalists. In the 1856 and 1860 series, the Republicans replaced the Democrats who had become the heirs of the Jeffersonians and in 1928–1932, the Democrats in turn replaced the Republicans. Between each shift, the critical elections served to reinforce the majority party which was successful in adapting itself to new times and new conditions. Thus in 1824–1828, the Jacksonian Democrats picked up the reigns from their Jeffersonian predecessors; in 1892–1896 the Republicans were able to reconstitute their party coalition to maintain their majority position and even strengthen it. In 1956–1960 the Democrats were able to do the same thing. The old coalition put together by FDR and the New Deal, which underwent severe strains in the late 1940's and early 1950's, was recon-

THE PERIODS OF AMERICAN POLITICAL HISTORY

| Year | 1830 | 1840 | 1850 | 1860 | 1870 | 1880 | 1890 | 1900 | 1910 | 1920 | 1930 | 1940 | 1950 | 1960 | 1970 |
|---|---|---|---|---|---|---|---|---|---|---|---|---|---|---|---|
| *Century* | | | | Nineteenth | | | | | | Twentieth | | | | | |
| *Generation* | | 7 | | 8 | | | 9 | | | 10 | | | 11 | | |

| *Frontier Stage* | Rural-Land Frontier | Urban-Industrial Frontier | Metropolitan-Technological Frontier |
|---|---|---|---|

| *Economic Period* | 1st Transition | **Free Enterprise** | Concentrated Enterprise | 2nd Transition | Regulated Enterprise |
|---|---|---|---|---|---|

| *Critical Elections (and majority party)* | 1856 DEM | 1892 GOP | 1928 GOP | 1956 GOP |
|---|---|---|---|---|
| | 1860 GOP | 1896 GOP | 1932 DEM | 1960 DEM |

*Major Generational Concerns* ___(g con't)___(h)___ ___(1)___ ___(j)___(2)___(3)___(4)___(k)

g) institutionalization of reform
h) social response to an industrial society
i) first assault on evils of industralization
j) reformation of the industrial system
2) WWI—first world involvement
3) WWII—end of isolation
4) Cold War
k) response to metropolitan frontier

| *Form of Federal-State Relations* | Formative Period | Cooperation via land grants | "Cooperative Federalism" |
|---|---|---|---|

stituted and reshaped by Adlai Stevenson and John F. Kennedy to give the Democrats an even stronger majority than before, which made the programs of the 1960's possible.

With this record in mind, it is not unreasonable to forecast a continued Democratic majority through 1980 though with persistent and increasing erosion of that majority as the 1970's wear on. During the 1980's, we may expect another set of critical elections which will very likely elevate a new party to majority status; perhaps a reconstituted Republican party, perhaps some party whose existence is as yet unforeseen. In the interim, the Republican party will no doubt win the presidency once or twice, something that has happened in every generation in the past, by capitalizing on some particular individual with great national appeal. More significantly, it will probably gain power at the state and local levels. Republican governors in increasing numbers across the country . . . will be

trying to make positive records to strengthen themselves and their party for the immediate future and for long range gains. These vigorous young chief executives will be open to positive programs with political appeal and will seek to actively participate in their formulation.

THE GREAT SOCIETY AND THE PARTNERSHIP

Our present position in the generational cycle has certain immediate implications for the role of the states and their . . . agencies in our system of government. . . . As the Great Society programs begin to take shape in the field as well as in legislation, we can see the way in which they are continuing old traditions of intergovernmental relations and moving into some new areas. As in the past, all governments are deeply and significantly involved in virtually every phase of the Great Society. This is true even of those programs which at first glance appear to be unilateral federal programs or federal-local programs designed to by-pass the states. Though the news media frequently give the impression that all creativity and decision-making are centered in Washington these days, this is most emphatically not so. Indeed, as recent articles in *Time* and *Fortune* have pointed out, one of the major concerns of the present national administration is that the new programs serve to build up the various centers of power in this country. President Johnson has characterized this concern as a new "creative federalism" but it really falls four square within the great tradition of noncentralization. Necessity alone is likely to enhance this concern as both population and programs grow too great for centralized direction. Talk of greater decentralization is even heard in Washington which, though bearing implications inimicable to the idea of noncentralized government, still represents a significant shift in emphasis.

At the same time, the press of new programs involving so many different agencies at each level of government as well as coordination across the levels, has created new demands for better intergovernmental coordination and for simplification in program administration. Some of these demands will no doubt disappear as the new programs become more routinized and those responsible for administering them develop patterns of administration and cooperation that can endure. Indeed, once routinization sets in, many of those with a stake in the programs will find that the very multiplicity of agencies and complexity of procedures serves their purposes better than any streamlining would. Nevertheless, over the next fourteen years, there will be considerable emphasis on improving administration and simplifying coordination if only because the amount of government activity in our society has now reached the point where it is virtually impossible to introduce any new programs without involving so many agencies on every level of government that some sorting out seems to be both necessary and inevitable. The development of computer technology and its application to government will almost certainly have a major impact in this regard.

The burden for this streamlining will fall on all levels of government just as the programs do. Indeed, fragmentation at the state and local level, enhanced as it is by federal grants which frequently allow state and local agencies to develop channels of support that by-pass their general governments, will require at least as much attention as the need for coordination at the federal level. The drive for streamlining may serve, if properly managed, to strengthen the general governments of the states and even of their localities, upgrading their abilities while giving them more control over the activities within their jurisdictions.

Still, as in the past, much of the burden of bringing together the various strands of governmental activity will fall on the local authorities. Following today's conventional patterns of thought which tend to accept bureaucratic principles of hierarchy, we tend to believe that coordination must inevitably come from the top. In fact, the very magnitude of governmental operations would make it impossible for any single center of control to develop at the top even if our system operated as a single pyramid. The empirical evidence has shown time and again that energetic local leaders are best able to ascertain which governmental agencies and programs (regardless of level) need to be coordinated for local purposes and to take the steps necessary to do so. In many cases, local leaders have been able to draw federal or state agencies that have proved to be uncoordinable at the top together into effective local partnerships. In doing so, they reflect the administrative benefits of America's traditional patterns of political "interference" in administration. There is good reason to believe that the nation's policy makers will discover the viability of this non-hierarchical pattern of controlling bureaucracy over the next half generation and begin to consciously make use of it in new ways.

Dealing with administrative difficulties will be only one aspect of the fulfillment of current programmatic innovations over the next half generation. The shape of the programs will also be subject to refinement and development, partly by remedial action at the congressional level and to a great extent, through implementing action at the state and local levels. If present trends continue, the shaping will emphasize more and more planning, greater equalization of public benefits, and great emphasis on collective action.

. . . Not only will the requirement for planning to qualify for federal aid grow, but there are likely to be greater efforts to implement the plans that are produced. It is unclear whether these efforts will be successful, at least partly because so many of the plans that are prepared, while meeting the symbolic demands placed upon them, really do not reflect the basic values and fundamental interests of the American people.

One of the elements that may promote greater implementation of plans is the quest for equalization which is part of the Great Society's theoretical foundation. As of now, there is still a coincidence between the policies of those who seek this equalization within the framework of the traditional American desire to provide equality of opportunity for all and the aspirations of those who believe that we must strive for something approaching equality of condition instead. However, there is a tendency built into certain of the Great Society programs that supports the notion of equality of condition going beyond simple provision of equality of opportunity, and, increasingly, public discussion is being couched in such equalitarian terms. . . . The issue will be joined as the new programs move toward fulfillment and the outcome will have decisive consequences for the role of government in American society.

Finally, the notion of collective action,

which is closely related to the drive for equality of condition, is likely to be pressed by unofficial and some official spokesmen for the new programs. I use the term collective action advisedly, but it would not be entirely amiss to use the term collectivism to describe the more radical versions of Great Society policy. Again, there is a tension between those who advocate collective action in the cooperative spirit that falls with the American tradition of individualism and partnership and those who are willing—even eager—to move toward real collectivism in order to secure their equalizing and planning goals.

Emphasis on planning for good or ill means a concomitant de-emphasis on market decisions or on letting nature take its course. This is not to say that planning cannot be used in conjunction with free decision-making; indeed many planners have concluded that it is best used to aid "nature" or "the market," not to try to replace them. But the thrust of many leading supporters of planning today seems to be away from that kind of planning toward the notion that all decisions should be preplanned and in line with some overall plan.

By the same token, the thrust for equalization makes the maintenance of legitimate distinctions and differences more difficult. This not only operates to limit the choices of individuals and groups but also the possibilities for state and local diversity. It is always difficult to separate the setting of necessary new standards from the drive for standardization, to determine what is necessary and what goes beyond necessity. This difficulty is enhanced when there is a lack of concern for diversity. This will be a recurring problem for the next half generation, particularly in regard to state and local differences within the federal system. In major fields like education, public welfare, and employment security, we see the drive for standardization going full force today as the leading spokesmen for the new programs in those fields argue that differences among the states are detrimental to the national welfare. Coupled with this is the notion that local distinctiveness or uniqueness is to be valued only where it does not extend into policy areas. States and localities could possibly lose the right to opt out of national programs, changing the old system whereby they were simply encouraged to opt in.

It should be recognized that the aforementioned possibilities may remain more theoretical than practical. For example, whatever the possibilities, the states and their subdivisions have never chosen to opt out of the great federal grant programs created since the New Deal or even earlier, primarily because enactment of those programs has itself reflected the existence of a national consensus spread nationwide. There is no reason to believe that this will be any different in the future.

At the same time, the very multiplication of federal aid programs available opens up many more choices for the states and localities. There are already so many grant-in-aid programs available from Washington that most states, if not all, are picking and choosing among them. It is true that the great grant programs covering highways, public health, and now education, are universally accepted and utilized but the myriad of smaller programs are being selected by the states and localities increasingly on the basis of their own overall policy decisions.

Beyond the question of simply participating in the programs, the states and their local subdivisions increasingly determine how much federal money they will use, often not taking all available for them because they are unwilling to divert their own resources from other programs which they consider to be of higher priority to match the federal grants fully. In this way, the states and their subdivisions have actually developed greater flexibility within the framework of the grant programs now than in the past. In some cases, this has led to counter-pressures for federal grants that do not require local matching in order to virtually insure the states' participation on the assumption that they will willingly take something that does not cost them anything. There may be increasing pressures along these and similar lines in the political arena.

## TO 1980 AND BEYOND

Within the policy framework projected above, we can make certain specific projections for the immediate future:

(1) *All governments will continue to grow* — in size, expenditures, and scope of activities. With the possible exception of two decades in the middle of the 19th century, government has grown consistently in all three categories since the establishment of the Republic. There is nothing on the horizon to indicate that this trend will be reversed. On the contrary, as the role of government in our society grows greater, so governments must continue to grow. For the moment, it seems as if governmental growth is primarily federal growth, but appearances are deceiving. One of the important discoveries of the new thinking about federalism is that, since the sum total of power in American society is constantly growing, government can grow without increasing its relative share of that power and the federal government can grow without decreasing the power available to state and local government.

We are presently in a period of dramatic growth in federal activity, accompanied by a certain growth in federal expenditures. This growth period, however, has not extended to the field of federal employment which has remained more or less stable for nearly half a generation. The 2.6 million workers employed by the federal government is actually 100,000 less than were employed in 1946. Moreover, federal growth is accompanied by state and local growth of equal magnitude. While the federal budget is increasing, so are state and local budgets, to hold the relative federal and state-local shares of governmental expenditure nearly constant. (Within the states, on the other hand, state expenditures are growing markedly in relation to local expenditures).

221

State and local employment rolls are increasing even more rapidly, up 4.7 million since 1946 to 8 million today.

So long as the press of world affairs requires the federal government to devote something like 50 percent of its budget to paying for current military expenditures and another 20 percent to paying interest and costs from past wars, it is unlikely that spectacular federal growth in the domestic field will continue for more than brief periods. On the contrary, the major growth in government over the next half generation will continue to take place at the state and local levels as it has since the end of World War II. The states and their localities presently account for two thirds of the total governmental expenditure for domestic purposes and are likely to continue to do so unless there is a radical decline in world tensions. This may be obscured by the great growth in actual dollars appropriated by Congress that we can reasonably expect. Fiscal experts are predicting an annual federal budget of $175 billion by 1976. If such a figure is reached—and it does not seem in the least implausible—it will be paralleled, no doubt, by annual state-local expenditures of close to $125 billion.

As governments grow, administrative decision-making will continue to occupy an increasingly important role in our lives. Legislatures will continue to set broad policy goals in their legislation and to prescribe the outlines for administrative regulations. Both of these activities are likely to become even more significant in shaping the administrative decisions, primarily because legislatures will also work to devise means to oversee the administrative agencies and check their discretionary activities in crucial ways. Congress is already discussing potential reforms along these lines and the state legislatures are being encouraged to do the same by a growing number of legislative reform groups. The next fourteen years are likely to see an intensification of the drive to improve and strengthen legislatures just as the last half of the previous generation was devoted to the development of administrative techniques to handle big government.

Within the bureaucracy, there will be greater emphasis on the use of trained professionals. Routine administrative operations are being increasingly taken over by computers so that the percentage of skilled specialists in the overall civil service at all levels of government is likely to increase. Increase in expertise will inevitably strengthen the administrative branches vis-a-vis the legislature unless the legislatures follow through with programs presently under discussion to acquire experts of their own. At the same time, increased expertise at the state and local levels will not only improve the quality of their governmental services but will put the states and localities in a better position to negotiate with their federal counterparts. Not only will these professionals share the same professional values and long-range aspirations, with a consequent easing of communications, but they will also enable their governments to negotiate from positions of greater strength. This has been true of established programs in the past whereby the states and localities have gained greater control over cooperative programs whenever they have developed greater expertise to handle them. Certainly the field of education provides a superb example of how this is so. Today the real repository of educational expertise is at the state and local level. As long as this remains the case, federal aid will be of an assisting variety rather than a threat to state and local autonomy.

(2) *Sharing will be equally important in the future and will even seem to increase.* Since intergovernmental cooperation is already pervasive, it is difficult to talk about an increase in sharing. In fact, the amount of sharing will grow in absolute terms as government activity increases without changing the basic degree of sharing. There will no doubt be changes in the respective roles of different governments and government agencies in specific cases, and new forms of sharing are likely to develop. Re-

gional arrangements are beginning to loom large on the governmental scene ranging from such long term organizations as the Appalachian Regional Commission to this Conference. This new regionalism is promoting new kinds of cooperation in at least two ways; an increase in subnational planning and programs to deal with problems involving more than one state and the involvement of both the federal government and the states in joint policy-making at the very beginning of new programs. Various approaches to regional cooperation are likely to be tried with increasing frequency over the next half generation, with varying degrees of success.

The character of sharing over the next half generation is more difficult to forecast. One could simply conclude that old patterns will continue with minor adjustments. There are, however, some problems, well-nigh perennial ones, which make the issue somewhat more problematical. It is entirely possible that the widespread recognition of sharing will lead to the use of sharing devices as a means to achieve de facto centralization. If the smaller governments are forced into a position where they must cooperate without really participating in decision making, simply on the grounds that cooperation is expected of them, sharing will be formally preserved without achieving the goals for which it is intended.

In addition, there is the question of direct federal-local relations and even more vital, that of federal-private relations. One of the characteristics of Great Society programs has been the increased emphasis on federal aid to anybody. Thus the federal government is not only developing more programs in which localities can deal directly with Washington to gain assistance, but is revising older programs to allow selective direct federal-local relations where none existed before. Though there are some tendencies to the contrary, it is likely that such relationships will continue to grow in the immediate future.

In a more radical vein, traditional concepts of federalism are being challenged by notions of pluralism whereby great national associations or corporations with powerful means to influence Congress are given responsibilities that might otherwise have been allocated to state or local governments. In some cases, there is every justification for this. In others, the issue is unclear. For example, the use of private industries to run Job Corps centers under federal contracts may or may not be the best way for the federal government to provide assistance to impoverished youth who need additional training. Federal-private relations are also a form of sharing and unquestionably help to perpetuate noncentralized government. At the same time, they may alter the shape of the system if they proliferate over the next fourteen years. There will be, almost certainly, pressures for their proliferation, particularly since the large corporations that have grown great as a result of federal defense spending are beginning to seek alternative ways to continue to draw upon the federal treasury for their profits in an effort to lessen their dependence on defense contracts. In one sense, this is all to the good, since it will make future disarmament efforts easier on the economy. However, if these efforts are not fitted into the federal system, the states and localities may suffer from them.

(3) *The states will have to act constantly and with greater vigor to maintain their traditional position as the keystones in the American governmental arch.* The continued central role of the states is no longer a foregone conclusion within the framework of American federalism. While it is not seriously possible to conceive of the states not playing a major role, the significance of their role will depend to a very great extent upon their responses over the next half generation to the challenges which confront them. Now that the federal government is meeting little public objection to its involvement in the range of domestic activities and direct federal relations with the localities are becoming equally accepted, it is possible that the role of the localities will be emphasized at the expense of the states.

223

However, the very thrust towards regionalism indicates that sheer federal-local relations will not be sufficient to handle the dispersal of power and operational activity which is considered desirable in this country. The localities cannot confront the powerful federal government alone, nor can overall policy be made in Washington for the country as a whole. Moreover, the states, by their sheer existence, have developed concrete patterns of politics and culture which infuse their localities with unique ways of doing things. Hence, they do not stand at a particular disadvantage in defining a positive place for themselves in the new federalism. But, in order to do so, they will have to function like general governments and indeed, like central governments. It will no longer be possible for them to rely simply upon their role as conduits funneling federal aid to their localities or local requests to Washington, nor will they profit by acting as simply another set of local governments. Rather, their strength lies in the fact that they are general governments with central government responsibilities toward their local subdivisions.

The governors of the states show every indication of recognizing this and of seeking to capitalize on it. Such recent actions as the Interstate Compact on Education, which is a clear attempt on the part of the governors to gain some measure of general control over educational programs within their states that have previously been highly fragmented, is one good example of this new recognition of their role. The Appalachia program, which channels decision-making through the general organs of state government rather than through the specialized agencies, is another. The political situation of the next fourteen years which will encourage Republican governors to make records in their states is likely to stimulate this kind of response. Democratic governors will be forced to respond in kind if only in self defense.

The states will have additional advantages in defining their position because of the nation's population growth. The sheer population size of the country is making the dispersion of political and administrative decisions necessary and desirable now, in the way that the problem of territorial size made such a dispersion necessary and desirable in the past. At the same time, the constant growth of population in the fixed number of states offers each state greater opportunity for internal viability. One need only look at the States of California and New York to see how this is so. States of some 18 million people, they are more populous than all but a few of the sovereign nations of the world and have larger budgets than all but five of them. California maintains an educational plant larger than that of any country with the exception of the Soviet Union. Such states are able to draw upon many kinds of skills found within their borders simply because they have enough people to produce a variety of talents. While they may never become as large as their giant sisters, sheer passage of time will enable most states to reach a stage in population growth that will give them greater flexibility as well as more money with which to function, thus adding to their potential for self-directed action. Even today, the Rocky Mountain states have populations equal to or greater than 29 sovereign nations.

(4) *Localities will have to struggle for policy — as distinct from administrative — control of the new programs.* Despite the fact that federal-local relations are increasing and are likely to increase, the localities are not assured that these relations will continue to emphasize local decision-making with outside financial and technical assistance as in the past. The evidence is that the present pattern will be continued. Nevertheless, the localities will have to compete against the pressures for excessive equalitarian leveling and collectivist action that could make local control a relatively hollow achievement. These pressures will continue to be directed toward eliminating the policy-making powers of local government, particularly in the realms of housing, zon-

ing, and urban development. The growth of expertise at the local level could offset these pressures unless the new urban professionals themselves identify with these centralizing goals.

In their efforts, the localities would be wise to place increased reliance upon their states. The major pressures for direct federal-local relations that bypass the states come from the nation's largest cities, ones whose populations equal or exceed the populations of many states, and who consequently have sufficient self-sufficiency and expertise to work directly with Washington without being at a great disadvantage. As the nation's population decentralizes within the metropolitan areas and within the belts of urban settlement that are forming in various parts of the country, more people will be living in smaller units of local government. Since the chances for local consolidation have diminished and indeed, the value of such consolidation has become increasingly suspect, there will be relatively few local units capable of dealing directly with Washington, simply by virtue of their lack of appropriate personnel. The states will provide assistance in most cases for a certain price, namely a "say" in local decisions. While this price is not likely to be great—the states are also committed to the principle of local control—it will give the localities additional need to define their positions as well. . . .

By 1980 Americans will be on their way to discover new problems for government to deal with. While it will take a decade or more for those problems to find their way onto the national stage as programs, the states and localities of the nation will be apt to confront them or at least to formulate and refine them in the years of the 9th decade of this century. It is hard to forecast what those problems will be. It is possible that the irresistable momentum of planning and government activity will continue to stimulate a drive for more planning and more government intervention into the lives of the citizenry. Or it may be that Americans will seek solutions which call for limiting or shifting government's role. The combination of social and technological developments as yet unforeseen will be a decisive influence here. . . .

The next half generation promises to be as eventful as the previous one—indeed, as the entire 20th century has been to date. Its very eventfulness makes prediction well-nigh impossible and forecasting very difficult. At the same time, the very complexity of our century makes some degree of planning necessary. Looking at government's role in the future, one must tread a sharp line between uttering simple banalities and predicting beyond reasonable knowledge. This becomes possible only because our political system has shown a tremendous ability to adapt itself to radical changes while changing relatively little in its own right. In a century of change, our political system has served as a rock of stability. There is no reason to believe that it cannot continue to do so provided we understand it and use it wisely.

# Suggestions For Reading

The beginnings of the literature of American federalism antedate the United States by at least a century. However it is only in recent years that empirical studies of the operations of the federal system have come into their own. Prior to that, the major emphasis in the field was placed on theoretical and constitutional questions. This brief list of readings that follows draws from both traditions.

*The Federalist* remains the great classic of American federalist thought and the starting point for the study of the political idea of federalism. It is available in numerous editions. Martin Diamond is the foremost contemporary interpreter of *The Federalist*. His chapter in Leo Strauss and Joseph Cropsey, eds., *History of Political Philosophy*; his article "Democracy and The Federalist: A Reconsideration of the Framers' Intent," *American Political Science Review* (March, 1959); and his chapter in Robert A. Goldwin, ed., *A Nation of States* (1963), "The Fe eralist's View of Federalism," are basic to the understanding of the origins of the American system. Recently, the works of the anti-federalists have come in for serious attention. Two anthologies of their writings are especially useful: John D. Lewis, ed., *Anti-Federalists versus Federalists* (1961) and Alpheus Thomas Mason, ed., *The States' Rights Debate: Anti-Federalism and the Constitution* (1964). Jackson Turner Main analyses anti-federalist thought in *The Anti-Federalists: Critics of the Constitution, 1781–1788* (1961). David G. Smith's *The Convention and the Constitution* (1965) is perhaps the best short synthesis of recent scholarly interpretations of the creation of the American constitutional structure.

Two other studies of the ideas of the formative period of American federalism deserve attention: Carl L. Becker, *The Declaration of Independence* (1922) and Andrew C. McLaughlin, *The Foundations of American Constitutionalism* (1961) both examine the empirical and theoretical bases for the emergence of federalism in America. Perry Miller is the most authoritative interpreter of the theological roots of the federal idea. Particularly important are his *The New England Mind* (2 vols., 1939, 1953) and *Errand into the Wilderness* (1956).

Classical nineteenth century studies dealing with the question of federalism include James Bryce, *The American Commonwealth* (1888), Alexis de Toqueville, *Democracy in America* (1835), and Woodrow Wilson, *Congressional Government* (1885). All three are notable for combining theoretical analysis with basically empirical concerns. Among the more important theoretical works written in the nineteenth century are those of John C. Calhoun, a selection of which is available in *Calhoun: Basic Documents* (1952) edited by John M. Anderson and Alexander Stephens, *A Constitutional View of the War Between the States* (1868). Both reflect classic "states-rights" positions. A well-known nationalist argument of the same general period which rests on similar premises is offered by John W. Burgess in "The American Commonwealth" *Political Science Quarterly* (1886). Though there is a vast historical literature which deals indirectly with specific aspects of intergovernmental relations in the nineteenth century, the history of federalism before 1913 as such has been much neglected. Daniel J. Elazar's studies, *The American Partnership: Intergovernmental Cooperation in the Nineteenth Century United States* (1962) and "Urban Problems and the Federal Government: A Historical Inquiry," *Political Science Quarterly* (December 1967) represent efforts to examine that period from the vantage point of the sharing hypothesis. Two earlier works, John Bell Sanborn's *Congressional Grants of Land in Aid of Railways* (1899) and Mathias N. Orfield's *Federal Land Grants to the States With Special Reference to Minnesota* (1915) examine aspects of the early federal aid system from an almost contemporary perspective. William B. Hessetine, *Lincoln and the War Governors* (1955) and Curtis Arthur Amlund, *Federalism in the Southern Confederacy* (1966) offer views of federal-state relations on both sides during the Civil War.

The rise of massive intergovernmental programs in the twentieth century has led to growing scholarly interest in the problems of federalism and intergovernmental relations. Among the earliest efforts to come to grips with the new scene was Austin Macdonald, *Federal Aid* (1928). The New Deal brought forth a number of theoretical and empirical studies including George C. S. Benson, *The New Centralization* (1941) which worried about the changes taking place, Jane Perry Clark, *The Rise of a New Federalism* (1938) which analysed those changes; and Edward B. Corwin, "National-State Cooperation—Its Present Possibilities," *Yale Law Journal* (1937) which endorsed them. V. O. Key, Jr., *The Administration of Federal Grants-in-Aid* (1937), and a special issue of the *Annals of the American Academy of Political and Social Science* on Intergovernmental Relations (1940) provided the first empirical studies of the expanded role of the federal government. Both remain especially useful works.

Since World War II, a number of very important general works have been published. William Anderson's, *The Nation and the States: Rivals or Partners?* (1955) was one of the first to generalize about cooperative federalism from an empirical-historical as well as a constitutional perspective. That same year Arthur W. Macmahon edited the results of a Columbia University conference as *Federalism: Mature and Emergent*, a landmark in synthesizing empirical studies with emerging theoretical perspectives. W. Brooke Graves, one of the first to devote his career to the study of federalism has summarized his life's work in *American Intergovernmental Relations* (1964), a compendious review of the entire field. In an attempt to formulate a theory of the geographic diffusion of power, Arthur Maas edited a collection of papers titled *Area and Power* (1959). *A Nation of States* (1963) edited by Robert A. Goldwin offers a convenient anthology of current popular theories of federalism set alongside recent empirical studies. The overall study of the federal system undertaken by Morton Grodzins and his associates in the late 1950's has produced a number of important works, the most significant of which were those of Grodzins himself. His major work, *The American System: A New View of Government in the United States* (1966), summarizes much of that study and offers the most sophisticated of the comprehensive views to emerge in recent years. Daniel J. Elazar's, *American Federalism: A View From the States* (1966) is, in many respects, a complementary work. In 1965, a second issue of the *Annals* devoted to intergovernmental relations was published which, like the first, did much to summarize the current state of knowledge in the field.

More specialized studies of various aspects of the federal system have also begun to appear in the past two decades. The first of these came from students of public administration concerned with the implementation of federal aid programs and their impact on the states and localities. The series of ten individually-authored monographs edited by William Anderson and Edward Weidner under the general title *Intergovernmental Relations in Minnesota* and published between 1946 and 1960 still stands as the most comprehensive and detailed scholarly review of the cooperative system from the vantage point of the states.

The field of public law was the second to be considered by the "new breed" of students of federalism. Edward Corwin pioneered in expanding the study of constitutional questions of federalism beyond the limits of normative theory. His many publications remain important landmarks in the evolution of the study of public law. See, for example, his *The Commerce Power versus States'-Rights* (1936). Henry M. Hart and Herbert Wechsler summarize the general relationship of federal and state law in *The Federal Courts and the Federal System* (1953). The decisions of the United States Supreme Court not only contribute heavily to shaping federal-state relations but also serve as vehicles for the enunciation of theories of federalism at different periods in American history. Two basic constitutional histories covering the Court's role are Carl Brent Swisher, *American Constitutional Development* (1954) and Alfred H. Kelly and Winfred A. Harbison, *The American Constitution* (1963). Both contain much about federalism. More recent studies that emphasize the behavioralistic approach included John R. Schmidhauser, *The Supreme Court as Final Arbiter in Federal State Relations: 1789–1957* (1958) and John D. Sprague, *Voting Patterns of the United States Supreme Court: Cases in Federalism 1889–1959* (1968). For other aspects of federalism and the courts, see Walter F. Murphy, "Lower Court Checks on Supreme Court Power," *American Political Science Review* (December 1959).

The politics of federalism, as such, has been one of the least explored aspects of the American system. Grodzins' work remains preeminent in this regard. Herbert Agar's *The Price of Union* (1950), though weak in its analysis of the origins of the Constitution is a superb study of the way in which the political aspects of the federal system work to forge the compromises that hold this heterogeneous nation together. Arthur N. Holcombe's study of American political developments in light of the Constitution, *Our More Perfect Union* (1959) is an equally important work. V. O. Key, Jr., *American State Politics: An Introduction* (1956) devotes considerable space to the political effects of federalism on the states. The autonomy of the states in the system is well illustrated in the various chapters of Herbert Jacob and Kenneth N. Vines, eds., *Politics in the American States* (1965). Theodore H. White's books on *The Making of the President* (1961, 1965) offer valuable insights into the workings of politics in the federal system.

An increasing number of studies of specific functions and issues are to be found every year. Among the more interesting ones are Ernest R. Bartley, *The Tidelands Oil Controversy: A Legal and Historical Analysis* (1953); Glenn E. Brooks, *When Governors Convene: The Governors' Conference and National Politics* (1961). Robert J. Morgan, *Governing Soil Conservation* (Baltimore: The Johns Hopkins

Press, n.d.); Roscoe C. Martin, Guthrie S. Birkhead, Jesse Burkhead and Frank J. Munger, *River Basin Administration and the Delaware* (Syracuse: Syracuse University Press, 1960); Martha Derthick, *The National Guard in Politics* (Cambridge, Mass.: Harvard University Press, 1965) and the 12 volume Syracuse series on "The Economics and Politics of Public Education" (Syracuse: Syracuse University Press, 1962).

Government-sponsored studies have contributed greatly to our knowledge of the workings and problems of the federal system. The most important of these is the sixteen volume study of the Commission on Intergovernmental Relations (1953) known as the Kestnbaum Commission after its chairman. The subcommittees on intergovernmental relations of the House and Senate committees on government operations have both maintained a watchful eye on the operations of the federal system for the past decade or more. Both periodically publish the results of their labors as hearings or committee prints. Their publications are especially useful as sources of data on the attitudes of federal, state, and local officials toward each other, the programs they administer, and the federal system generally. The House subcommittee, under its chairman, Congressman L. H. Fountain of North Carolina, began hearings to that end in 1956. The Senate subcommittee, under Senator Edward M. Muskie of Maine, has been conducting a series of hearings to explore "Creative Federalism" since 1966. Because of the pervasiveness of intergovernmental collaboration, virtually every Congressional committee conducts some investigations of interest to students of American federalism, hence their published hearings and committee prints are often excellent sources of data for specific functional areas. The Advisory Commission on Intergovernmental Relations is another excellent source of materials. The over sixty commission staff and information reports deal with a wide range of current problems in intergovernmental relations and the Commission's annual report is becoming a major source of information on the overall state of American federalism.

Major state publications on American federalism include the special studies issued by the Council of State Governments; that agency's two periodicals: *State Government* (quarterly) and *State Government News* (monthly); and the biennial *Book of the States*. Individual states periodically issue studies and reports on aspects of their relations with the federal government or their local subdivisions. Bureaus of governmental research at state universities are particularly important sources of specialized studies in the intergovernmental field. The *Britannica Book of the Year* features an annual review of "Developments in the States" which focuses on intergovernmental relations. The Tax Foundation publishes an annual compendium of fiscal data as *Facts and Figures on Government Finance*.

Recent discussions of the values of federalism include a defense of traditional states' rights by James J. Kilpatrick in *The Sovereign States* (1956) and an argument based on the premises of cooperative federalism by Nelson A. Rockefeller in *The Future of Federalism* (1962). Contrasting arguments about the theory underlying the federal idea can be found in James MacGregor Burns, *The Deadlock of Democracy* (1963), who follows the path of Jacobin democracy and Walter Lippman, *The Public Philosophy* (1955), who argues for the federalist or Madisonian path.

123456789